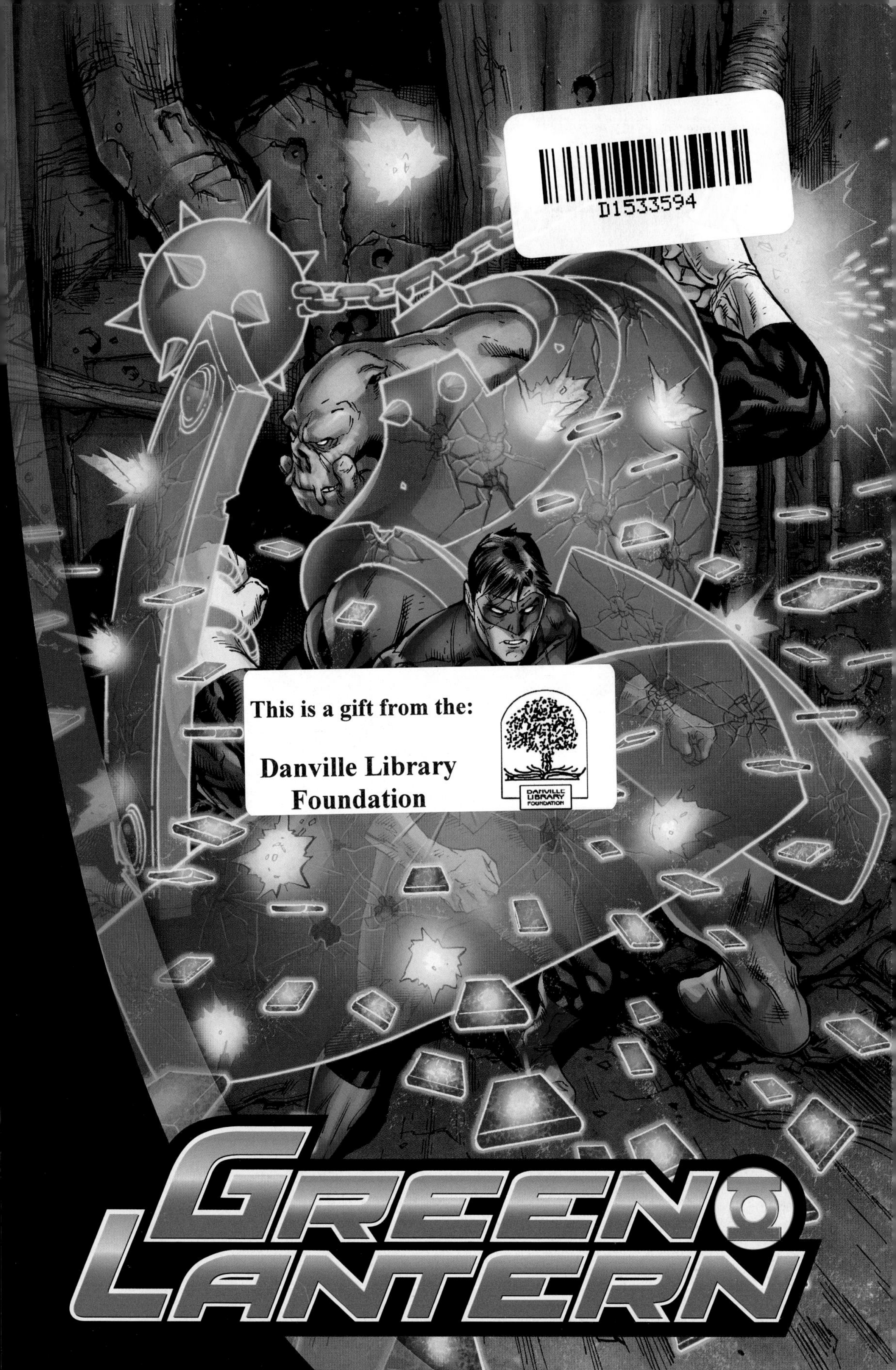

GREEN LANTERN

VOLUME 4 **DARK DAYS**

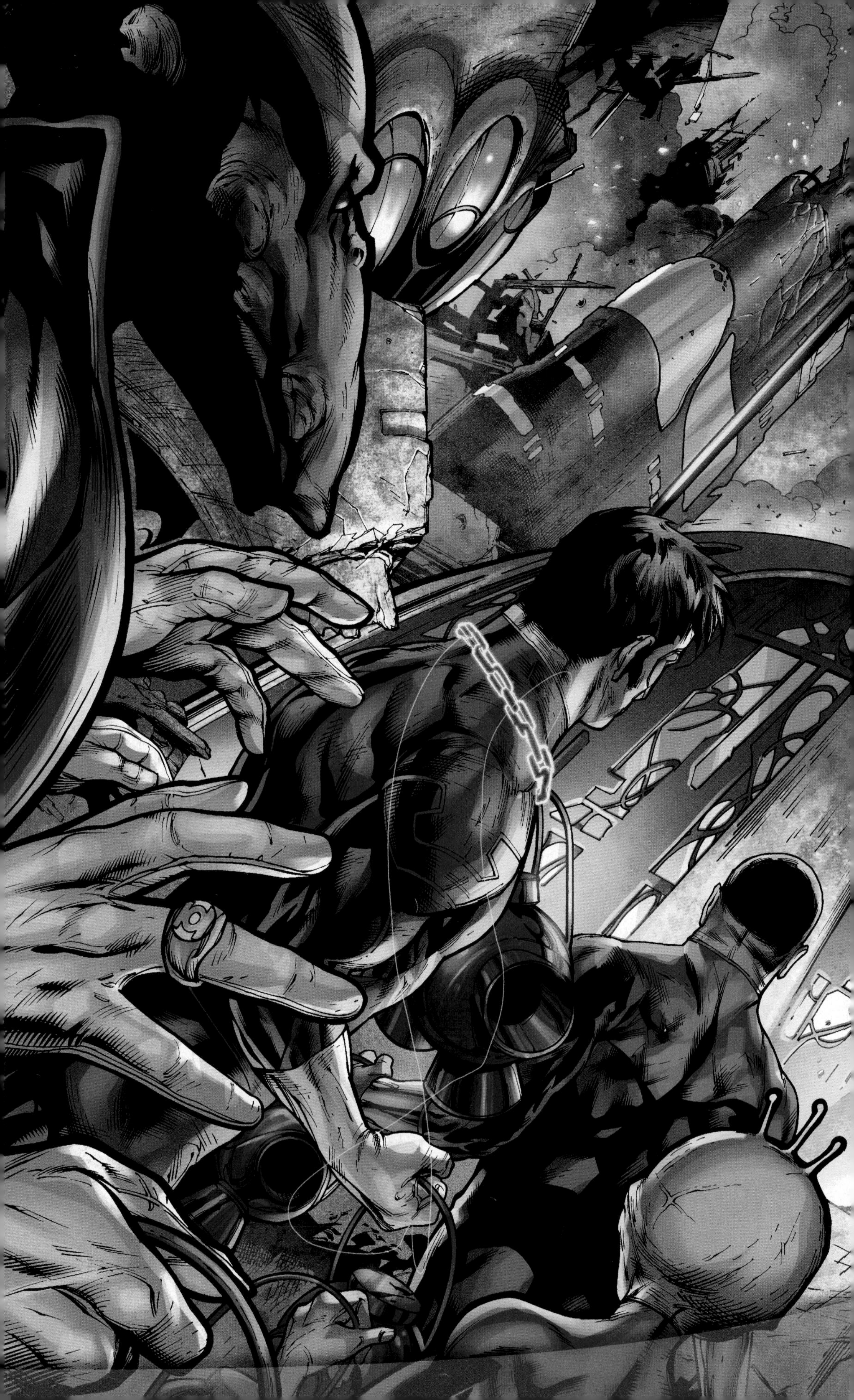

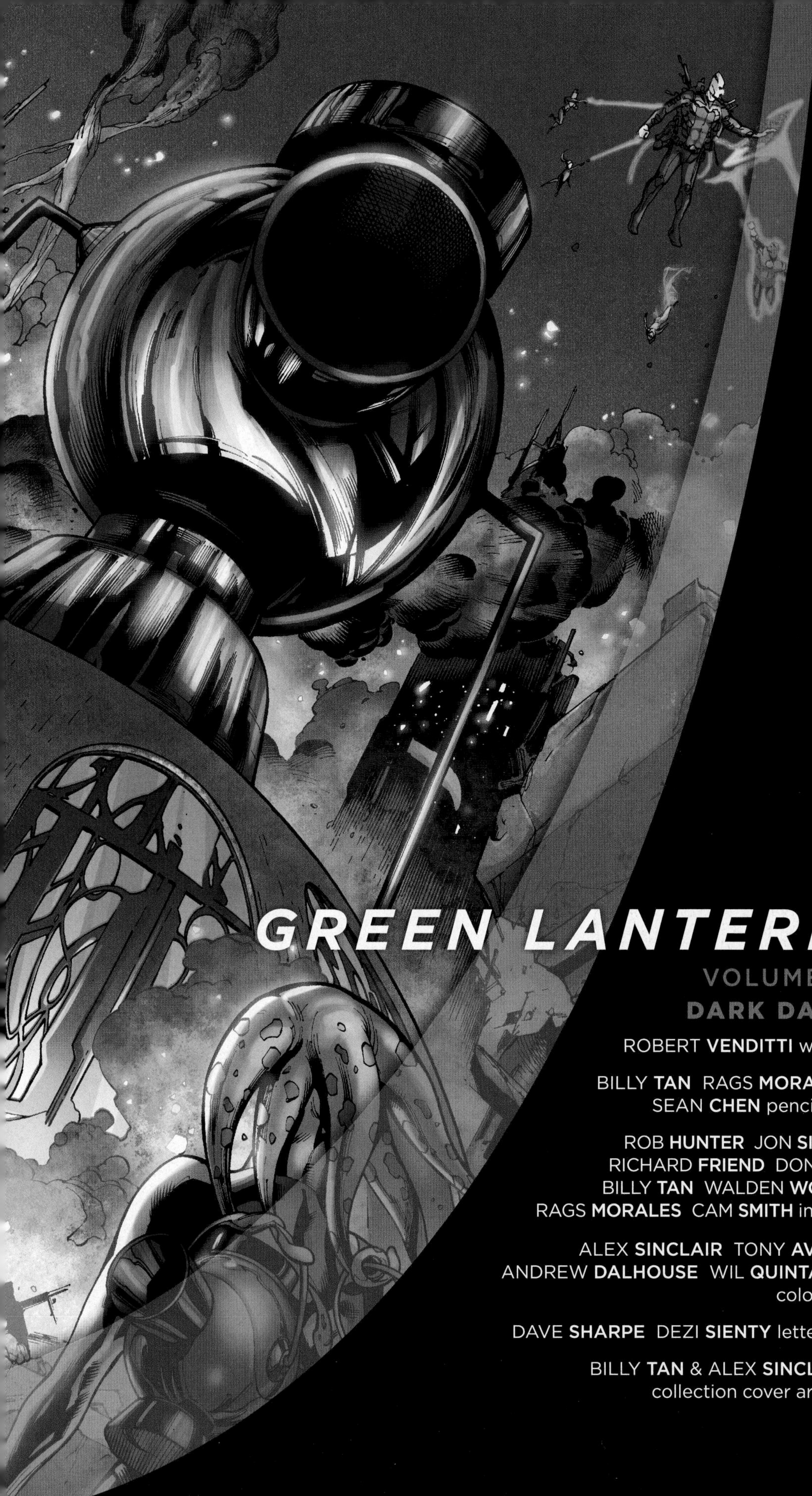

GREEN LANTERN

VOLUME 4

DARK DAYS

ROBERT **VENDITTI** writer

BILLY **TAN** RAGS **MORALES**
SEAN **CHEN** pencillers

ROB **HUNTER** JON **SIBAL**
RICHARD **FRIEND** DON **HO**
BILLY **TAN** WALDEN **WONG**
RAGS **MORALES** CAM **SMITH** inkers

ALEX **SINCLAIR** TONY **AVIÑA**
ANDREW **DALHOUSE** WIL **QUINTANA**
colorists

DAVE **SHARPE** DEZI **SIENTY** letterers

BILLY **TAN** & ALEX **SINCLAIR**
collection cover artists

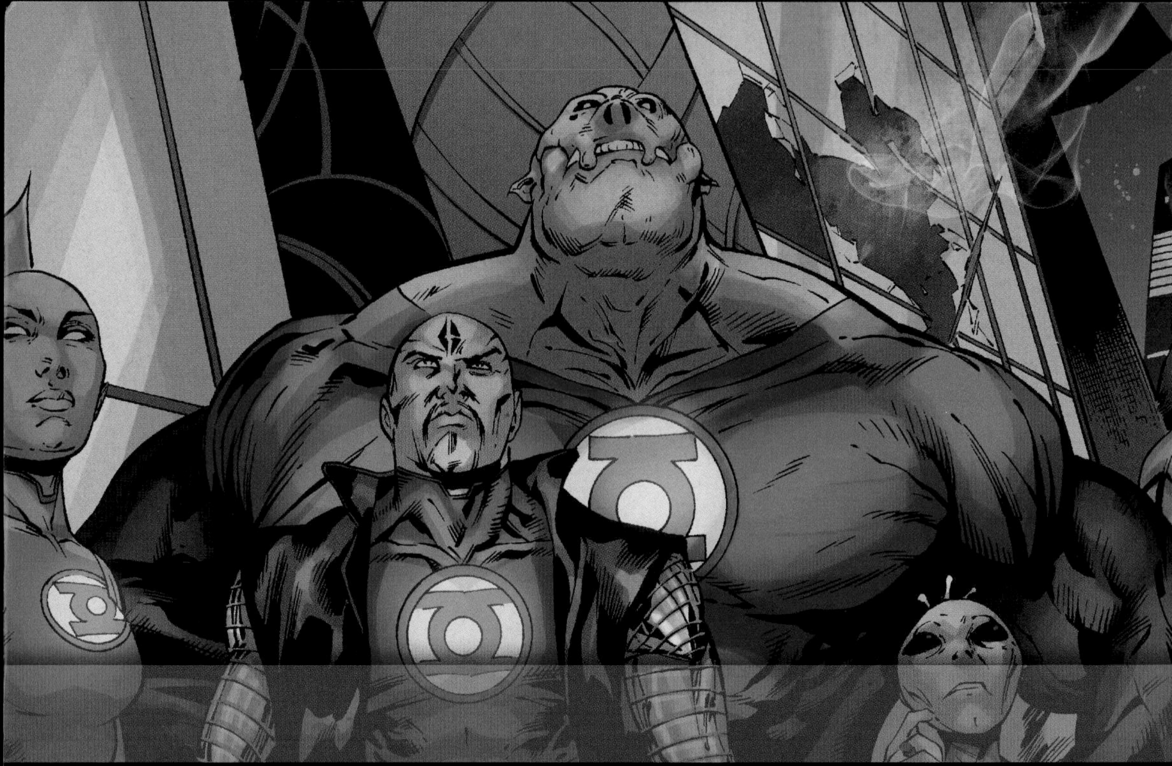

MATT IDELSON Editor – Original Series CHRIS CONROY Associate Editor – Original Series RACHEL PINNELAS Editor
ROBBIN BROSTERMAN Design Director – Books ROBBIE BIEDERMAN Publication Design

BOB HARRAS Senior VP – Editor-in-Chief, DC Comics

DIANE NELSON President DAN DIDIO and JIM LEE Co-Publishers GEOFF JOHNS Chief Creative Officer
AMIT DESAI Senior VP – Marketing and Franchise Management
AMY GENKINS Senior VP – Business and Legal Affairs NAIRI GARDINER Senior VP – Finance
JEFF BOISON VP – Publishing Planning MARK CHIARELLO VP – Art Direction and Design
JOHN CUNNINGHAM VP – Marketing TERRI CUNNINGHAM VP – Editorial Administration
LARRY GANEM VP – Talent Relations and Services ALISON GILL Senior VP – Manufacturing and Operations
HANK KANALZ Senior VP – Vertigo and Integrated Publishing JAY KOGAN VP – Business and Legal Affairs, Publishing
JACK MAHAN VP – Business Affairs, Talent NICK NAPOLITANO VP – Manufacturing Administration SUE POHJA VP – Book Sales
FRED RUIZ VP – Manufacturing Operations COURTNEY SIMMONS Senior VP – Publicity BOB WAYNE Senior VP – Sales

GREEN LANTERN VOLUME 4: DARK DAYS

Published by DC Comics.

DC Comics, 1700 Broadway, New York, NY 10019
A Warner Bros. Entertainment Company.
Printed by RR Donnelley, Salem, VA, USA. 9/26/14. First Printing.

ISBN: 978-1-4012-4942-7

SUSTAINABLE FORESTRY INITIATIVE
Certified Chain of Custody
20% Certified Forest Content,
80% Certified Sourcing
www.sfiprogram.org
SFI-01042
APPLIES TO TEXT STOCK ONLY

Library of Congress Cataloging-in-Publication Data

Venditti, Robert, author.
Green Lantern. Volume 4, Dark Days / Robert Venditti ; illustrated by Billy Tan.
pages cm
ISBN 978-1-4012-4942-7
1. Graphic novels. I. Tan, Billy, illustrator. II. Title. III. Title: Dark Days.
PN6728.G74V46 2014
741.5'973—dc23
2013049632

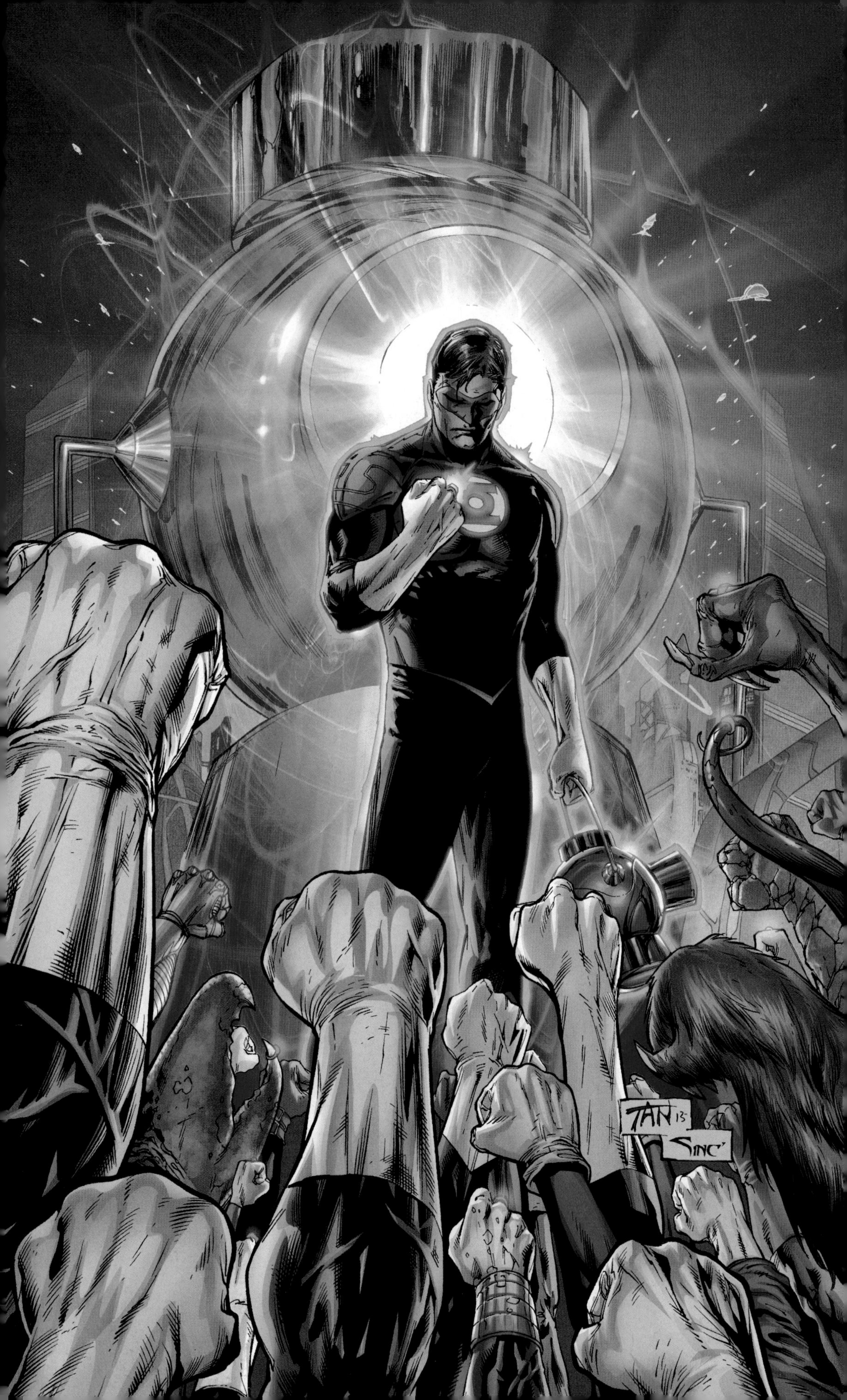
TAN 13
SINC'

ROBERT VENDITTI writer **BILLY TAN** penciller **RICHARD FRIEND** inker
cover art by **BILLY TAN & ALEX SINCLAIR**

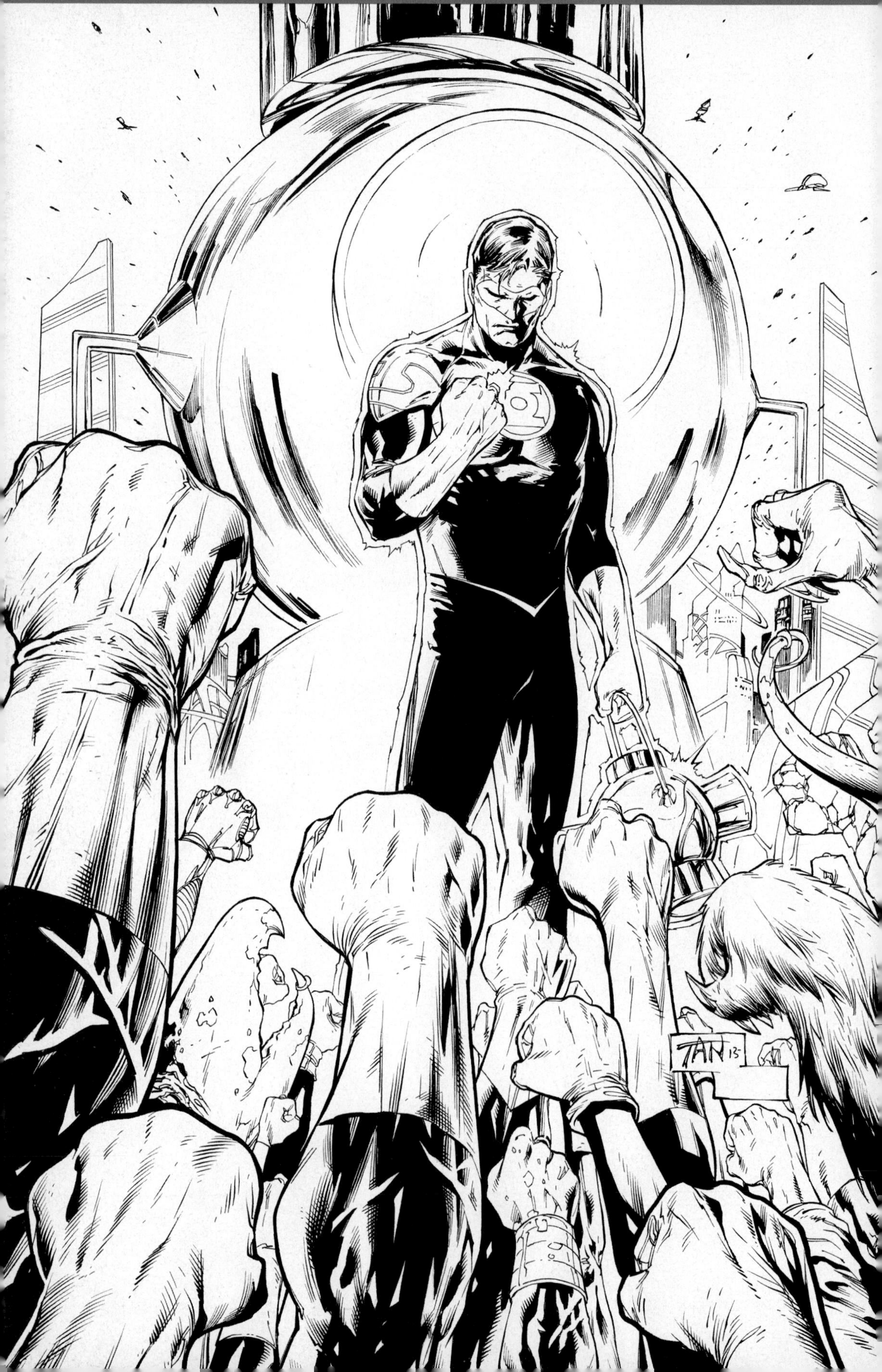

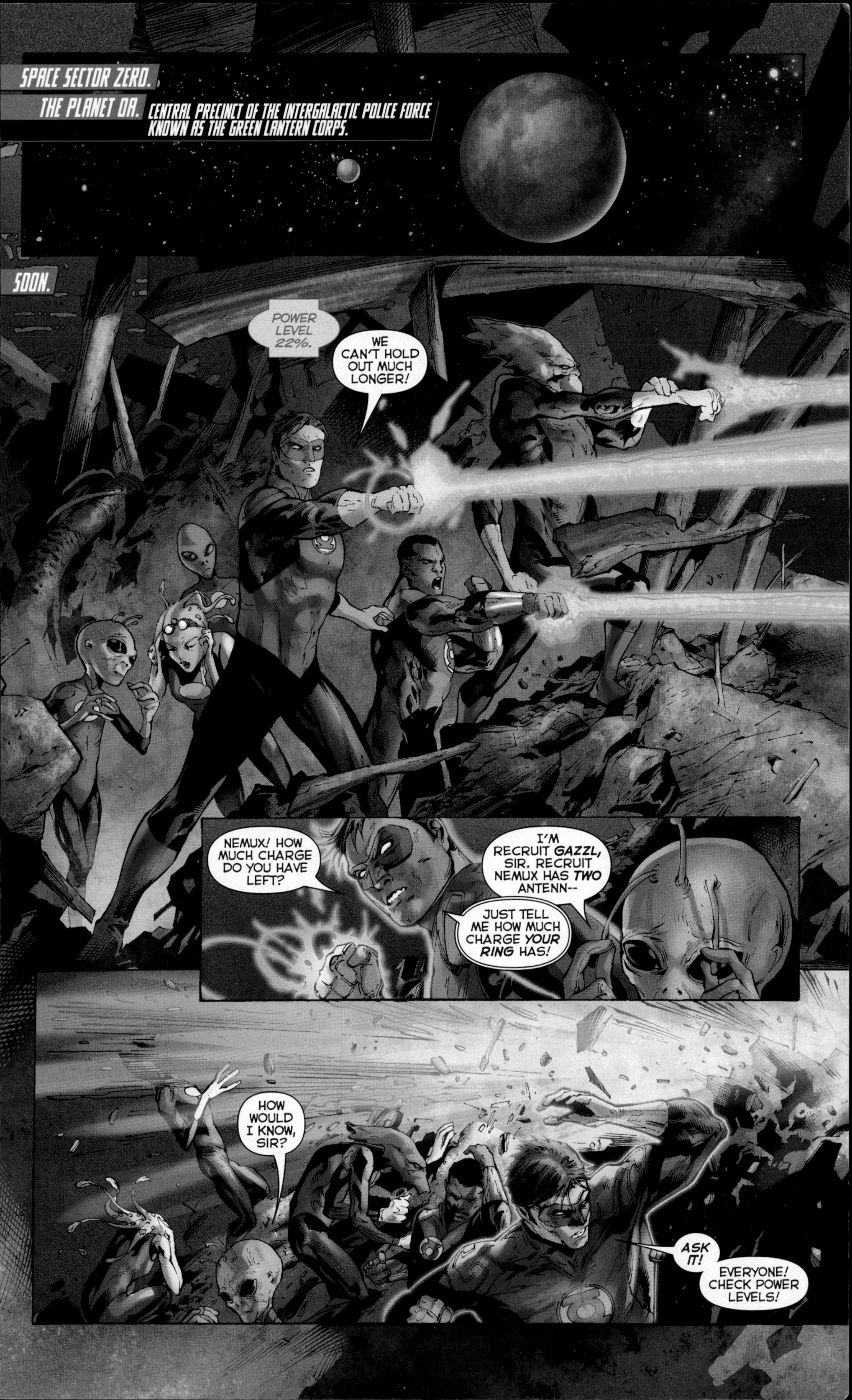
SPACE SECTOR ZERO.
THE PLANET OA.
CENTRAL PRECINCT OF THE INTERGALACTIC POLICE FORCE KNOWN AS THE GREEN LANTERN CORPS.
SOON.
POWER LEVEL 22%.
WE CAN'T HOLD OUT MUCH LONGER!
NEMUX! HOW MUCH CHARGE DO YOU HAVE LEFT?
I'M RECRUIT GAZZL, SIR. RECRUIT NEMUX HAS TWO ANTENN--
JUST TELL ME HOW MUCH CHARGE YOUR RING HAS!
HOW WOULD I KNOW, SIR?
ASK IT!
EVERYONE! CHECK POWER LEVELS!

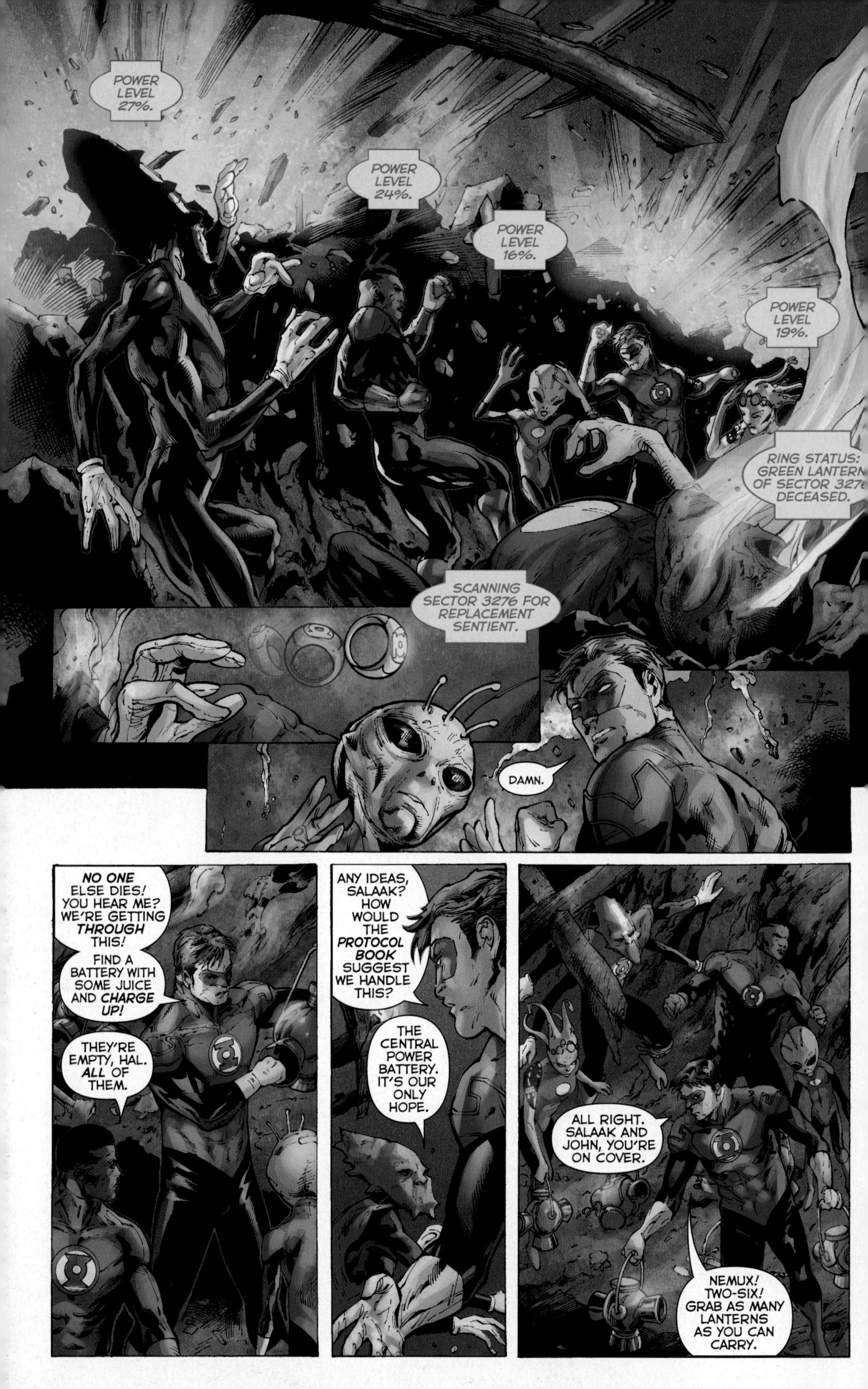
POWER LEVEL 27%.
POWER LEVEL 24%.
POWER LEVEL 16%.
POWER LEVEL 19%.
RING STATUS: GREEN LANTERN OF SECTOR 3276 DECEASED.
SCANNING SECTOR 3276 FOR REPLACEMENT SENTIENT.
DAMN.
NO ONE ELSE DIES! YOU HEAR ME? WE'RE GETTING THROUGH THIS!
FIND A BATTERY WITH SOME JUICE AND CHARGE UP!
THEY'RE EMPTY, HAL. ALL OF THEM.
ANY IDEAS, SALAAK? HOW WOULD THE PROTOCOL BOOK SUGGEST WE HANDLE THIS?
THE CENTRAL POWER BATTERY. IT'S OUR ONLY HOPE.
ALL RIGHT. SALAAK AND JOHN, YOU'RE ON COVER.
NEMUX! TWO-SIX! GRAB AS MANY LANTERNS AS YOU CAN CARRY.

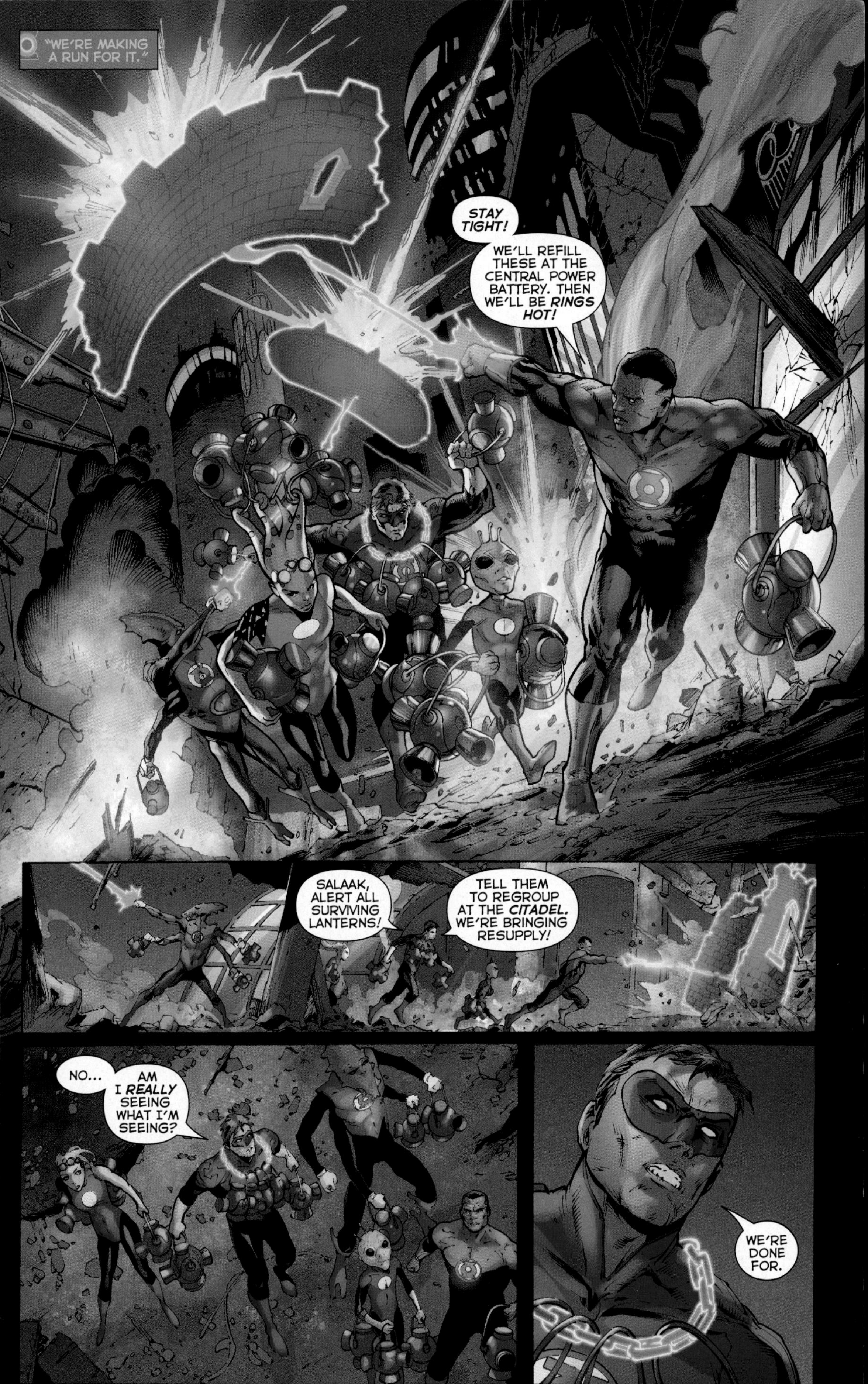
"WE'RE MAKING A RUN FOR IT."
STAY TIGHT!
WE'LL REFILL THESE AT THE CENTRAL POWER BATTERY. THEN WE'LL BE RINGS HOT!
SALAAK, ALERT ALL SURVIVING LANTERNS!
TELL THEM TO REGROUP AT THE CITADEL. WE'RE BRINGING RESUPPLY!
NO...
AM I REALLY SEEING WHAT I'M SEEING?
WE'RE DONE FOR.

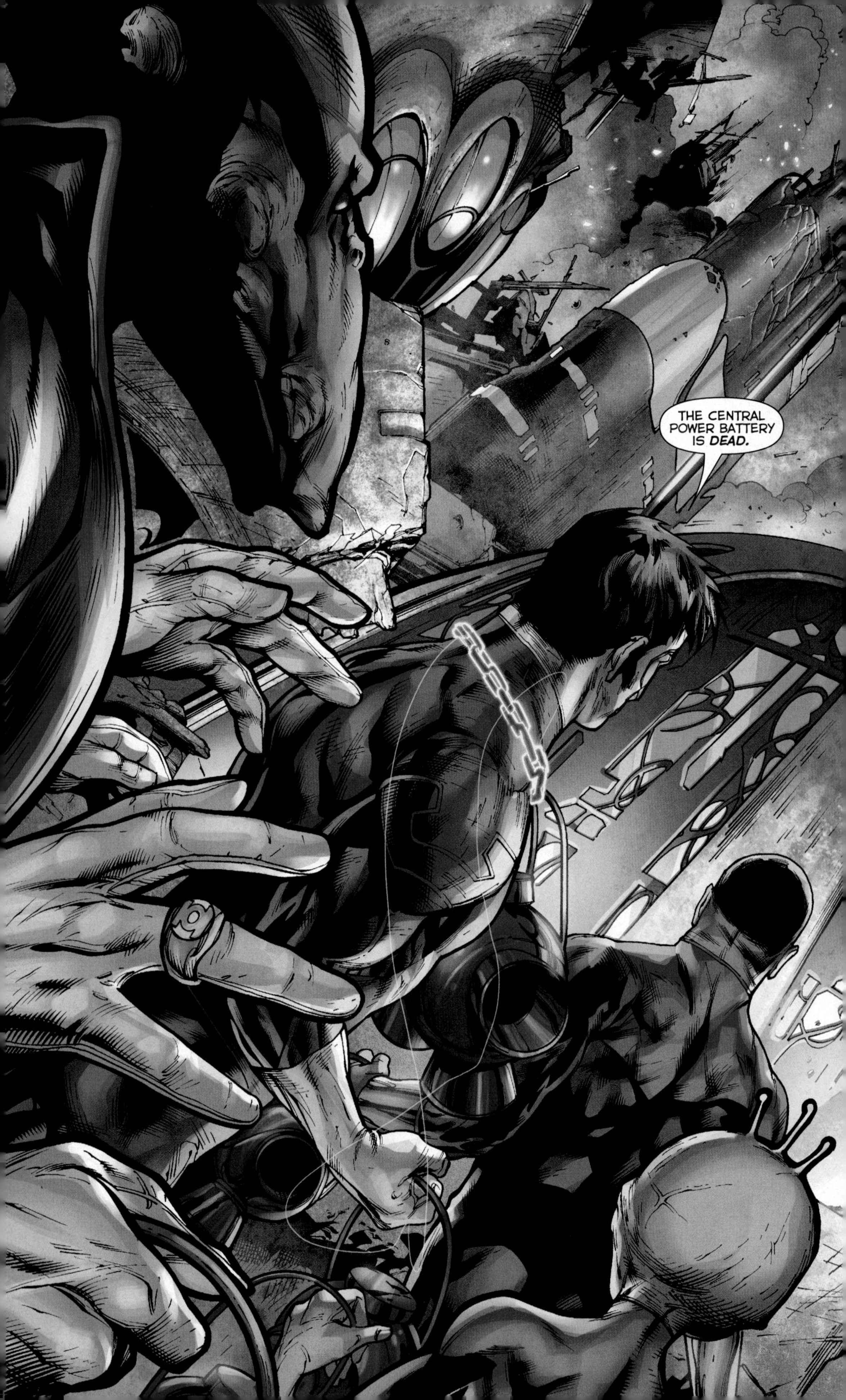
THE CENTRAL POWER BATTERY IS *DEAD.*

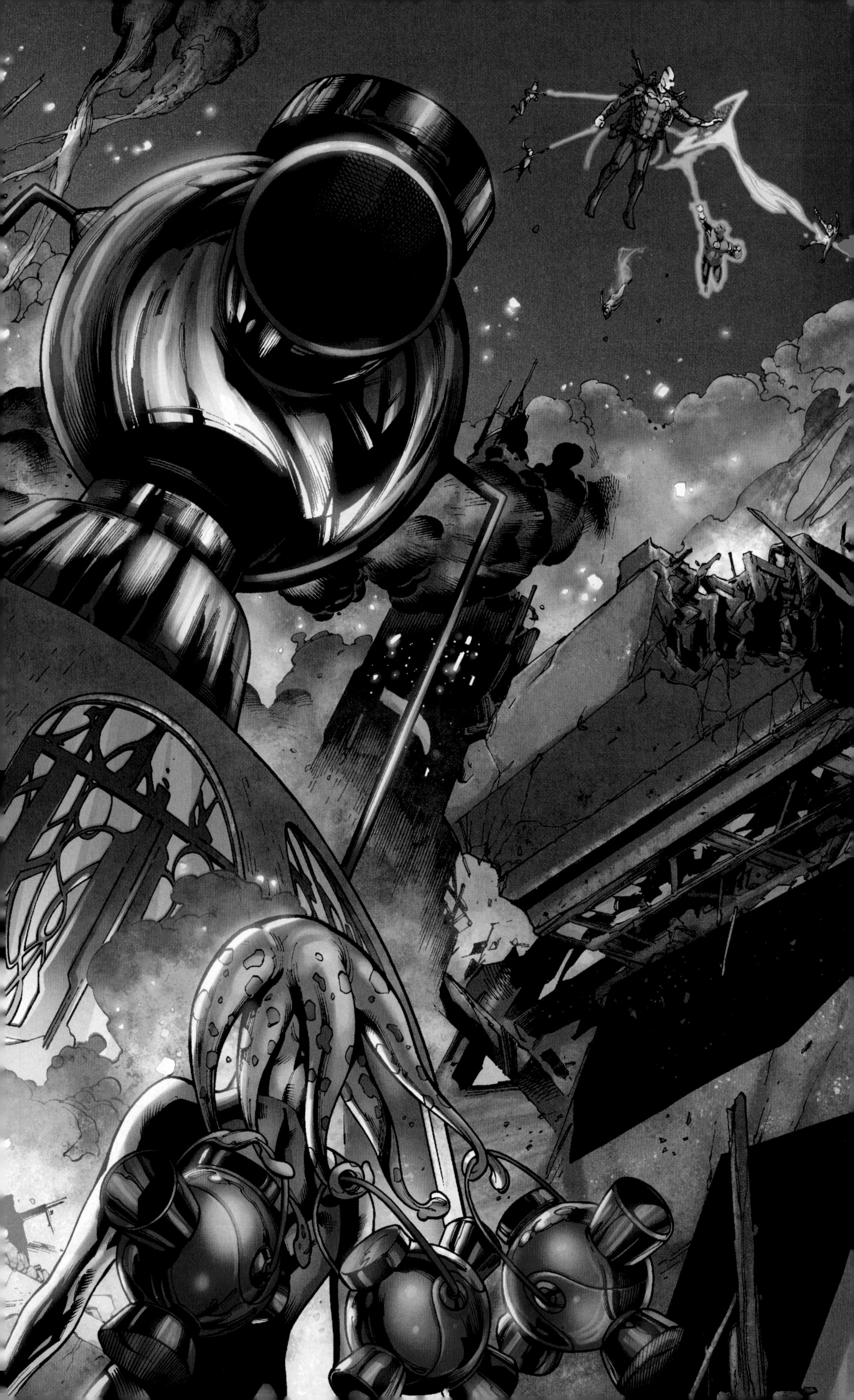

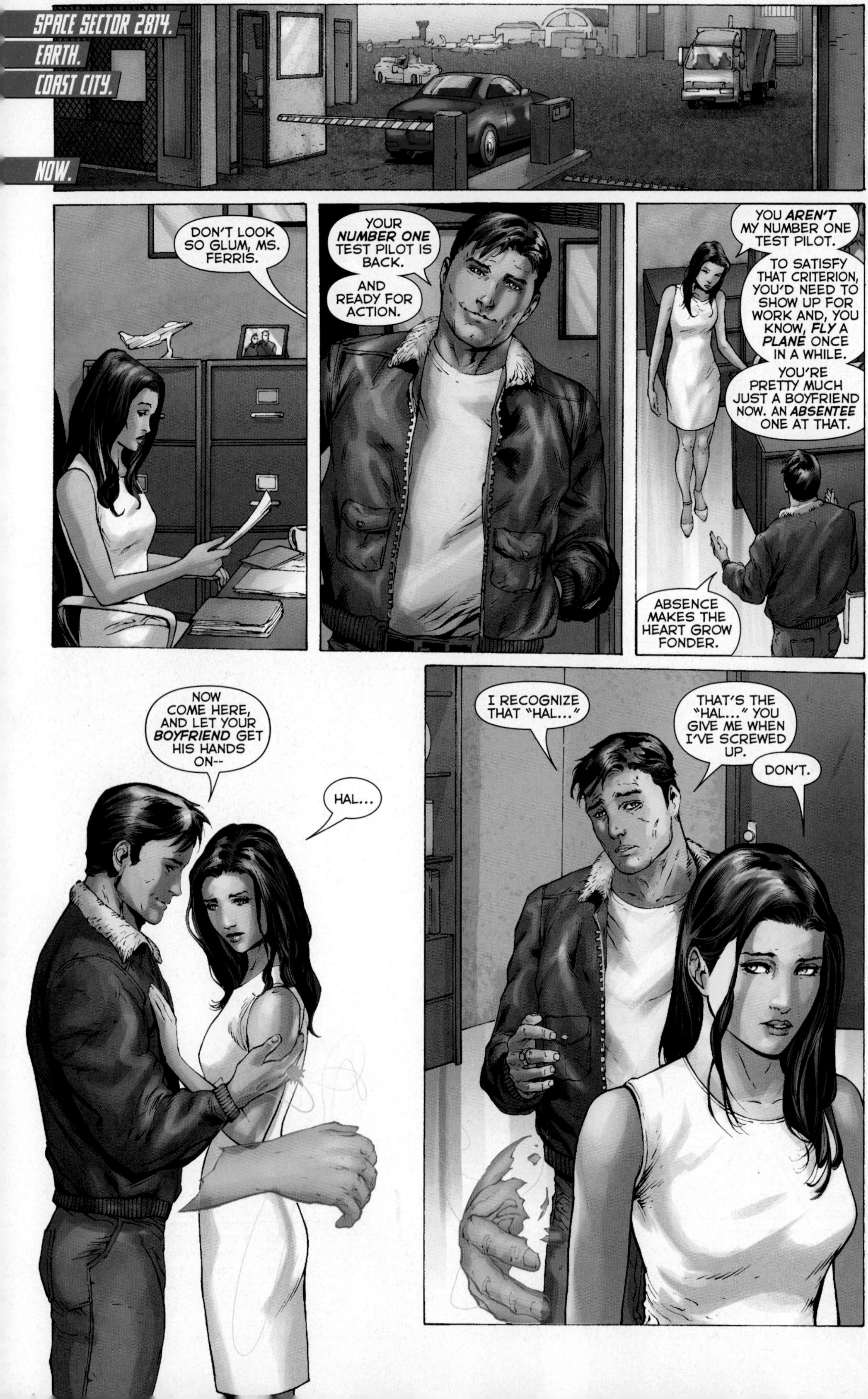
SPACE SECTOR 2814.
EARTH.
COAST CITY.
NOW.
DON'T LOOK SO GLUM, MS. FERRIS.
YOUR NUMBER ONE TEST PILOT IS BACK.
AND READY FOR ACTION.
YOU AREN'T MY NUMBER ONE TEST PILOT.
TO SATISFY THAT CRITERION, YOU'D NEED TO SHOW UP FOR WORK AND, YOU KNOW, FLY A PLANE ONCE IN A WHILE.
YOU'RE PRETTY MUCH JUST A BOYFRIEND NOW. AN ABSENTEE ONE AT THAT.
ABSENCE MAKES THE HEART GROW FONDER.
NOW COME HERE, AND LET YOUR BOYFRIEND GET HIS HANDS ON--
HAL...
I RECOGNIZE THAT "HAL..."
THAT'S THE "HAL..." YOU GIVE ME WHEN I'VE SCREWED UP.
DON'T.

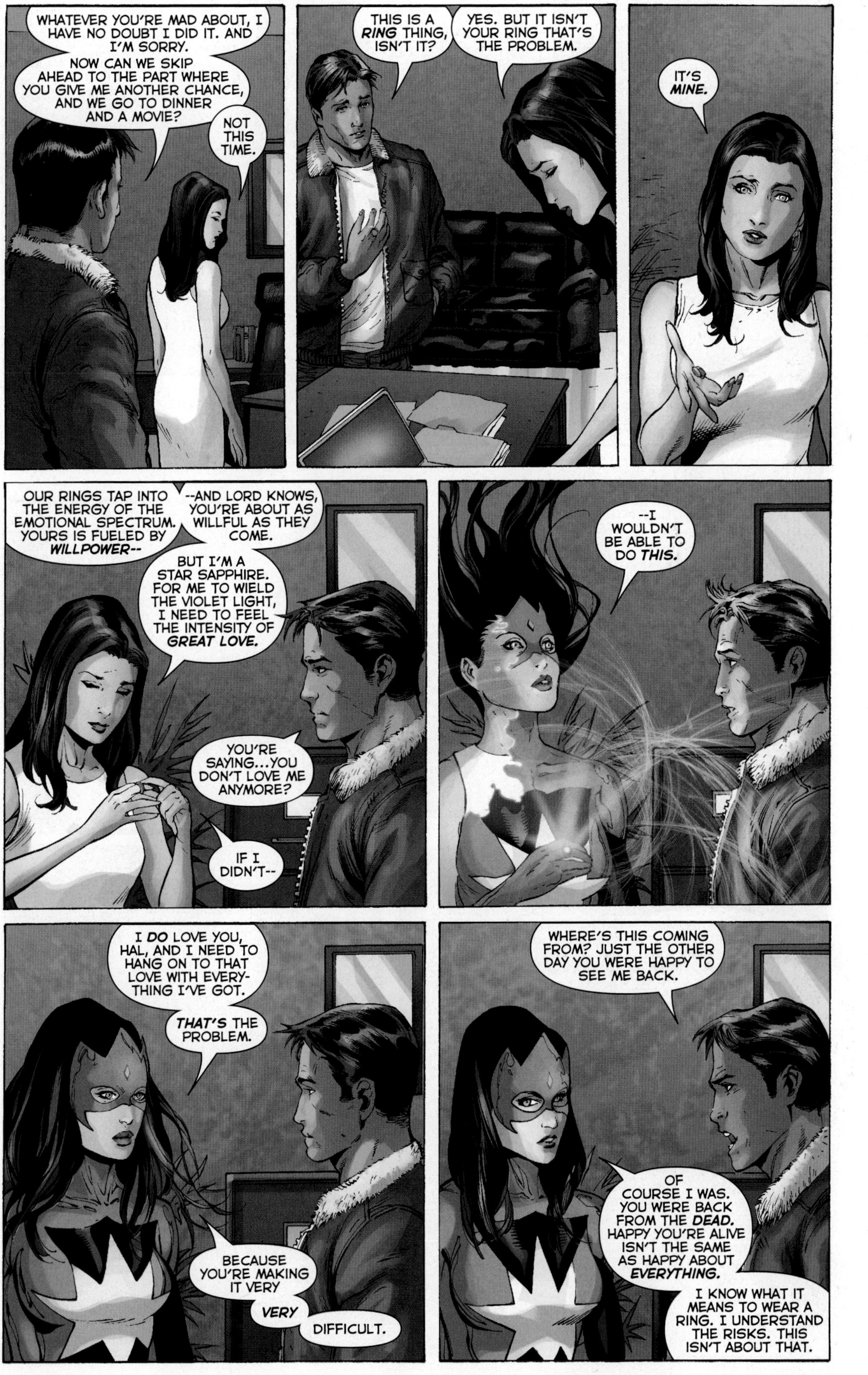
WHATEVER YOU'RE MAD ABOUT, I HAVE NO DOUBT I DID IT. AND I'M SORRY.
NOW CAN WE SKIP AHEAD TO THE PART WHERE YOU GIVE ME ANOTHER CHANCE, AND WE GO TO DINNER AND A MOVIE?
NOT THIS TIME.
THIS IS A RING THING, ISN'T IT?
YES. BUT IT ISN'T YOUR RING THAT'S THE PROBLEM.
IT'S MINE.
OUR RINGS TAP INTO THE ENERGY OF THE EMOTIONAL SPECTRUM. YOURS IS FUELED BY WILLPOWER--
--AND LORD KNOWS, YOU'RE ABOUT AS WILLFUL AS THEY COME.
BUT I'M A STAR SAPPHIRE. FOR ME TO WIELD THE VIOLET LIGHT, I NEED TO FEEL THE INTENSITY OF GREAT LOVE.
YOU'RE SAYING...YOU DON'T LOVE ME ANYMORE?
IF I DIDN'T--
--I WOULDN'T BE ABLE TO DO THIS.
I DO LOVE YOU, HAL, AND I NEED TO HANG ON TO THAT LOVE WITH EVERY-THING I'VE GOT.
THAT'S THE PROBLEM.
BECAUSE YOU'RE MAKING IT VERY
VERY
DIFFICULT.
WHERE'S THIS COMING FROM? JUST THE OTHER DAY YOU WERE HAPPY TO SEE ME BACK.
OF COURSE I WAS. YOU WERE BACK FROM THE DEAD. HAPPY YOU'RE ALIVE ISN'T THE SAME AS HAPPY ABOUT EVERYTHING.
I KNOW WHAT IT MEANS TO WEAR A RING. I UNDERSTAND THE RISKS. THIS ISN'T ABOUT THAT.

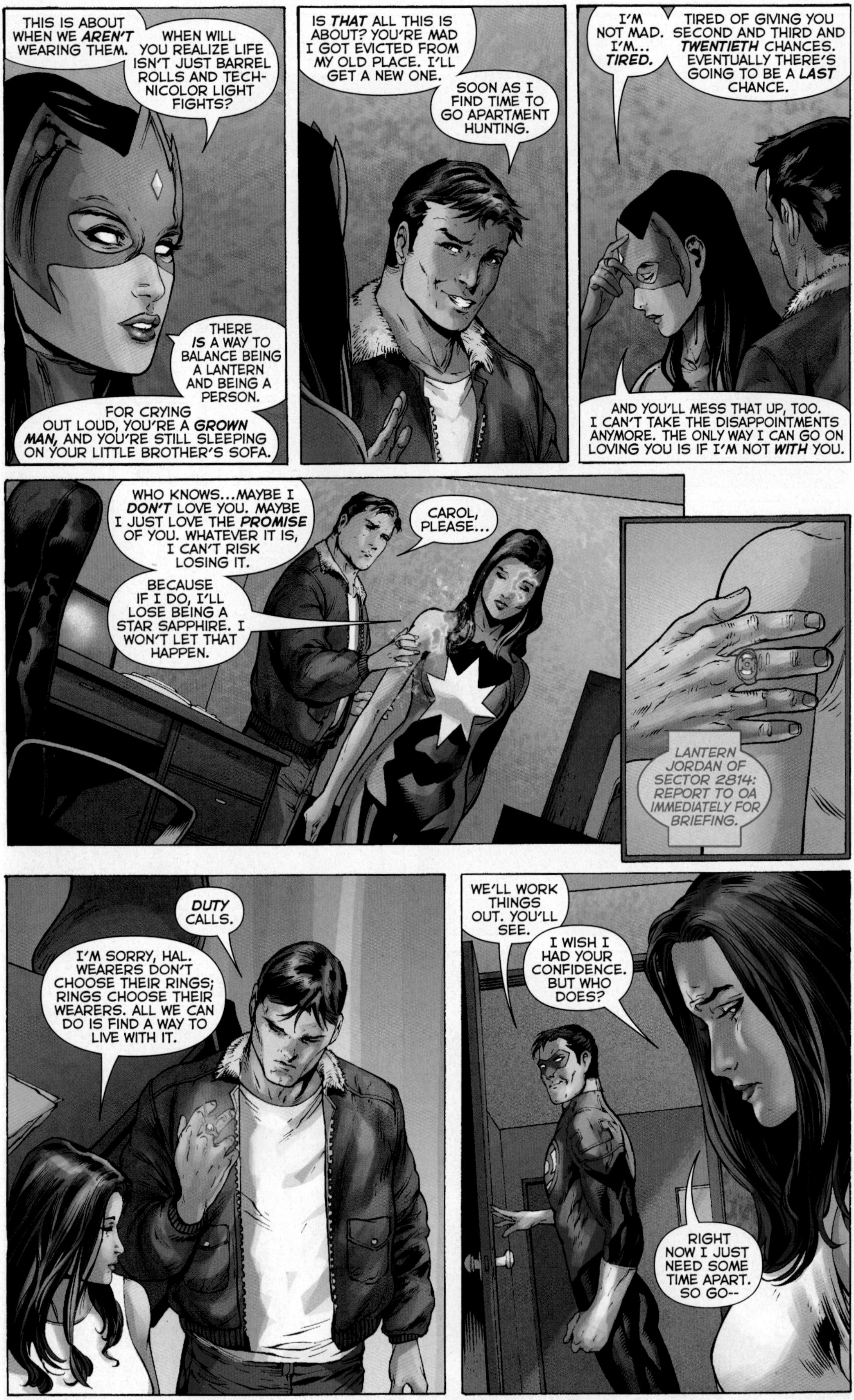
THIS IS ABOUT WHEN WE AREN'T WEARING THEM.
WHEN WILL YOU REALIZE LIFE ISN'T JUST BARREL ROLLS AND TECHNICOLOR LIGHT FIGHTS?
THERE IS A WAY TO BALANCE BEING A LANTERN AND BEING A PERSON.
FOR CRYING OUT LOUD, YOU'RE A GROWN MAN, AND YOU'RE STILL SLEEPING ON YOUR LITTLE BROTHER'S SOFA.
IS THAT ALL THIS IS ABOUT? YOU'RE MAD I GOT EVICTED FROM MY OLD PLACE. I'LL GET A NEW ONE.
SOON AS I FIND TIME TO GO APARTMENT HUNTING.
I'M NOT MAD. I'M... TIRED.
TIRED OF GIVING YOU SECOND AND THIRD AND TWENTIETH CHANCES. EVENTUALLY THERE'S GOING TO BE A LAST CHANCE.
AND YOU'LL MESS THAT UP, TOO. I CAN'T TAKE THE DISAPPOINTMENTS ANYMORE. THE ONLY WAY I CAN GO ON LOVING YOU IS IF I'M NOT WITH YOU.
WHO KNOWS...MAYBE I DON'T LOVE YOU. MAYBE I JUST LOVE THE PROMISE OF YOU. WHATEVER IT IS, I CAN'T RISK LOSING IT.
CAROL, PLEASE...
BECAUSE IF I DO, I'LL LOSE BEING A STAR SAPPHIRE. I WON'T LET THAT HAPPEN.
LANTERN JORDAN OF SECTOR 2814: REPORT TO OA IMMEDIATELY FOR BRIEFING.
DUTY CALLS.
I'M SORRY, HAL. WEARERS DON'T CHOOSE THEIR RINGS; RINGS CHOOSE THEIR WEARERS. ALL WE CAN DO IS FIND A WAY TO LIVE WITH IT.
WE'LL WORK THINGS OUT. YOU'LL SEE.
I WISH I HAD YOUR CONFIDENCE. BUT WHO DOES?
RIGHT NOW I JUST NEED SOME TIME APART. SO GO--

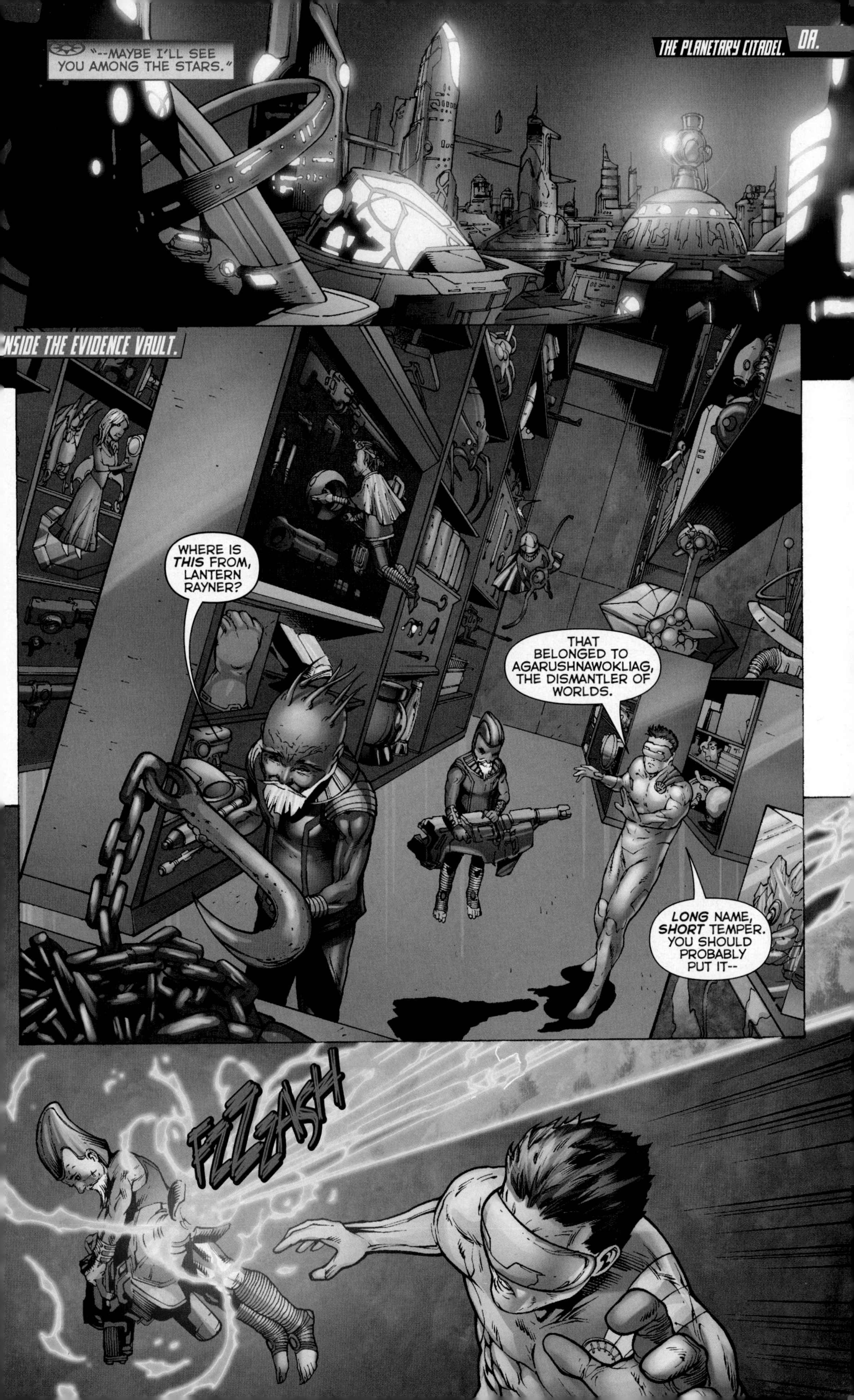
"--MAYBE I'LL SEE YOU AMONG THE STARS."
THE PLANETARY CITADEL. OA.
INSIDE THE EVIDENCE VAULT.
WHERE IS THIS FROM, LANTERN RAYNER?
THAT BELONGED TO AGARUSHNAWOKLIAG, THE DISMANTLER OF WORLDS.
LONG NAME, SHORT TEMPER. YOU SHOULD PROBABLY PUT IT--
FZZZASH

THAT WAS *EXHILARATING!*

FOR *YOU*, MAYBE...

YOU ASKED TO SEE ME, GUARDIANS?

JUST A HEADS-UP--I ALREADY RECEIVED MY SCOLDING FOR TODAY.

WE HAVE NO INTENTION OF REPRIMANDING YOU, LANTERN JORDAN. WE WISH TO *PROMOTE* YOU.

YOU ARE THE NEW CORPS LEADER.

EFFECTIVE IMMEDIATELY.

YOU'VE BEEN LOCKED IN A BOX FOR *BILLIONS* OF YEARS, SO LET ME CLEAR UP ANY MISCONCEPTIONS YOU HAVE ABOUT ME.

I WAS BOOTED FROM THE AIR FORCE FOR *DECKING* MY SUPERIOR OFFICER.

TRUST ME, I'M NOT LEADERSHIP MATERIAL.

WHAT HE SAID.

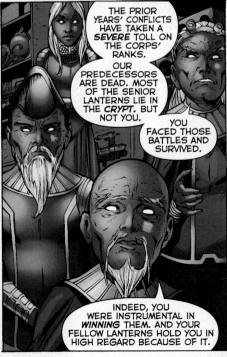

THE PRIOR YEARS' CONFLICTS HAVE TAKEN A *SEVERE* TOLL ON THE CORPS' RANKS.

OUR PREDECESSORS ARE DEAD. MOST OF THE SENIOR LANTERNS LIE IN THE *CRYPT.* BUT NOT YOU.

YOU FACED THOSE BATTLES AND SURVIVED.

INDEED, YOU WERE INSTRUMENTAL IN *WINNING* THEM. AND YOUR FELLOW LANTERNS HOLD YOU IN HIGH REGARD BECAUSE OF IT.

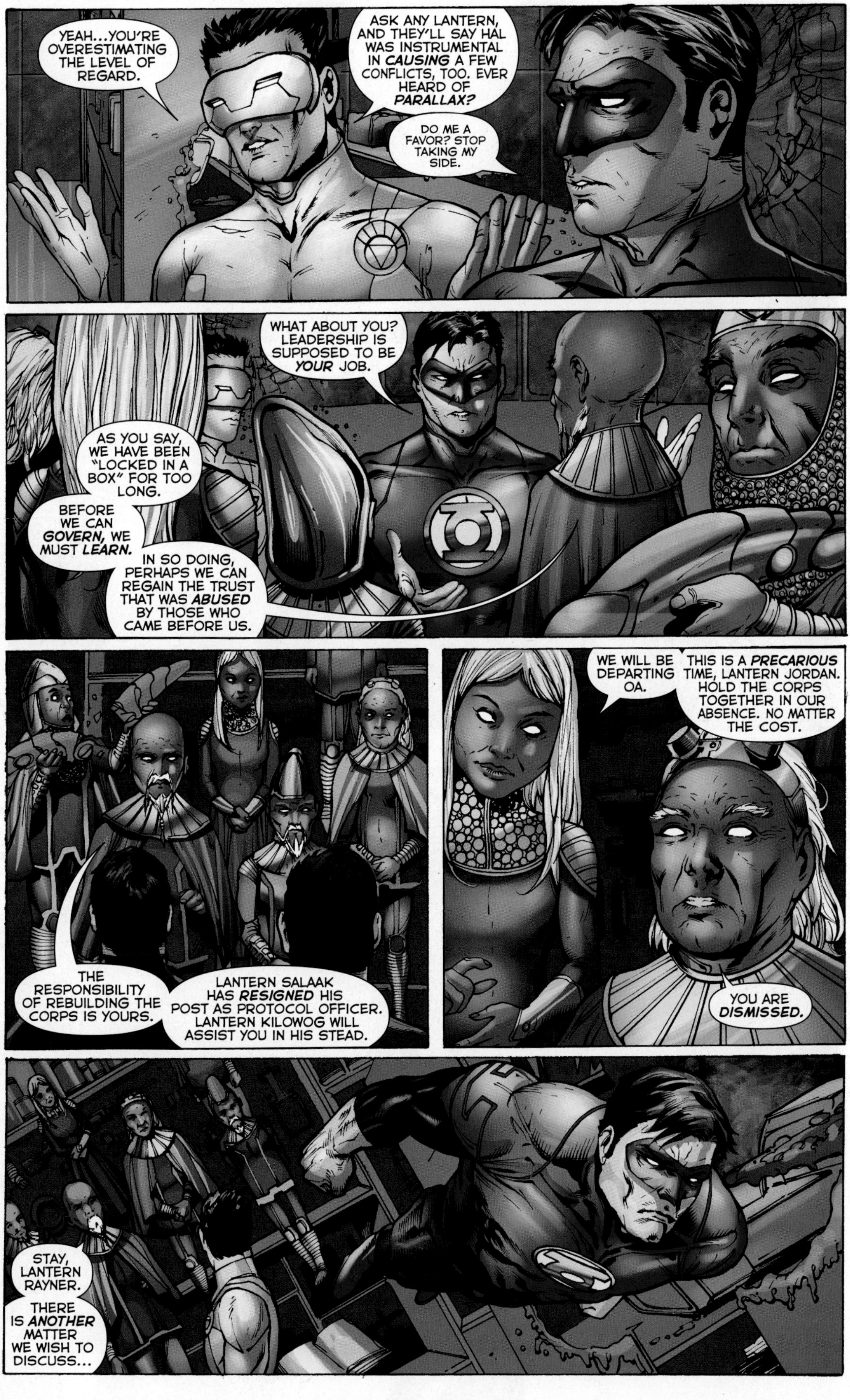
YEAH...YOU'RE OVERESTIMATING THE LEVEL OF REGARD.
ASK ANY LANTERN, AND THEY'LL SAY HAL WAS INSTRUMENTAL IN *CAUSING* A FEW CONFLICTS, TOO. EVER HEARD OF *PARALLAX?*
DO ME A FAVOR? STOP TAKING MY SIDE.
WHAT ABOUT YOU? LEADERSHIP IS SUPPOSED TO BE *YOUR* JOB.
AS YOU SAY, WE HAVE BEEN "LOCKED IN A BOX" FOR TOO LONG.
BEFORE WE CAN *GOVERN,* WE MUST *LEARN.*
IN SO DOING, PERHAPS WE CAN REGAIN THE TRUST THAT WAS *ABUSED* BY THOSE WHO CAME BEFORE US.
THE RESPONSIBILITY OF REBUILDING THE CORPS IS YOURS.
LANTERN SALAAK HAS *RESIGNED* HIS POST AS PROTOCOL OFFICER. LANTERN KILOWOG WILL ASSIST YOU IN HIS STEAD.
WE WILL BE DEPARTING OA.
THIS IS A *PRECARIOUS* TIME, LANTERN JORDAN. HOLD THE CORPS TOGETHER IN OUR ABSENCE. NO MATTER THE COST.
YOU ARE *DISMISSED.*
STAY, LANTERN RAYNER.
THERE IS *ANOTHER* MATTER WE WISH TO DISCUSS...

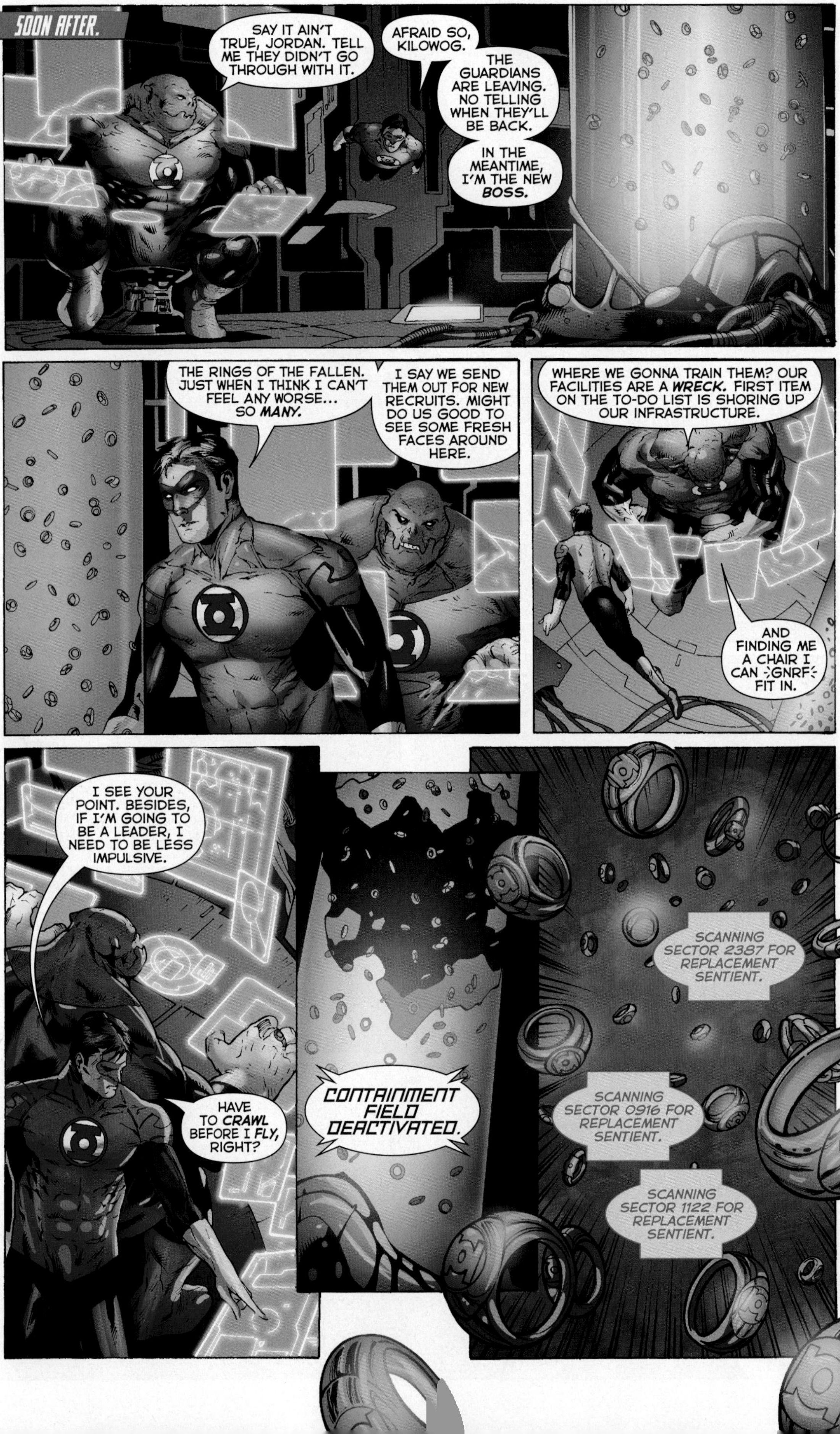
SOON AFTER.
SAY IT AIN'T TRUE, JORDAN. TELL ME THEY DIDN'T GO THROUGH WITH IT.
AFRAID SO, KILOWOG.
THE GUARDIANS ARE LEAVING. NO TELLING WHEN THEY'LL BE BACK.
IN THE MEANTIME, I'M THE NEW BOSS.
THE RINGS OF THE FALLEN. JUST WHEN I THINK I CAN'T FEEL ANY WORSE... SO MANY.
I SAY WE SEND THEM OUT FOR NEW RECRUITS. MIGHT DO US GOOD TO SEE SOME FRESH FACES AROUND HERE.
WHERE WE GONNA TRAIN THEM? OUR FACILITIES ARE A WRECK. FIRST ITEM ON THE TO-DO LIST IS SHORING UP OUR INFRASTRUCTURE.
AND FINDING ME A CHAIR I CAN -GNRF- FIT IN.
I SEE YOUR POINT. BESIDES, IF I'M GOING TO BE A LEADER, I NEED TO BE LESS IMPULSIVE.
HAVE TO CRAWL BEFORE I FLY, RIGHT?
CONTAINMENT FIELD DEACTIVATED.
SCANNING SECTOR 2387 FOR REPLACEMENT SENTIENT.
SCANNING SECTOR 0916 FOR REPLACEMENT SENTIENT.
SCANNING SECTOR 1122 FOR REPLACEMENT SENTIENT.

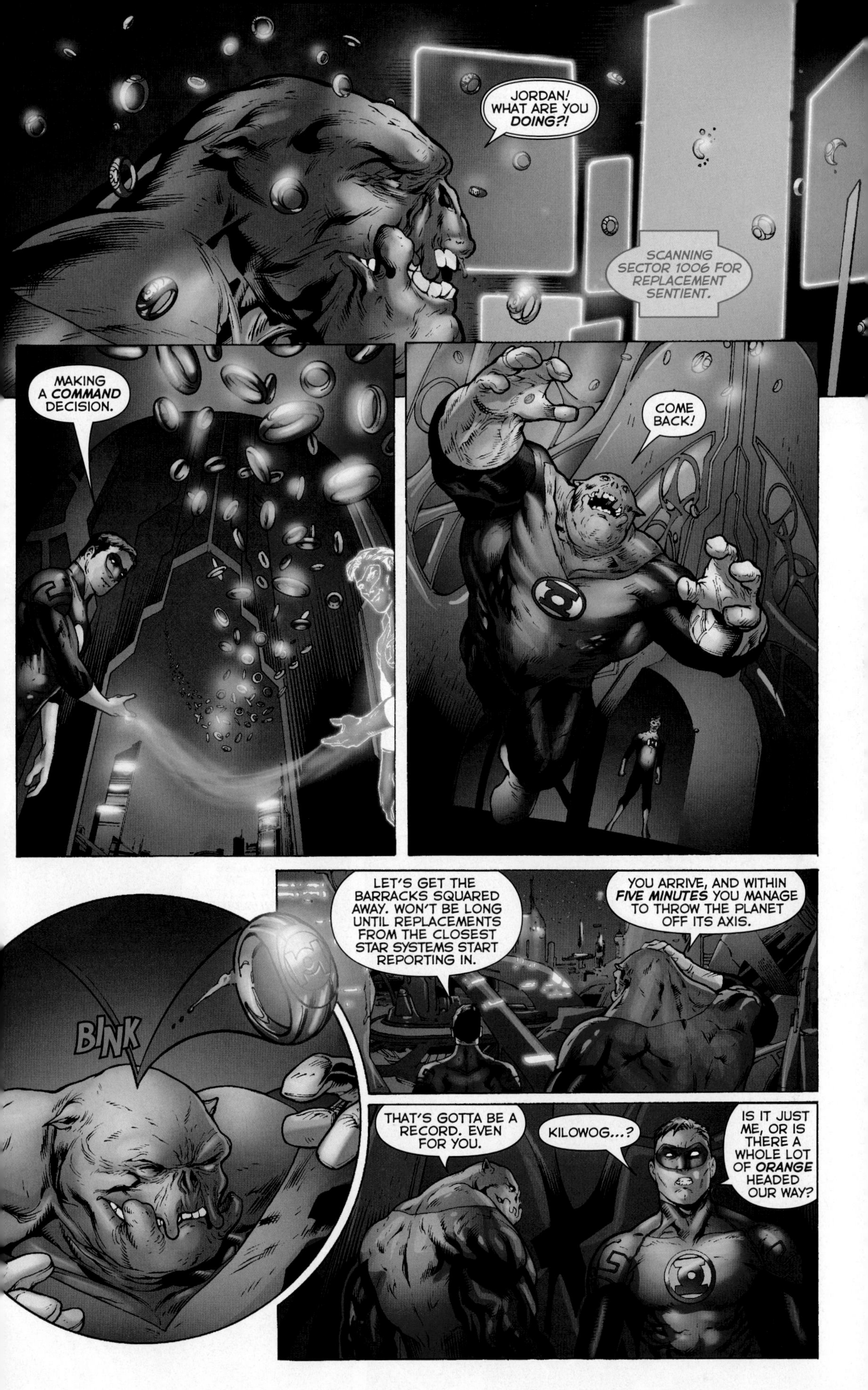
JORDAN! WHAT ARE YOU DOING?!
SCANNING SECTOR 1006 FOR REPLACEMENT SENTIENT.
MAKING A COMMAND DECISION.
COME BACK!
BINK
LET'S GET THE BARRACKS SQUARED AWAY. WON'T BE LONG UNTIL REPLACEMENTS FROM THE CLOSEST STAR SYSTEMS START REPORTING IN.
YOU ARRIVE, AND WITHIN FIVE MINUTES YOU MANAGE TO THROW THE PLANET OFF ITS AXIS.
THAT'S GOTTA BE A RECORD. EVEN FOR YOU.
KILOWOG...?
IS IT JUST ME, OR IS THERE A WHOLE LOT OF ORANGE HEADED OUR WAY?

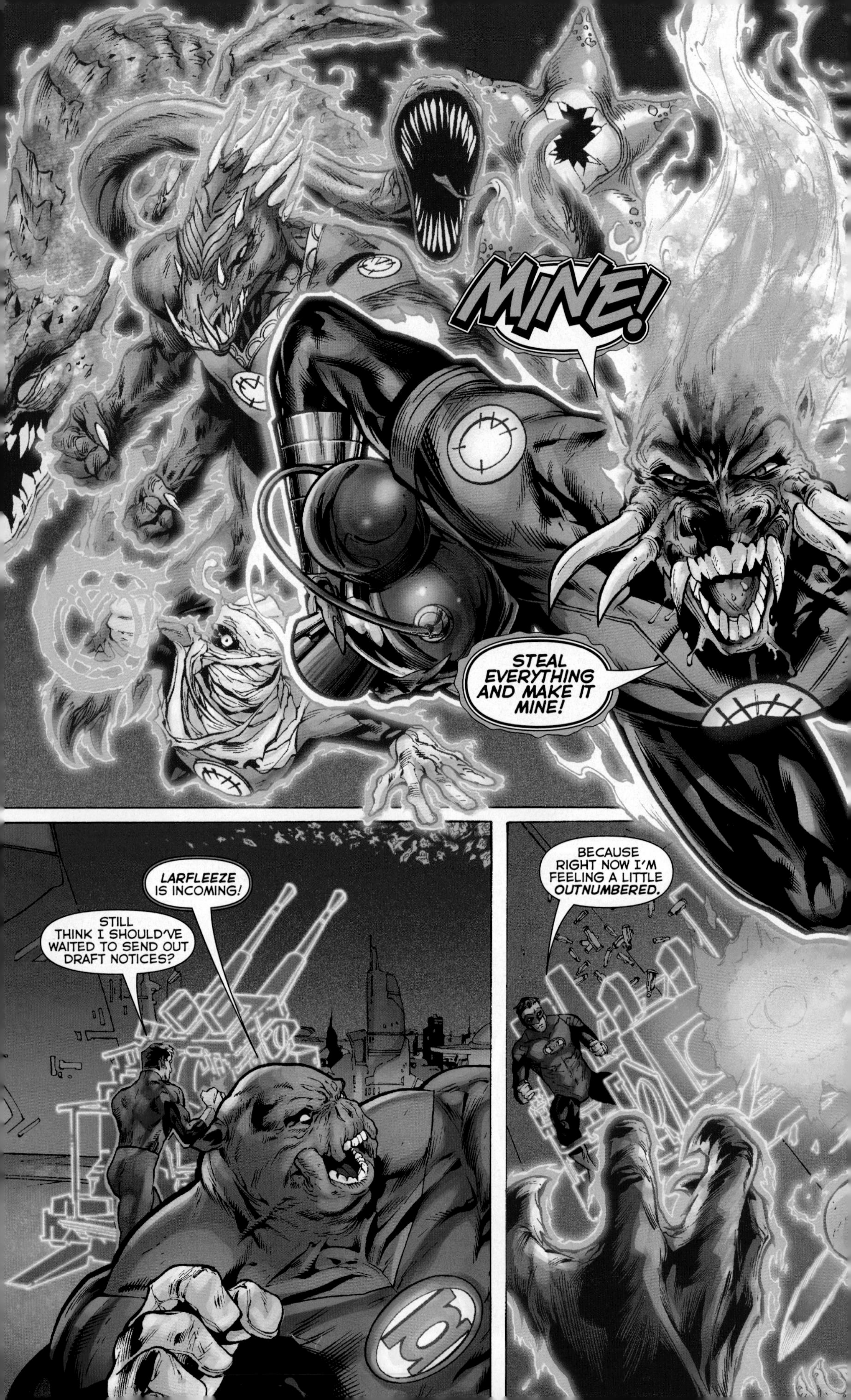
MINE!
STEAL EVERYTHING AND MAKE IT MINE!
LARFLEEZE IS INCOMING!
STILL THINK I SHOULD'VE WAITED TO SEND OUT DRAFT NOTICES?
BECAUSE RIGHT NOW I'M FEELING A LITTLE OUTNUMBERED.

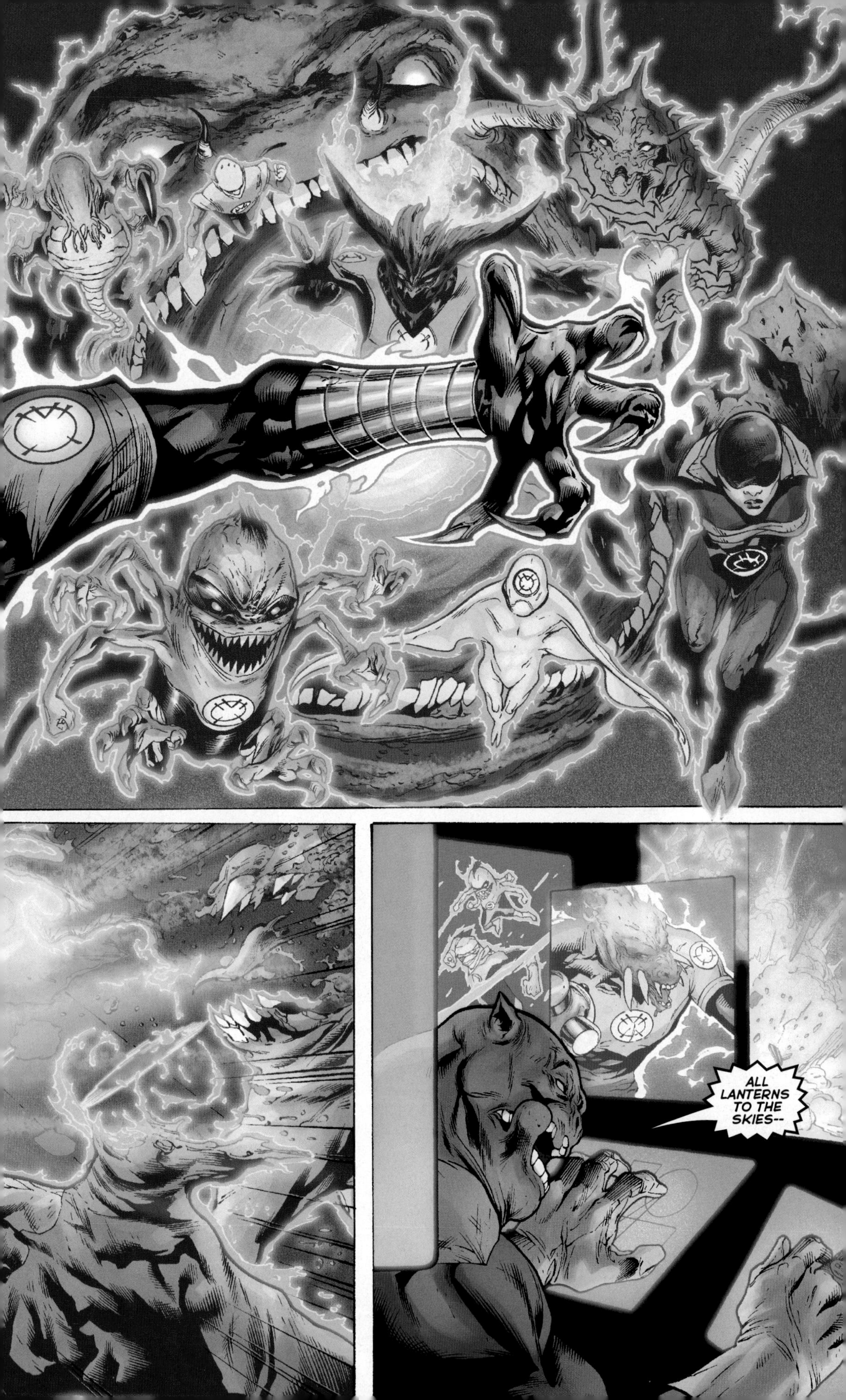
ALL LANTERNS TO THE SKIES--

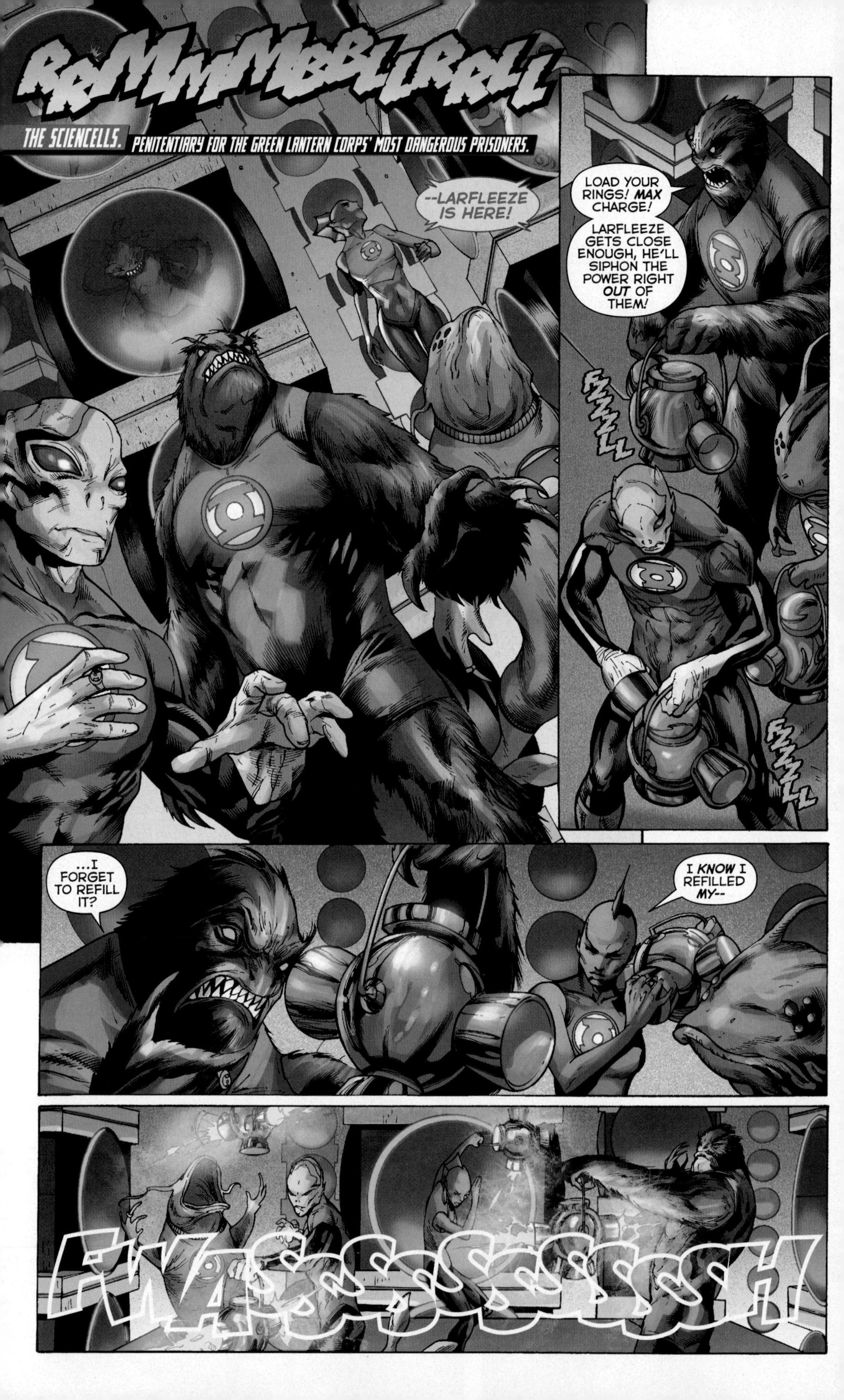

RRRMMMMBBLLRRRLL
THE SCIENCELLS. PENITENTIARY FOR THE GREEN LANTERN CORPS' MOST DANGEROUS PRISONERS.
--LARFLEEZE IS HERE!
LOAD YOUR RINGS! MAX CHARGE!
LARFLEEZE GETS CLOSE ENOUGH, HE'LL SIPHON THE POWER RIGHT OUT OF THEM!
FZZZZLL
FZZZZLL
...I FORGET TO REFILL IT?
I KNOW I REFILLED MY--
FWASSSSSSSH

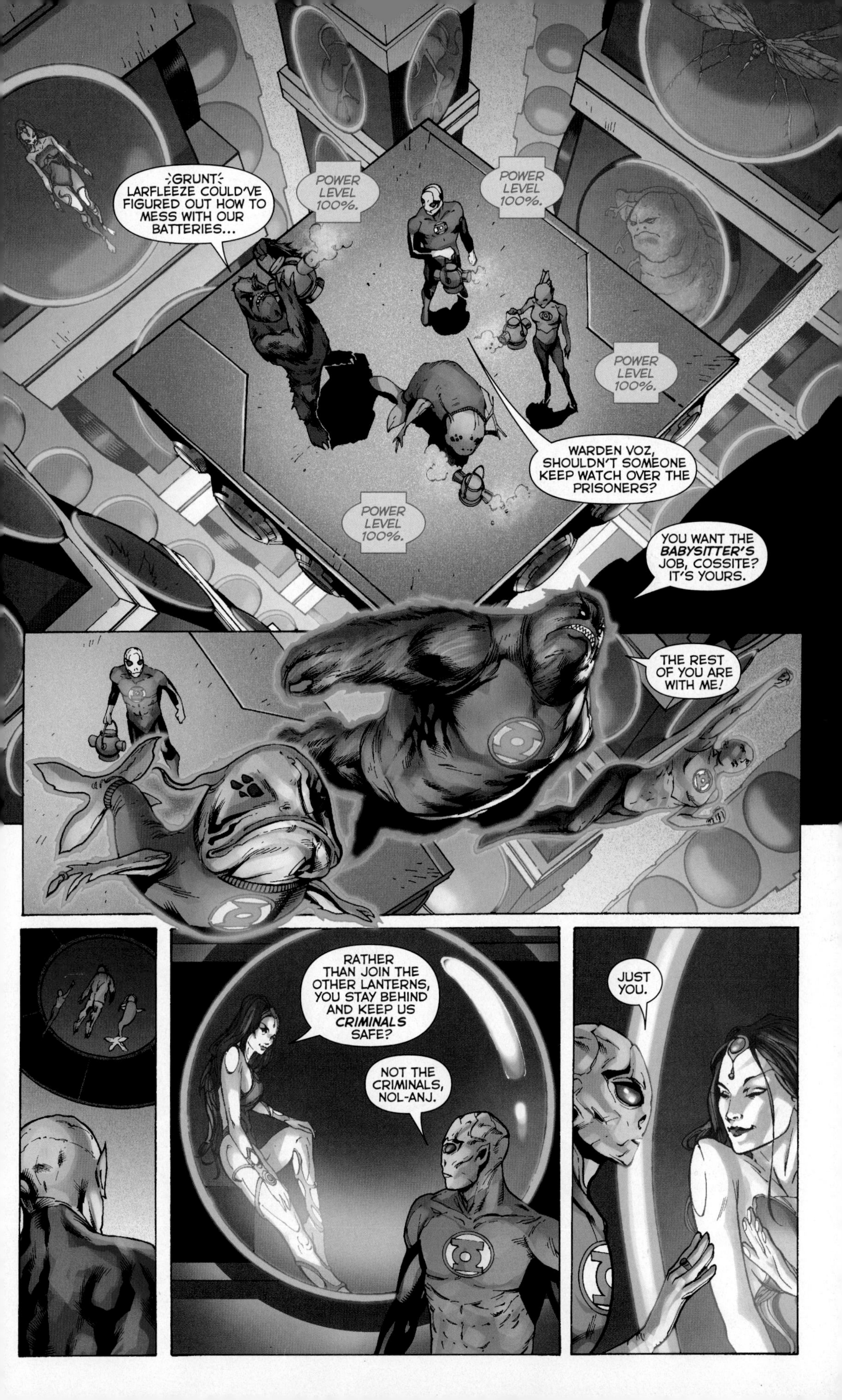
-GRUNT- LARFLEEZE COULD'VE FIGURED OUT HOW TO MESS WITH OUR BATTERIES...
POWER LEVEL 100%.
POWER LEVEL 100%.
POWER LEVEL 100%.
WARDEN VOZ, SHOULDN'T SOMEONE KEEP WATCH OVER THE PRISONERS?
POWER LEVEL 100%.
YOU WANT THE BABYSITTER'S JOB, COSSITE? IT'S YOURS.
THE REST OF YOU ARE WITH ME!
RATHER THAN JOIN THE OTHER LANTERNS, YOU STAY BEHIND AND KEEP US CRIMINALS SAFE?
NOT THE CRIMINALS, NOL-ANJ.
JUST YOU.

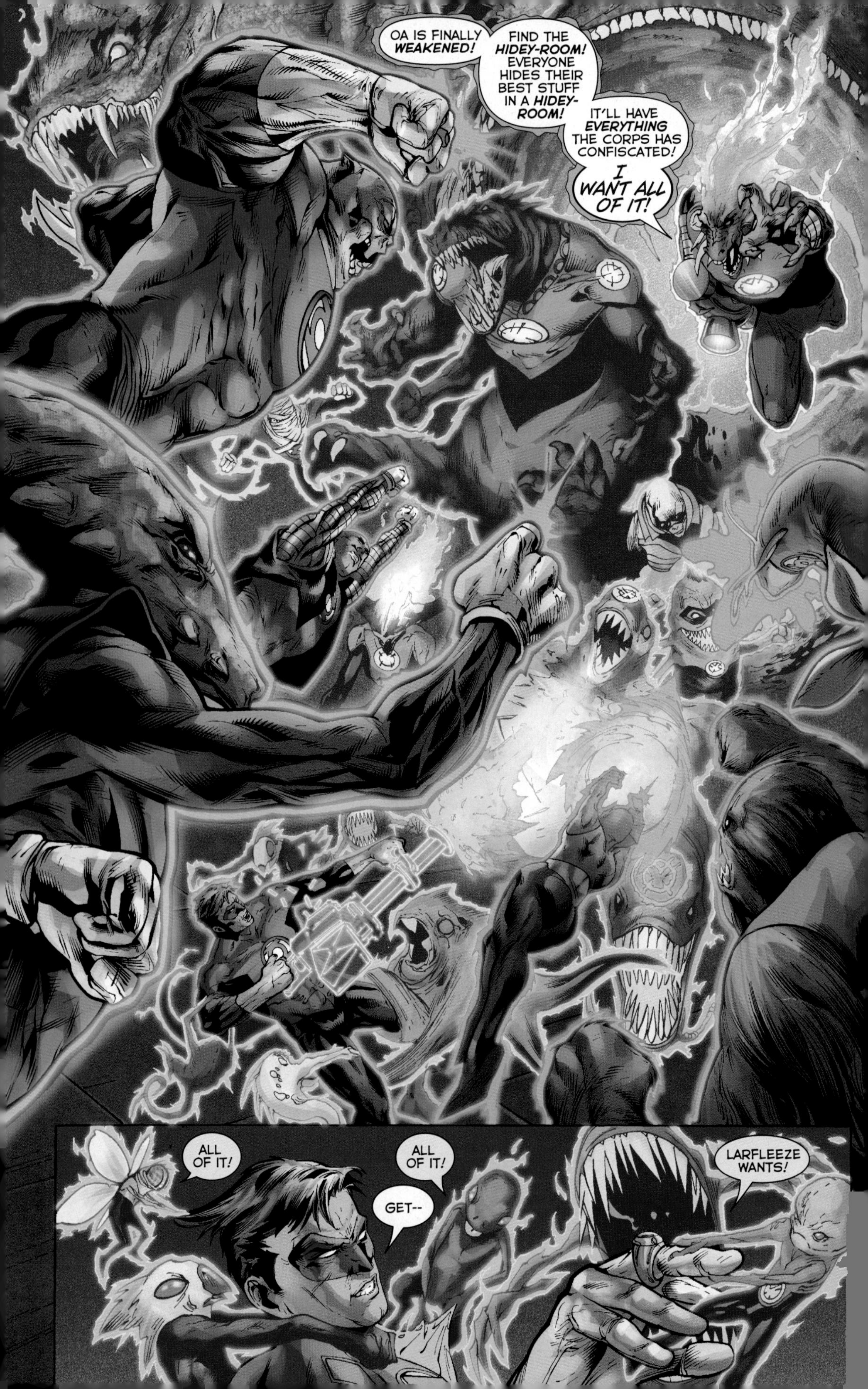
OA IS FINALLY WEAKENED!
FIND THE HIDEY-ROOM! EVERYONE HIDES THEIR BEST STUFF IN A HIDEY-ROOM!
IT'LL HAVE EVERYTHING THE CORPS HAS CONFISCATED!
I WANT ALL OF IT!
ALL OF IT!
ALL OF IT!
GET--
LARFLEEZE WANTS!

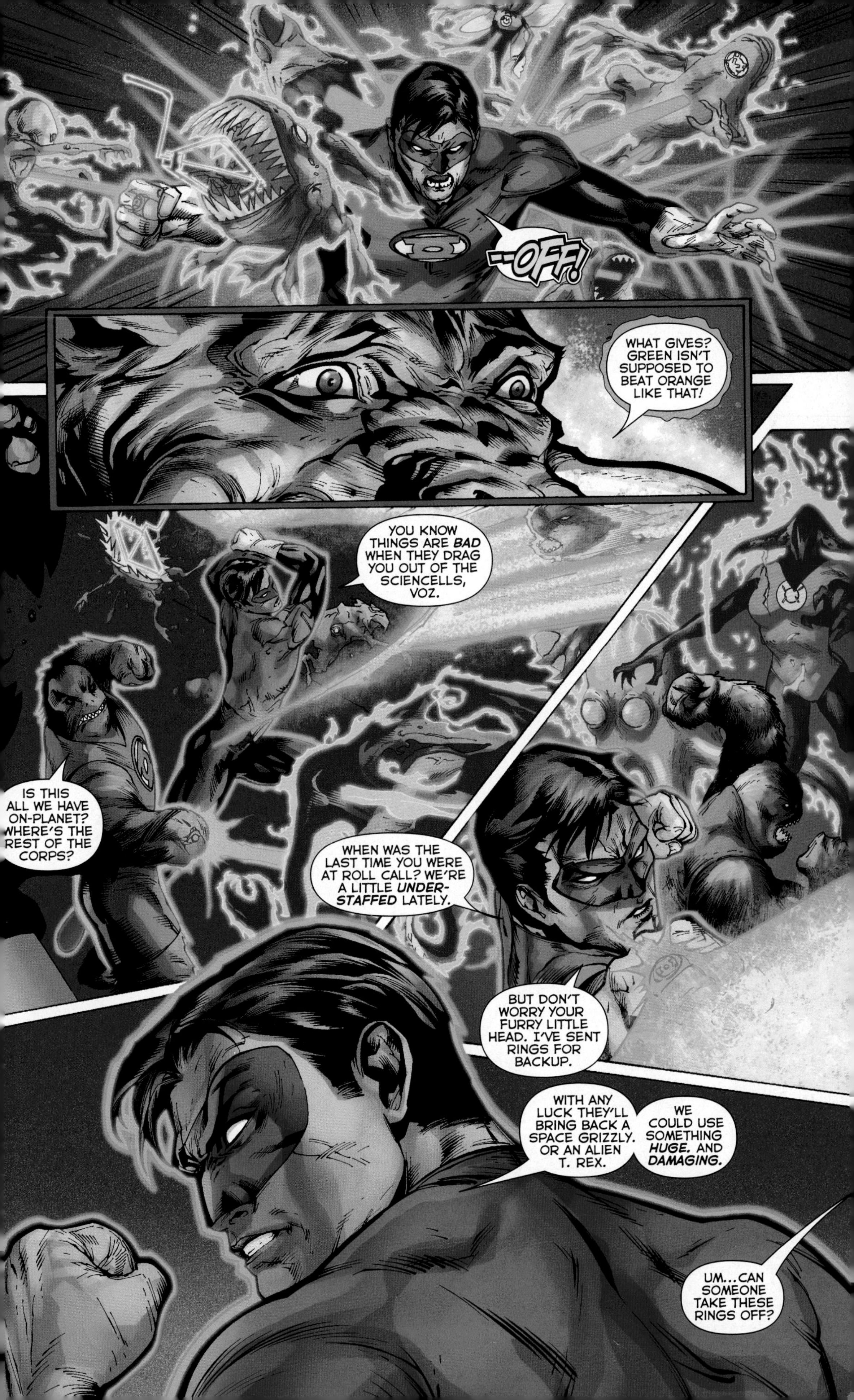
--OFF!
WHAT GIVES? GREEN ISN'T SUPPOSED TO BEAT ORANGE LIKE THAT!
YOU KNOW THINGS ARE BAD WHEN THEY DRAG YOU OUT OF THE SCIENCELLS, VOZ.
IS THIS ALL WE HAVE ON-PLANET? WHERE'S THE REST OF THE CORPS?
WHEN WAS THE LAST TIME YOU WERE AT ROLL CALL? WE'RE A LITTLE UNDER-STAFFED LATELY.
BUT DON'T WORRY YOUR FURRY LITTLE HEAD. I'VE SENT RINGS FOR BACKUP.
WITH ANY LUCK THEY'LL BRING BACK A SPACE GRIZZLY. OR AN ALIEN T. REX.
WE COULD USE SOMETHING HUGE. AND DAMAGING.
UM...CAN SOMEONE TAKE THESE RINGS OFF?

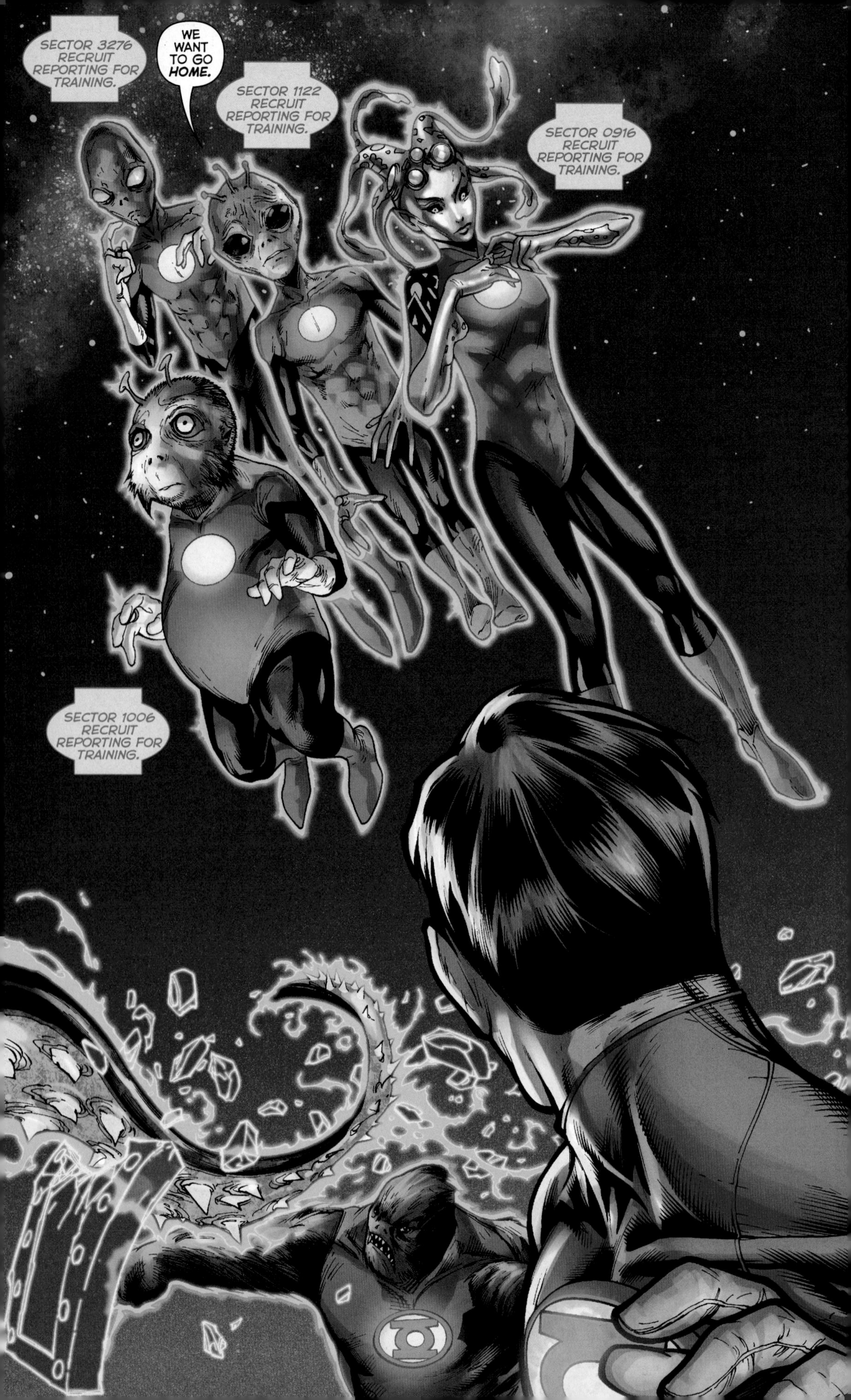
SECTOR 3276 RECRUIT REPORTING FOR TRAINING.
WE WANT TO GO HOME.
SECTOR 1122 RECRUIT REPORTING FOR TRAINING.
SECTOR 0916 RECRUIT REPORTING FOR TRAINING.
SECTOR 1006 RECRUIT REPORTING FOR TRAINING.

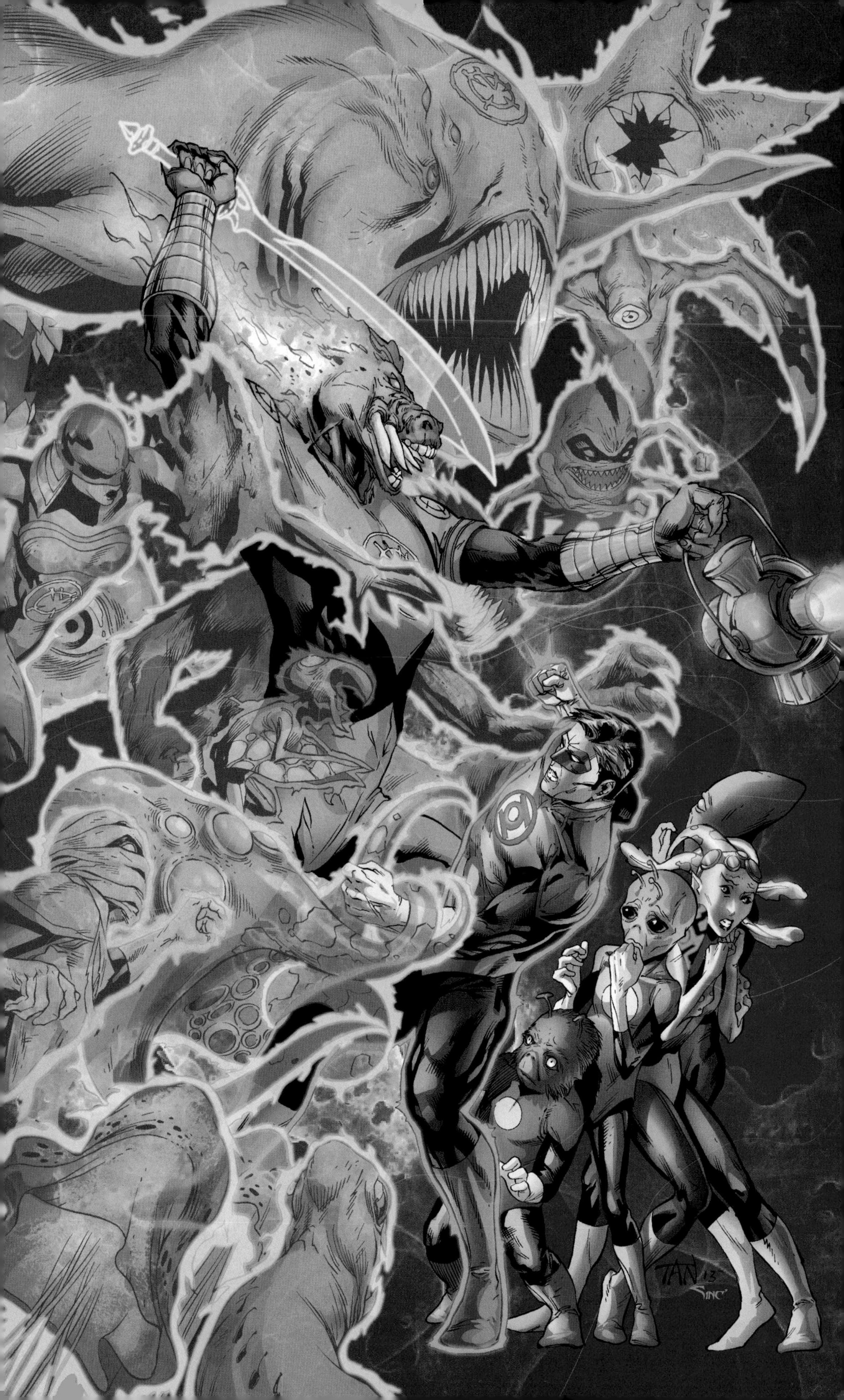

ROBERT VENDITTI writer **BILLY TAN** penciller **ROB HUNTER & JON SIBAL** inkers
cover art by **BILLY TAN & ALEX SINCLAIR**

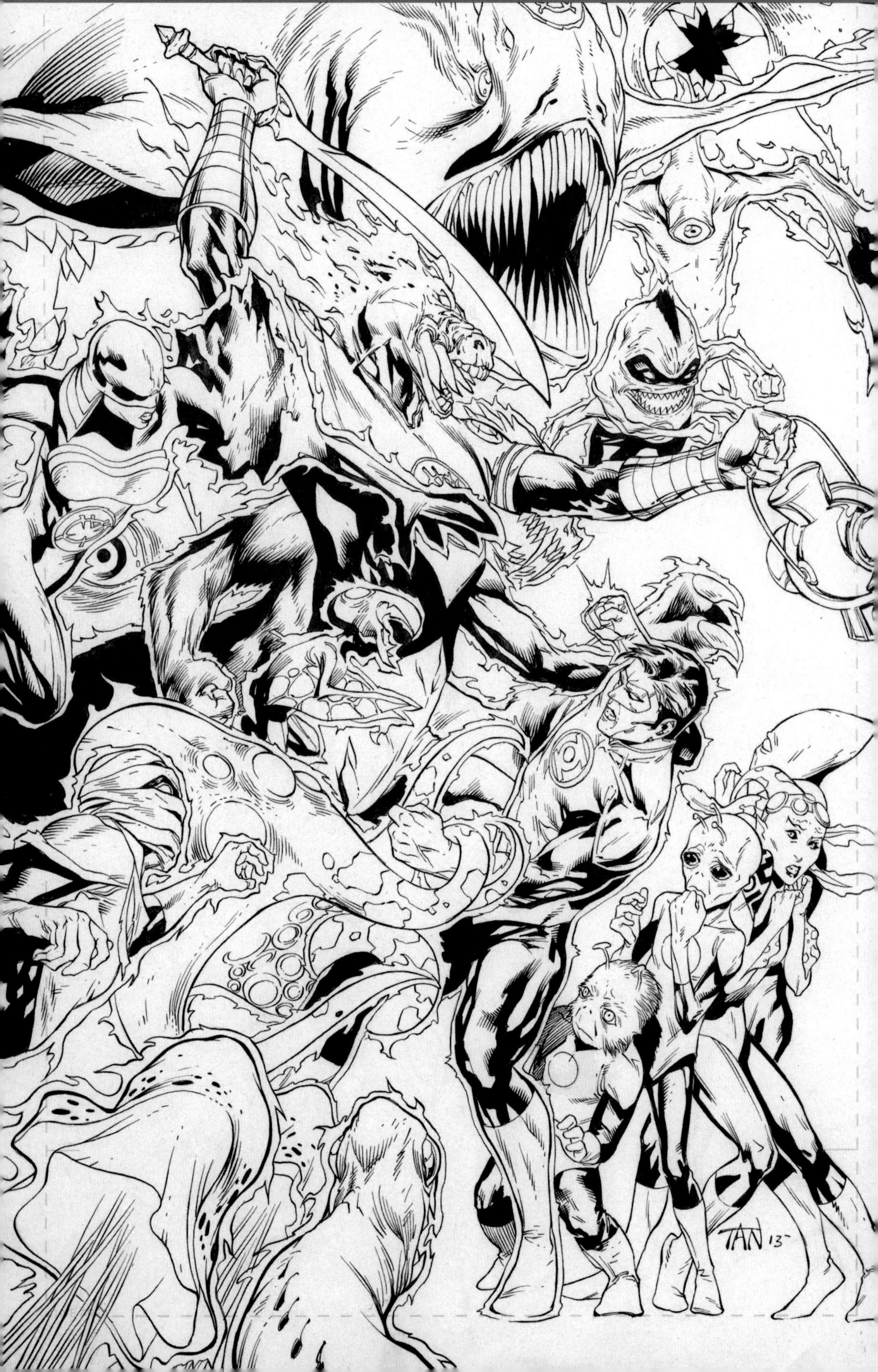
TAN 13

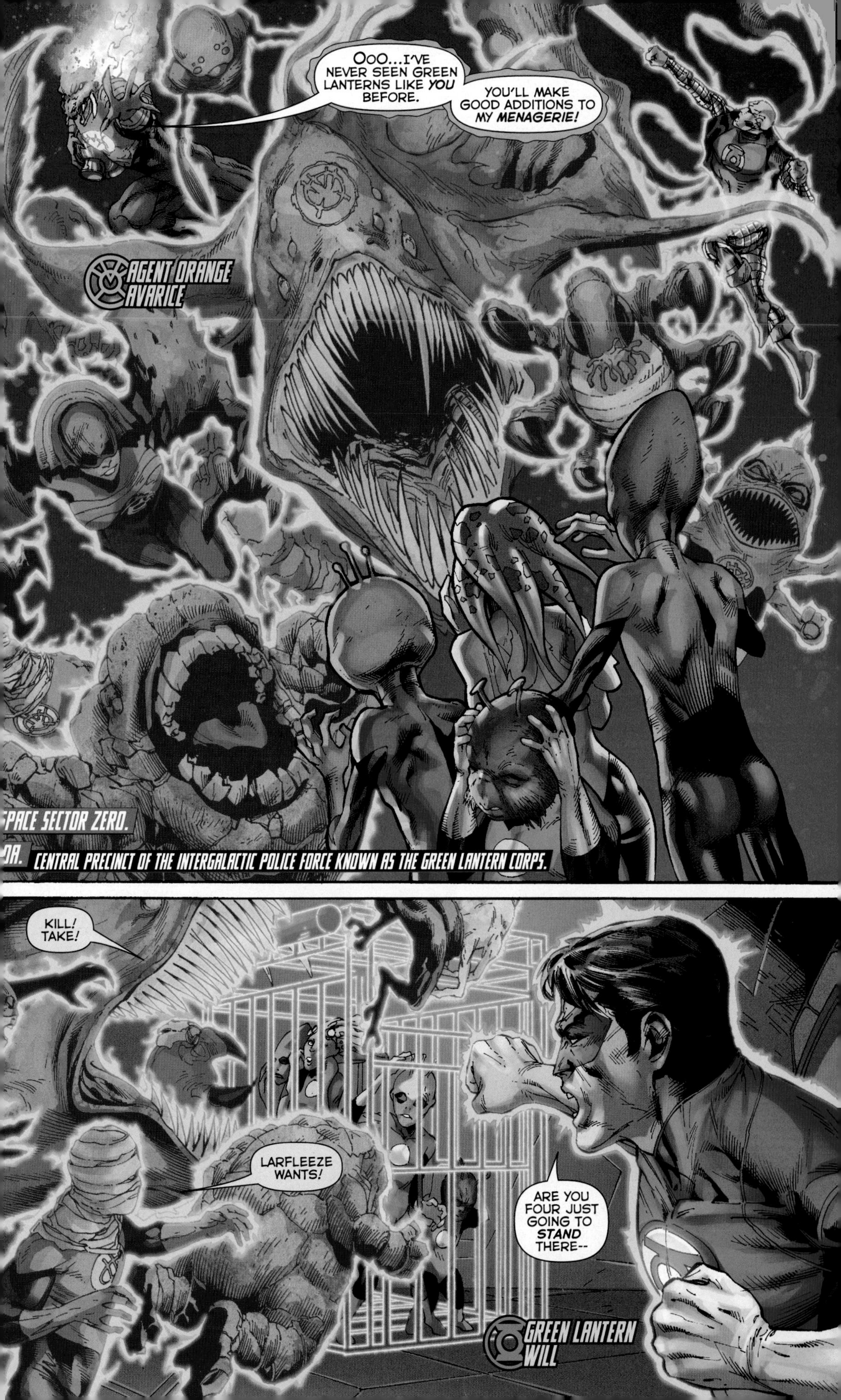

OOO...I'VE NEVER SEEN GREEN LANTERNS LIKE YOU BEFORE.
YOU'LL MAKE GOOD ADDITIONS TO MY MENAGERIE!
AGENT ORANGE AVARICE
SPACE SECTOR ZERO.
OA. CENTRAL PRECINCT OF THE INTERGALACTIC POLICE FORCE KNOWN AS THE GREEN LANTERN CORPS.
KILL! TAKE!
LARFLEEZE WANTS!
ARE YOU FOUR JUST GOING TO STAND THERE--
GREEN LANTERN WILL

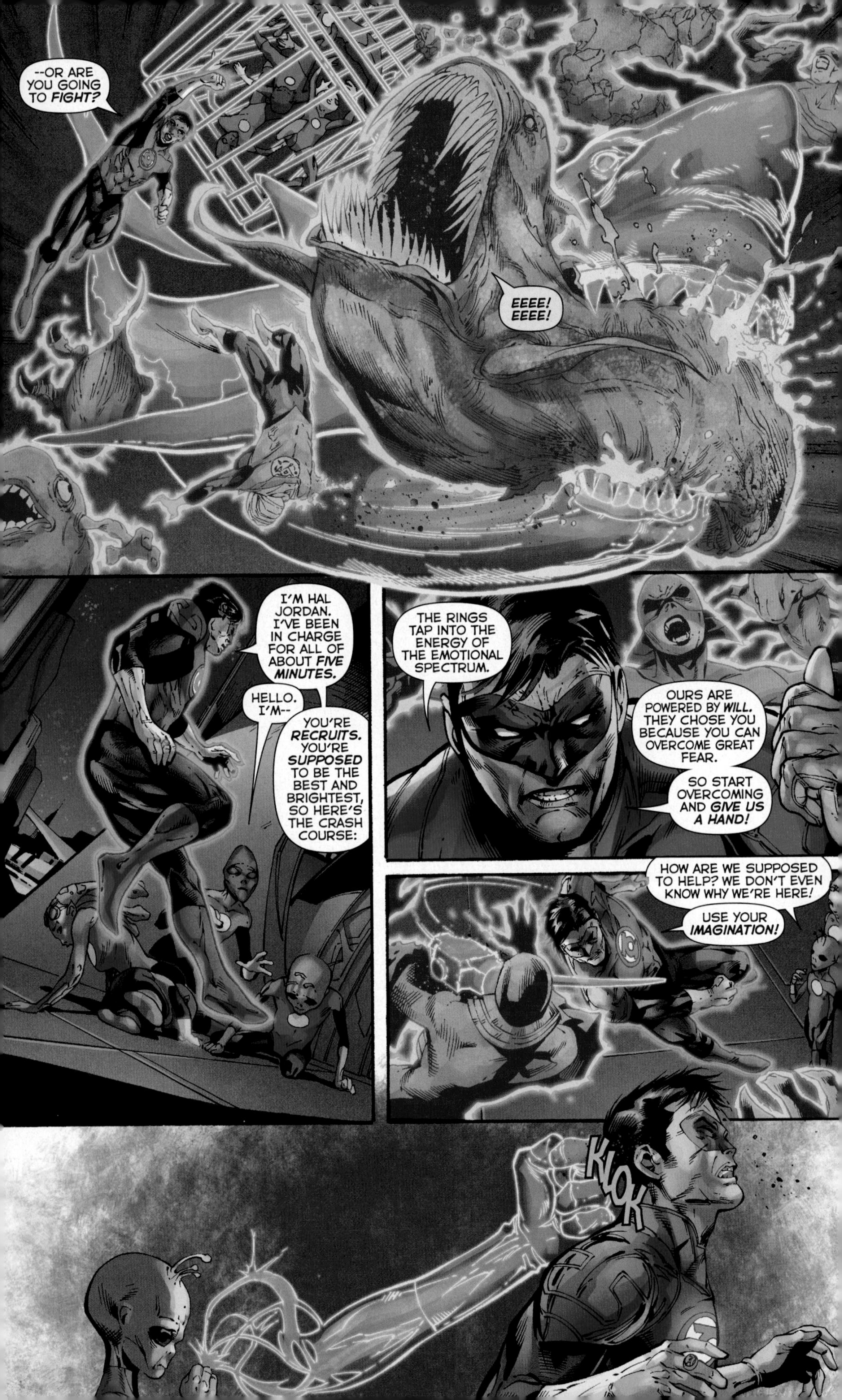
--OR ARE YOU GOING TO *FIGHT?*
EEEE! EEEE!
I'M HAL JORDAN. I'VE BEEN IN CHARGE FOR ALL OF ABOUT *FIVE MINUTES.*
HELLO. I'M--
YOU'RE *RECRUITS.* YOU'RE *SUPPOSED* TO BE THE BEST AND BRIGHTEST, SO HERE'S THE CRASH COURSE:
THE RINGS TAP INTO THE ENERGY OF THE EMOTIONAL SPECTRUM.
OURS ARE POWERED BY *WILL.* THEY CHOSE YOU BECAUSE YOU CAN OVERCOME GREAT FEAR.
SO START OVERCOMING AND *GIVE US A HAND!*
HOW ARE WE SUPPOSED TO HELP? WE DON'T EVEN KNOW WHY WE'RE HERE!
USE YOUR *IMAGINATION!*
KLOK

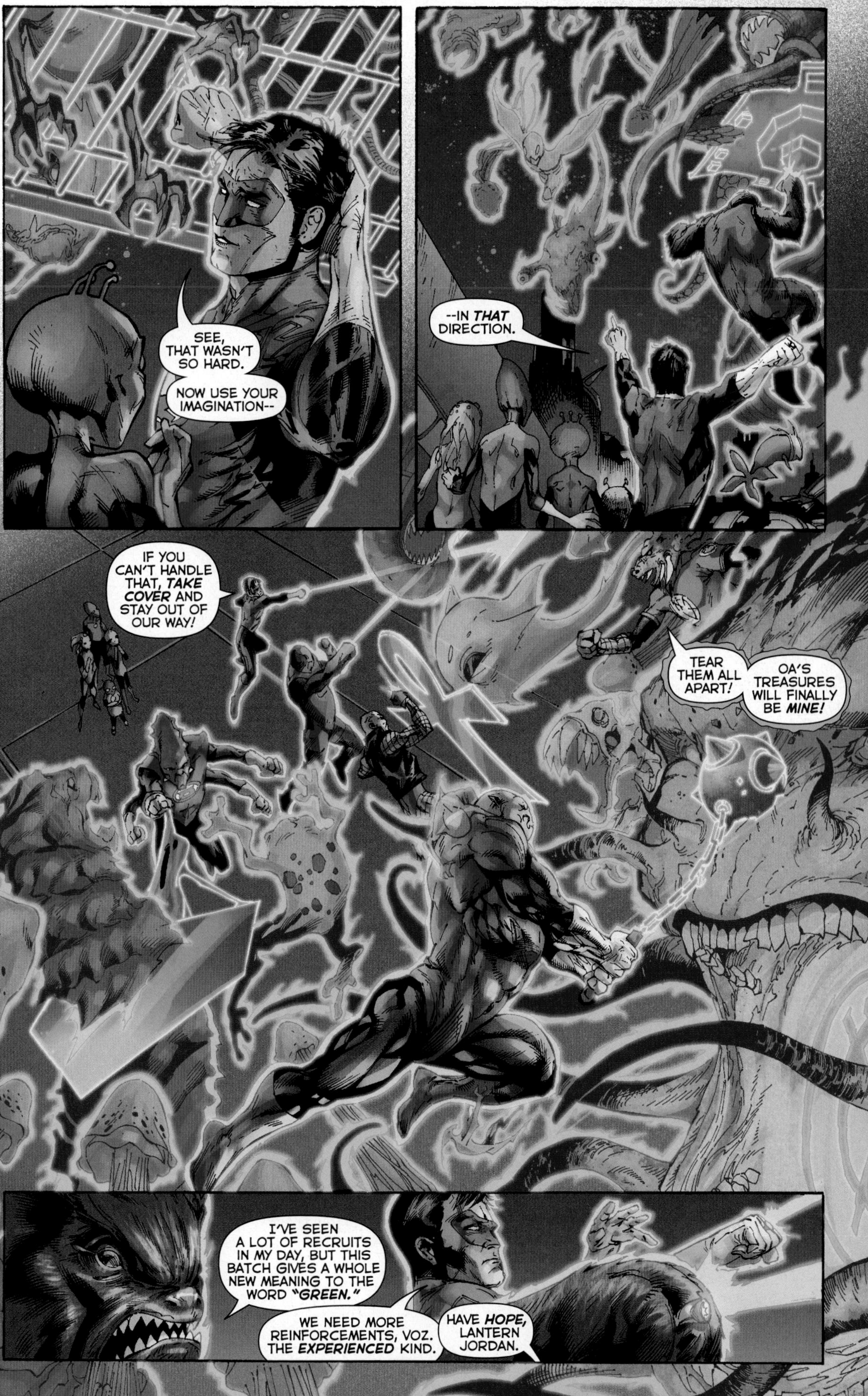
SEE, THAT WASN'T SO HARD.
NOW USE YOUR IMAGINATION--
--IN *THAT* DIRECTION.
IF YOU CAN'T HANDLE THAT, *TAKE COVER* AND STAY OUT OF OUR WAY!
TEAR THEM ALL APART!
OA'S TREASURES WILL FINALLY BE *MINE!*
I'VE SEEN A LOT OF RECRUITS IN MY DAY, BUT THIS BATCH GIVES A WHOLE NEW MEANING TO THE WORD *"GREEN."*
WE NEED MORE REINFORCEMENTS, VOZ. THE *EXPERIENCED* KIND.
HAVE *HOPE,* LANTERN JORDAN.

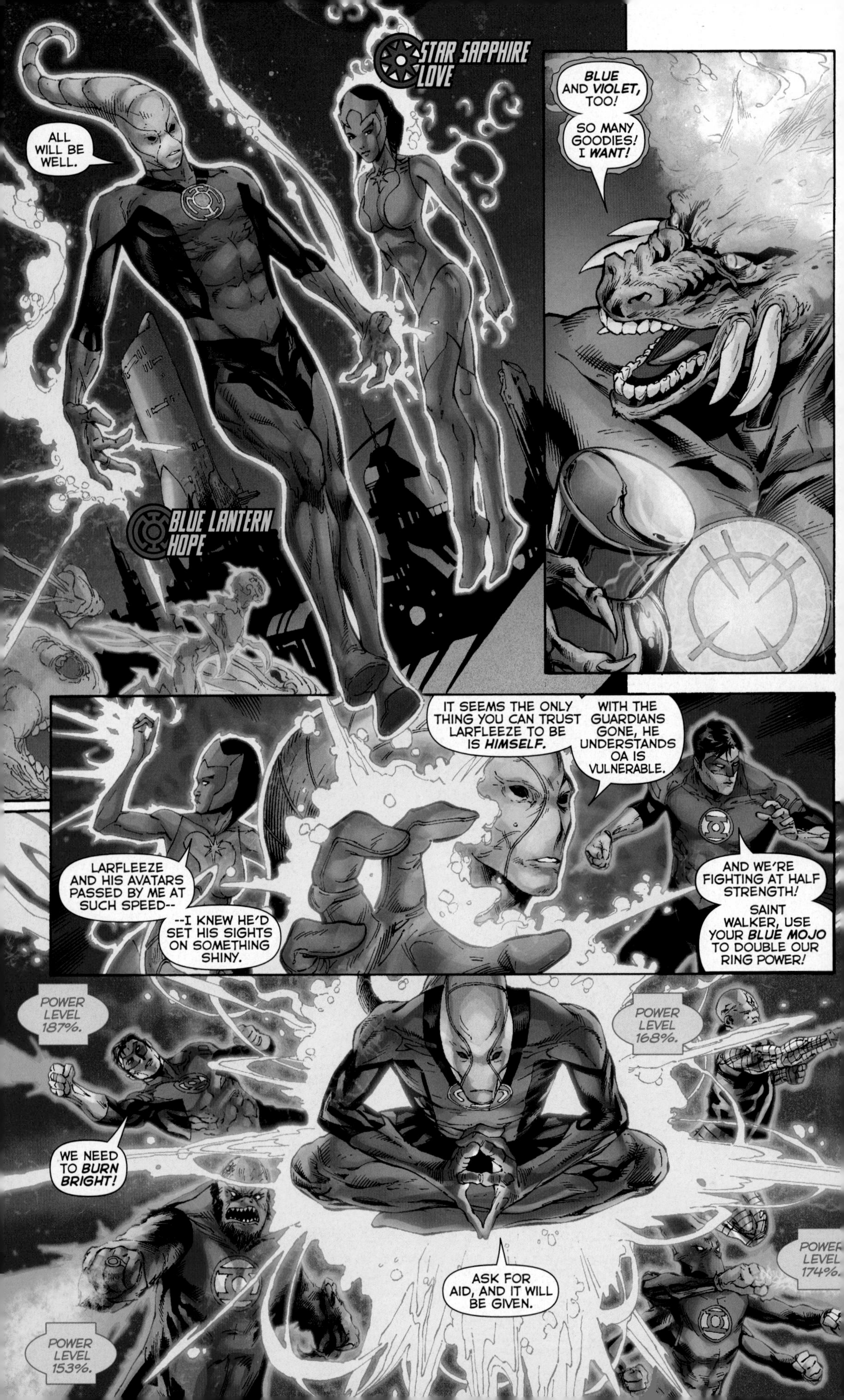
STAR SAPPHIRE LOVE
ALL WILL BE WELL.
BLUE LANTERN HOPE
BLUE AND VIOLET, TOO!
SO MANY GOODIES! I WANT!
IT SEEMS THE ONLY THING YOU CAN TRUST LARFLEEZE TO BE IS HIMSELF.
WITH THE GUARDIANS GONE, HE UNDERSTANDS OA IS VULNERABLE.
LARFLEEZE AND HIS AVATARS PASSED BY ME AT SUCH SPEED--
--I KNEW HE'D SET HIS SIGHTS ON SOMETHING SHINY.
AND WE'RE FIGHTING AT HALF STRENGTH!
SAINT WALKER, USE YOUR BLUE MOJO TO DOUBLE OUR RING POWER!
POWER LEVEL 187%.
POWER LEVEL 168%.
WE NEED TO BURN BRIGHT!
ASK FOR AID, AND IT WILL BE GIVEN.
POWER LEVEL 174%.
POWER LEVEL 153%.

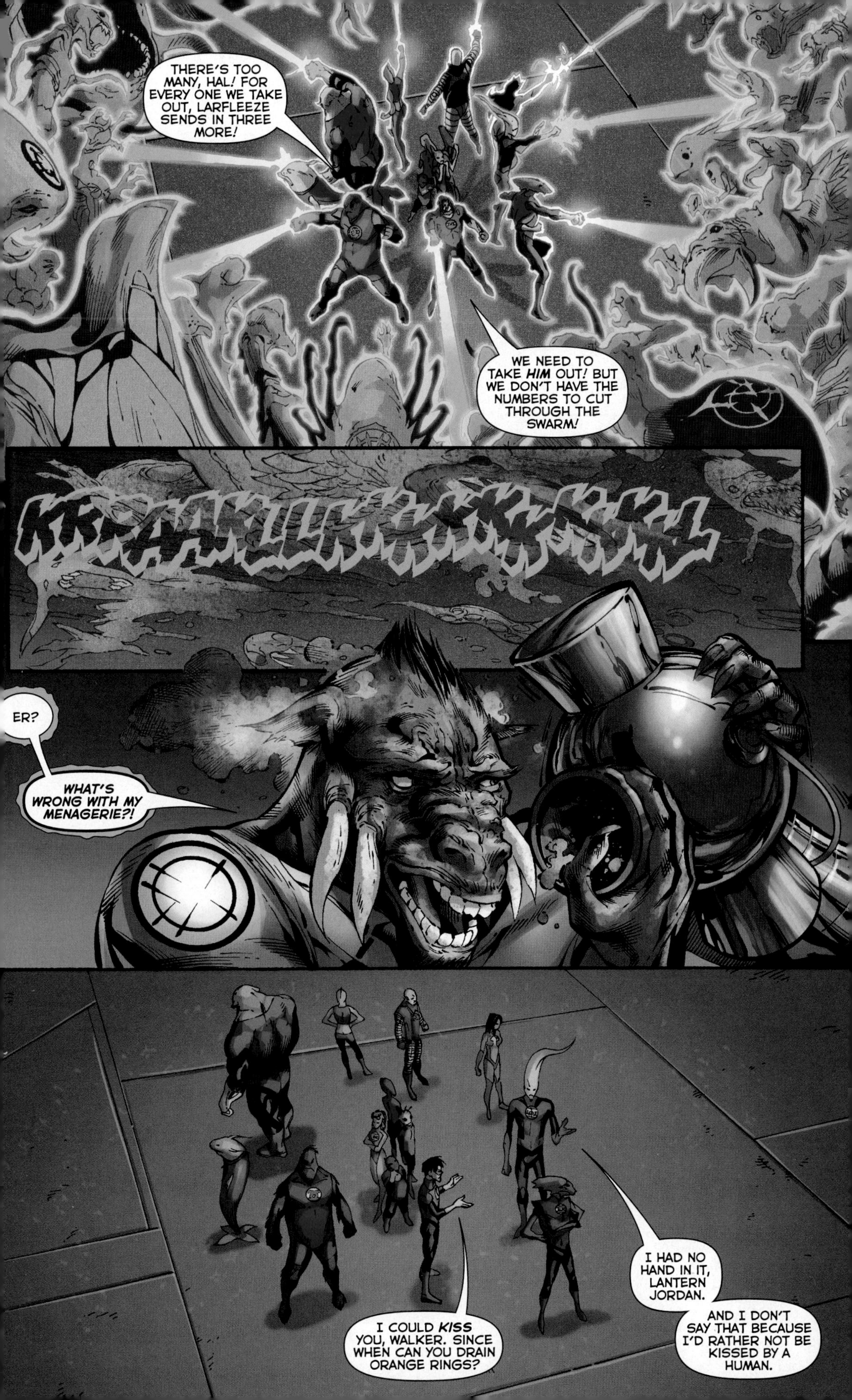
THERE'S TOO MANY, HAL! FOR EVERY ONE WE TAKE OUT, LARFLEEZE SENDS IN THREE MORE!
WE NEED TO TAKE HIM OUT! BUT WE DON'T HAVE THE NUMBERS TO CUT THROUGH THE SWARM!
ER?
WHAT'S WRONG WITH MY MENAGERIE?!
I COULD KISS YOU, WALKER. SINCE WHEN CAN YOU DRAIN ORANGE RINGS?
I HAD NO HAND IN IT, LANTERN JORDAN.
AND I DON'T SAY THAT BECAUSE I'D RATHER NOT BE KISSED BY A HUMAN.

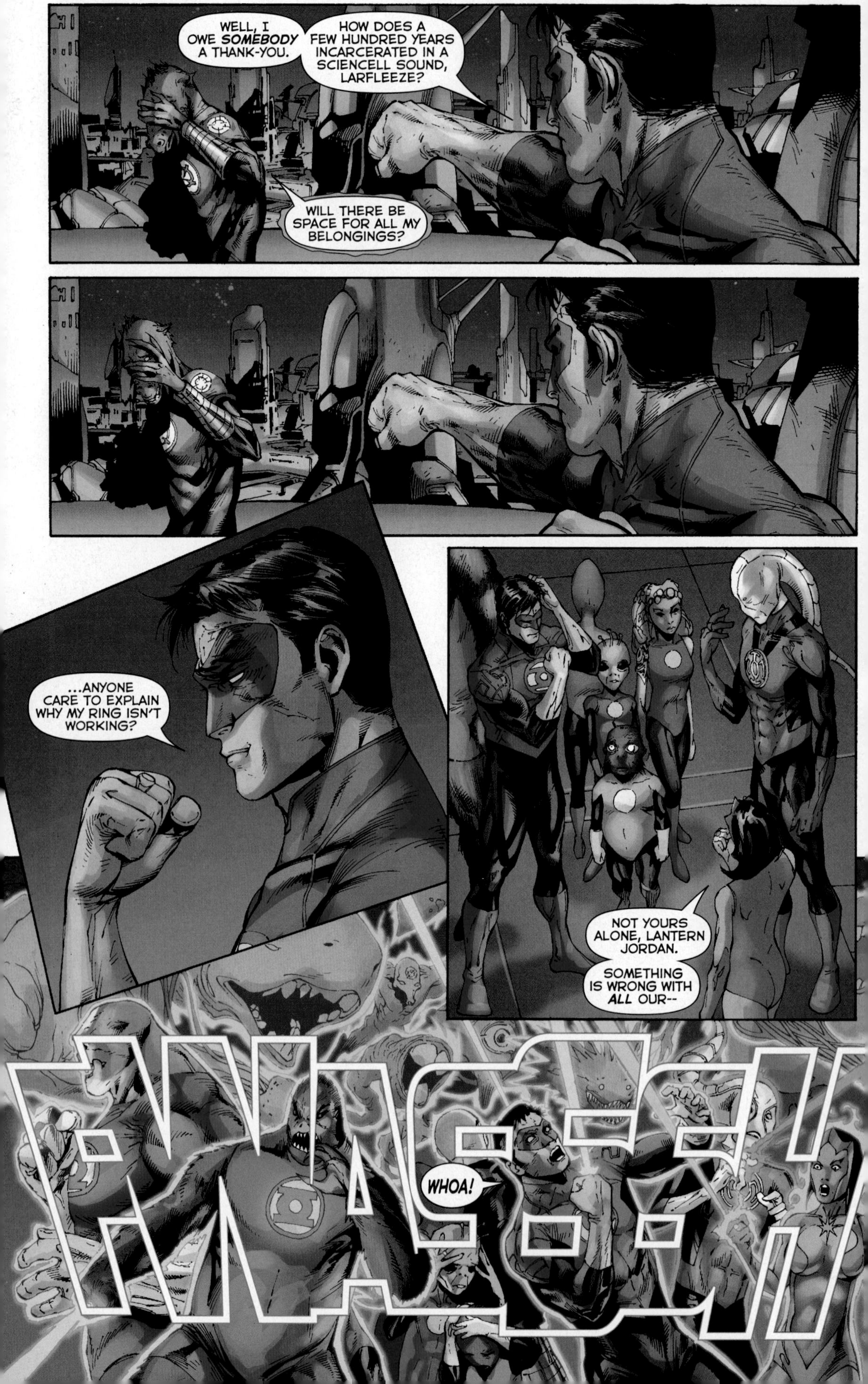
WELL, I OWE SOMEBODY A THANK-YOU.
HOW DOES A FEW HUNDRED YEARS INCARCERATED IN A SCIENCELL SOUND, LARFLEEZE?
WILL THERE BE SPACE FOR ALL MY BELONGINGS?
...ANYONE CARE TO EXPLAIN WHY MY RING ISN'T WORKING?
NOT YOURS ALONE, LANTERN JORDAN.
SOMETHING IS WRONG WITH ALL OUR--
WHOA!

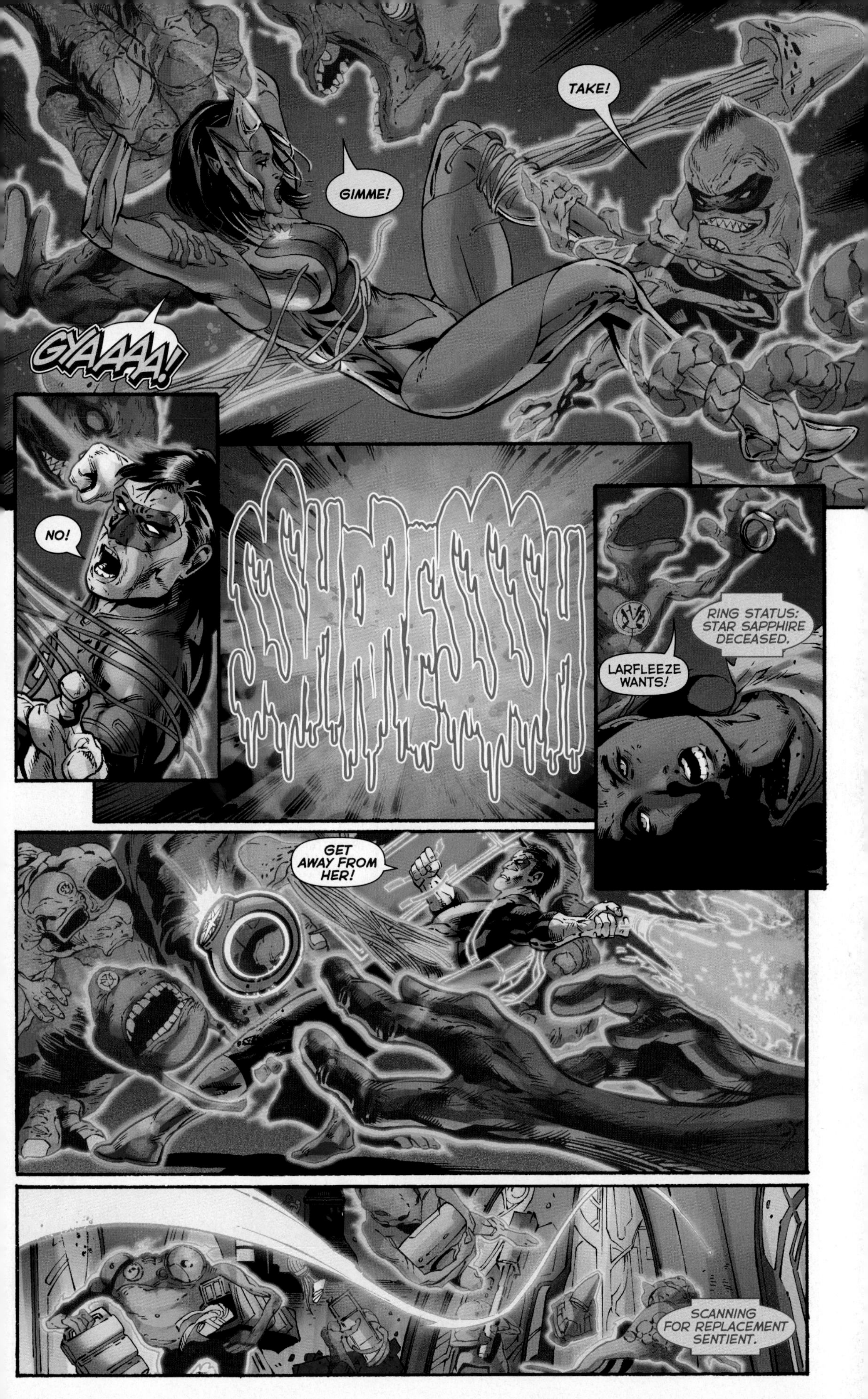
GIMME!
TAKE!
GYAAAA!
NO!
RING STATUS: STAR SAPPHIRE DECEASED.
LARFLEEZE WANTS!
GET AWAY FROM HER!
SCANNING FOR REPLACEMENT SENTIENT.

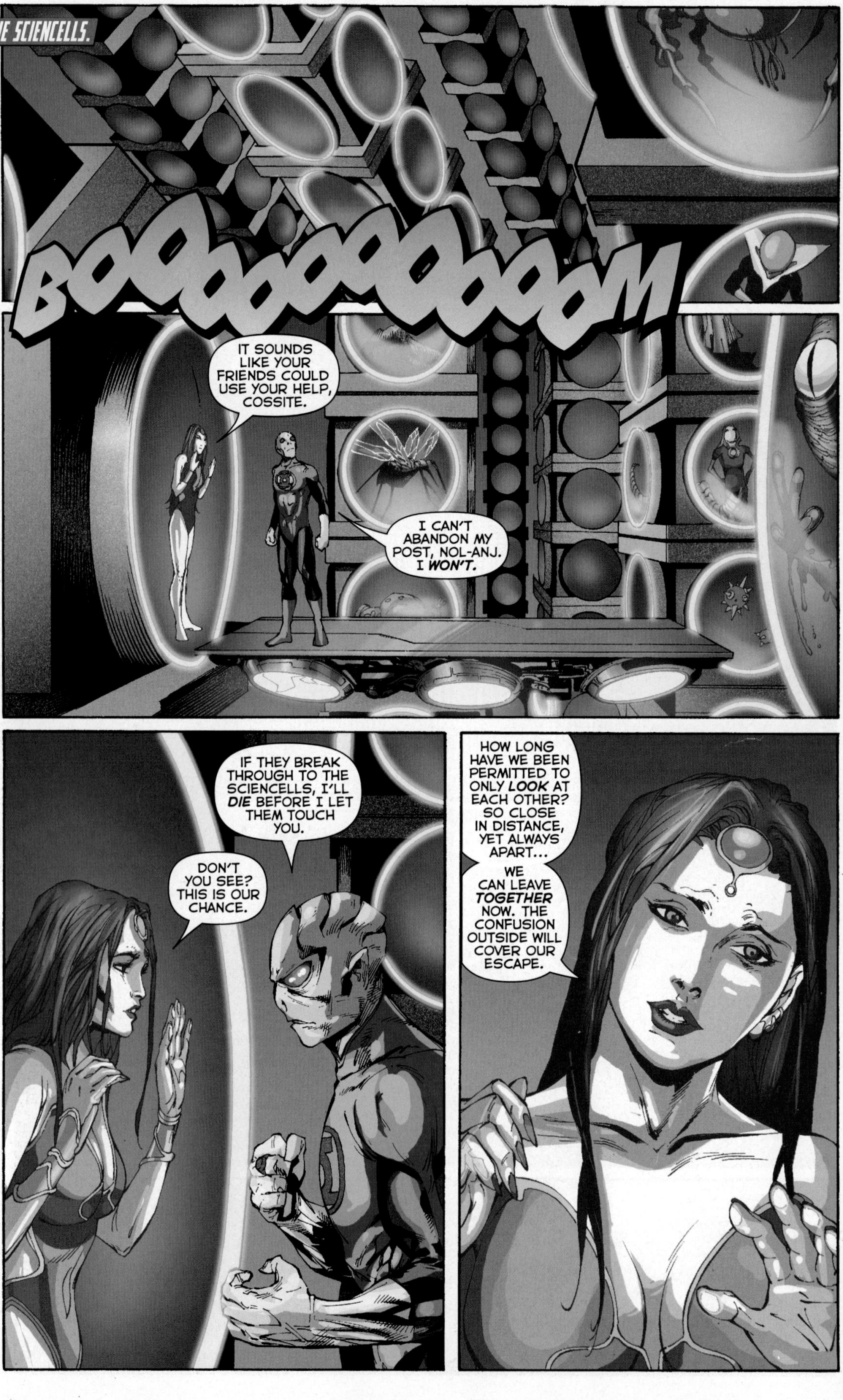
THE SCIENCELLS.
BOOOOOOOOOM
IT SOUNDS LIKE YOUR FRIENDS COULD USE YOUR HELP, COSSITE.
I CAN'T ABANDON MY POST, NOL-ANJ. I WON'T.
IF THEY BREAK THROUGH TO THE SCIENCELLS, I'LL DIE BEFORE I LET THEM TOUCH YOU.
DON'T YOU SEE? THIS IS OUR CHANCE.
HOW LONG HAVE WE BEEN PERMITTED TO ONLY LOOK AT EACH OTHER? SO CLOSE IN DISTANCE, YET ALWAYS APART...
WE CAN LEAVE TOGETHER NOW. THE CONFUSION OUTSIDE WILL COVER OUR ESCAPE.

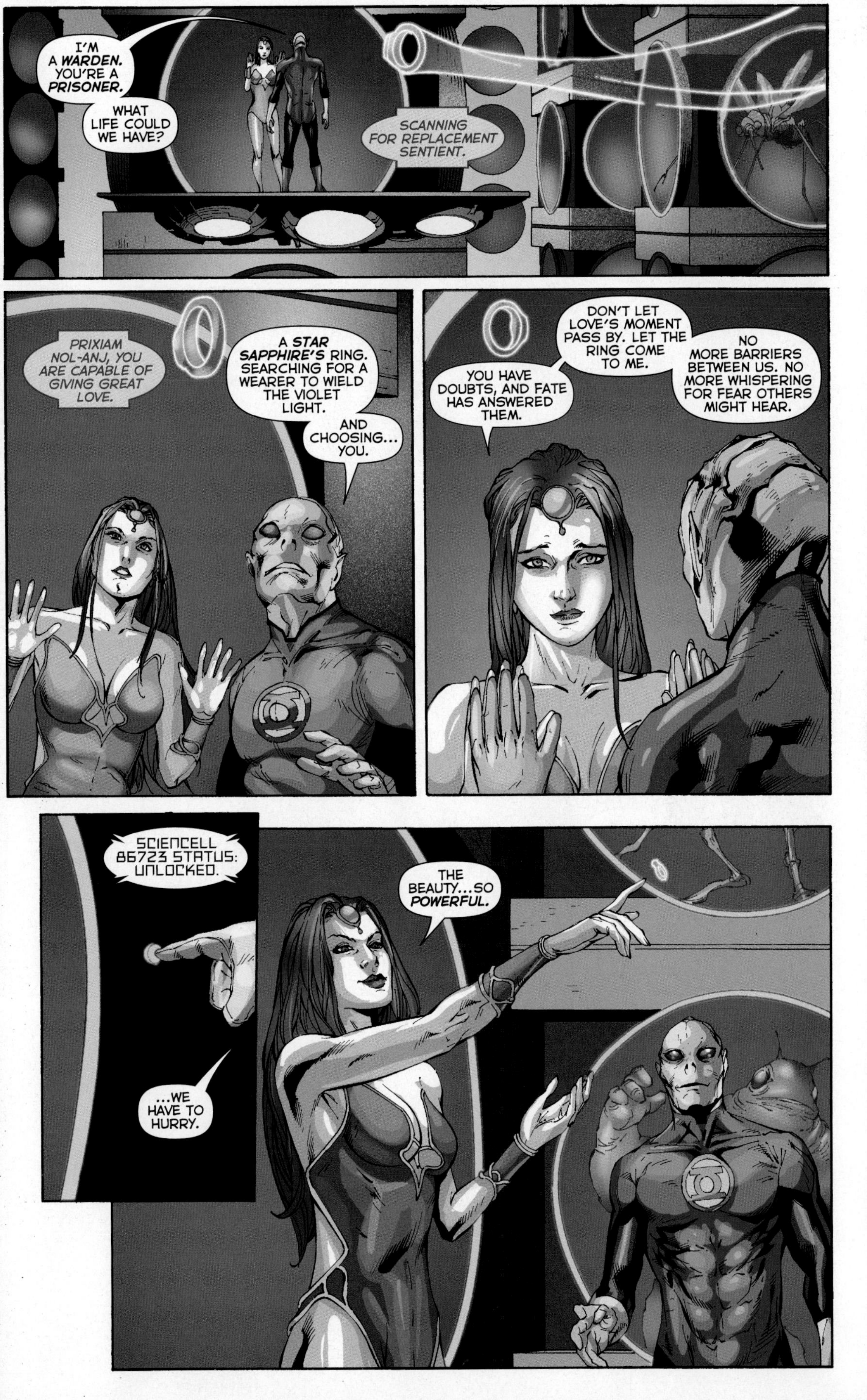
I'M A WARDEN. YOU'RE A PRISONER.
WHAT LIFE COULD WE HAVE?
SCANNING FOR REPLACEMENT SENTIENT.
PRIXIAM NOL-ANJ, YOU ARE CAPABLE OF GIVING GREAT LOVE.
A STAR SAPPHIRE'S RING. SEARCHING FOR A WEARER TO WIELD THE VIOLET LIGHT.
AND CHOOSING... YOU.
YOU HAVE DOUBTS, AND FATE HAS ANSWERED THEM.
DON'T LET LOVE'S MOMENT PASS BY. LET THE RING COME TO ME.
NO MORE BARRIERS BETWEEN US. NO MORE WHISPERING FOR FEAR OTHERS MIGHT HEAR.
SCIENCELL 86723 STATUS: UNLOCKED.
...WE HAVE TO HURRY.
THE BEAUTY...SO POWERFUL.

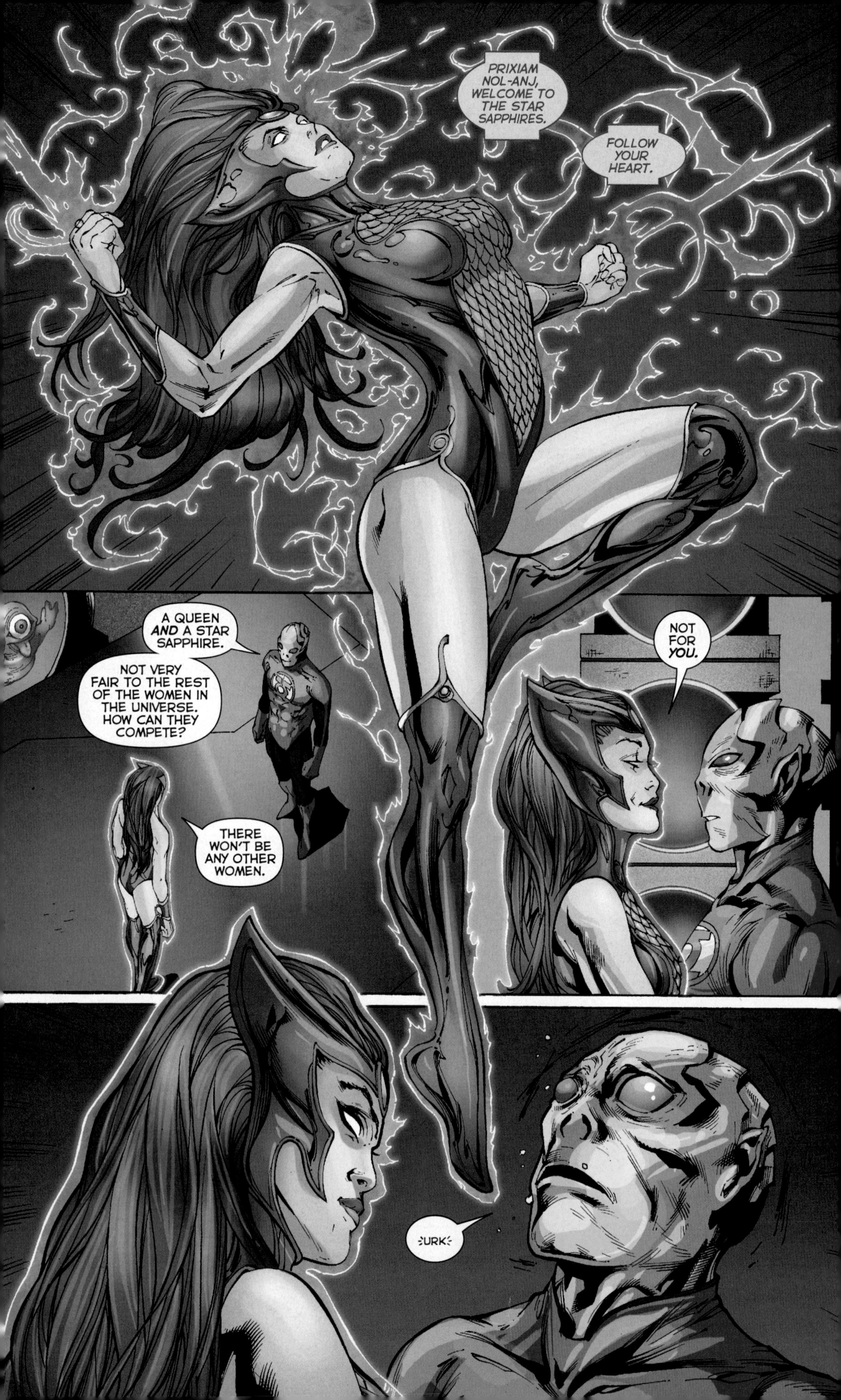
PRIXIAM NOL-ANJ, WELCOME TO THE STAR SAPPHIRES.
FOLLOW YOUR HEART.
A QUEEN AND A STAR SAPPHIRE.
NOT VERY FAIR TO THE REST OF THE WOMEN IN THE UNIVERSE. HOW CAN THEY COMPETE?
THERE WON'T BE ANY OTHER WOMEN.
NOT FOR YOU.
URK

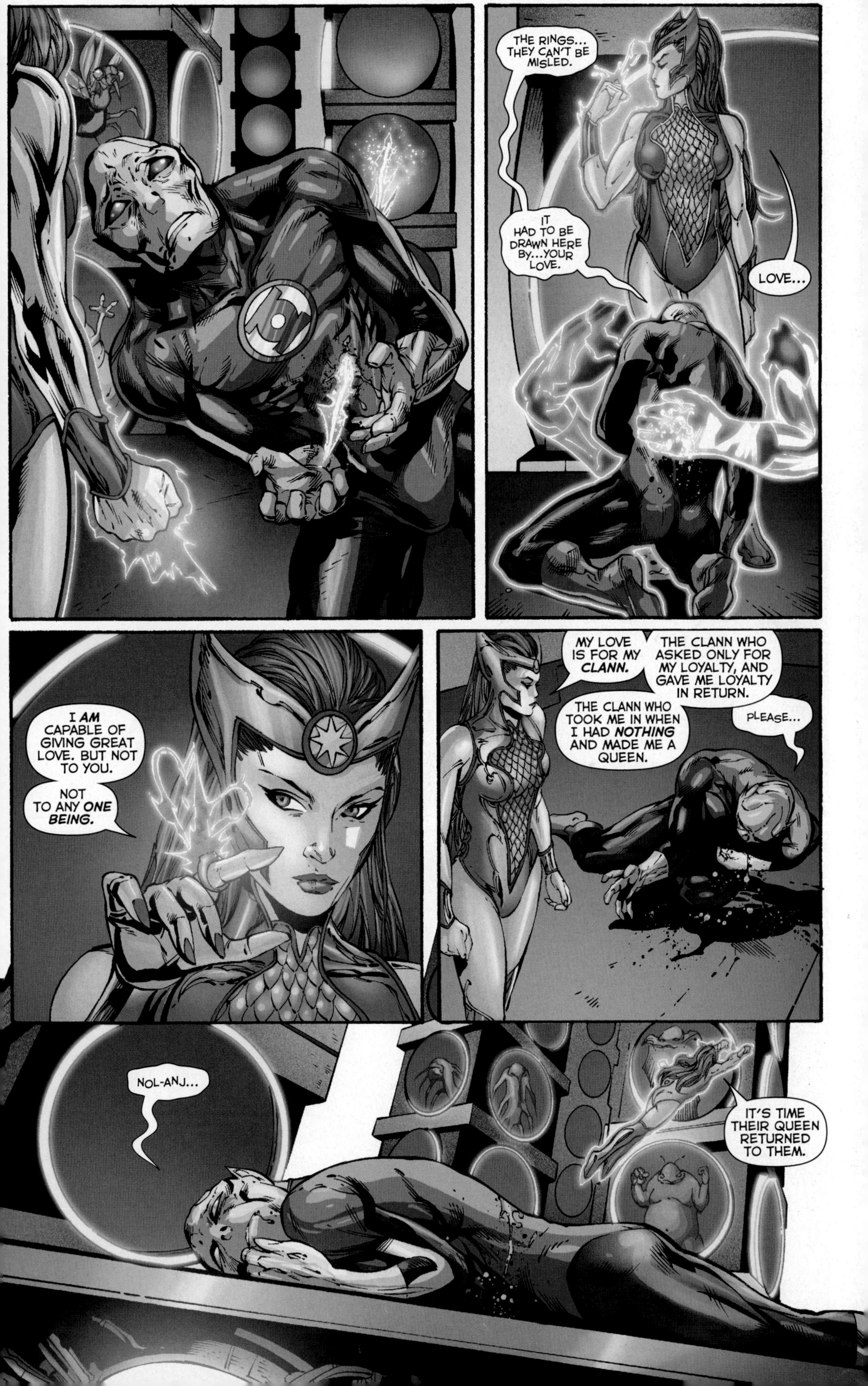
THE RINGS... THEY CAN'T BE MISLED.
IT HAD TO BE DRAWN HERE BY...YOUR LOVE.
LOVE...
I AM CAPABLE OF GIVING GREAT LOVE. BUT NOT TO YOU.
NOT TO ANY ONE BEING.
MY LOVE IS FOR MY CLANN.
THE CLANN WHO ASKED ONLY FOR MY LOYALTY, AND GAVE ME LOYALTY IN RETURN.
THE CLANN WHO TOOK ME IN WHEN I HAD NOTHING AND MADE ME A QUEEN.
PLEASE...
NOL-ANJ...
IT'S TIME THEIR QUEEN RETURNED TO THEM.

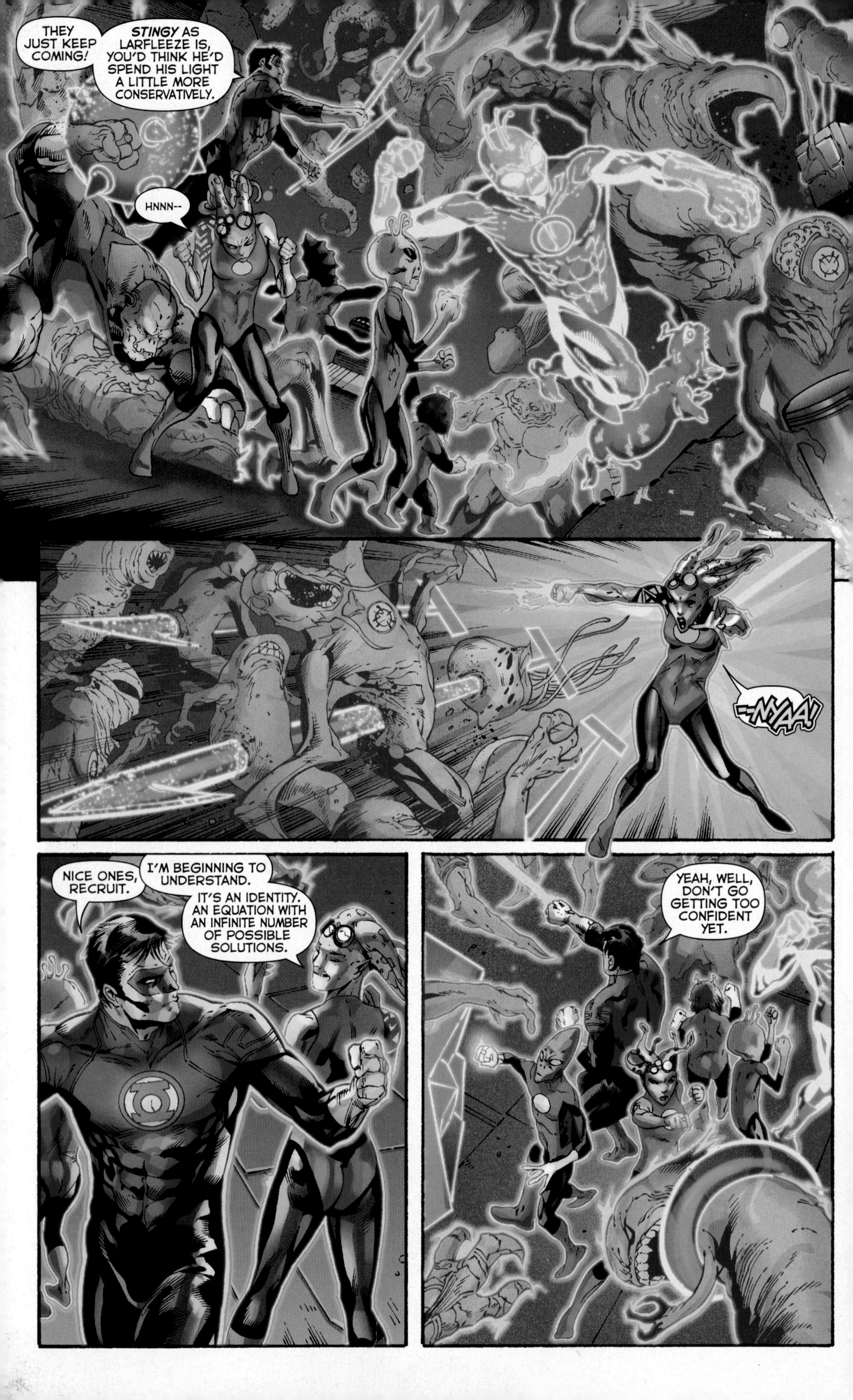
THEY JUST KEEP COMING!
STINGY AS LARFLEEZE IS, YOU'D THINK HE'D SPEND HIS LIGHT A LITTLE MORE CONSERVATIVELY.
HNNN--
--NYAA!
NICE ONES, RECRUIT.
I'M BEGINNING TO UNDERSTAND.
IT'S AN IDENTITY. AN EQUATION WITH AN INFINITE NUMBER OF POSSIBLE SOLUTIONS.
YEAH, WELL, DON'T GO GETTING TOO CONFIDENT YET.

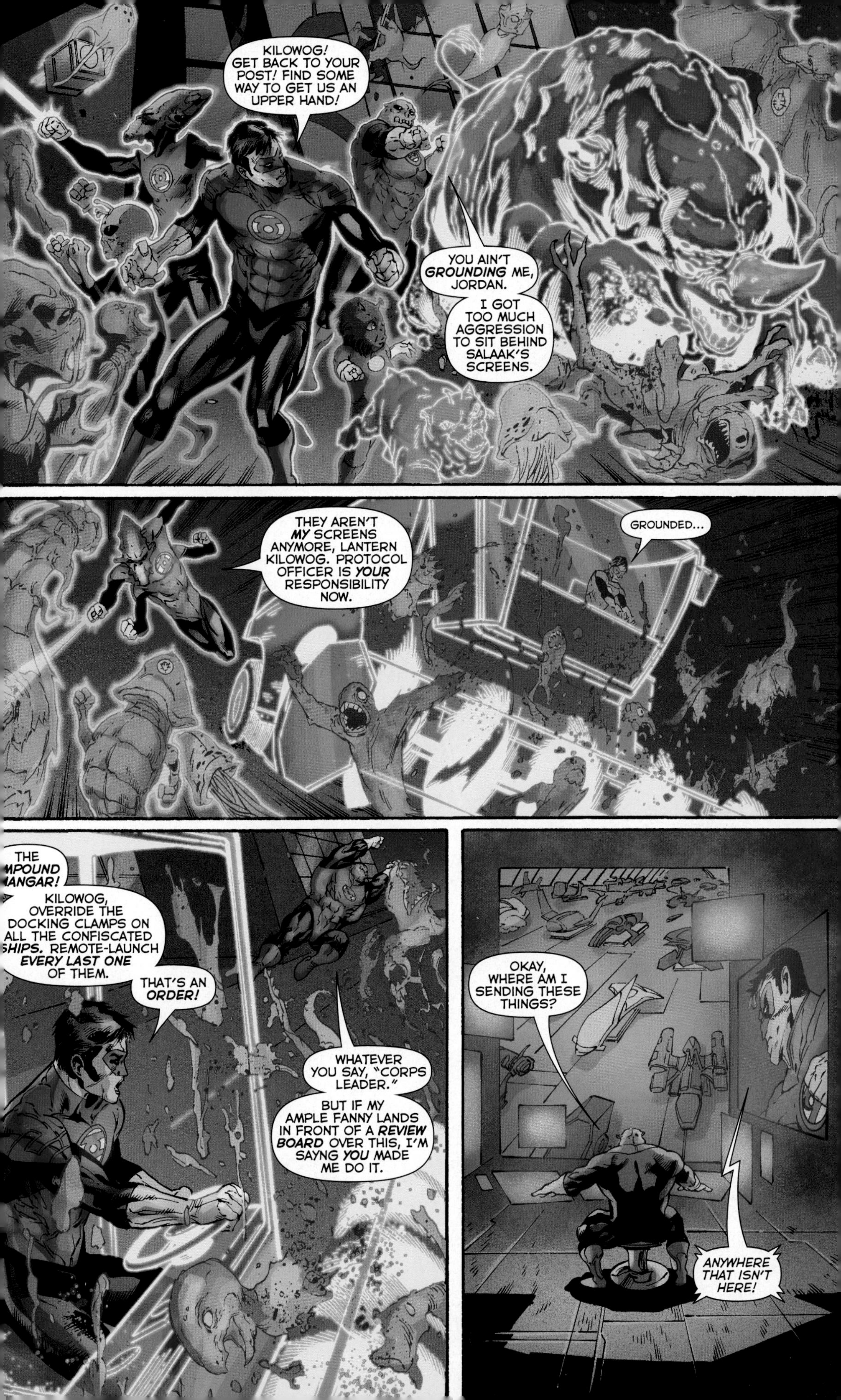
KILOWOG! GET BACK TO YOUR POST! FIND SOME WAY TO GET US AN UPPER HAND!
YOU AIN'T GROUNDING ME, JORDAN.
I GOT TOO MUCH AGGRESSION TO SIT BEHIND SALAAK'S SCREENS.
THEY AREN'T MY SCREENS ANYMORE, LANTERN KILOWOG. PROTOCOL OFFICER IS YOUR RESPONSIBILITY NOW.
GROUNDED...
THE MPOUND ANGAR!
KILOWOG, OVERRIDE THE DOCKING CLAMPS ON ALL THE CONFISCATED SHIPS. REMOTE-LAUNCH EVERY LAST ONE OF THEM.
THAT'S AN ORDER!
WHATEVER YOU SAY, "CORPS LEADER."
BUT IF MY AMPLE FANNY LANDS IN FRONT OF A REVIEW BOARD OVER THIS, I'M SAYING YOU MADE ME DO IT.
OKAY, WHERE AM I SENDING THESE THINGS?
ANYWHERE THAT ISN'T HERE!

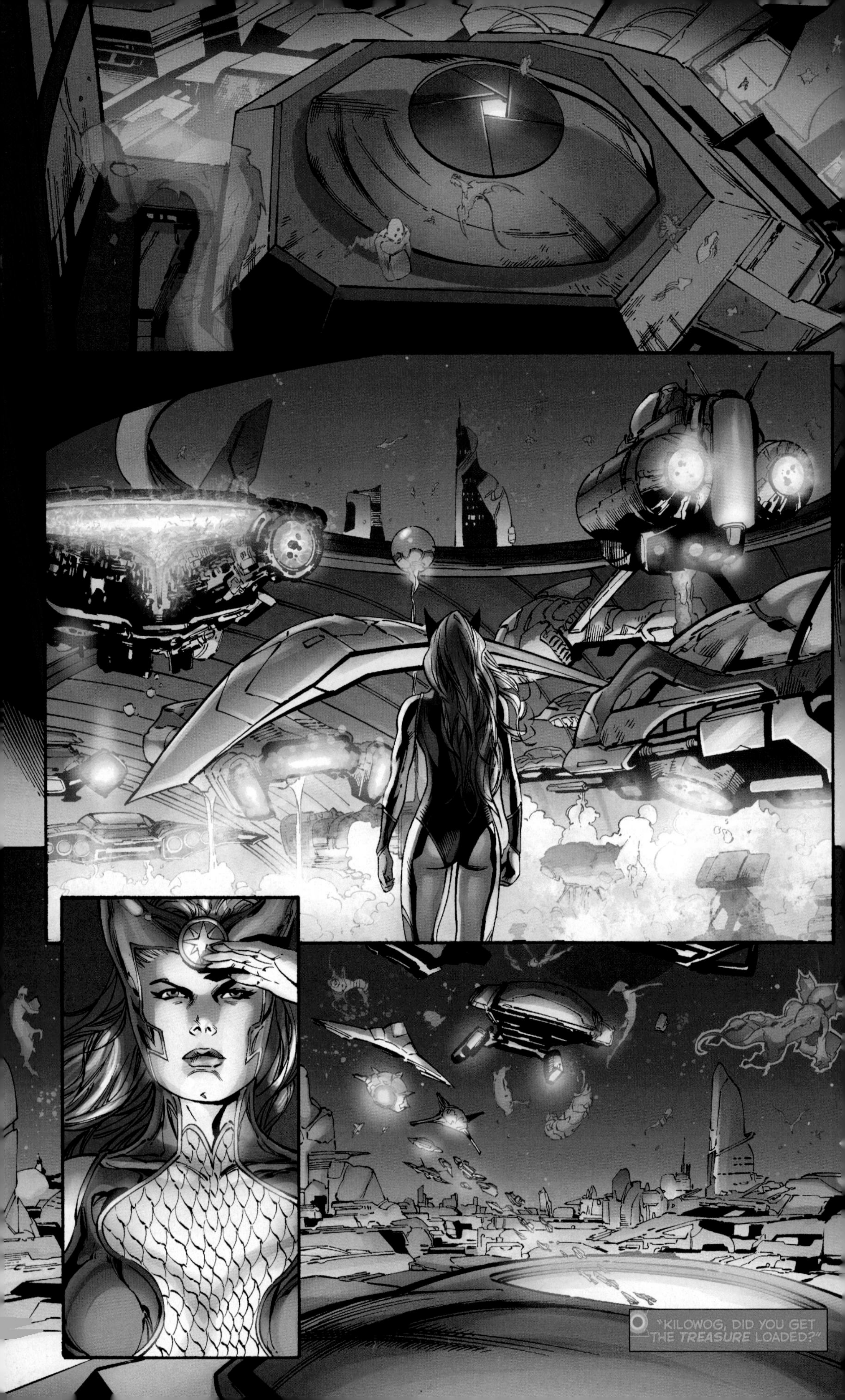
"KILOWOG, DID YOU GET THE *TREASURE* LOADED?"

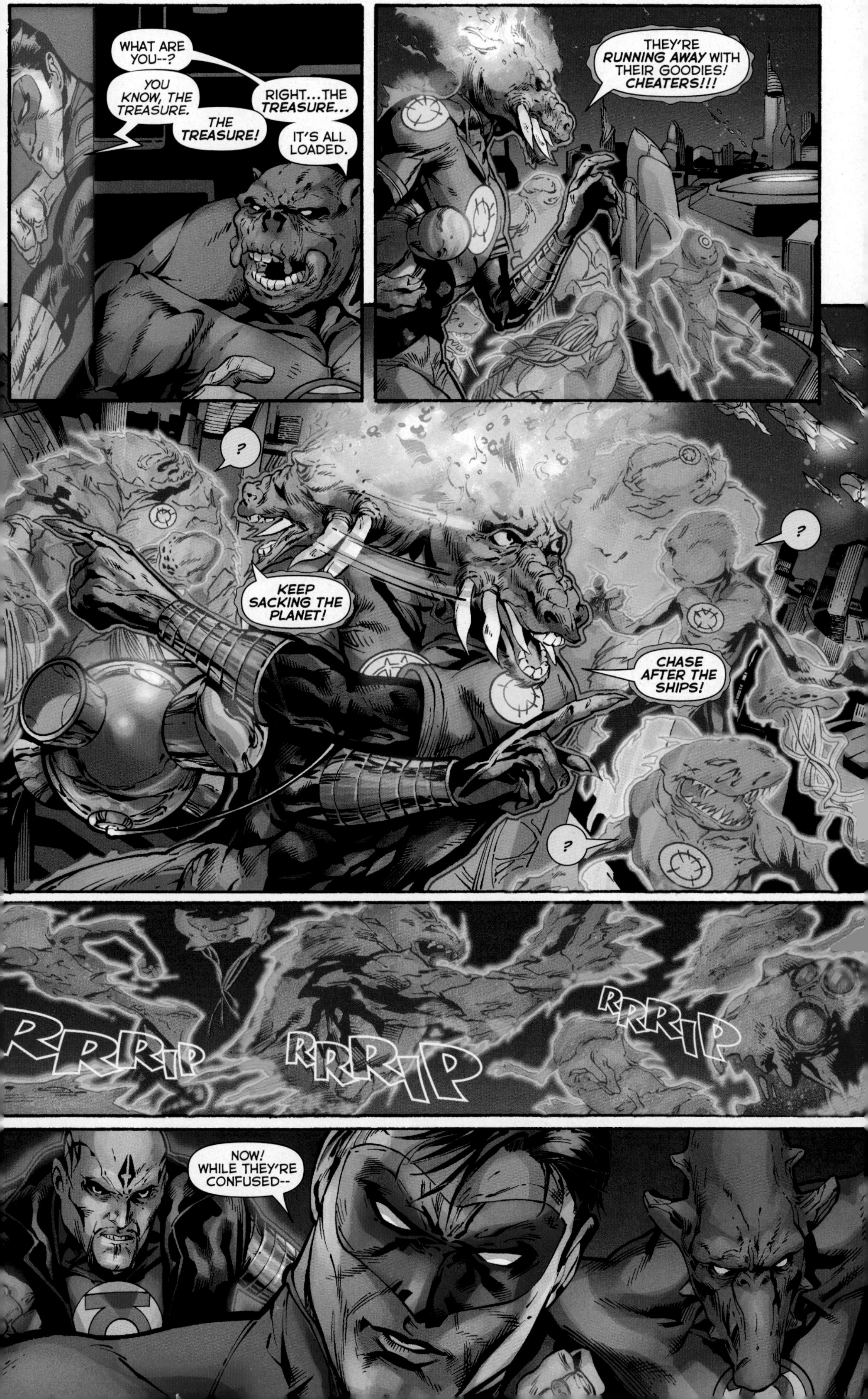
WHAT ARE YOU--?
YOU KNOW, THE TREASURE.
THE TREASURE!
RIGHT...THE TREASURE...
IT'S ALL LOADED.
THEY'RE RUNNING AWAY WITH THEIR GOODIES! CHEATERS!!!
?
KEEP SACKING THE PLANET!
?
CHASE AFTER THE SHIPS!
?
RRRRIP
RRRRIP
RRRRIP
NOW! WHILE THEY'RE CONFUSED--

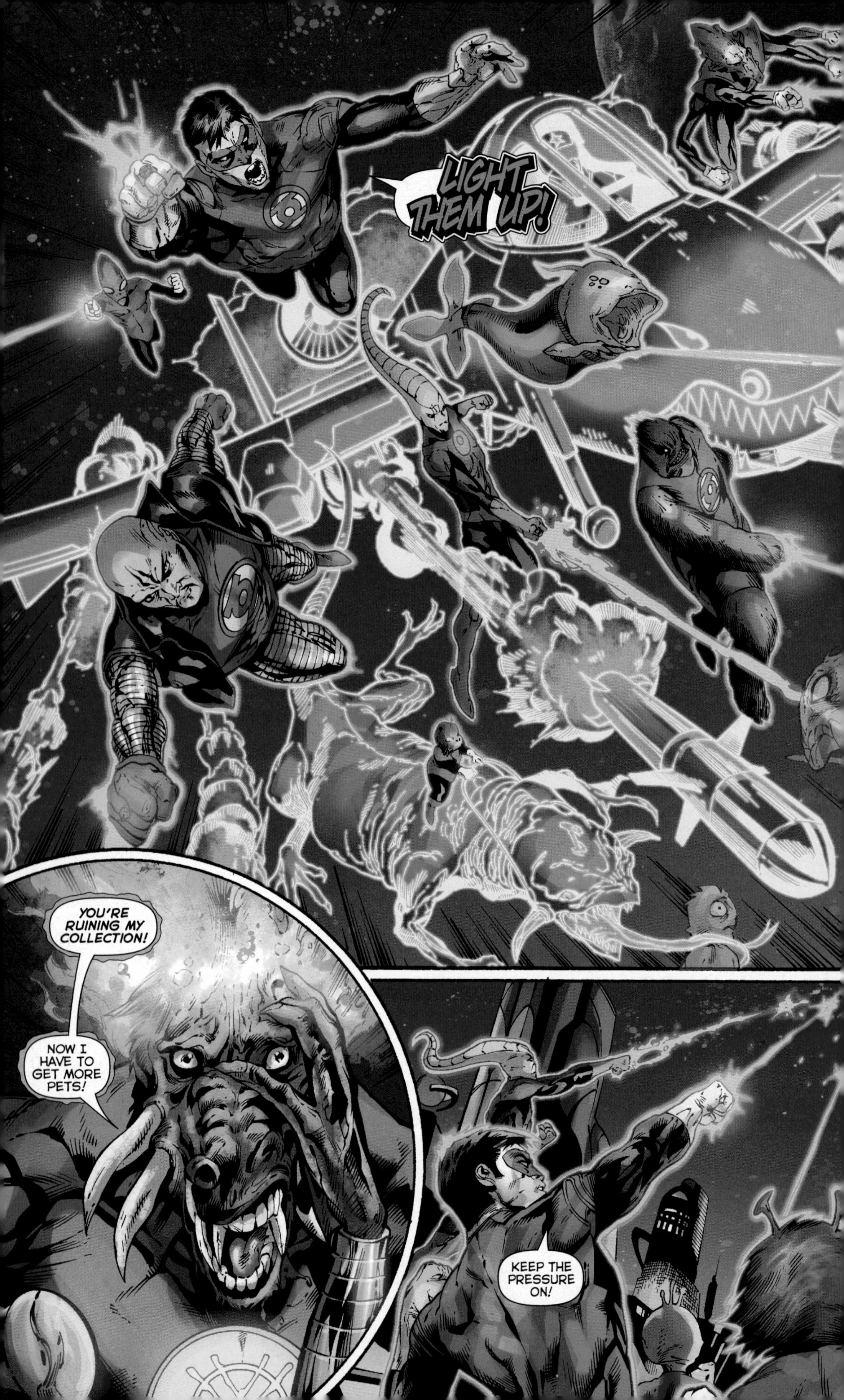
LIGHT THEM UP!
YOU'RE RUINING MY COLLECTION!
NOW I HAVE TO GET MORE PETS!
KEEP THE PRESSURE ON!

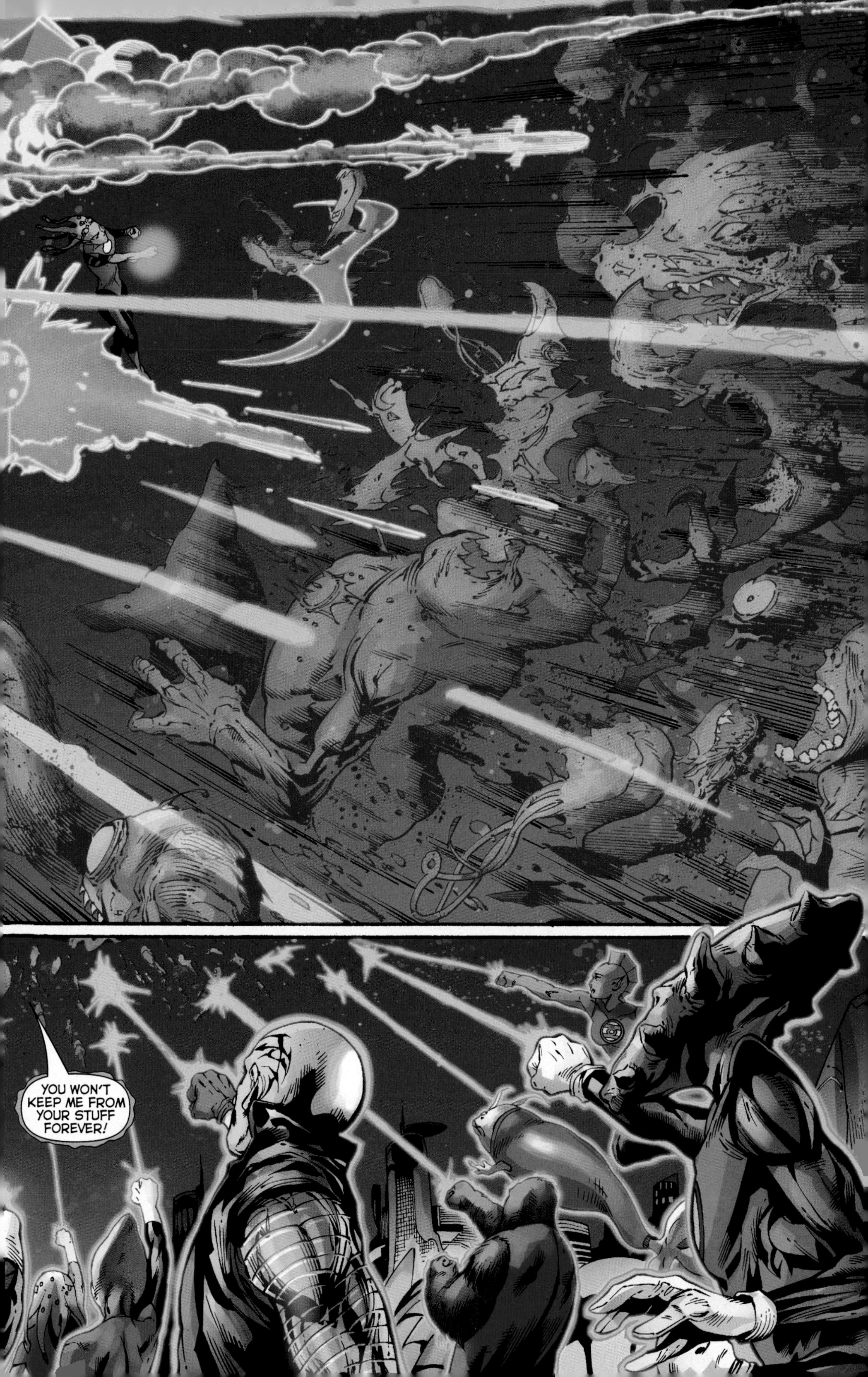
YOU WON'T KEEP ME FROM YOUR STUFF FOREVER!

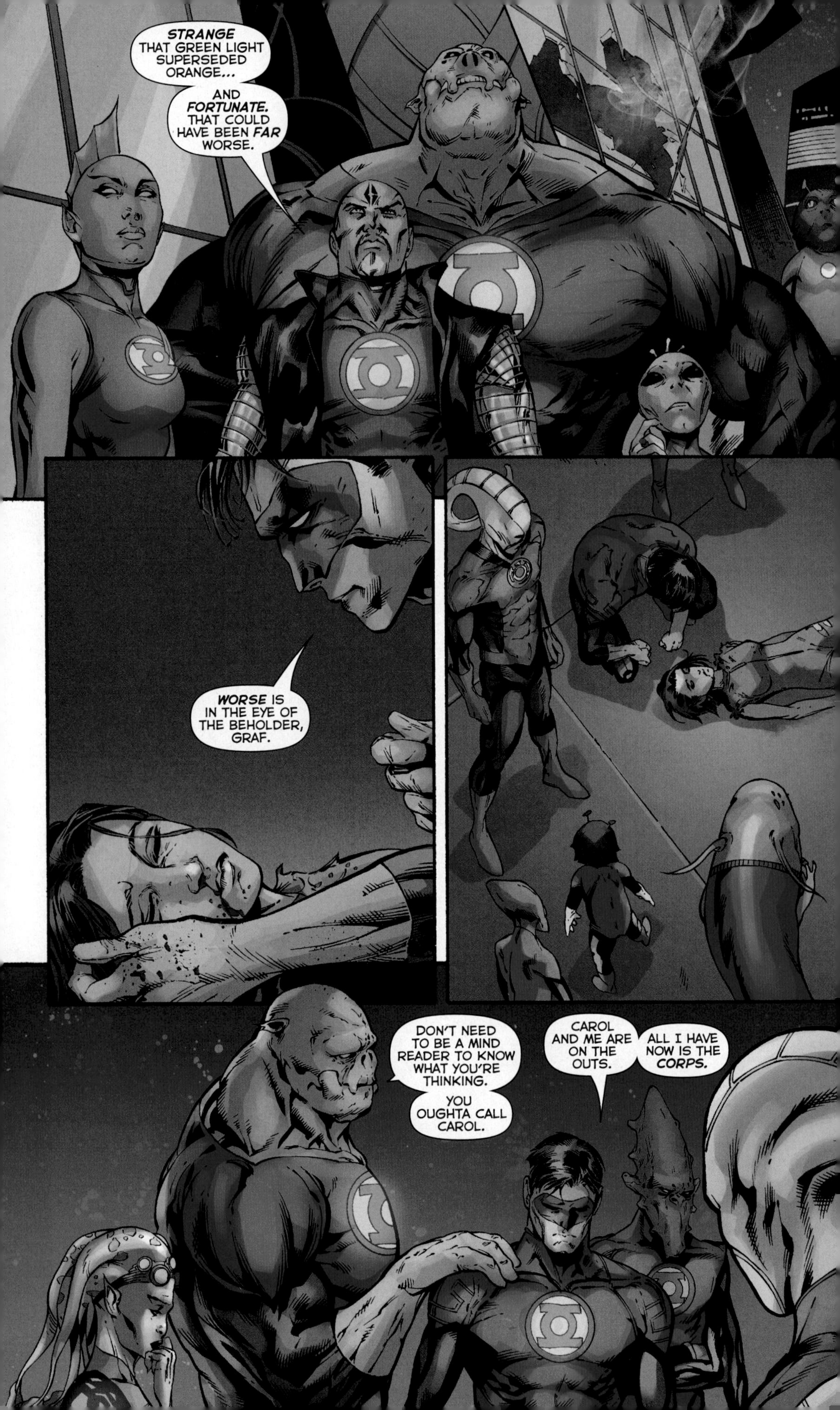
STRANGE THAT GREEN LIGHT SUPERSEDED ORANGE...
AND FORTUNATE. THAT COULD HAVE BEEN FAR WORSE.
WORSE IS IN THE EYE OF THE BEHOLDER, GRAF.
DON'T NEED TO BE A MIND READER TO KNOW WHAT YOU'RE THINKING.
YOU OUGHTA CALL CAROL.
CAROL AND ME ARE ON THE OUTS.
ALL I HAVE NOW IS THE CORPS.

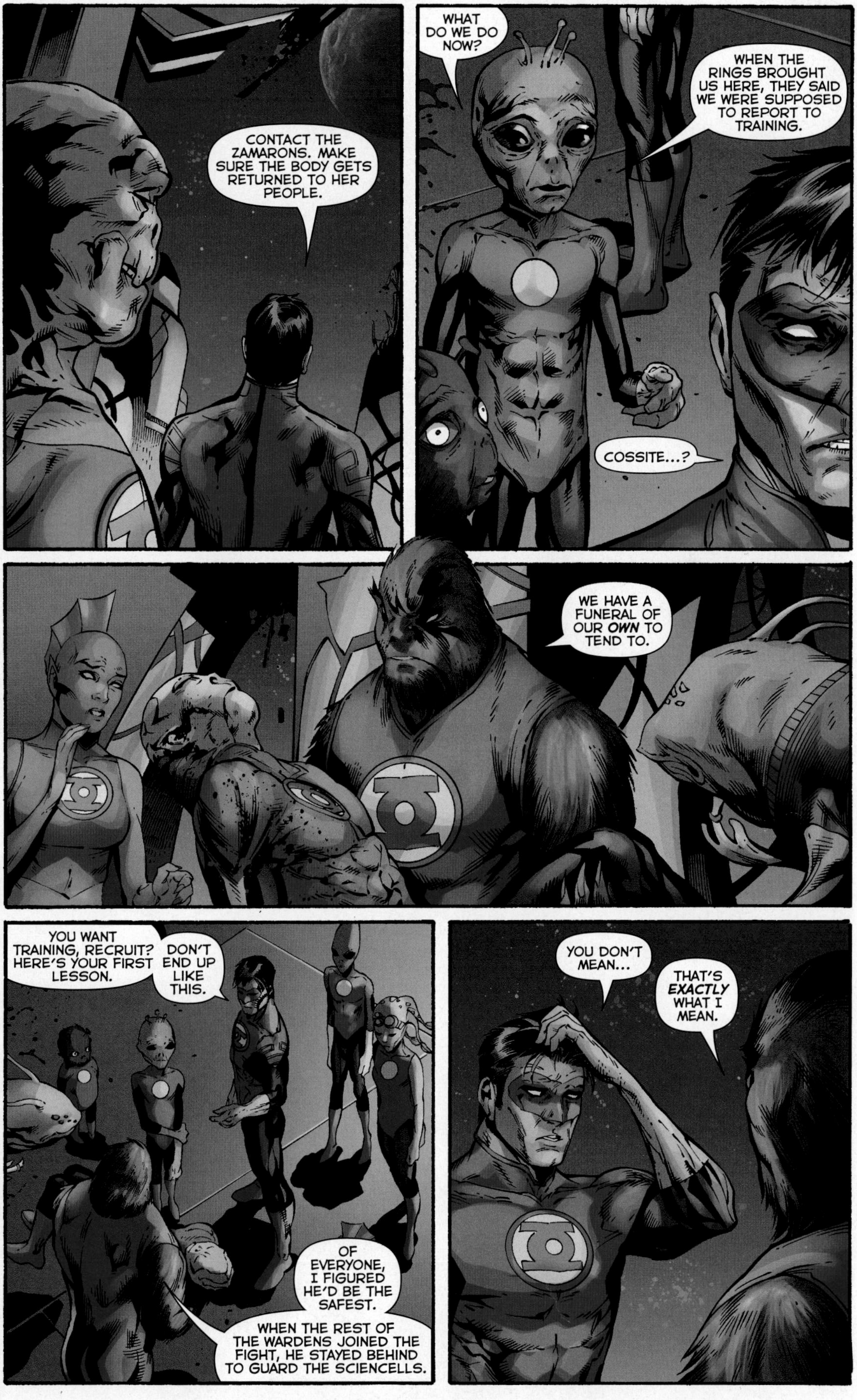
CONTACT THE ZAMARONS. MAKE SURE THE BODY GETS RETURNED TO HER PEOPLE.
WHAT DO WE DO NOW?
WHEN THE RINGS BROUGHT US HERE, THEY SAID WE WERE SUPPOSED TO REPORT TO TRAINING.
COSSITE...?
WE HAVE A FUNERAL OF OUR *OWN* TO TEND TO.
YOU WANT TRAINING, RECRUIT? HERE'S YOUR FIRST LESSON.
DON'T END UP LIKE THIS.
OF EVERYONE, I FIGURED HE'D BE THE SAFEST.
WHEN THE REST OF THE WARDENS JOINED THE FIGHT, HE STAYED BEHIND TO GUARD THE SCIENCELLS.
YOU DON'T MEAN...
THAT'S *EXACTLY* WHAT I MEAN.

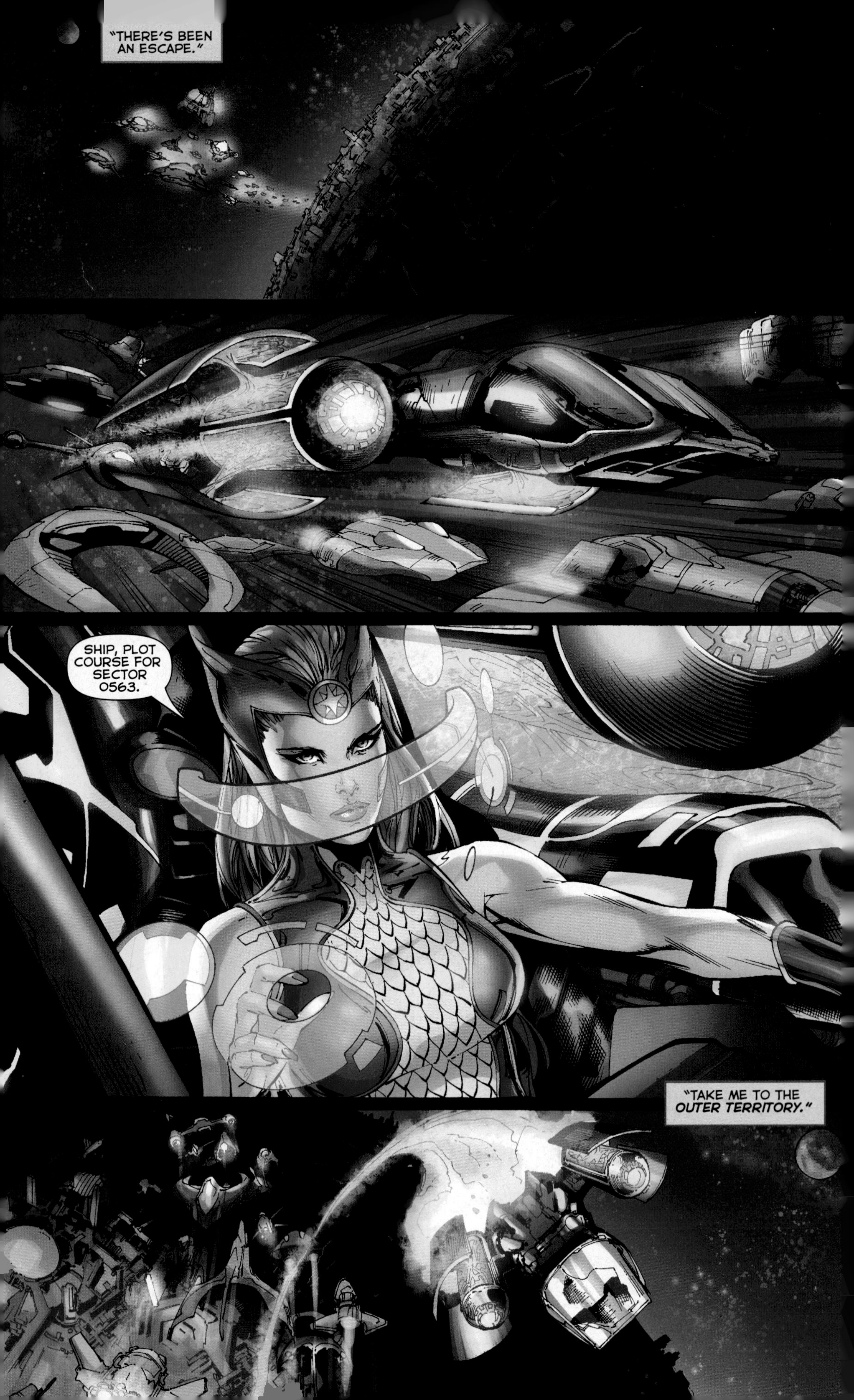
"THERE'S BEEN AN ESCAPE."
SHIP, PLOT COURSE FOR SECTOR 0563.
"TAKE ME TO THE OUTER TERRITORY."

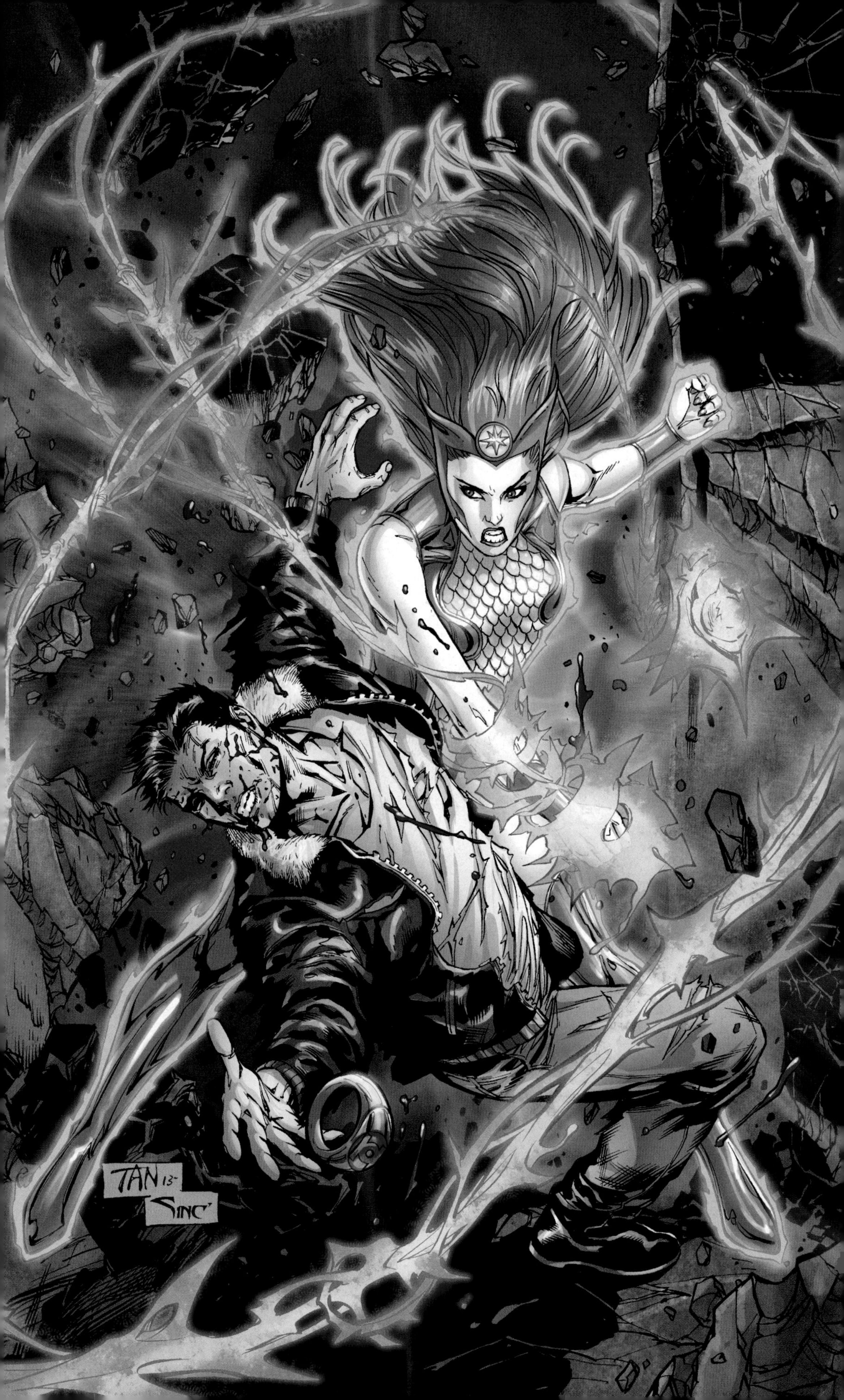
TAN 13
SINC'

ROBERT VENDITTI writer **BILLY TAN** penciller **ROB HUNTER** inker
cover art by **BILLY TAN & ALEX SINCLAIR**

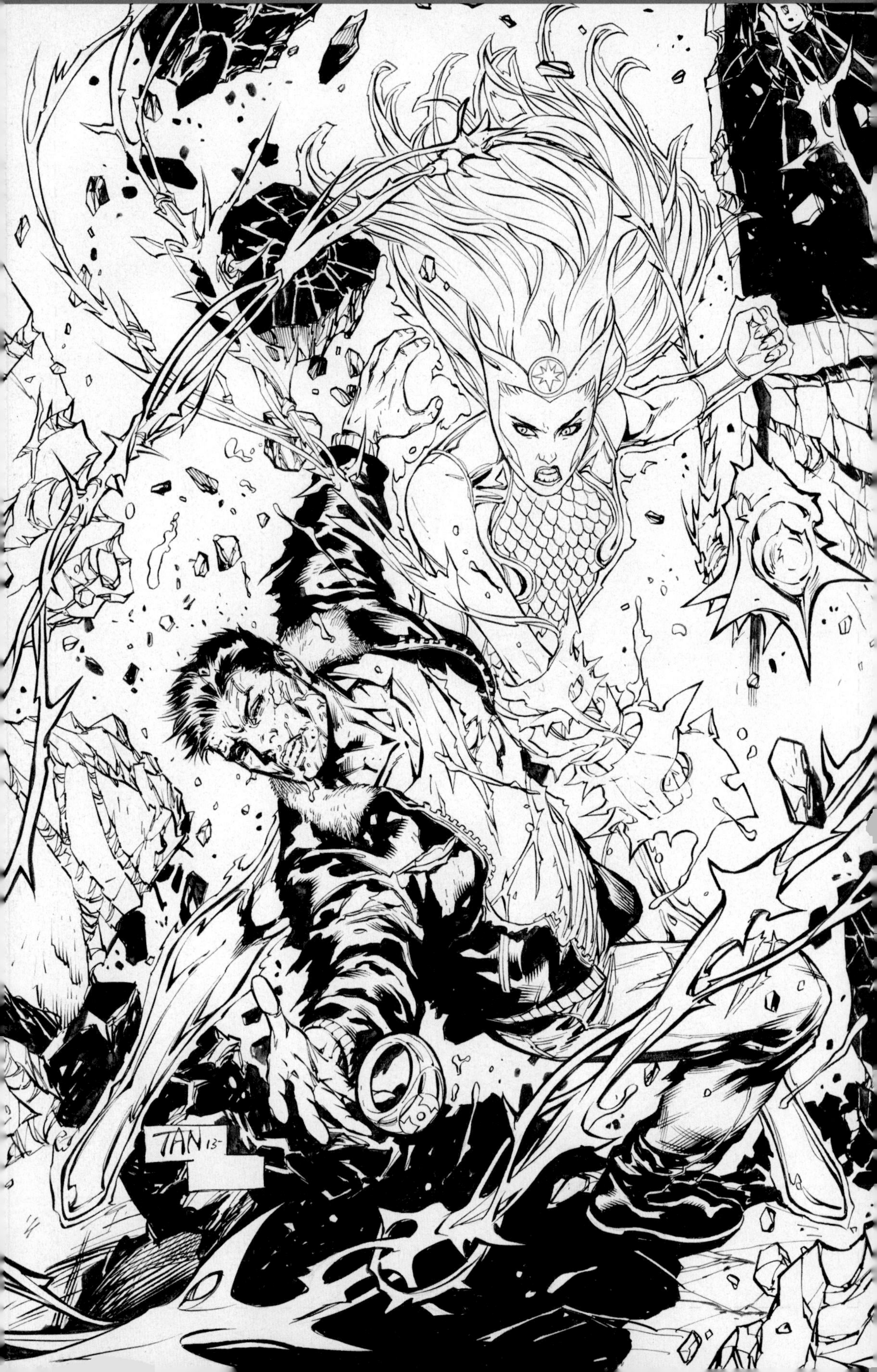
TAN 13

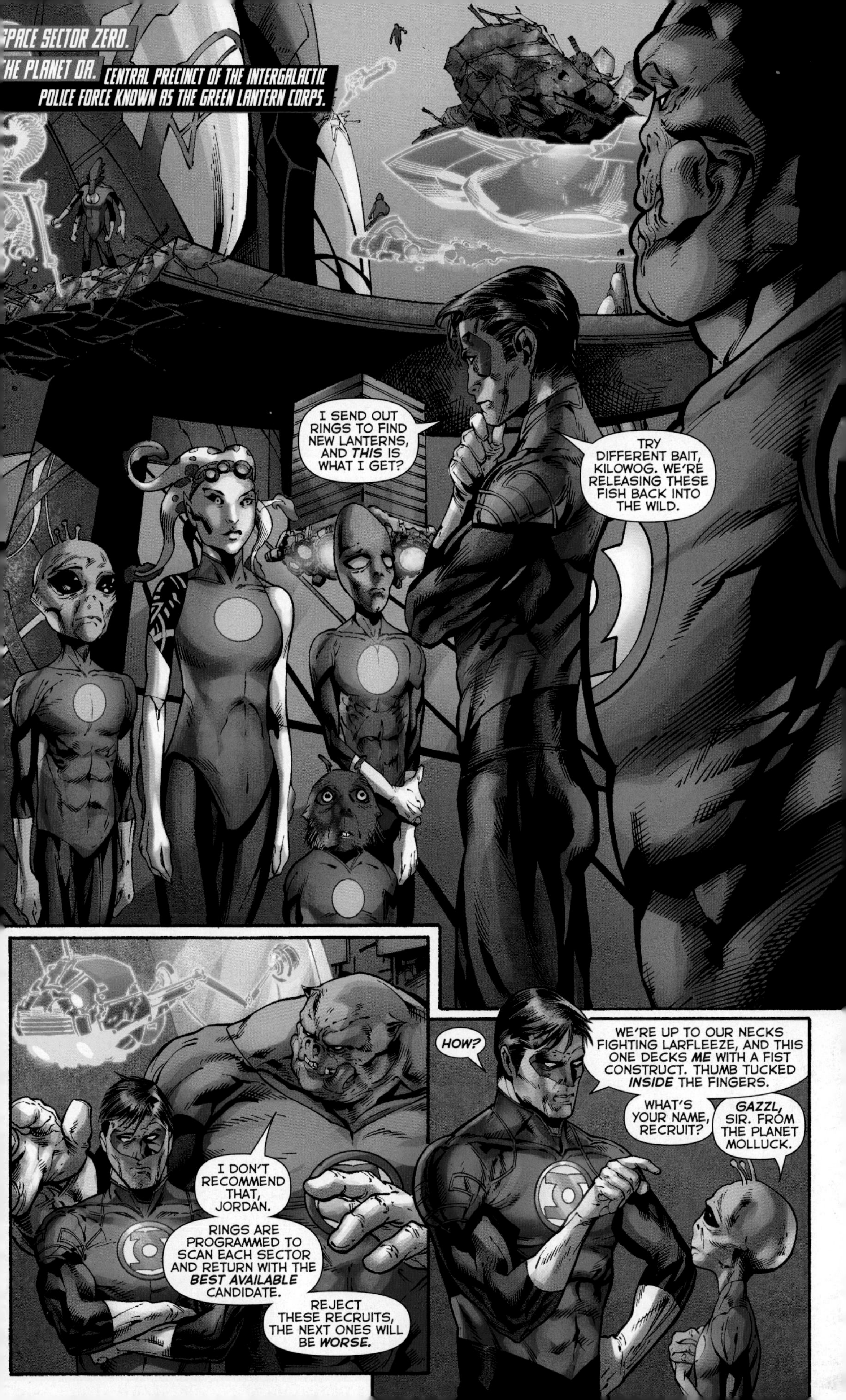
SPACE SECTOR ZERO.
THE PLANET OA.
CENTRAL PRECINCT OF THE INTERGALACTIC POLICE FORCE KNOWN AS THE GREEN LANTERN CORPS.
I SEND OUT RINGS TO FIND NEW LANTERNS, AND THIS IS WHAT I GET?
TRY DIFFERENT BAIT, KILOWOG. WE'RE RELEASING THESE FISH BACK INTO THE WILD.
I DON'T RECOMMEND THAT, JORDAN.
RINGS ARE PROGRAMMED TO SCAN EACH SECTOR AND RETURN WITH THE BEST AVAILABLE CANDIDATE.
REJECT THESE RECRUITS, THE NEXT ONES WILL BE WORSE.
HOW?
WE'RE UP TO OUR NECKS FIGHTING LARFLEEZE, AND THIS ONE DECKS ME WITH A FIST CONSTRUCT. THUMB TUCKED INSIDE THE FINGERS.
WHAT'S YOUR NAME, RECRUIT?
GAZZL, SIR. FROM THE PLANET MOLLUCK.

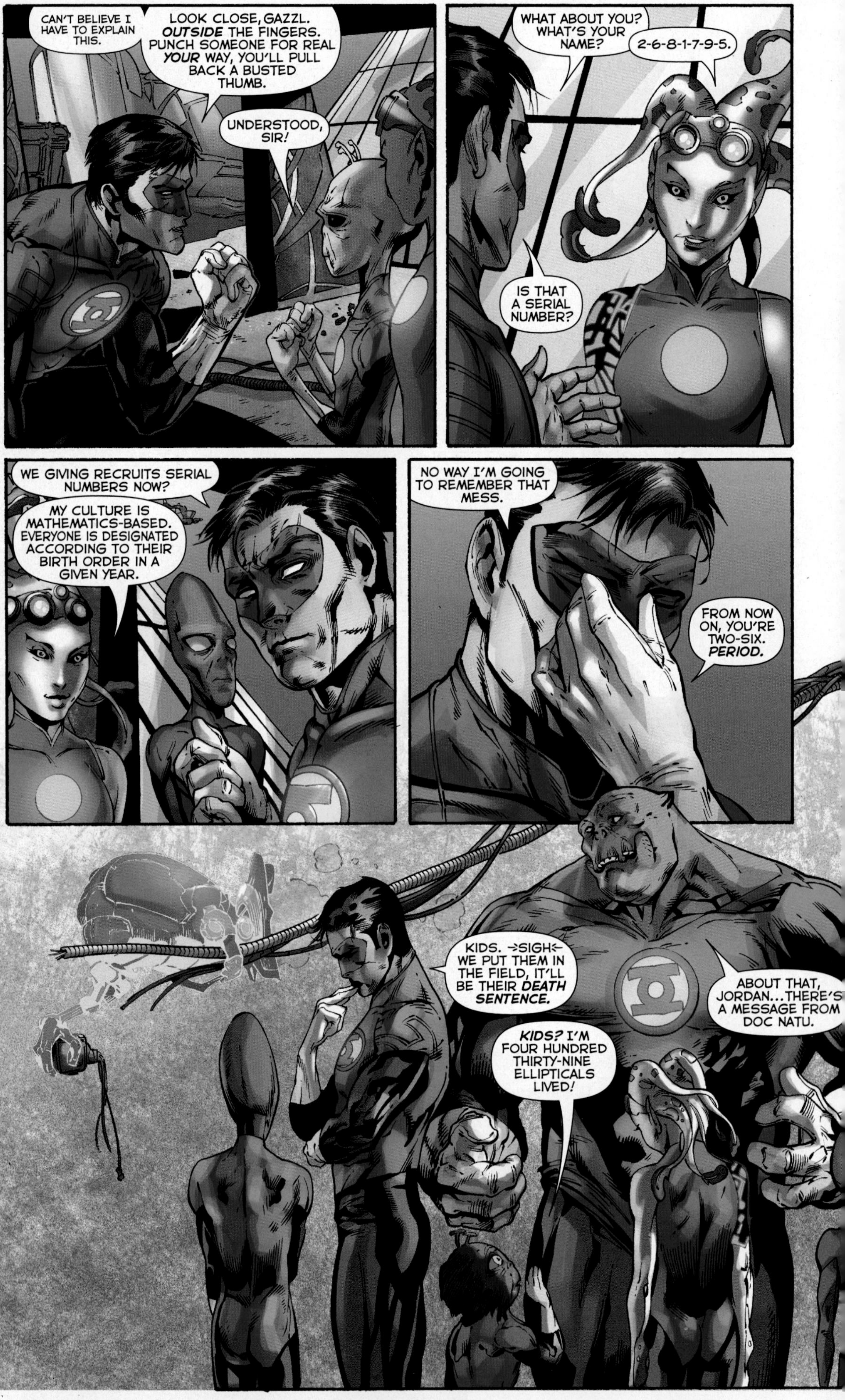

CAN'T BELIEVE I HAVE TO EXPLAIN THIS.
LOOK CLOSE, GAZZL. OUTSIDE THE FINGERS. PUNCH SOMEONE FOR REAL YOUR WAY, YOU'LL PULL BACK A BUSTED THUMB.
UNDERSTOOD, SIR!
WHAT ABOUT YOU? WHAT'S YOUR NAME?
2-6-8-1-7-9-5.
IS THAT A SERIAL NUMBER?
WE GIVING RECRUITS SERIAL NUMBERS NOW?
MY CULTURE IS MATHEMATICS-BASED. EVERYONE IS DESIGNATED ACCORDING TO THEIR BIRTH ORDER IN A GIVEN YEAR.
NO WAY I'M GOING TO REMEMBER THAT MESS.
FROM NOW ON, YOU'RE TWO-SIX. PERIOD.
KIDS. >SIGH< WE PUT THEM IN THE FIELD, IT'LL BE THEIR DEATH SENTENCE.
KIDS? I'M FOUR HUNDRED THIRTY-NINE ELLIPTICALS LIVED!
ABOUT THAT, JORDAN...THERE'S A MESSAGE FROM DOC NATU.

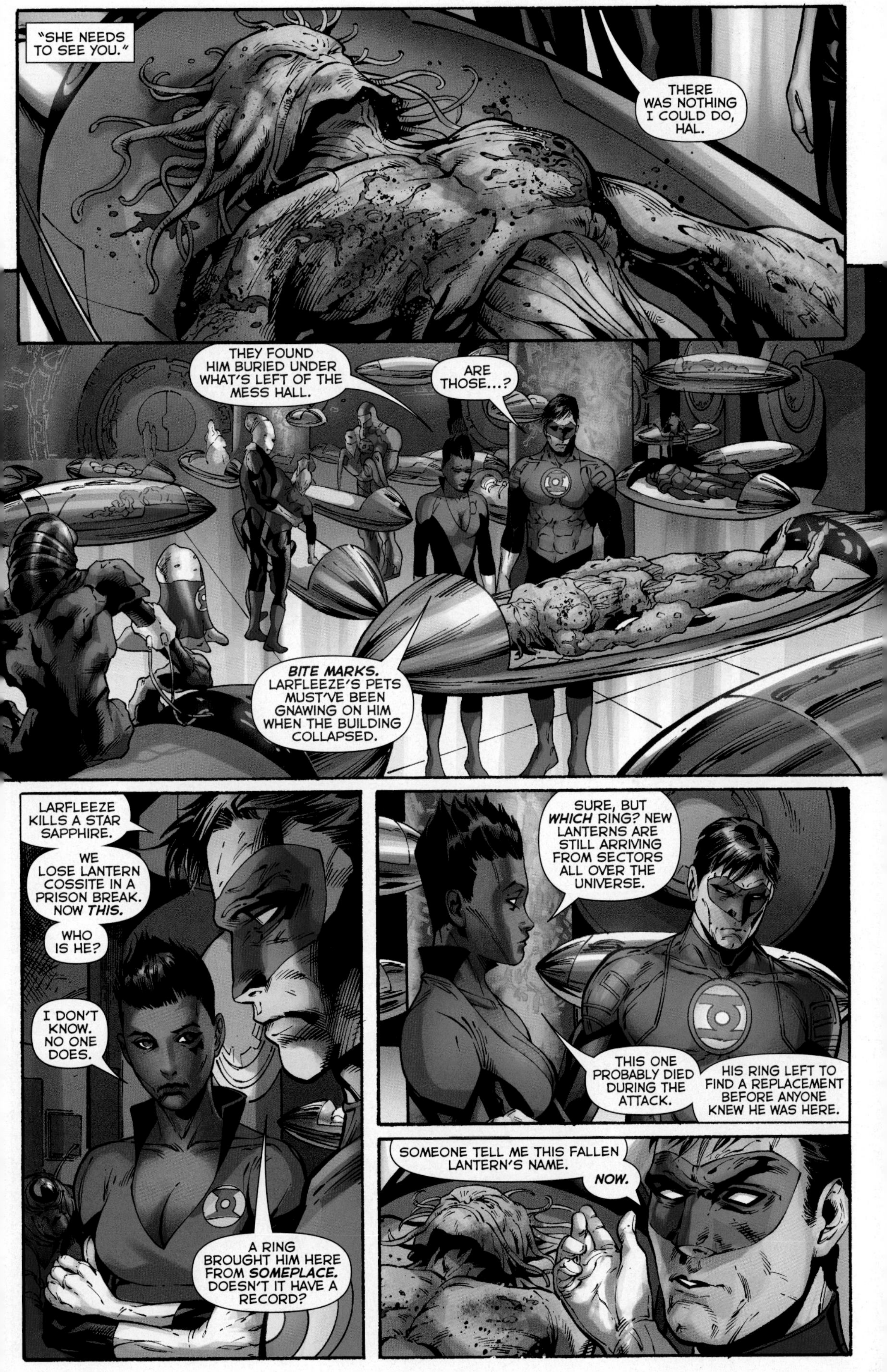

"SHE NEEDS TO SEE YOU."
THERE WAS NOTHING I COULD DO, HAL.
THEY FOUND HIM BURIED UNDER WHAT'S LEFT OF THE MESS HALL.
ARE THOSE...?
BITE MARKS. LARFLEEZE'S PETS MUST'VE BEEN GNAWING ON HIM WHEN THE BUILDING COLLAPSED.
LARFLEEZE KILLS A STAR SAPPHIRE.
WE LOSE LANTERN COSSITE IN A PRISON BREAK. NOW *THIS.*
WHO IS HE?
I DON'T KNOW. NO ONE DOES.
A RING BROUGHT HIM HERE FROM *SOMEPLACE.* DOESN'T IT HAVE A RECORD?
SURE, BUT *WHICH* RING? NEW LANTERNS ARE STILL ARRIVING FROM SECTORS ALL OVER THE UNIVERSE.
THIS ONE PROBABLY DIED DURING THE ATTACK.
HIS RING LEFT TO FIND A REPLACEMENT BEFORE ANYONE KNEW HE WAS HERE.
SOMEONE TELL ME THIS FALLEN LANTERN'S NAME.
NOW.

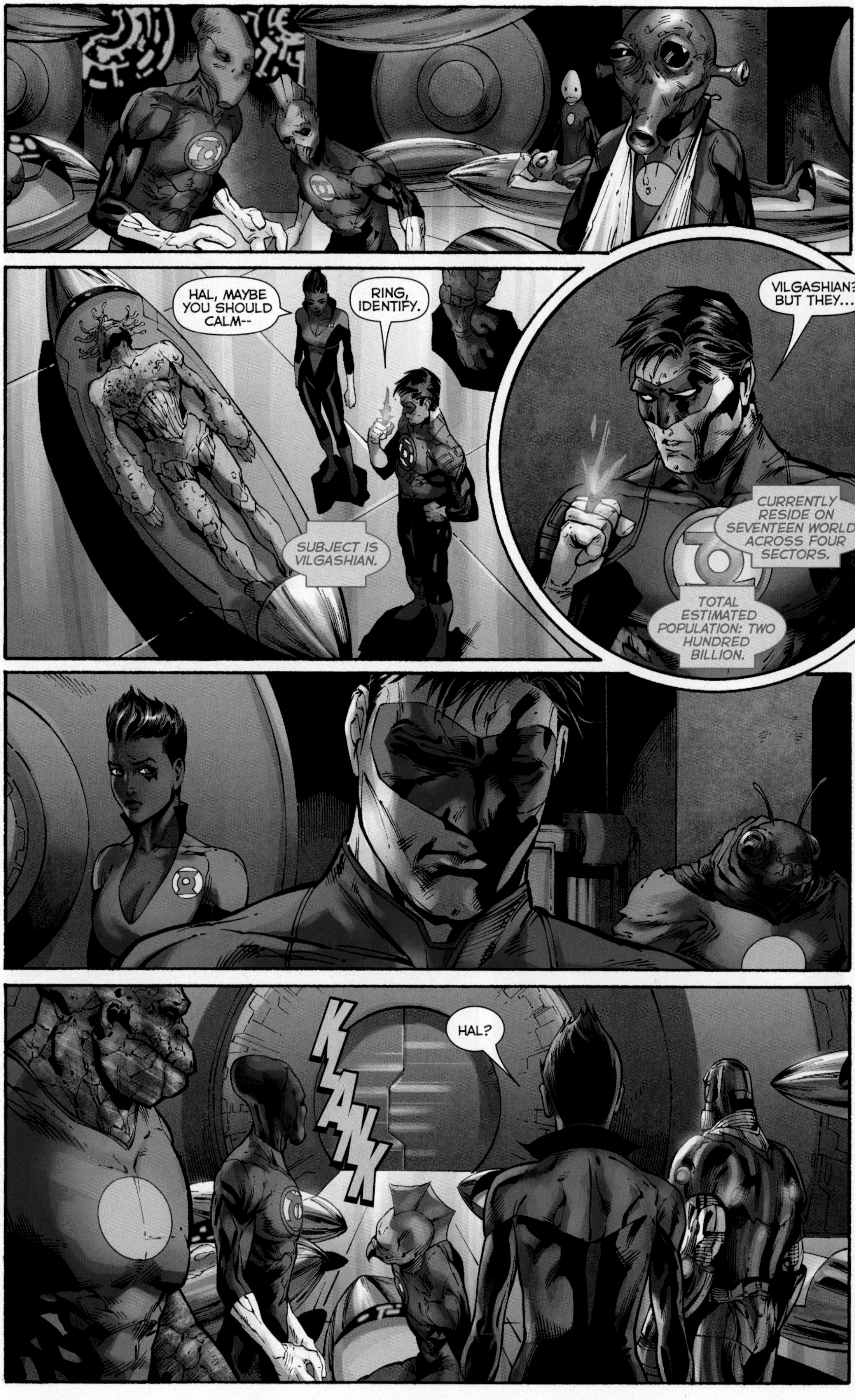
HAL, MAYBE YOU SHOULD CALM--
RING, IDENTIFY.
SUBJECT IS VILGASHIAN.
VILGASHIAN? BUT THEY...
CURRENTLY RESIDE ON SEVENTEEN WORLDS ACROSS FOUR SECTORS.
TOTAL ESTIMATED POPULATION: TWO HUNDRED BILLION.
KLANK
HAL?

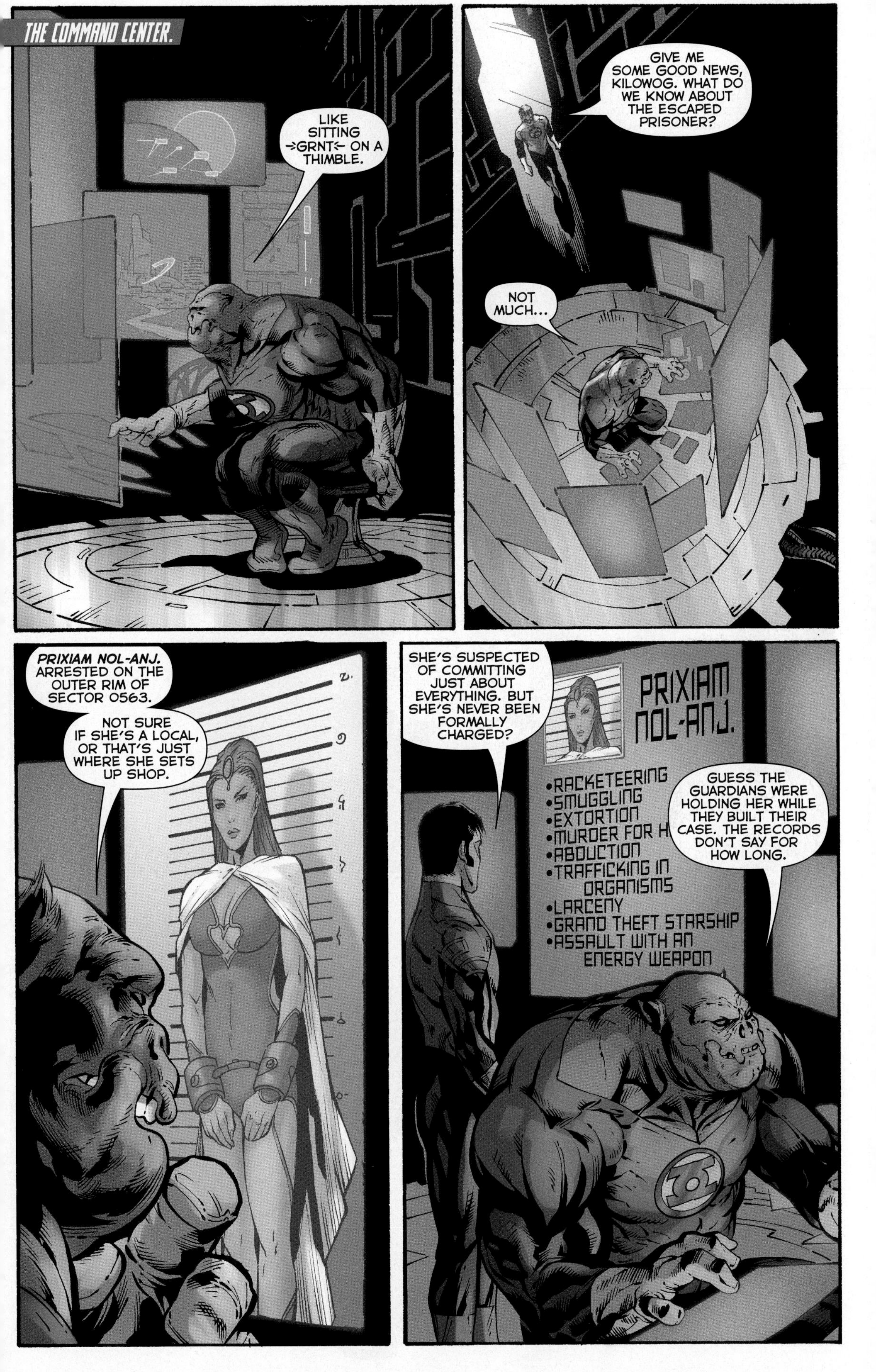
THE COMMAND CENTER.
LIKE SITTING ⇒GRNT⇐ ON A THIMBLE.
GIVE ME SOME GOOD NEWS, KILOWOG. WHAT DO WE KNOW ABOUT THE ESCAPED PRISONER?
NOT MUCH...
PRIXIAM NOL-ANJ. ARRESTED ON THE OUTER RIM OF SECTOR 0563.
NOT SURE IF SHE'S A LOCAL, OR THAT'S JUST WHERE SHE SETS UP SHOP.
SHE'S SUSPECTED OF COMMITTING JUST ABOUT EVERYTHING. BUT SHE'S NEVER BEEN FORMALLY CHARGED?
PRIXIAM NOL-ANJ.
•RACKETEERING
•SMUGGLING
•EXTORTION
•MURDER FOR H
•ABDUCTION
•TRAFFICKING IN ORGANISMS
•LARCENY
•GRAND THEFT STARSHIP
•ASSAULT WITH AN ENERGY WEAPON
GUESS THE GUARDIANS WERE HOLDING HER WHILE THEY BUILT THEIR CASE. THE RECORDS DON'T SAY FOR HOW LONG.

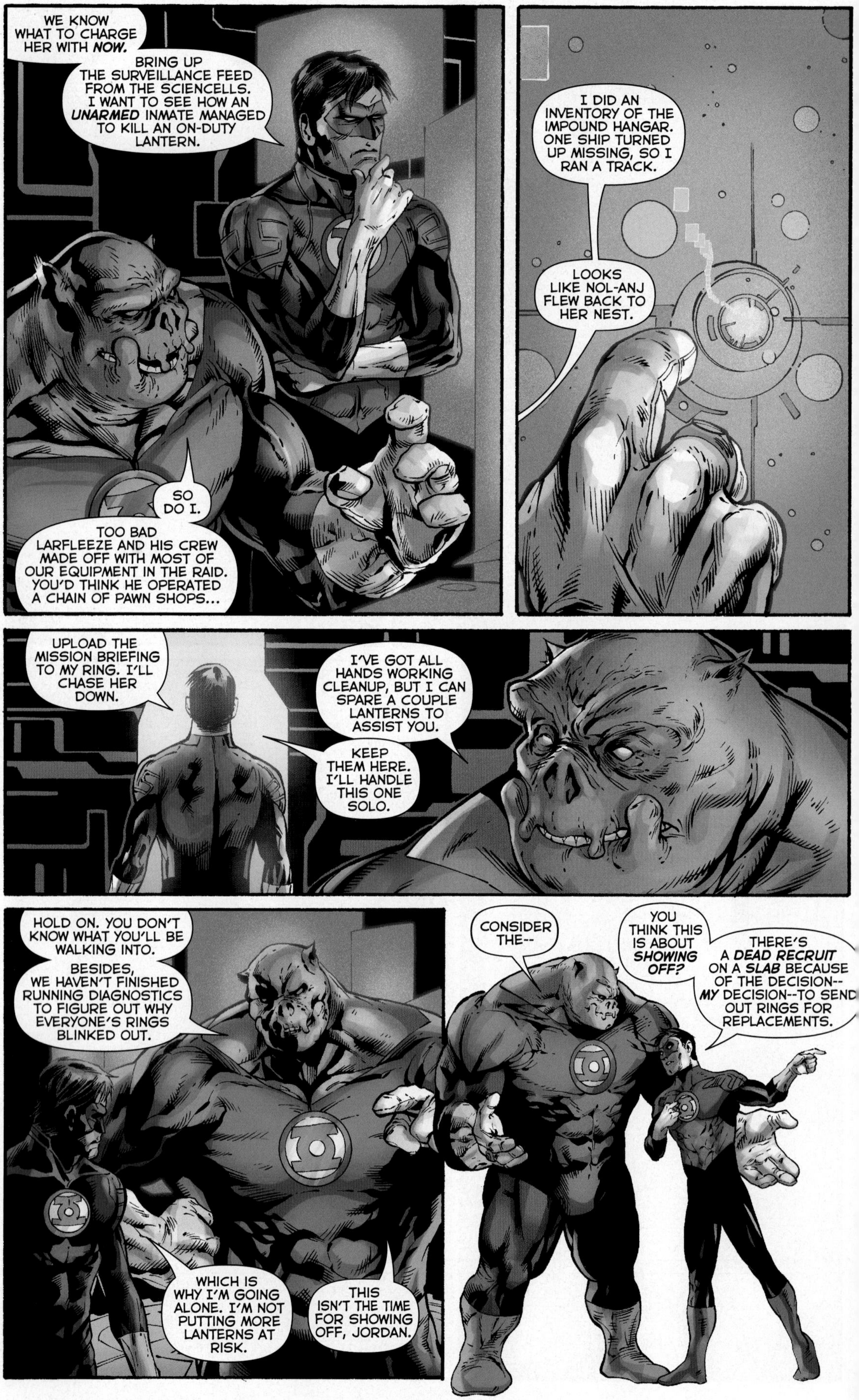

WE KNOW WHAT TO CHARGE HER WITH *NOW.*
BRING UP THE SURVEILLANCE FEED FROM THE SCIENCELLS. I WANT TO SEE HOW AN *UNARMED* INMATE MANAGED TO KILL AN ON-DUTY LANTERN.
SO DO I.
TOO BAD LARFLEEZE AND HIS CREW MADE OFF WITH MOST OF OUR EQUIPMENT IN THE RAID. YOU'D THINK HE OPERATED A CHAIN OF PAWN SHOPS...
I DID AN INVENTORY OF THE IMPOUND HANGAR. ONE SHIP TURNED UP MISSING, SO I RAN A TRACK.
LOOKS LIKE NOL-ANJ FLEW BACK TO HER NEST.
UPLOAD THE MISSION BRIEFING TO MY RING. I'LL CHASE HER DOWN.
I'VE GOT ALL HANDS WORKING CLEANUP, BUT I CAN SPARE A COUPLE LANTERNS TO ASSIST YOU.
KEEP THEM HERE. I'LL HANDLE THIS ONE SOLO.
HOLD ON. YOU DON'T KNOW WHAT YOU'LL BE WALKING INTO.
BESIDES, WE HAVEN'T FINISHED RUNNING DIAGNOSTICS TO FIGURE OUT WHY EVERYONE'S RINGS BLINKED OUT.
WHICH IS WHY I'M GOING ALONE. I'M NOT PUTTING MORE LANTERNS AT RISK.
THIS ISN'T THE TIME FOR SHOWING OFF, JORDAN.
CONSIDER THE--
YOU THINK THIS IS ABOUT *SHOWING OFF?*
THERE'S A *DEAD RECRUIT* ON A *SLAB* BECAUSE OF THE DECISION-- *MY* DECISION--TO SEND OUT RINGS FOR REPLACEMENTS.

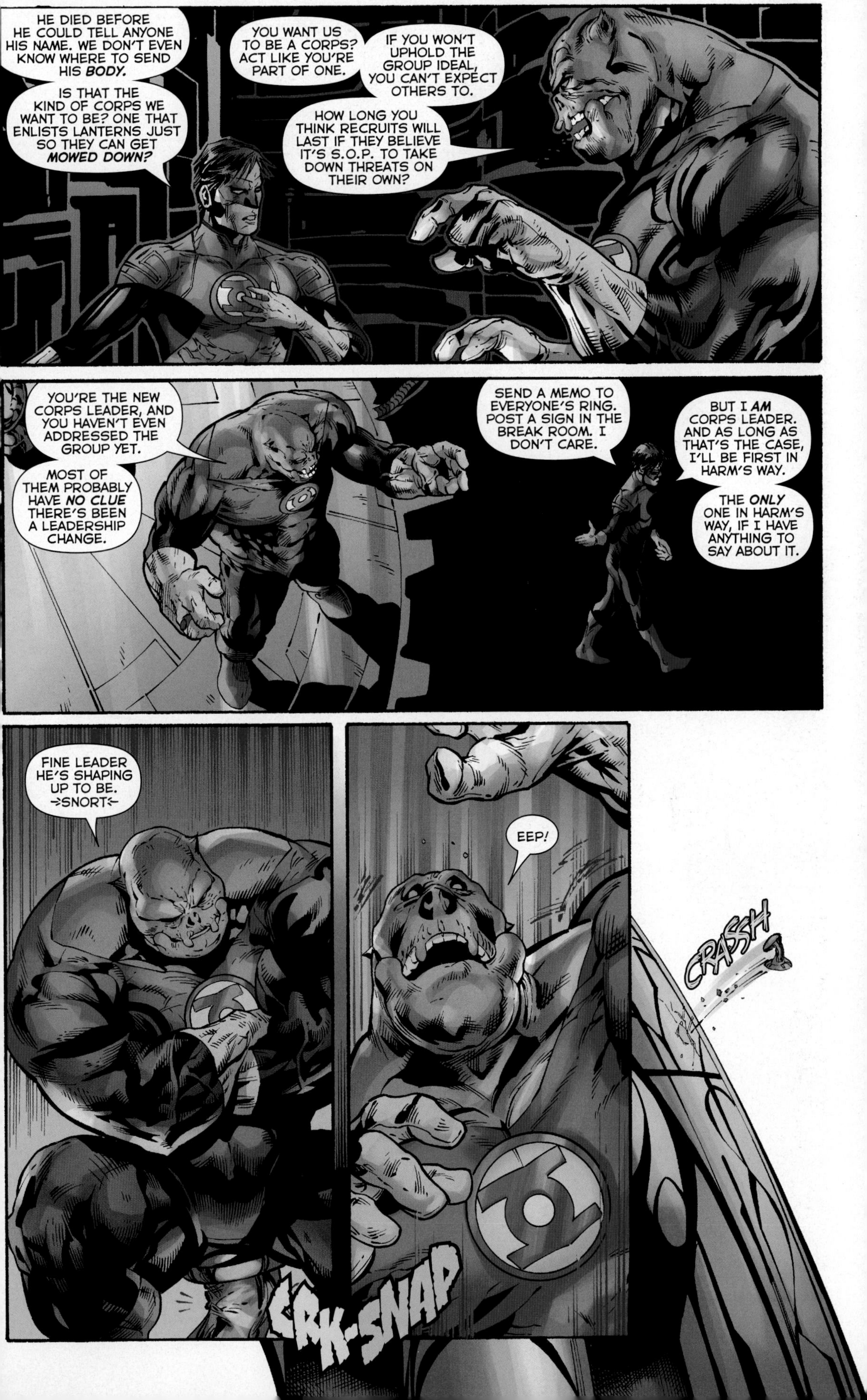
HE DIED BEFORE HE COULD TELL ANYONE HIS NAME. WE DON'T EVEN KNOW WHERE TO SEND HIS BODY.
IS THAT THE KIND OF CORPS WE WANT TO BE? ONE THAT ENLISTS LANTERNS JUST SO THEY CAN GET MOWED DOWN?
YOU WANT US TO BE A CORPS? ACT LIKE YOU'RE PART OF ONE.
IF YOU WON'T UPHOLD THE GROUP IDEAL, YOU CAN'T EXPECT OTHERS TO.
HOW LONG YOU THINK RECRUITS WILL LAST IF THEY BELIEVE IT'S S.O.P. TO TAKE DOWN THREATS ON THEIR OWN?
YOU'RE THE NEW CORPS LEADER, AND YOU HAVEN'T EVEN ADDRESSED THE GROUP YET.
MOST OF THEM PROBABLY HAVE NO CLUE THERE'S BEEN A LEADERSHIP CHANGE.
SEND A MEMO TO EVERYONE'S RING. POST A SIGN IN THE BREAK ROOM. I DON'T CARE.
BUT I AM CORPS LEADER. AND AS LONG AS THAT'S THE CASE, I'LL BE FIRST IN HARM'S WAY.
THE ONLY ONE IN HARM'S WAY, IF I HAVE ANYTHING TO SAY ABOUT IT.
FINE LEADER HE'S SHAPING UP TO BE. >SNORT<
EEP!
CRASSH
CRK-SNAP

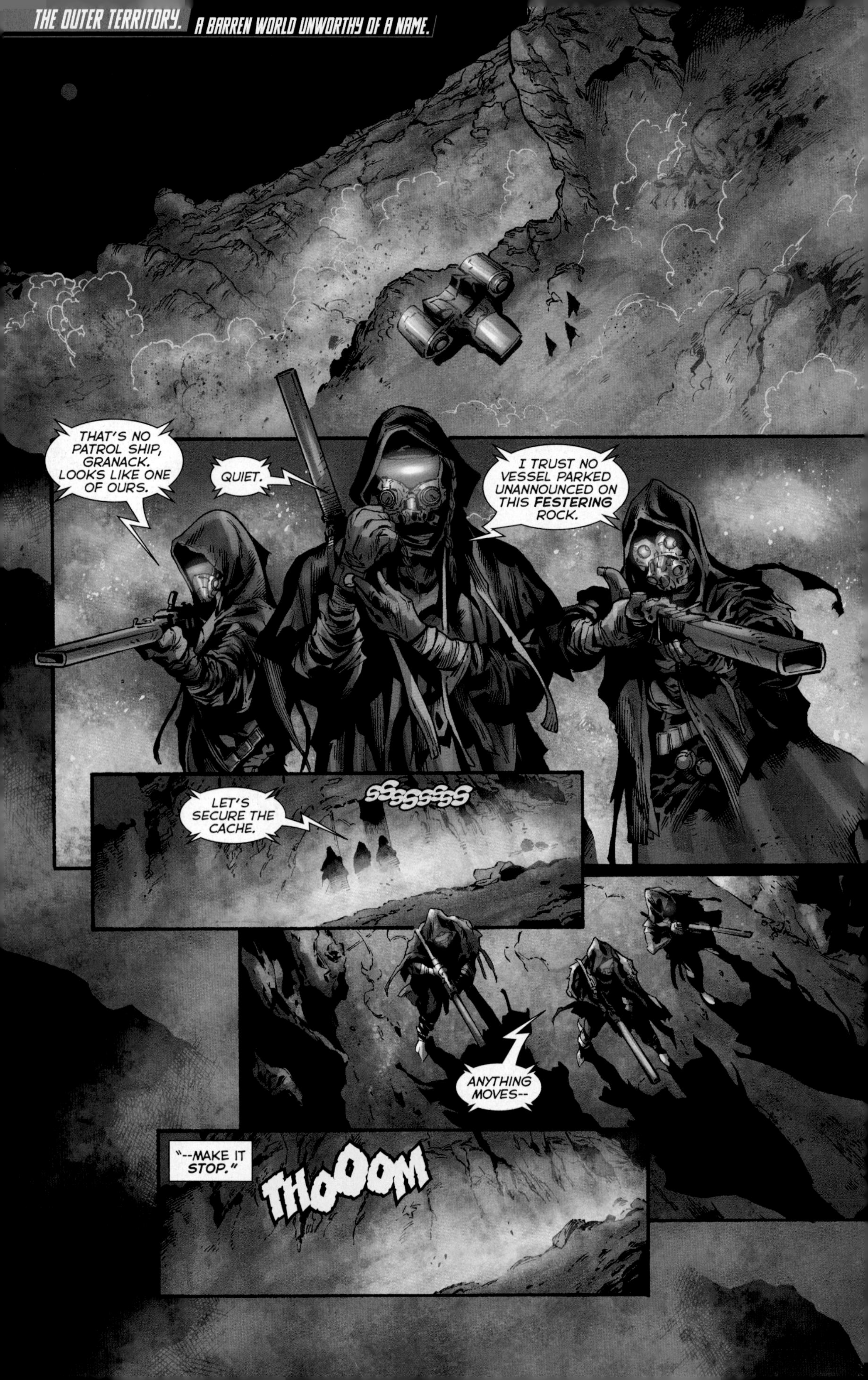
THE OUTER TERRITORY.
A BARREN WORLD UNWORTHY OF A NAME.
THAT'S NO PATROL SHIP, GRANACK. LOOKS LIKE ONE OF OURS.
QUIET.
I TRUST NO VESSEL PARKED UNANNOUNCED ON THIS FESTERING ROCK.
LET'S SECURE THE CACHE.
SSSSSSS
ANYTHING MOVES--
"--MAKE IT STOP."
THOOOM

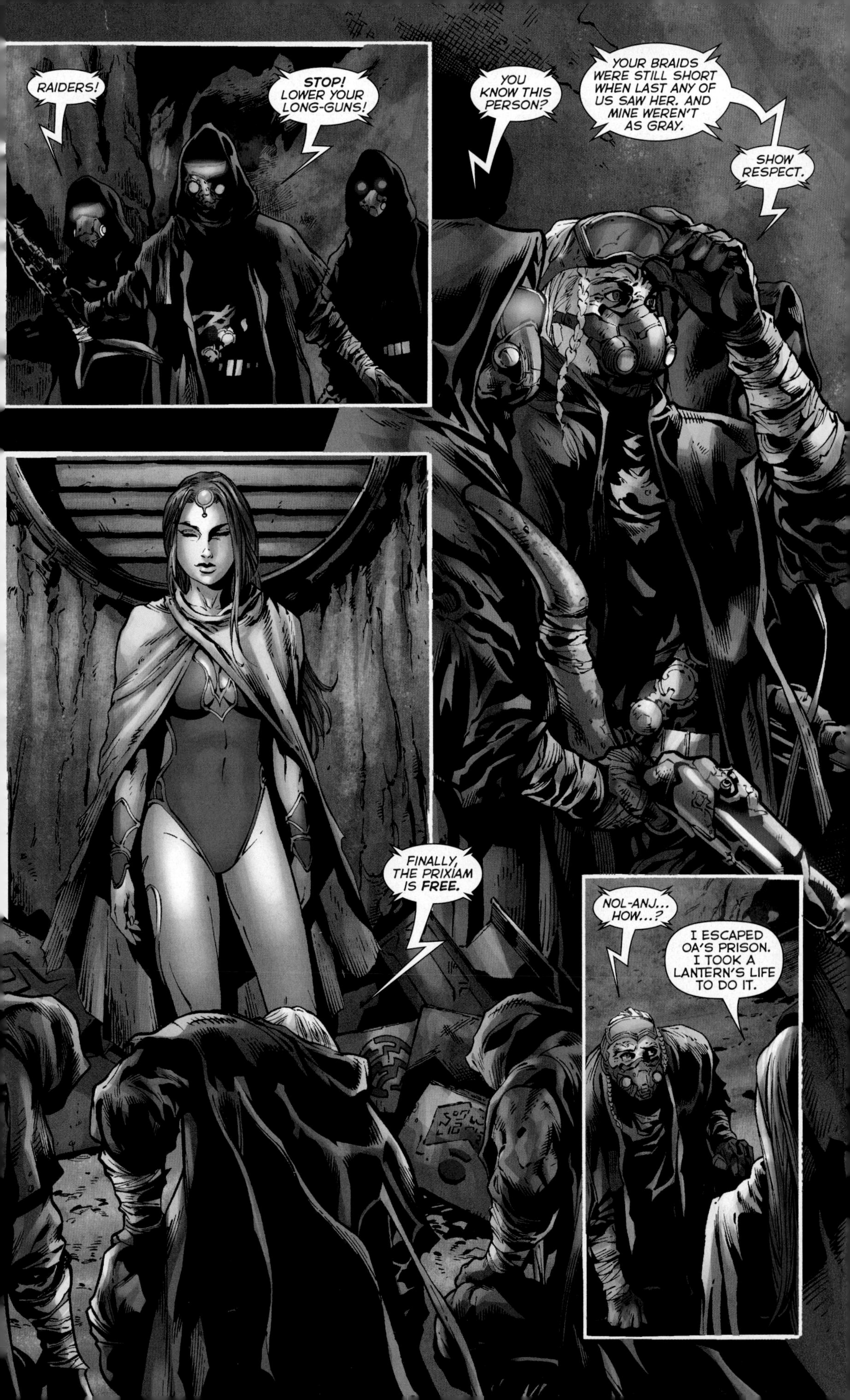
RAIDERS!
STOP! LOWER YOUR LONG-GUNS!
YOU KNOW THIS PERSON?
YOUR BRAIDS WERE STILL SHORT WHEN LAST ANY OF US SAW HER. AND MINE WEREN'T AS GRAY.
SHOW RESPECT.
FINALLY, THE PRIXIAM IS FREE.
NOL-ANJ... HOW...?
I ESCAPED OA'S PRISON. I TOOK A LANTERN'S LIFE TO DO IT.

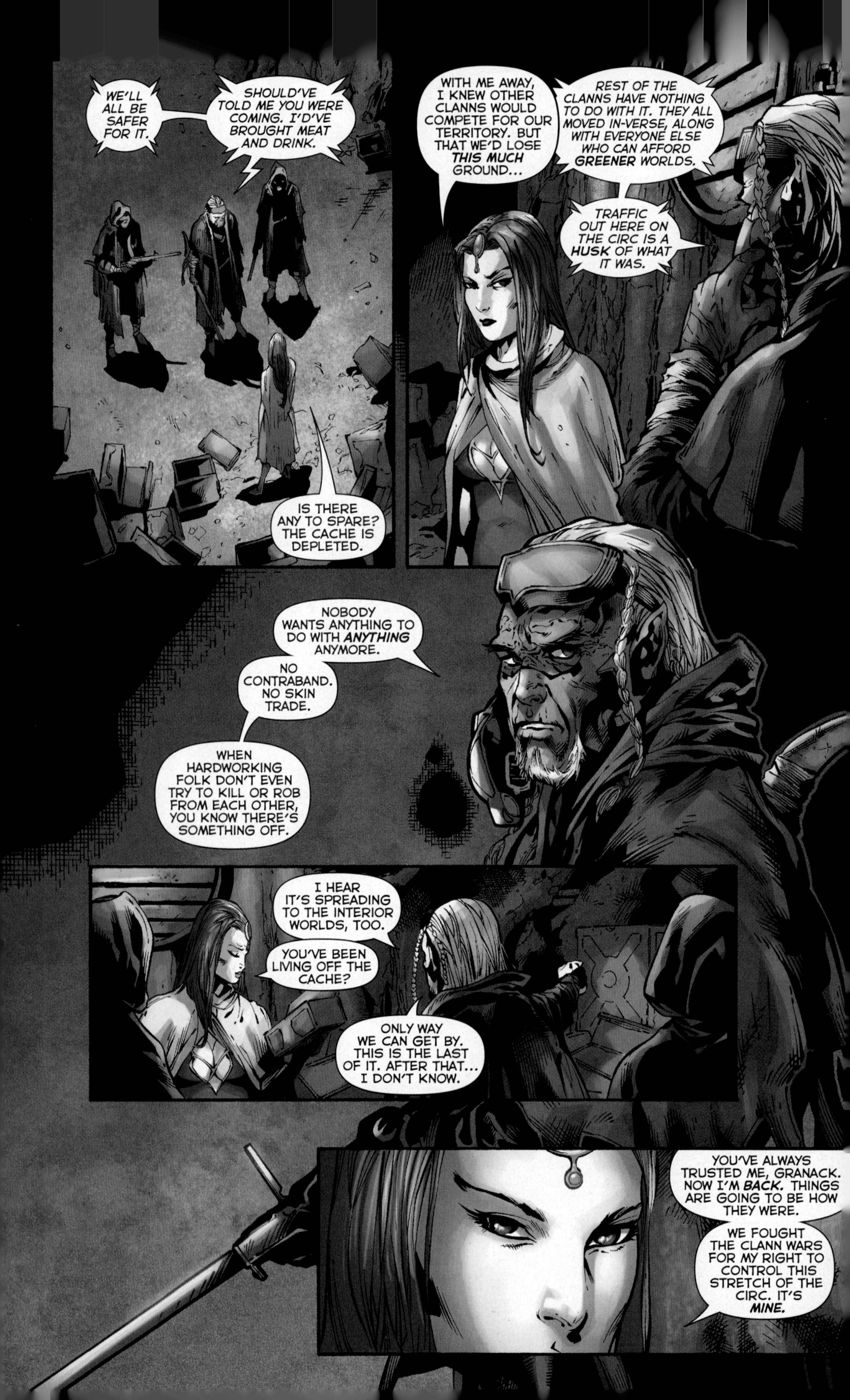
SHOULD'VE TOLD ME YOU WERE COMING. I'D'VE BROUGHT MEAT AND DRINK.
WE'LL ALL BE SAFER FOR IT.
IS THERE ANY TO SPARE? THE CACHE IS DEPLETED.
WITH ME AWAY, I KNEW OTHER CLANNS WOULD COMPETE FOR OUR TERRITORY. BUT THAT WE'D LOSE THIS MUCH GROUND...
REST OF THE CLANNS HAVE NOTHING TO DO WITH IT. THEY ALL MOVED IN-VERSE, ALONG WITH EVERYONE ELSE WHO CAN AFFORD GREENER WORLDS.
TRAFFIC OUT HERE ON THE CIRC IS A HUSK OF WHAT IT WAS.
NOBODY WANTS ANYTHING TO DO WITH ANYTHING ANYMORE.
NO CONTRABAND. NO SKIN TRADE.
WHEN HARDWORKING FOLK DON'T EVEN TRY TO KILL OR ROB FROM EACH OTHER, YOU KNOW THERE'S SOMETHING OFF.
I HEAR IT'S SPREADING TO THE INTERIOR WORLDS, TOO.
YOU'VE BEEN LIVING OFF THE CACHE?
ONLY WAY WE CAN GET BY. THIS IS THE LAST OF IT. AFTER THAT... I DON'T KNOW.
YOU'VE ALWAYS TRUSTED ME, GRANACK. NOW I'M BACK. THINGS ARE GOING TO BE HOW THEY WERE.
WE FOUGHT THE CLANN WARS FOR MY RIGHT TO CONTROL THIS STRETCH OF THE CIRC. IT'S MINE.

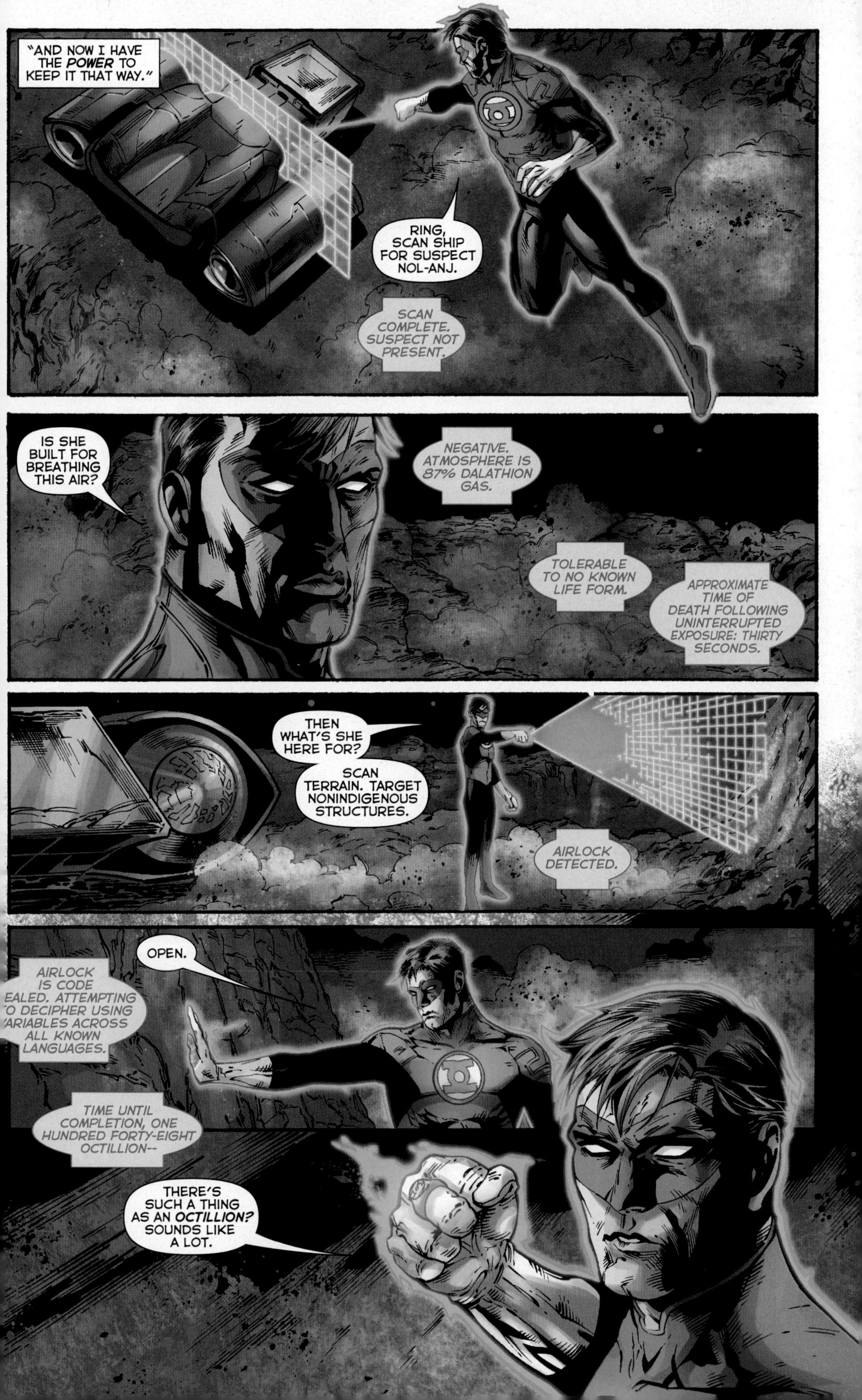
"AND NOW I HAVE THE *POWER* TO KEEP IT THAT WAY."
RING, SCAN SHIP FOR SUSPECT NOL-ANJ.
SCAN COMPLETE. SUSPECT NOT PRESENT.
IS SHE BUILT FOR BREATHING THIS AIR?
NEGATIVE. ATMOSPHERE IS 87% DALATHION GAS.
TOLERABLE TO NO KNOWN LIFE FORM.
APPROXIMATE TIME OF DEATH FOLLOWING UNINTERRUPTED EXPOSURE: THIRTY SECONDS.
THEN WHAT'S SHE HERE FOR?
SCAN TERRAIN. TARGET NONINDIGENOUS STRUCTURES.
AIRLOCK DETECTED.
OPEN.
AIRLOCK IS CODE EALED. ATTEMPTING TO DECIPHER USING ARIABLES ACROSS ALL KNOWN LANGUAGES.
TIME UNTIL COMPLETION, ONE HUNDRED FORTY-EIGHT OCTILLION--
THERE'S SUCH A THING AS AN *OCTILLION?* SOUNDS LIKE A LOT.

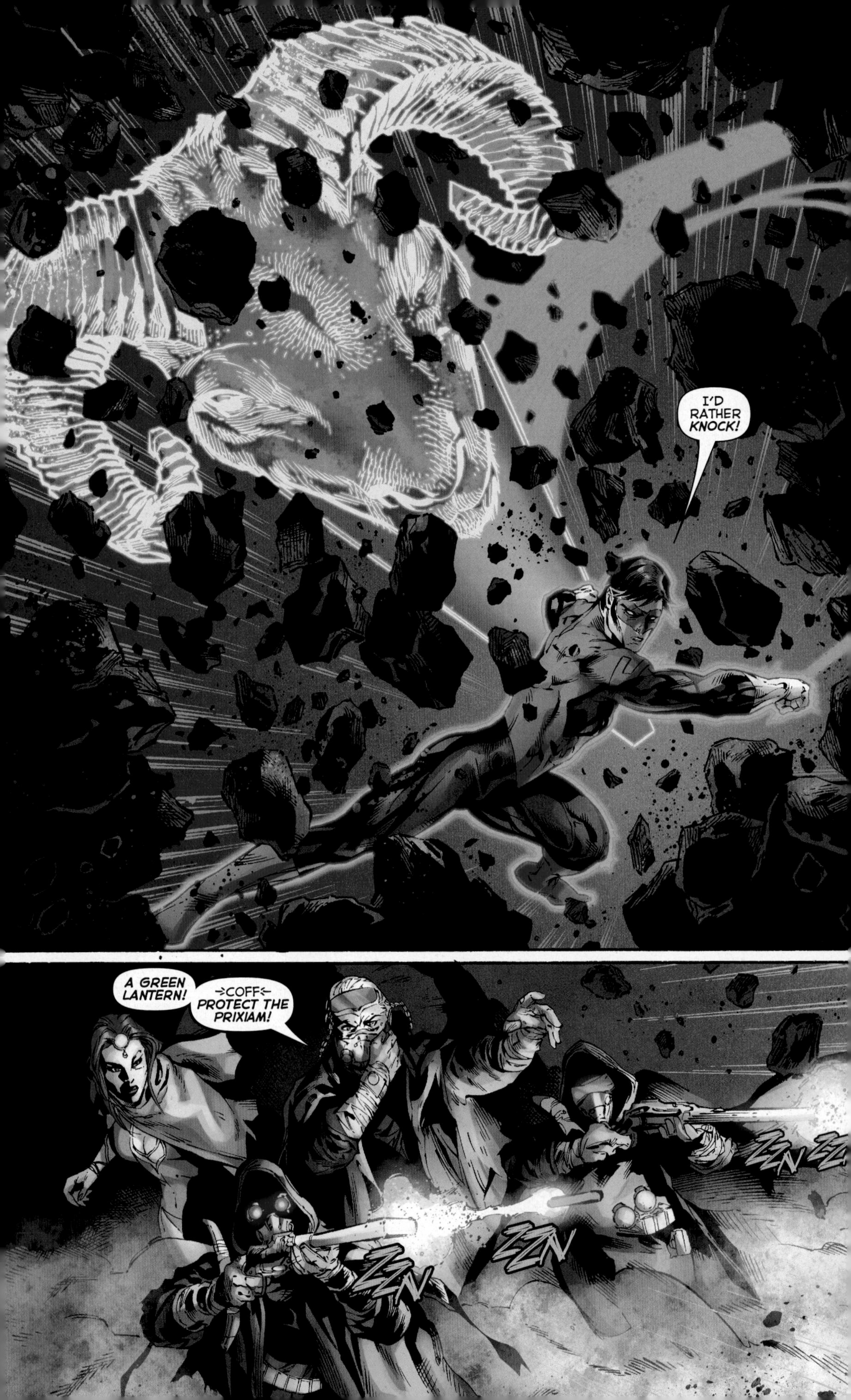
I'D RATHER KNOCK!
A GREEN LANTERN!
COFF
PROTECT THE PRIXIAM!
ZZN
ZZN
ZZN
ZZN

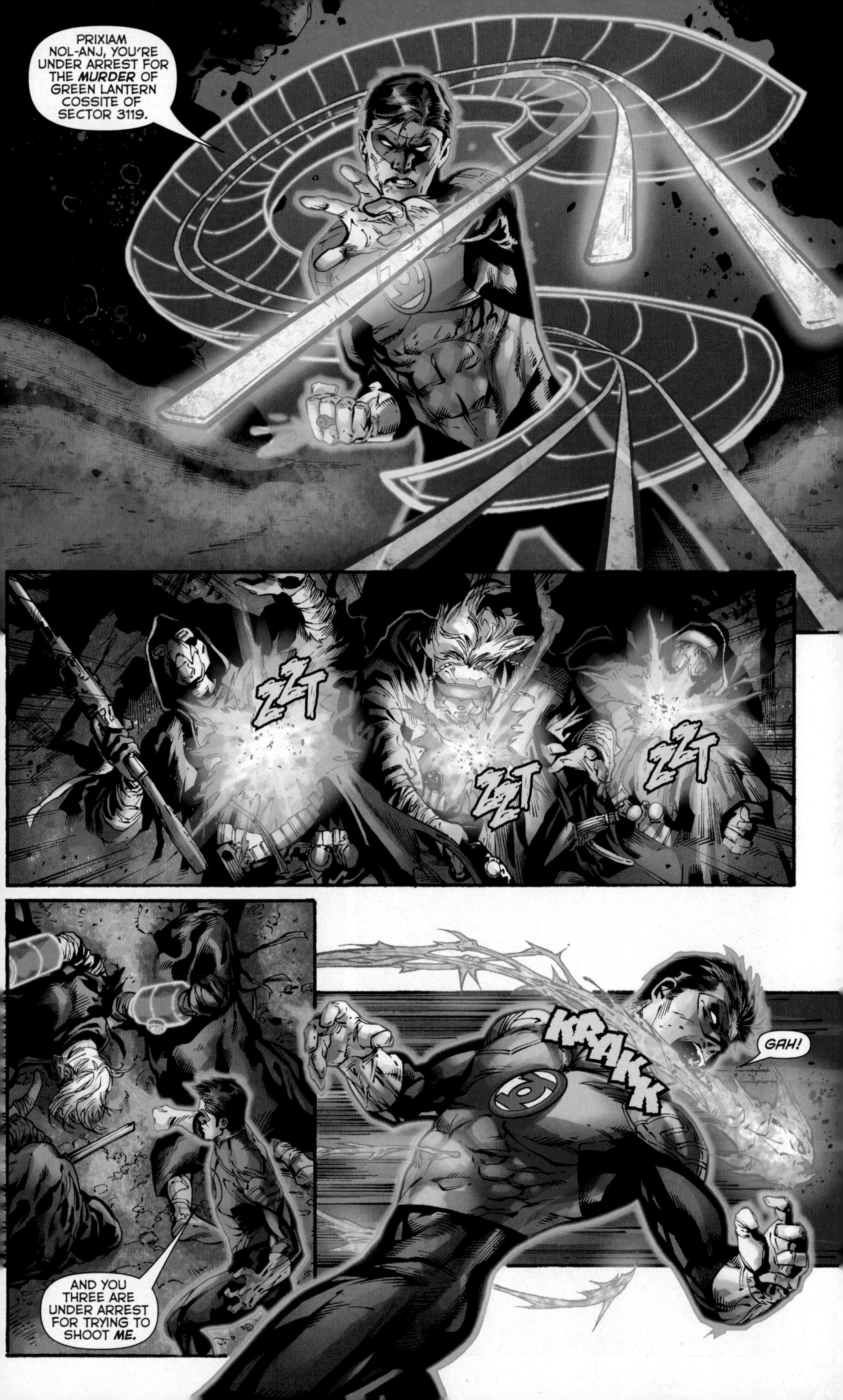
PRIXIAM NOL-ANJ, YOU'RE UNDER ARREST FOR THE *MURDER* OF GREEN LANTERN COSSITE OF SECTOR 3119.
ZZT
ZZT
ZZT
KRAKK
GAH!
AND YOU THREE ARE UNDER ARREST FOR TRYING TO SHOOT *ME.*

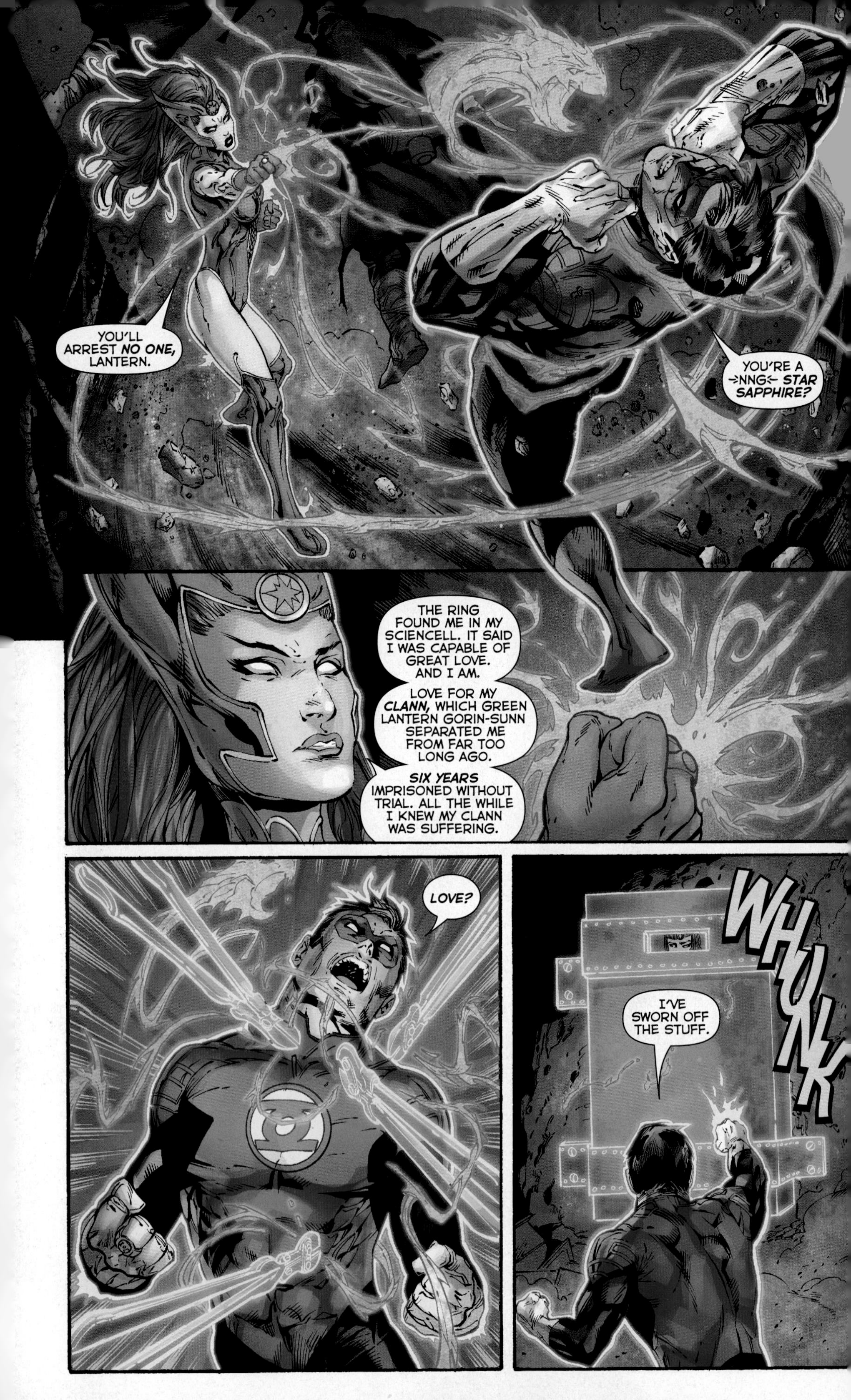
YOU'LL ARREST NO ONE, LANTERN.
YOU'RE A ⇒NNG⇐ STAR SAPPHIRE?
THE RING FOUND ME IN MY SCIENCELL. IT SAID I WAS CAPABLE OF GREAT LOVE. AND I AM.
LOVE FOR MY CLANN, WHICH GREEN LANTERN GORIN-SUNN SEPARATED ME FROM FAR TOO LONG AGO.
SIX YEARS IMPRISONED WITHOUT TRIAL. ALL THE WHILE I KNEW MY CLANN WAS SUFFERING.
LOVE?
I'VE SWORN OFF THE STUFF.
WHUNK

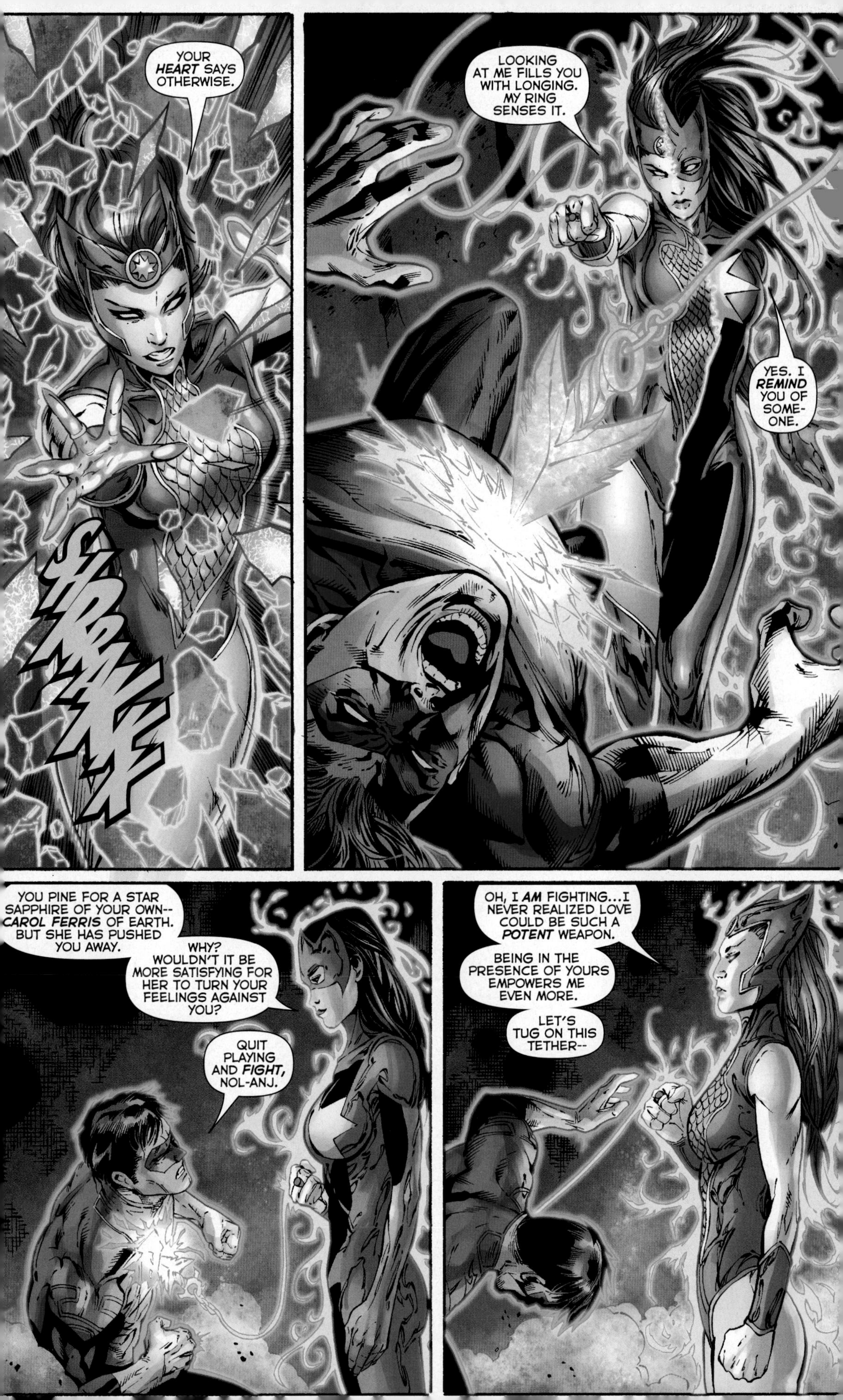
YOUR HEART SAYS OTHERWISE.
LOOKING AT ME FILLS YOU WITH LONGING. MY RING SENSES IT.
YES. I REMIND YOU OF SOME-ONE.
YOU PINE FOR A STAR SAPPHIRE OF YOUR OWN-- CAROL FERRIS OF EARTH. BUT SHE HAS PUSHED YOU AWAY.
WHY? WOULDN'T IT BE MORE SATISFYING FOR HER TO TURN YOUR FEELINGS AGAINST YOU?
QUIT PLAYING AND FIGHT, NOL-ANJ.
OH, I AM FIGHTING...I NEVER REALIZED LOVE COULD BE SUCH A POTENT WEAPON.
BEING IN THE PRESENCE OF YOURS EMPOWERS ME EVEN MORE.
LET'S TUG ON THIS TETHER--

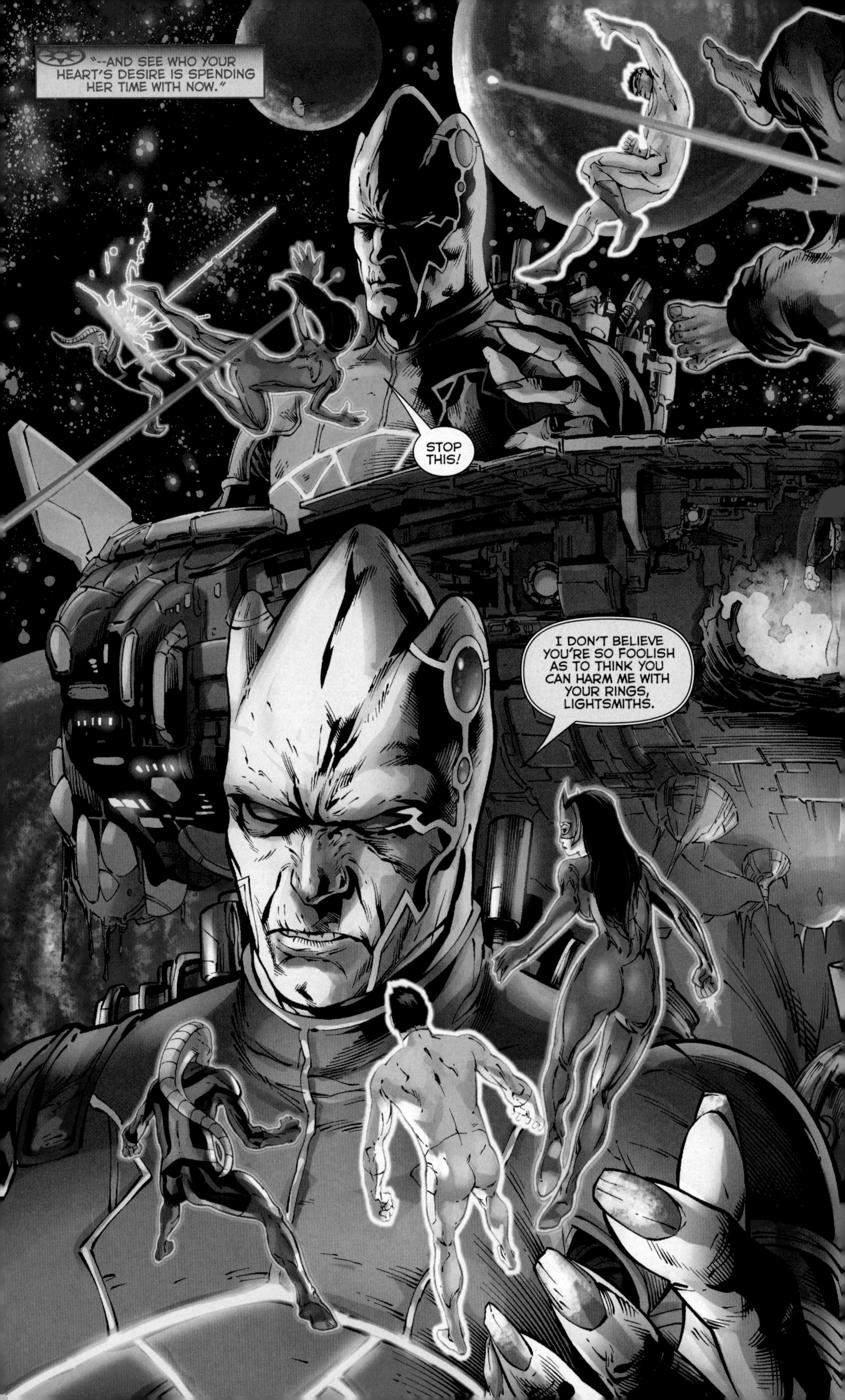
"--AND SEE WHO YOUR HEART'S DESIRE IS SPENDING HER TIME WITH NOW."
STOP THIS!
I DON'T BELIEVE YOU'RE SO FOOLISH AS TO THINK YOU CAN HARM ME WITH YOUR RINGS, LIGHTSMITHS.

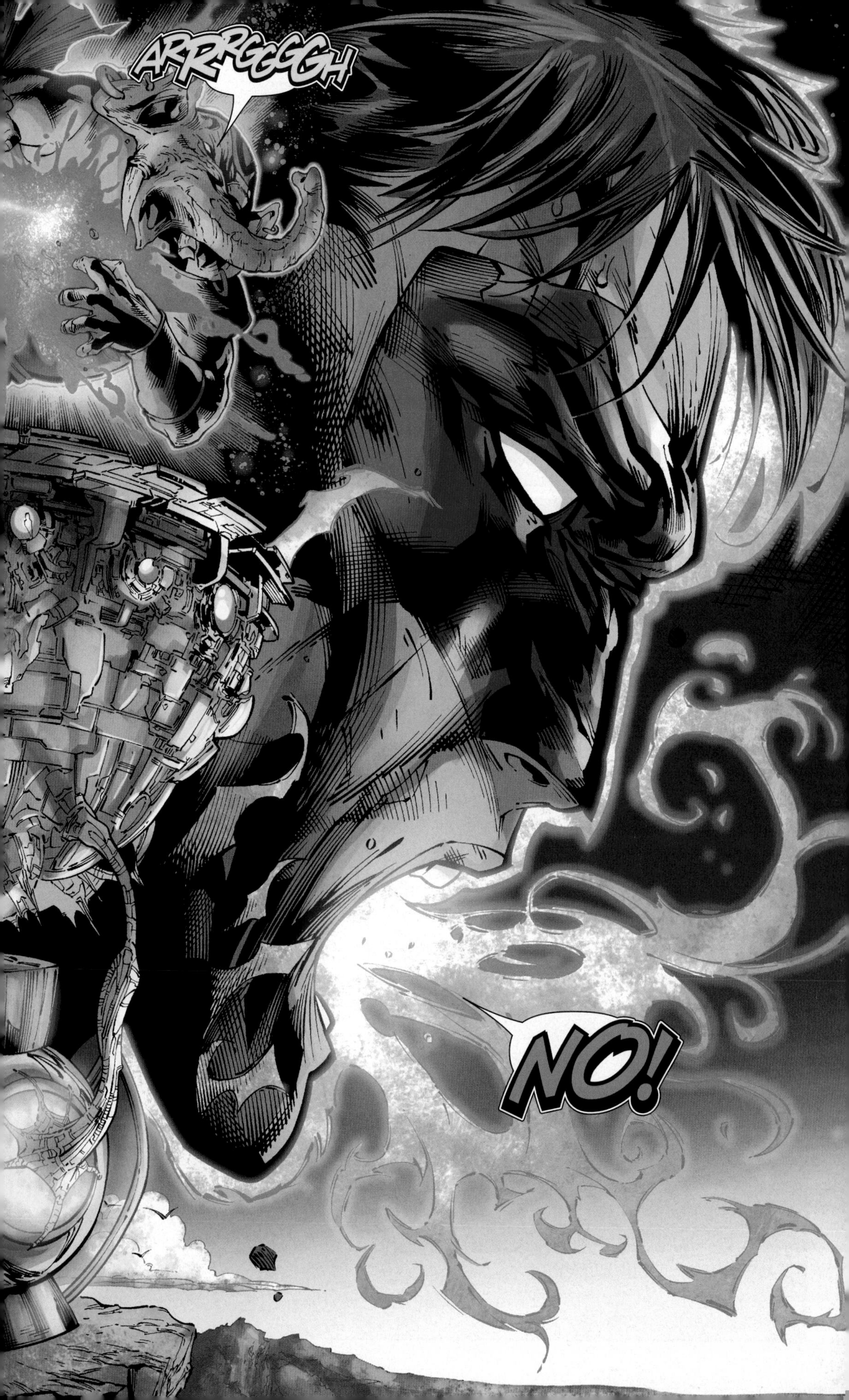
ARRRGGGGH
NO!

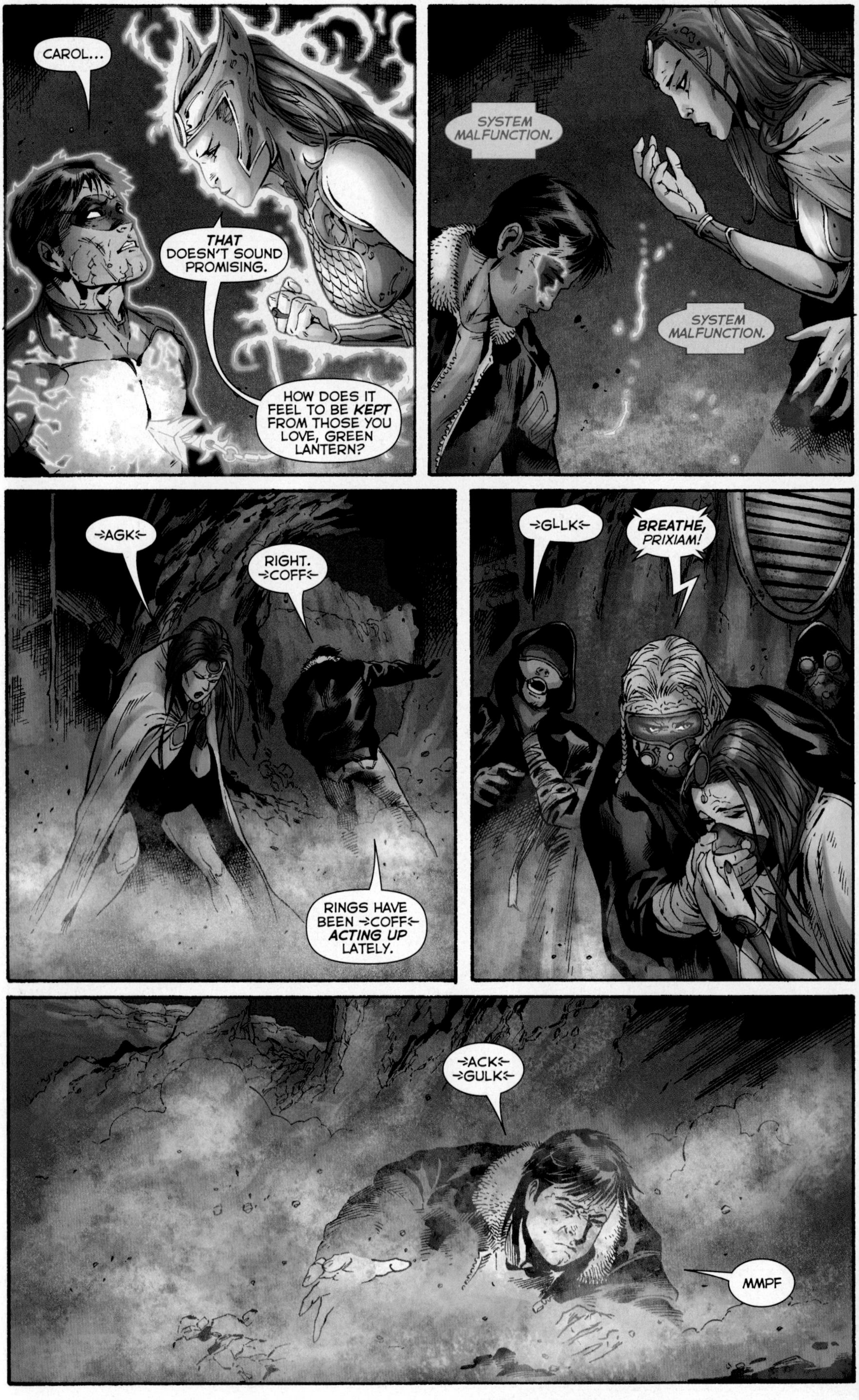
CAROL...
THAT DOESN'T SOUND PROMISING.
HOW DOES IT FEEL TO BE KEPT FROM THOSE YOU LOVE, GREEN LANTERN?
SYSTEM MALFUNCTION.
SYSTEM MALFUNCTION.
AGK
RIGHT. COFF
RINGS HAVE BEEN COFF ACTING UP LATELY.
GLLK
BREATHE, PRIXIAM!
ACK GULK
MMPF

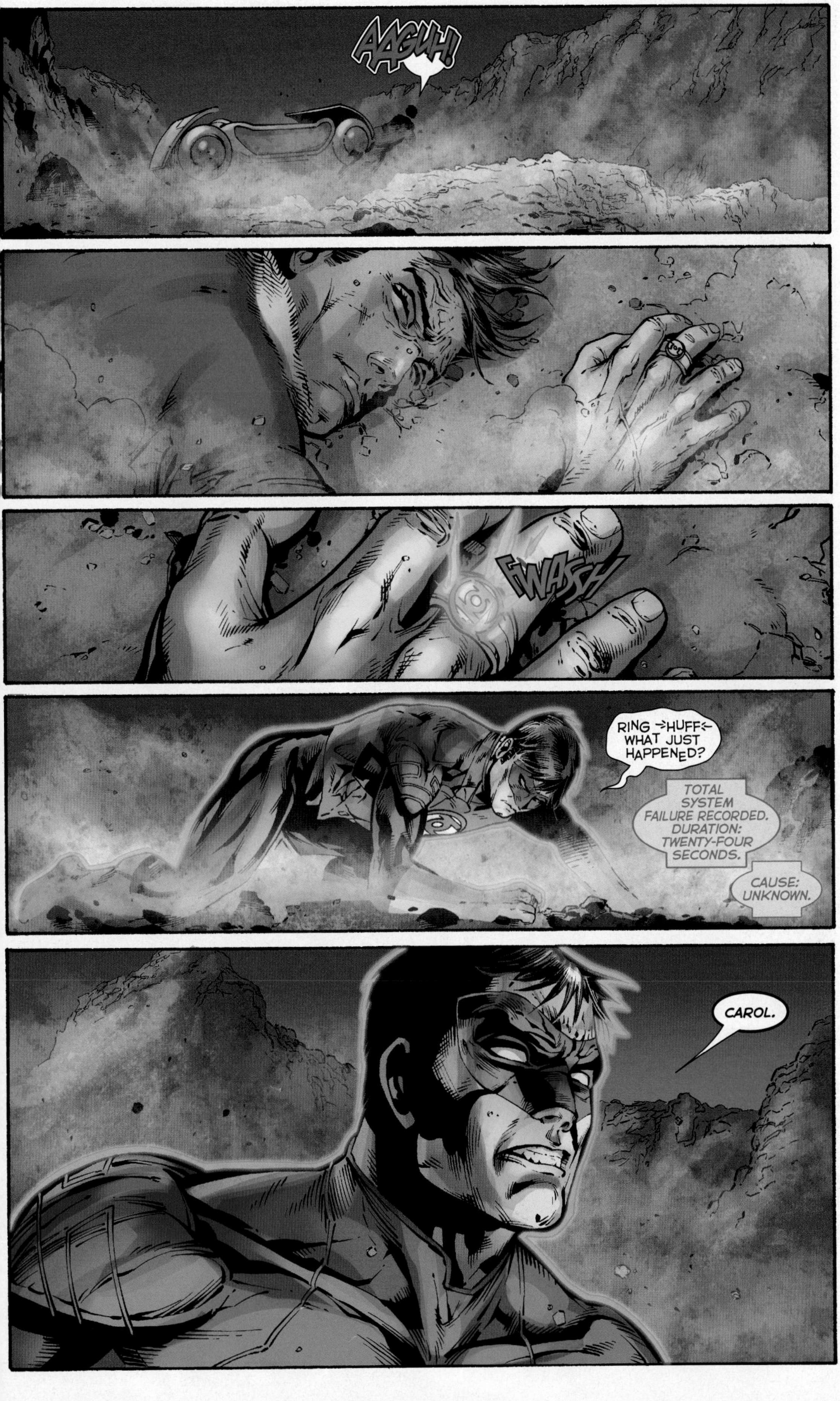
AAGUH!
FWASH
RING ⇾HUFF⇽ WHAT JUST HAPPENED?
TOTAL SYSTEM FAILURE RECORDED. DURATION: TWENTY-FOUR SECONDS.
CAUSE: UNKNOWN.
CAROL.

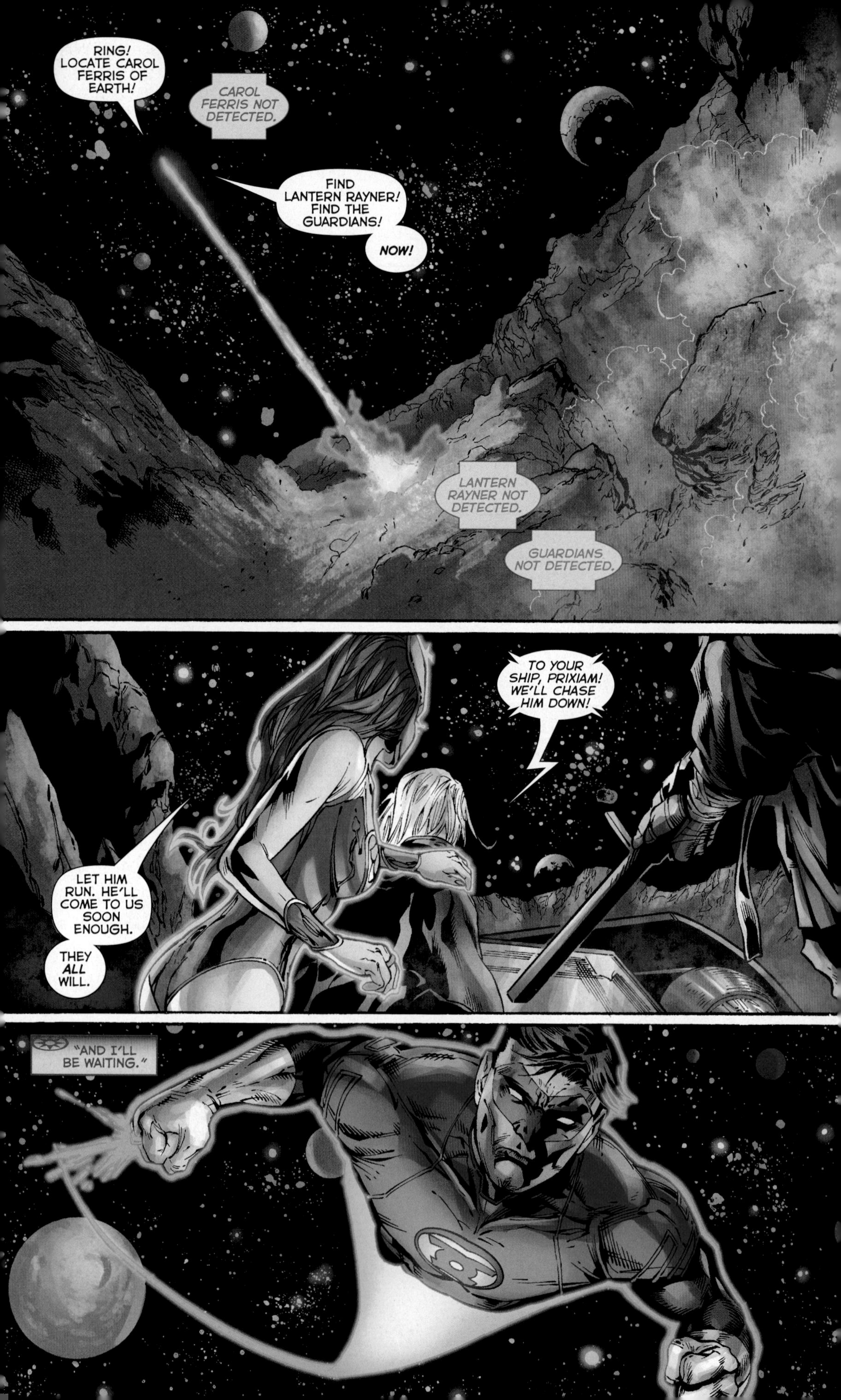
RING! LOCATE CAROL FERRIS OF EARTH!
CAROL FERRIS NOT DETECTED.
FIND LANTERN RAYNER! FIND THE GUARDIANS!
NOW!
LANTERN RAYNER NOT DETECTED.
GUARDIANS NOT DETECTED.
TO YOUR SHIP, PRIXIAM! WE'LL CHASE HIM DOWN!
LET HIM RUN. HE'LL COME TO US SOON ENOUGH.
THEY ALL WILL.
"AND I'LL BE WAITING."

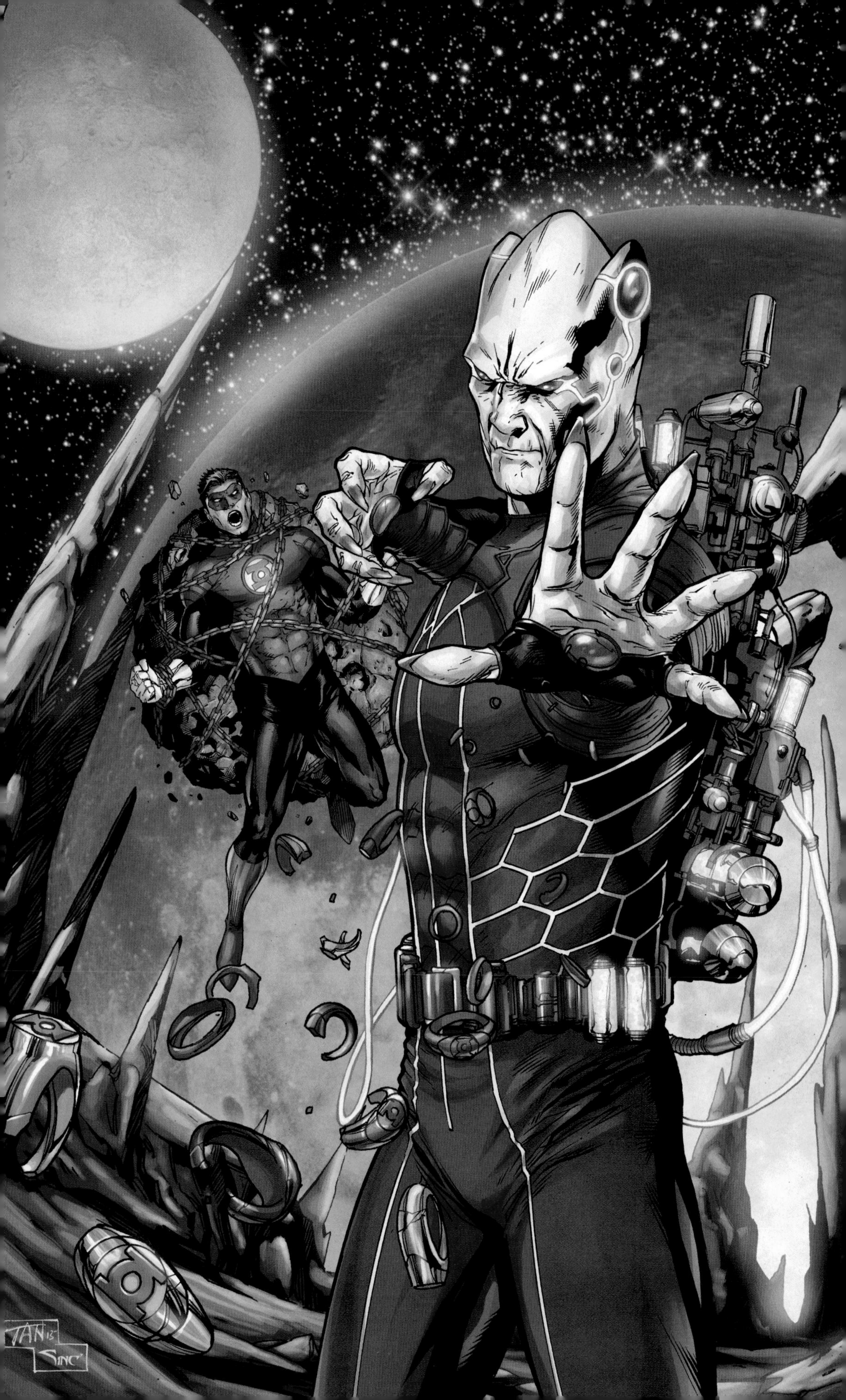

ROBERT VENDITTI writer RAGS MORALES penciller CAM SMITH with RAGS MORALES inkers
cover art by BILLY TAN & ALEX SINCLAIR

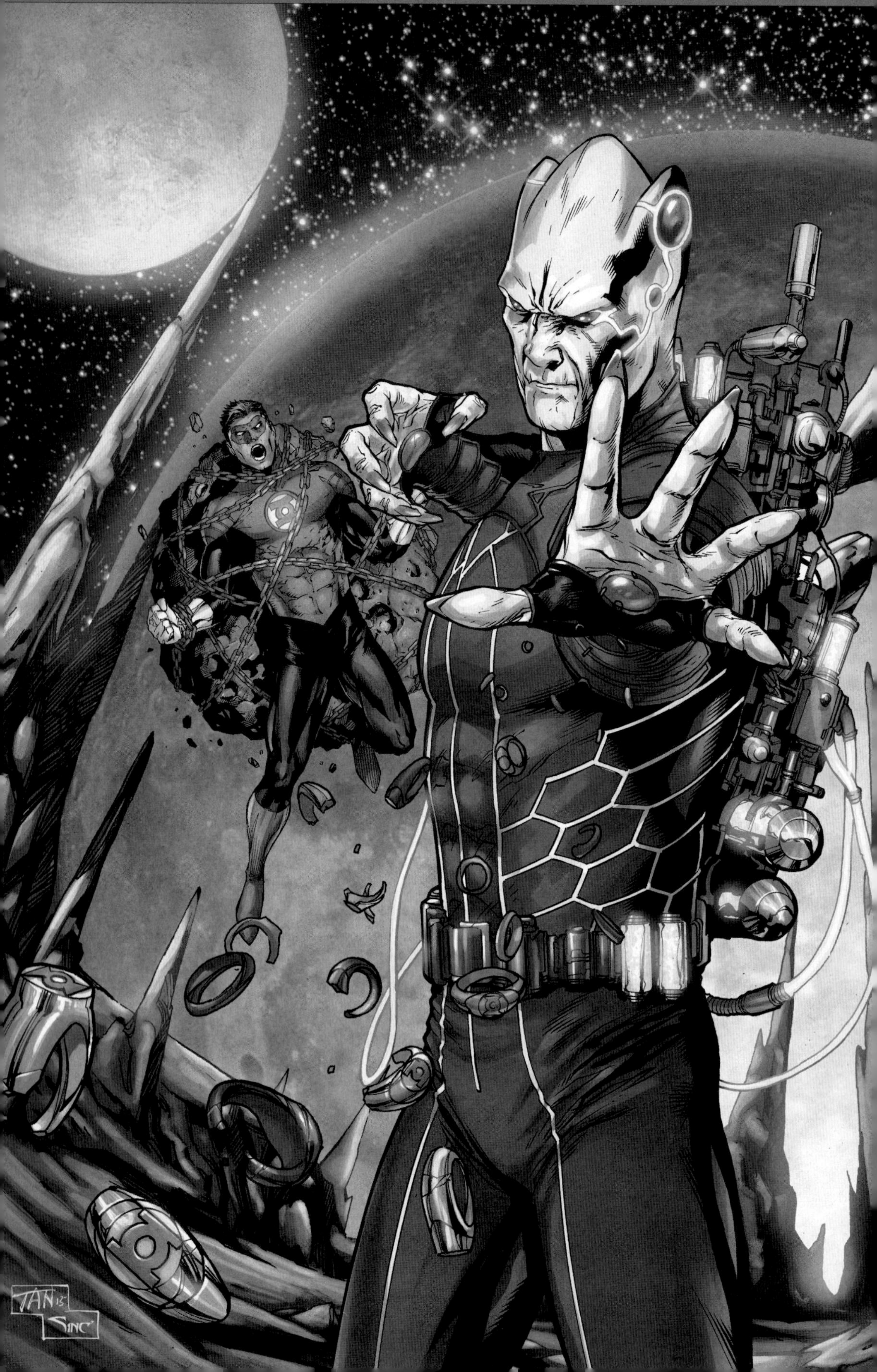

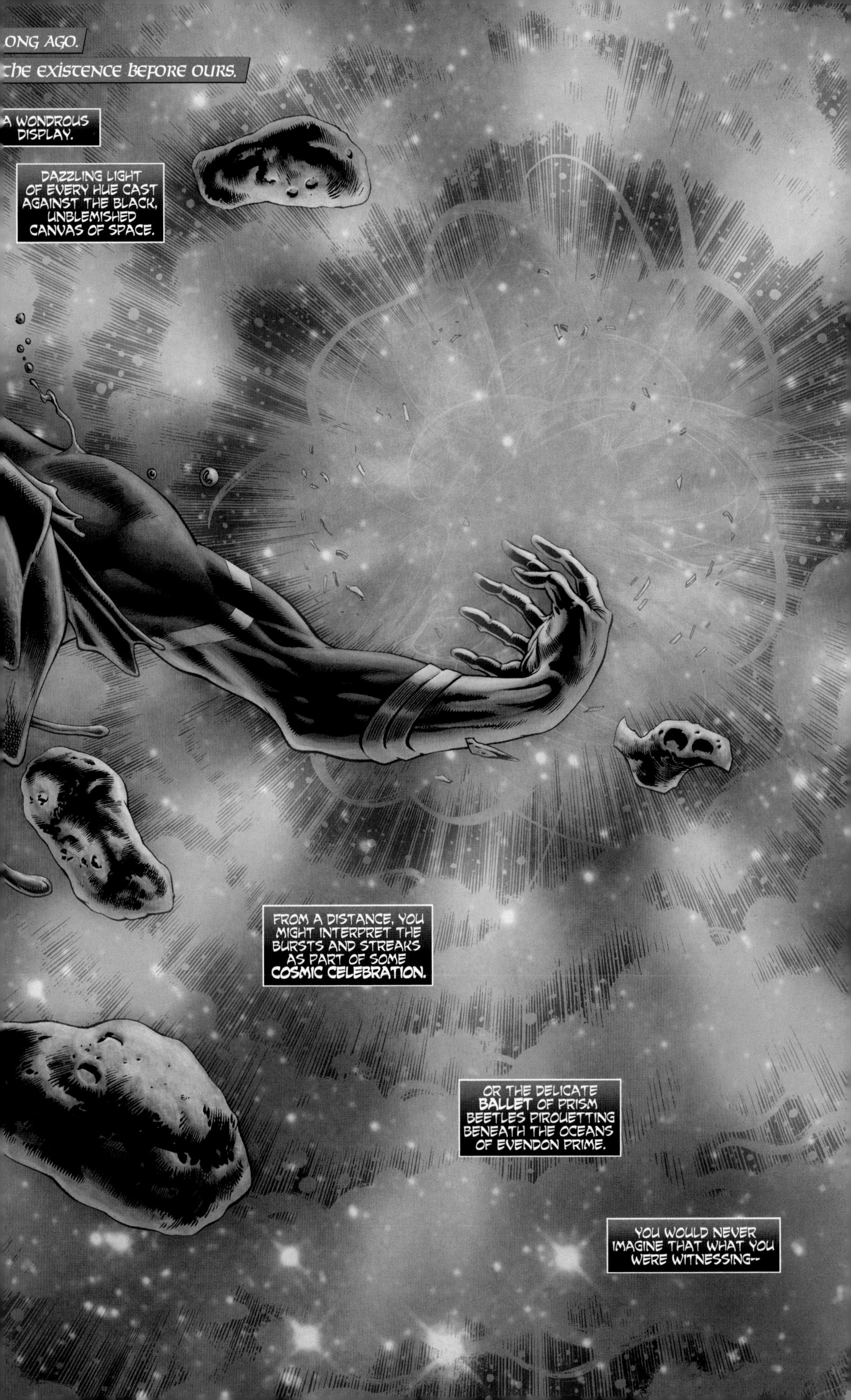
ONG AGO.
THE EXISTENCE BEFORE OURS.
A WONDROUS DISPLAY.
DAZZLING LIGHT OF EVERY HUE CAST AGAINST THE BLACK, UNBLEMISHED CANVAS OF SPACE.
FROM A DISTANCE, YOU MIGHT INTERPRET THE BURSTS AND STREAKS AS PART OF SOME COSMIC CELEBRATION.
OR THE DELICATE BALLET OF PRISM BEETLES PIROUETTING BENEATH THE OCEANS OF EVENDON PRIME.
YOU WOULD NEVER IMAGINE THAT WHAT YOU WERE WITNESSING--

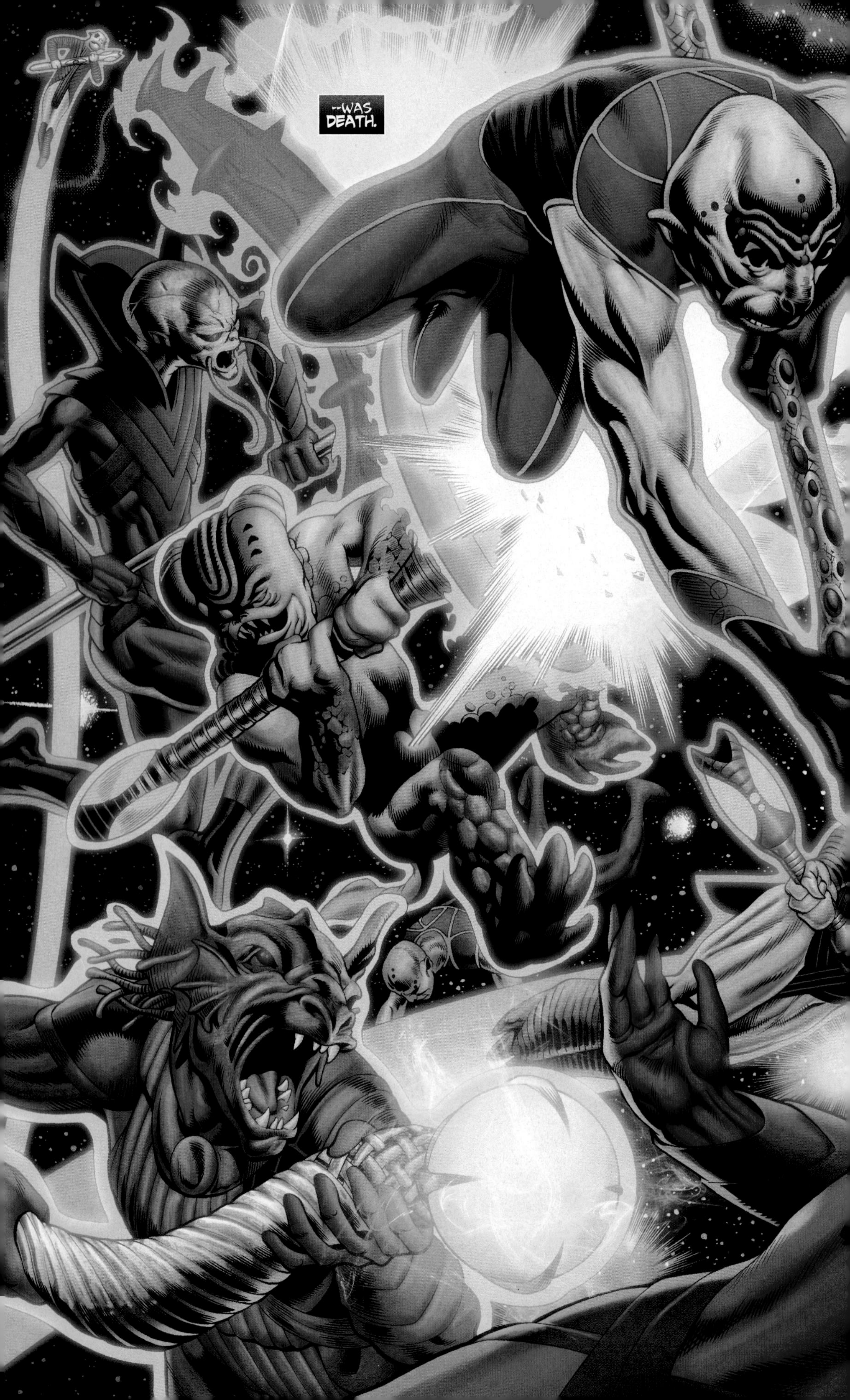
--WAS DEATH.

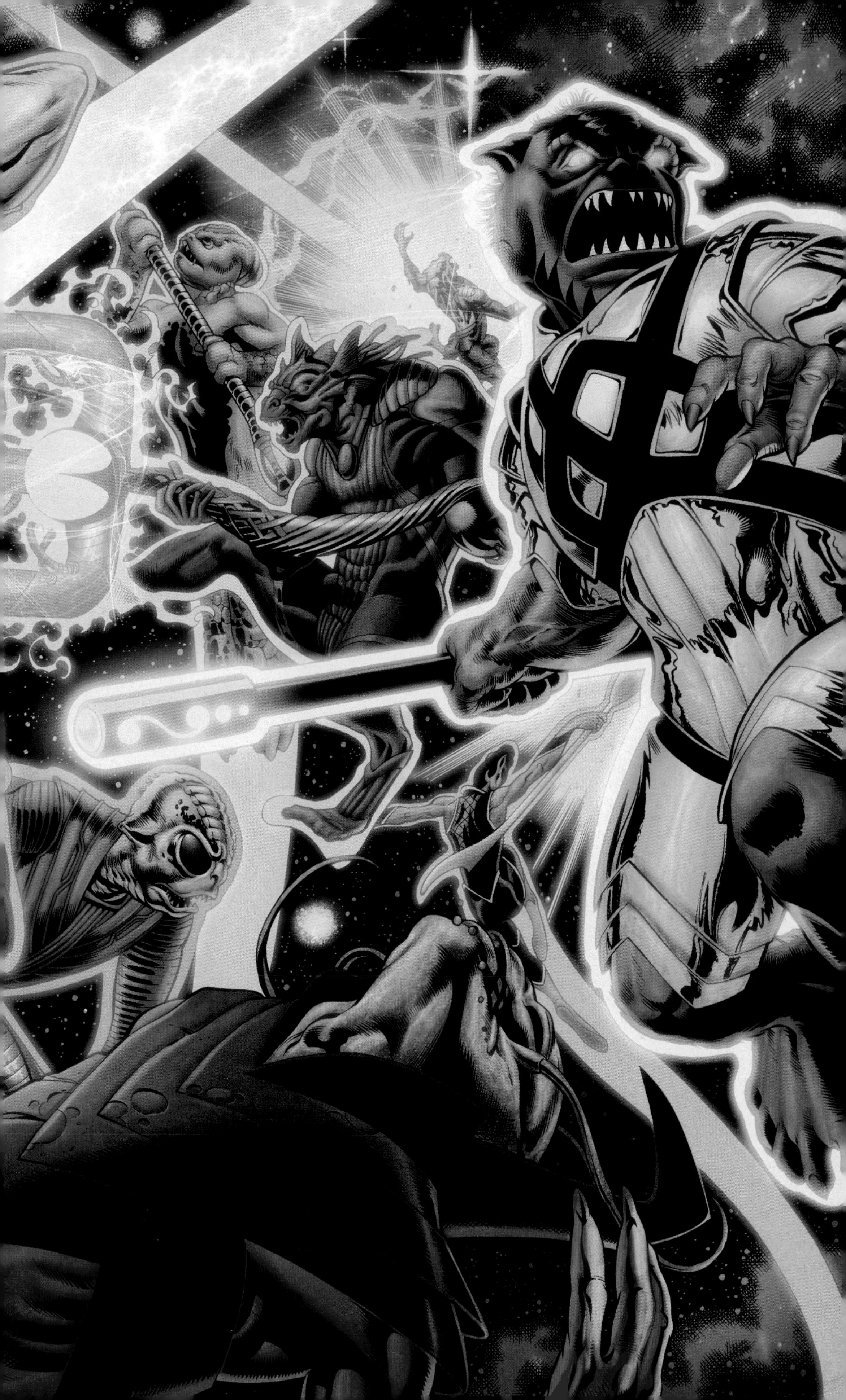

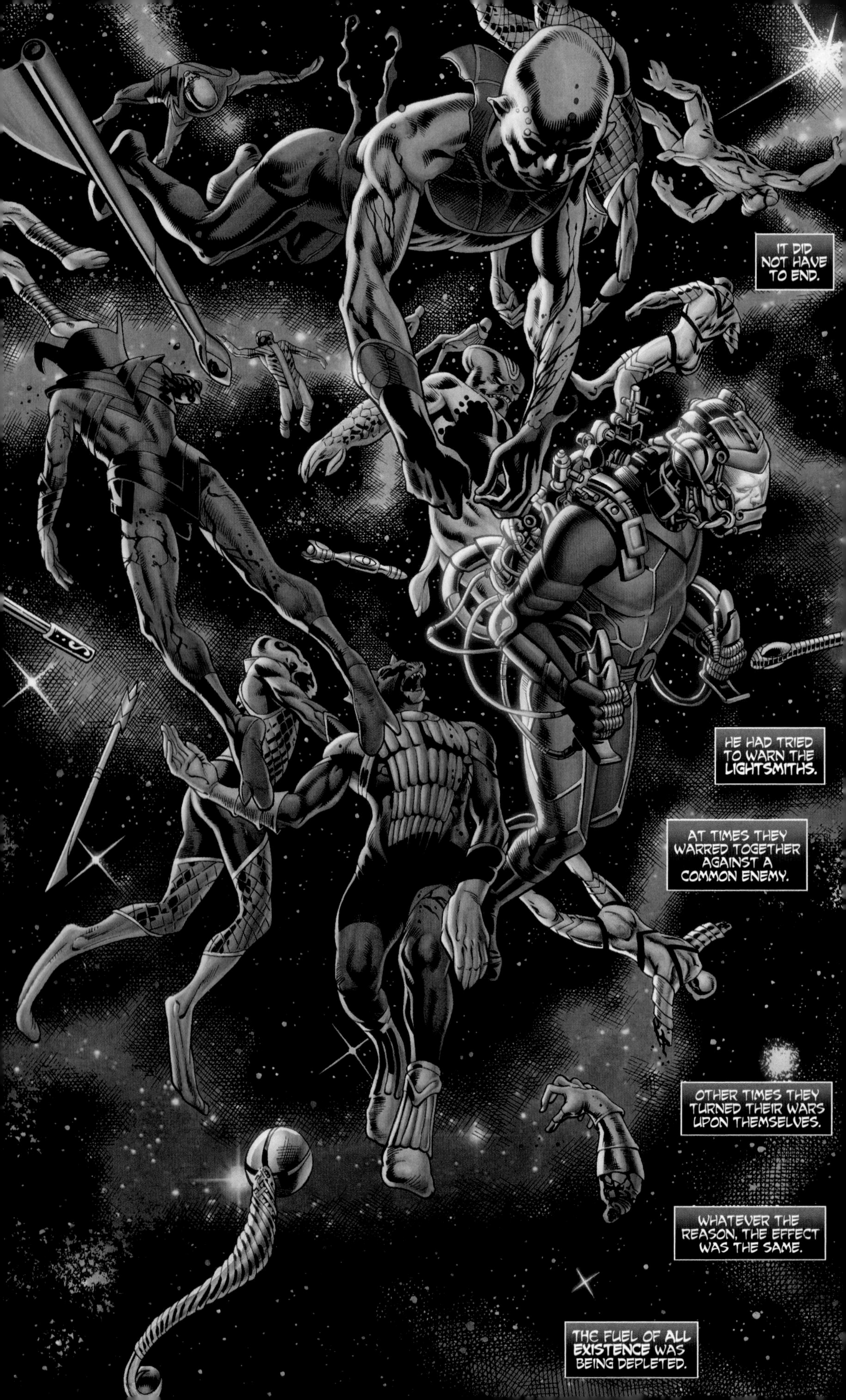
IT DID NOT HAVE TO END.
HE HAD TRIED TO WARN THE LIGHTSMITHS.
AT TIMES THEY WARRED TOGETHER AGAINST A COMMON ENEMY.
OTHER TIMES THEY TURNED THEIR WARS UPON THEMSELVES.
WHATEVER THE REASON, THE EFFECT WAS THE SAME.
THE FUEL OF ALL EXISTENCE WAS BEING DEPLETED.

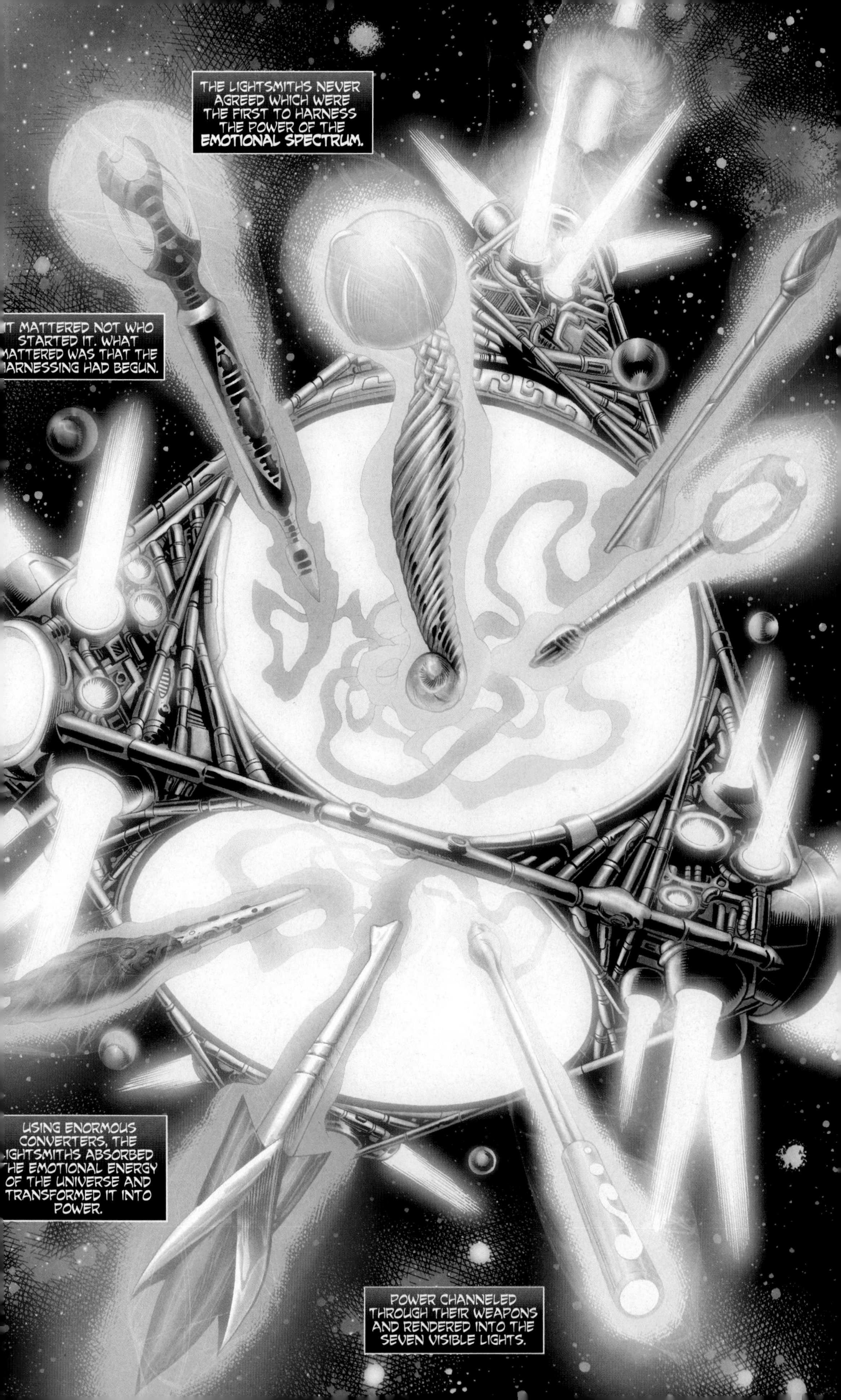
THE LIGHTSMITHS NEVER AGREED WHICH WERE THE FIRST TO HARNESS THE POWER OF THE **EMOTIONAL SPECTRUM.**
IT MATTERED NOT WHO STARTED IT. WHAT MATTERED WAS THAT THE HARNESSING HAD BEGUN.
USING ENORMOUS CONVERTERS, THE LIGHTSMITHS ABSORBED THE EMOTIONAL ENERGY OF THE UNIVERSE AND TRANSFORMED IT INTO POWER.
POWER CHANNELED THROUGH THEIR WEAPONS AND RENDERED INTO THE SEVEN VISIBLE LIGHTS.

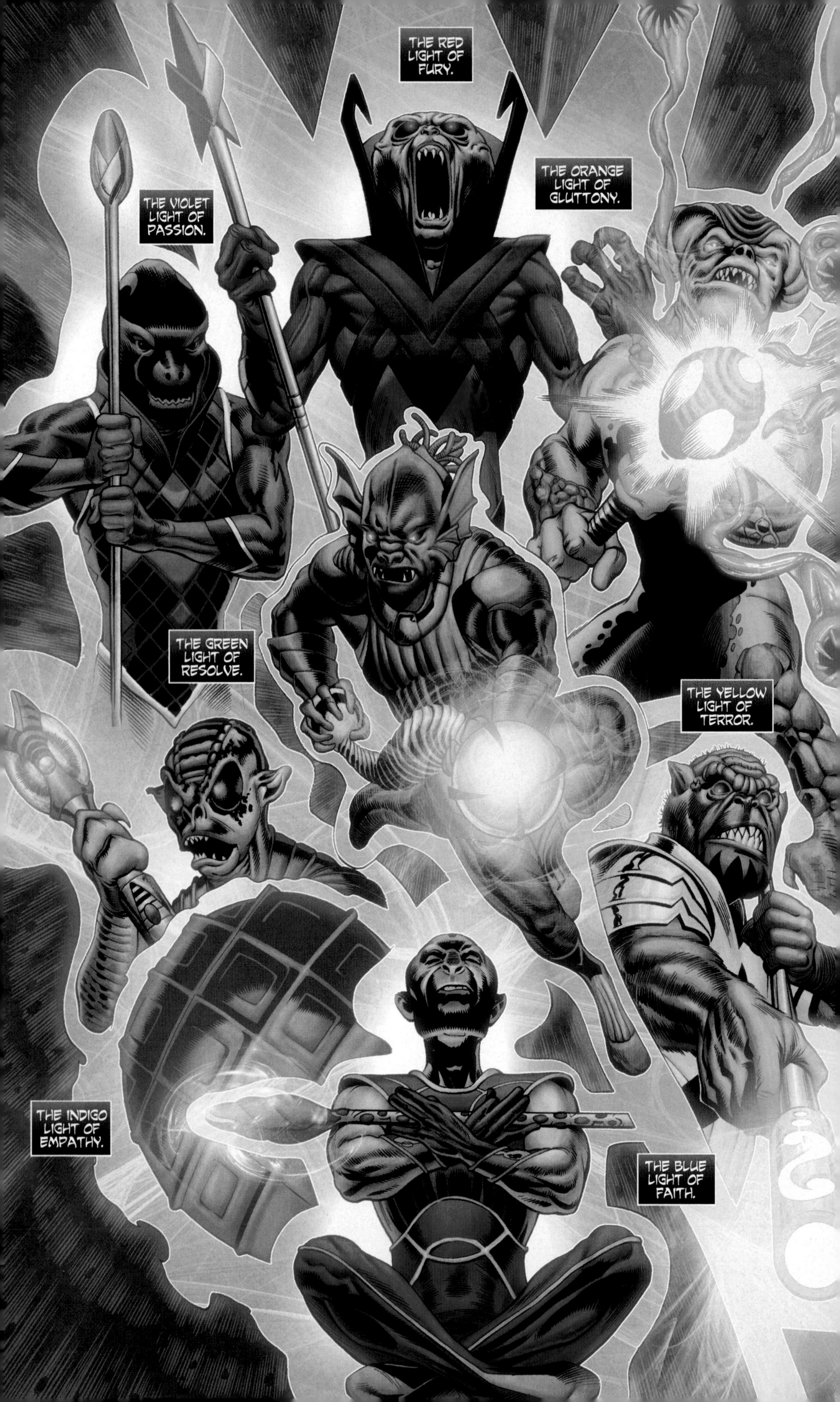

THE RED LIGHT OF FURY.
THE ORANGE LIGHT OF GLUTTONY.
THE VIOLET LIGHT OF PASSION.
THE GREEN LIGHT OF RESOLVE.
THE YELLOW LIGHT OF TERROR.
THE INDIGO LIGHT OF EMPATHY.
THE BLUE LIGHT OF FAITH.

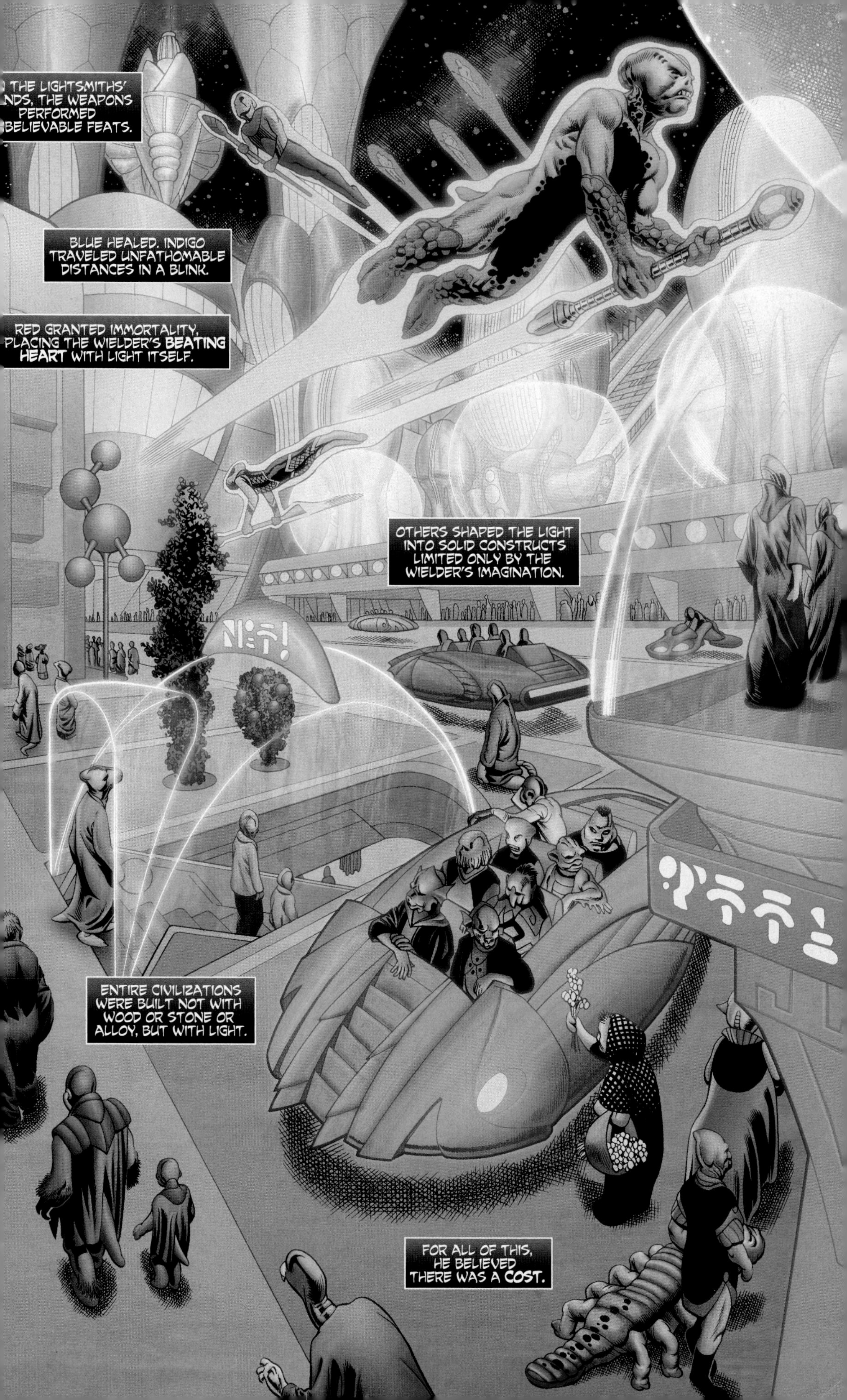

THE LIGHTSMITHS' NDS, THE WEAPONS PERFORMED BELIEVABLE FEATS.
BLUE HEALED. INDIGO TRAVELED UNFATHOMABLE DISTANCES IN A BLINK.
RED GRANTED IMMORTALITY, PLACING THE WIELDER'S BEATING HEART WITH LIGHT ITSELF.
OTHERS SHAPED THE LIGHT INTO SOLID CONSTRUCTS LIMITED ONLY BY THE WIELDER'S IMAGINATION.
ENTIRE CIVILIZATIONS WERE BUILT NOT WITH WOOD OR STONE OR ALLOY, BUT WITH LIGHT.
FOR ALL OF THIS, HE BELIEVED THERE WAS A COST.

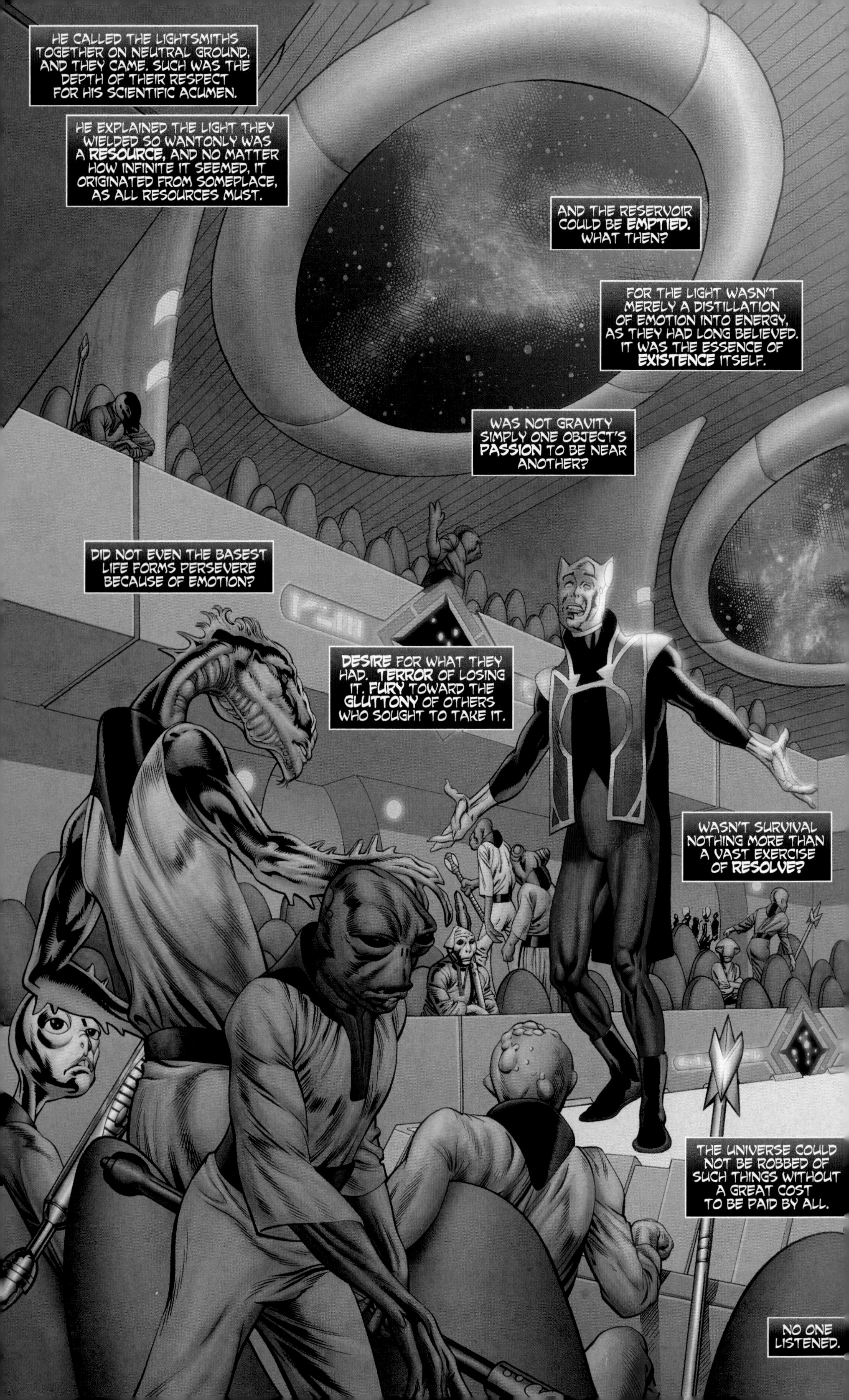

HE CALLED THE LIGHTSMITHS TOGETHER ON NEUTRAL GROUND, AND THEY CAME. SUCH WAS THE DEPTH OF THEIR RESPECT FOR HIS SCIENTIFIC ACUMEN.
HE EXPLAINED THE LIGHT THEY WIELDED SO WANTONLY WAS A RESOURCE, AND NO MATTER HOW INFINITE IT SEEMED, IT ORIGINATED FROM SOMEPLACE, AS ALL RESOURCES MUST.
AND THE RESERVOIR COULD BE EMPTIED. WHAT THEN?
FOR THE LIGHT WASN'T MERELY A DISTILLATION OF EMOTION INTO ENERGY, AS THEY HAD LONG BELIEVED. IT WAS THE ESSENCE OF EXISTENCE ITSELF.
WAS NOT GRAVITY SIMPLY ONE OBJECT'S PASSION TO BE NEAR ANOTHER?
DID NOT EVEN THE BASEST LIFE FORMS PERSEVERE BECAUSE OF EMOTION?
DESIRE FOR WHAT THEY HAD. TERROR OF LOSING IT. FURY TOWARD THE GLUTTONY OF OTHERS WHO SOUGHT TO TAKE IT.
WASN'T SURVIVAL NOTHING MORE THAN A VAST EXERCISE OF RESOLVE?
THE UNIVERSE COULD NOT BE ROBBED OF SUCH THINGS WITHOUT A GREAT COST TO BE PAID BY ALL.
NO ONE LISTENED.

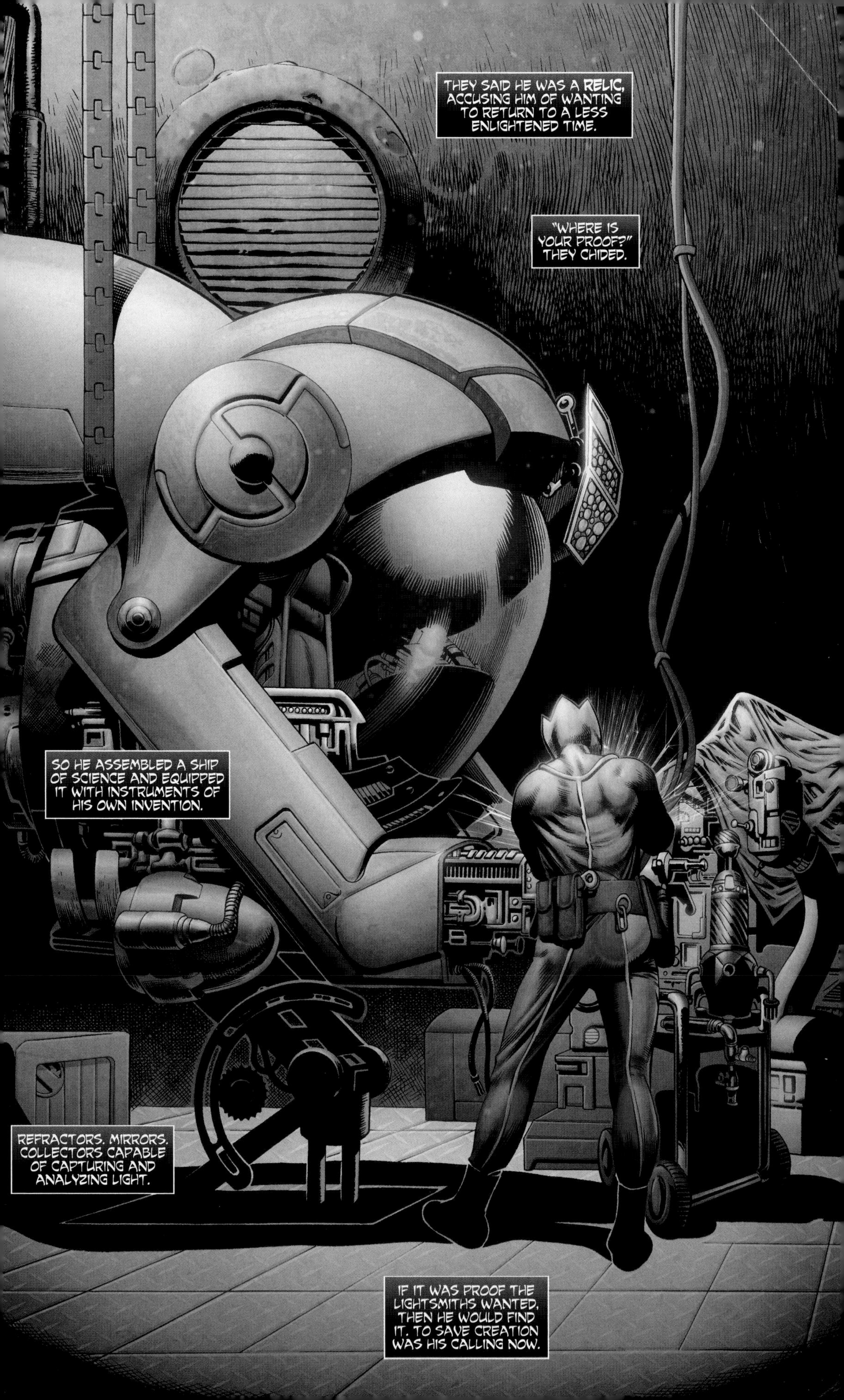
THEY SAID HE WAS A RELIC, ACCUSING HIM OF WANTING TO RETURN TO A LESS ENLIGHTENED TIME.
"WHERE IS YOUR PROOF?" THEY CHIDED.
SO HE ASSEMBLED A SHIP OF SCIENCE AND EQUIPPED IT WITH INSTRUMENTS OF HIS OWN INVENTION.
REFRACTORS. MIRRORS. COLLECTORS CAPABLE OF CAPTURING AND ANALYZING LIGHT.
IF IT WAS PROOF THE LIGHTSMITHS WANTED, THEN HE WOULD FIND IT. TO SAVE CREATION WAS HIS CALLING NOW.

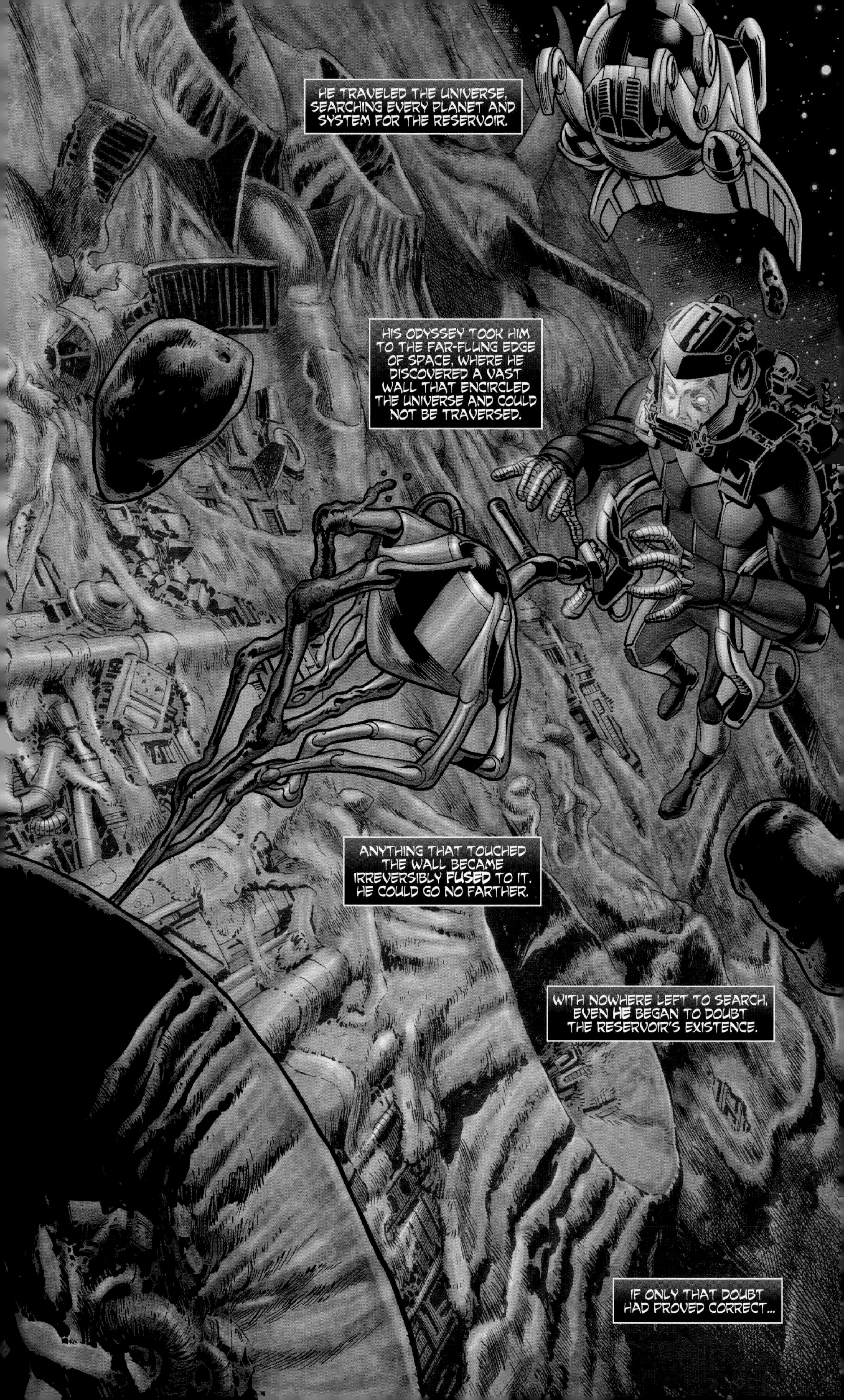
HE TRAVELED THE UNIVERSE, SEARCHING EVERY PLANET AND SYSTEM FOR THE RESERVOIR.
HIS ODYSSEY TOOK HIM TO THE FAR-FLUNG EDGE OF SPACE, WHERE HE DISCOVERED A VAST WALL THAT ENCIRCLED THE UNIVERSE AND COULD NOT BE TRAVERSED.
ANYTHING THAT TOUCHED THE WALL BECAME IRREVERSIBLY FUSED TO IT. HE COULD GO NO FARTHER.
WITH NOWHERE LEFT TO SEARCH, EVEN HE BEGAN TO DOUBT THE RESERVOIR'S EXISTENCE.
IF ONLY THAT DOUBT HAD PROVED CORRECT...

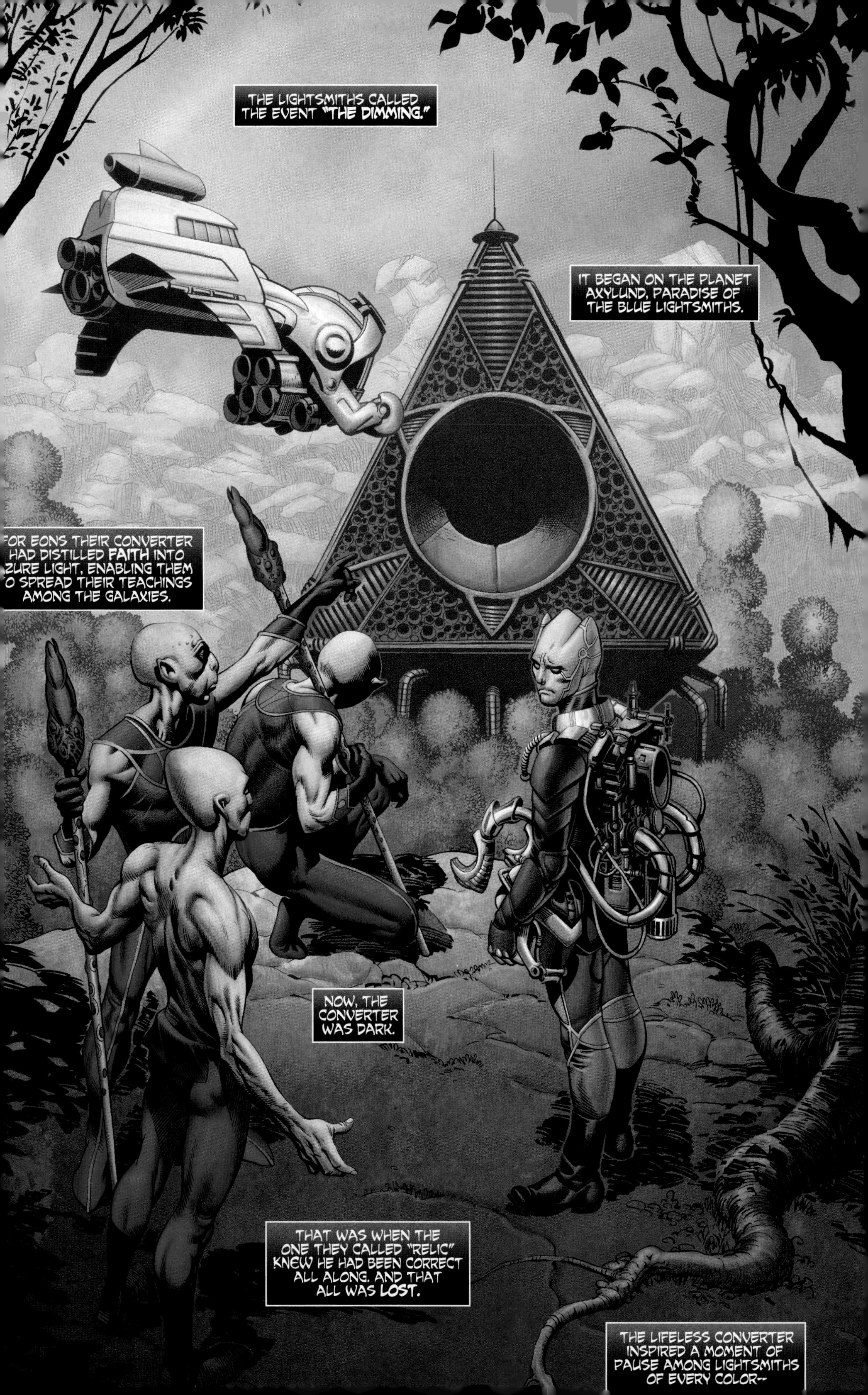

THE LIGHTSMITHS CALLED THE EVENT "THE DIMMING."
IT BEGAN ON THE PLANET AXYLUND, PARADISE OF THE BLUE LIGHTSMITHS.
FOR EONS THEIR CONVERTER HAD DISTILLED FAITH INTO ZURE LIGHT, ENABLING THEM O SPREAD THEIR TEACHINGS AMONG THE GALAXIES.
NOW, THE CONVERTER WAS DARK.
THAT WAS WHEN THE ONE THEY CALLED "RELIC" KNEW HE HAD BEEN CORRECT ALL ALONG. AND THAT ALL WAS LOST.
THE LIFELESS CONVERTER INSPIRED A MOMENT OF PAUSE AMONG LIGHTSMITHS OF EVERY COLOR--

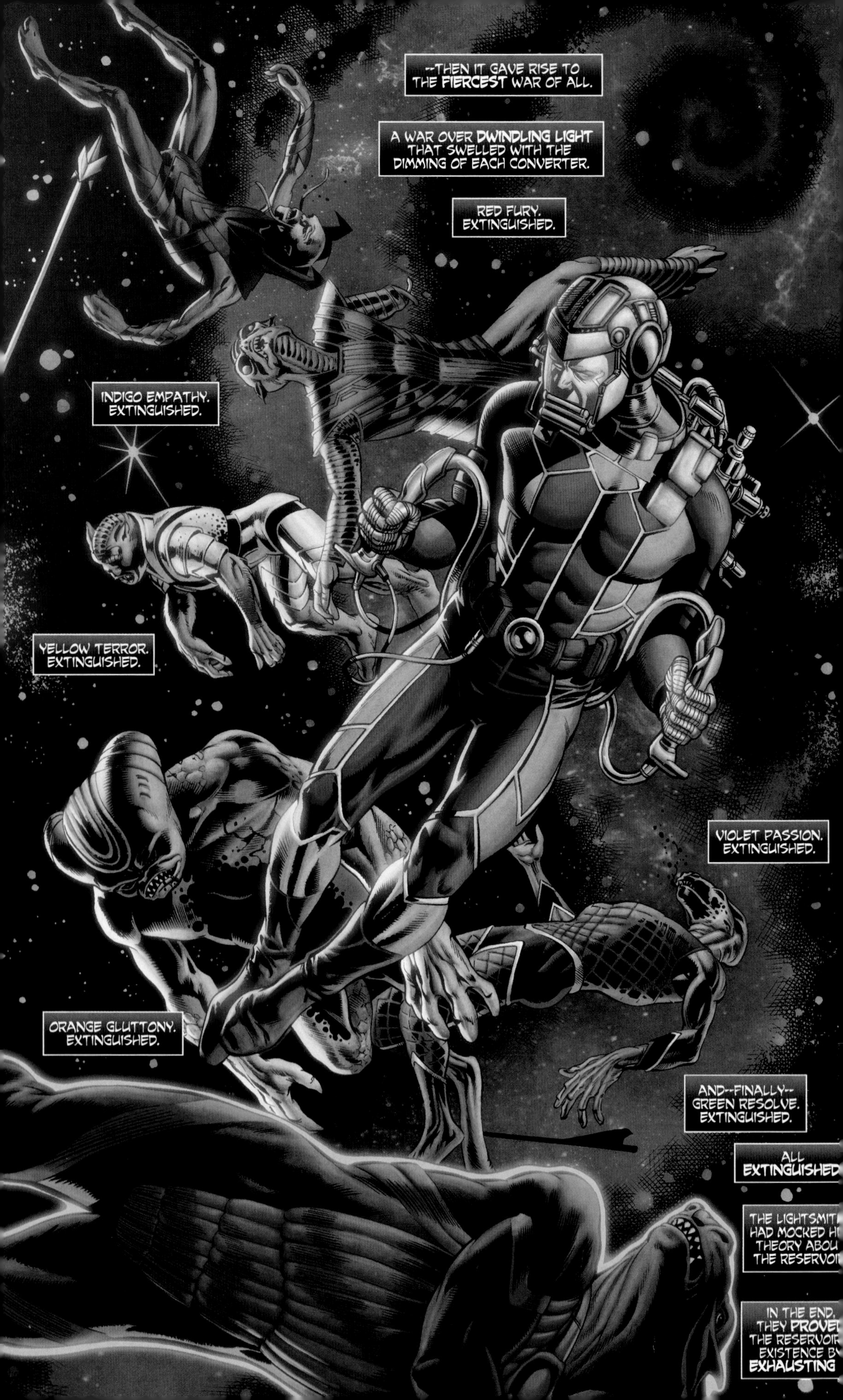
--THEN IT GAVE RISE TO THE FIERCEST WAR OF ALL.
A WAR OVER DWINDLING LIGHT THAT SWELLED WITH THE DIMMING OF EACH CONVERTER.
RED FURY. EXTINGUISHED.
INDIGO EMPATHY. EXTINGUISHED.
YELLOW TERROR. EXTINGUISHED.
VIOLET PASSION. EXTINGUISHED.
ORANGE GLUTTONY. EXTINGUISHED.
AND--FINALLY--GREEN RESOLVE. EXTINGUISHED.
ALL EXTINGUISHED
THE LIGHTSMIT HAD MOCKED H THEORY ABOU THE RESERVOI
IN THE END. THEY PROVE THE RESERVOIR EXISTENCE B EXHAUSTING

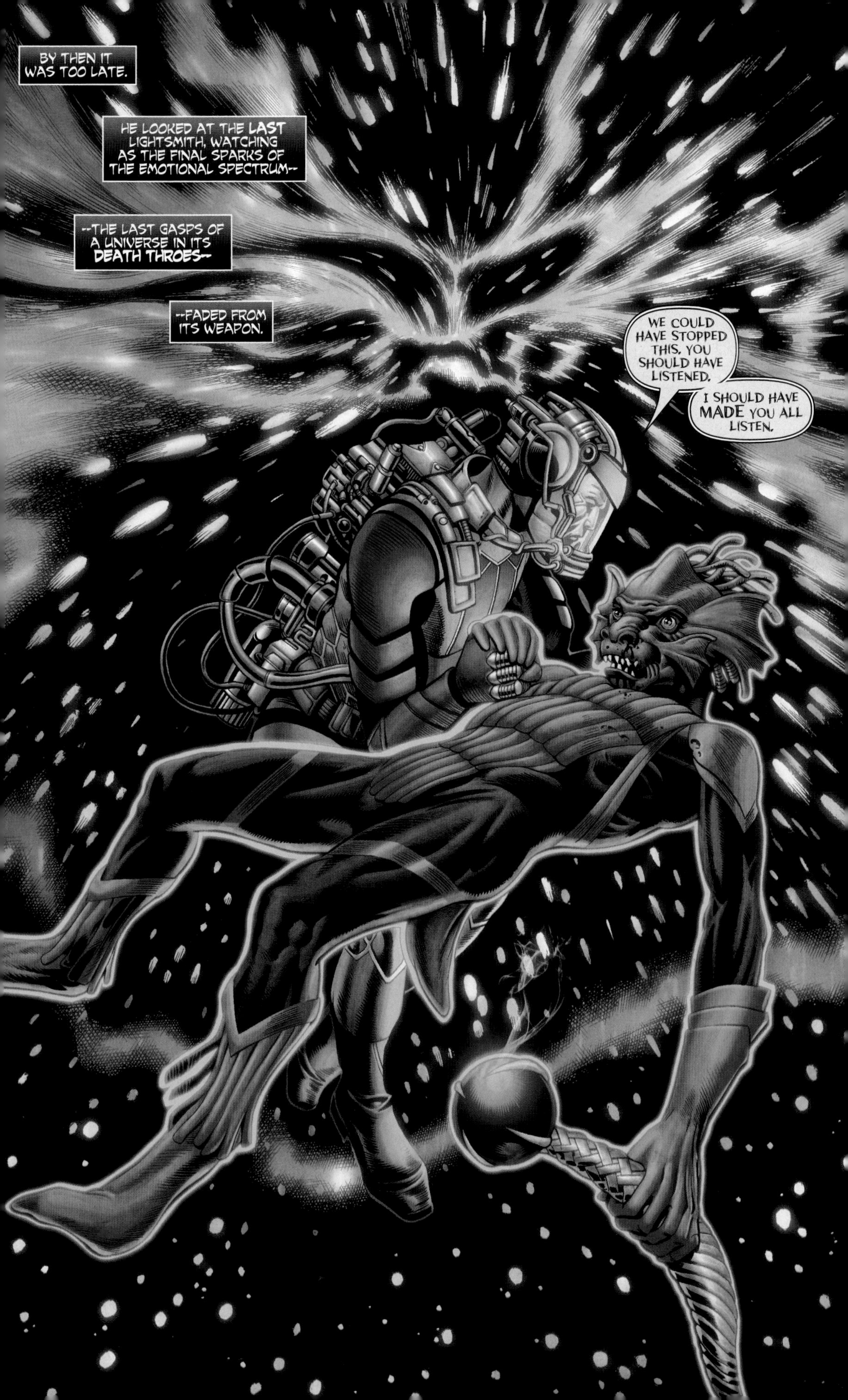
BY THEN IT WAS TOO LATE.
HE LOOKED AT THE LAST LIGHTSMITH, WATCHING AS THE FINAL SPARKS OF THE EMOTIONAL SPECTRUM--
--THE LAST GASPS OF A UNIVERSE IN ITS DEATH THROES--
--FADED FROM ITS WEAPON.
WE COULD HAVE STOPPED THIS. YOU SHOULD HAVE LISTENED.
I SHOULD HAVE MADE YOU ALL LISTEN.

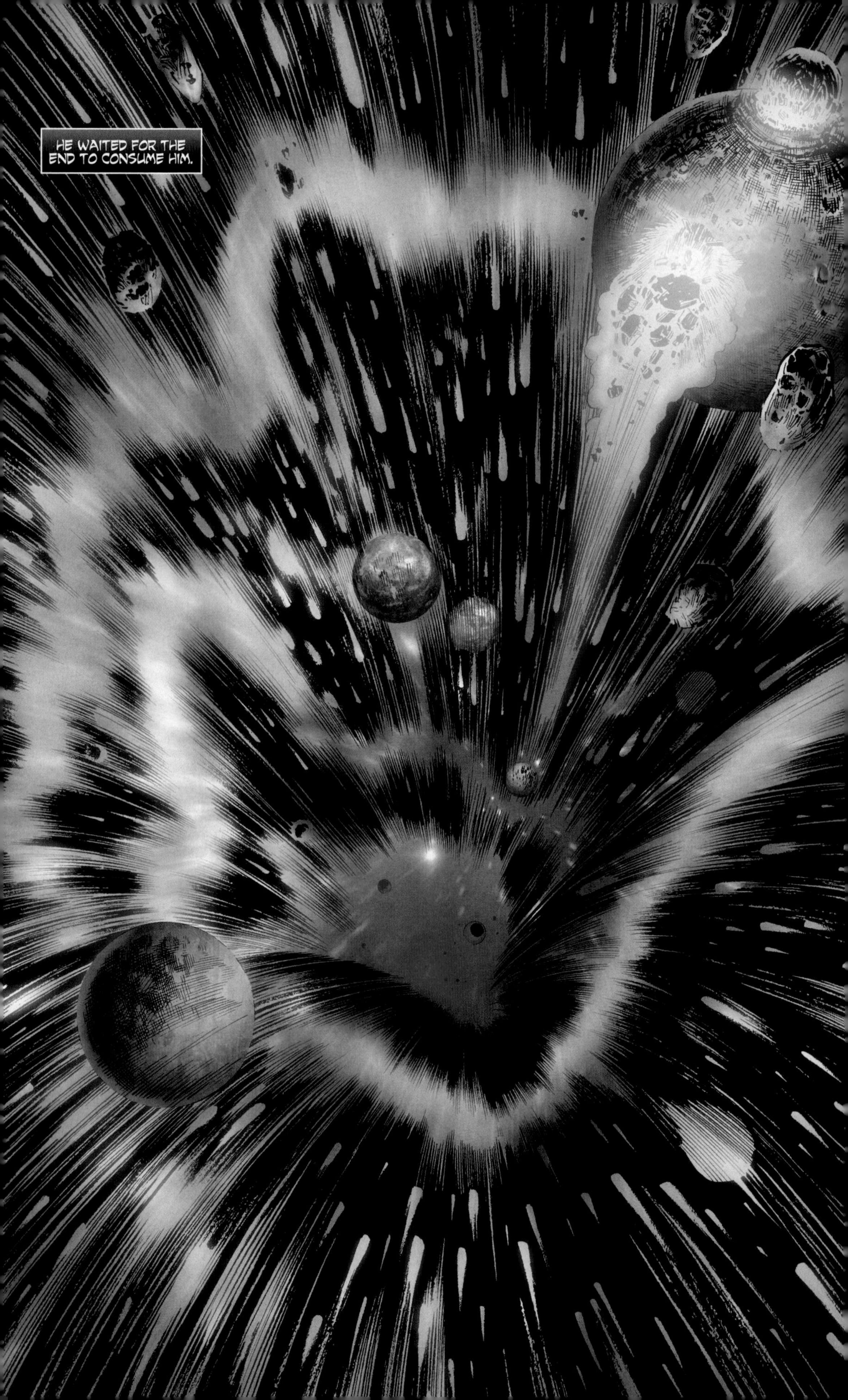
HE WAITED FOR THE END TO CONSUME HIM.

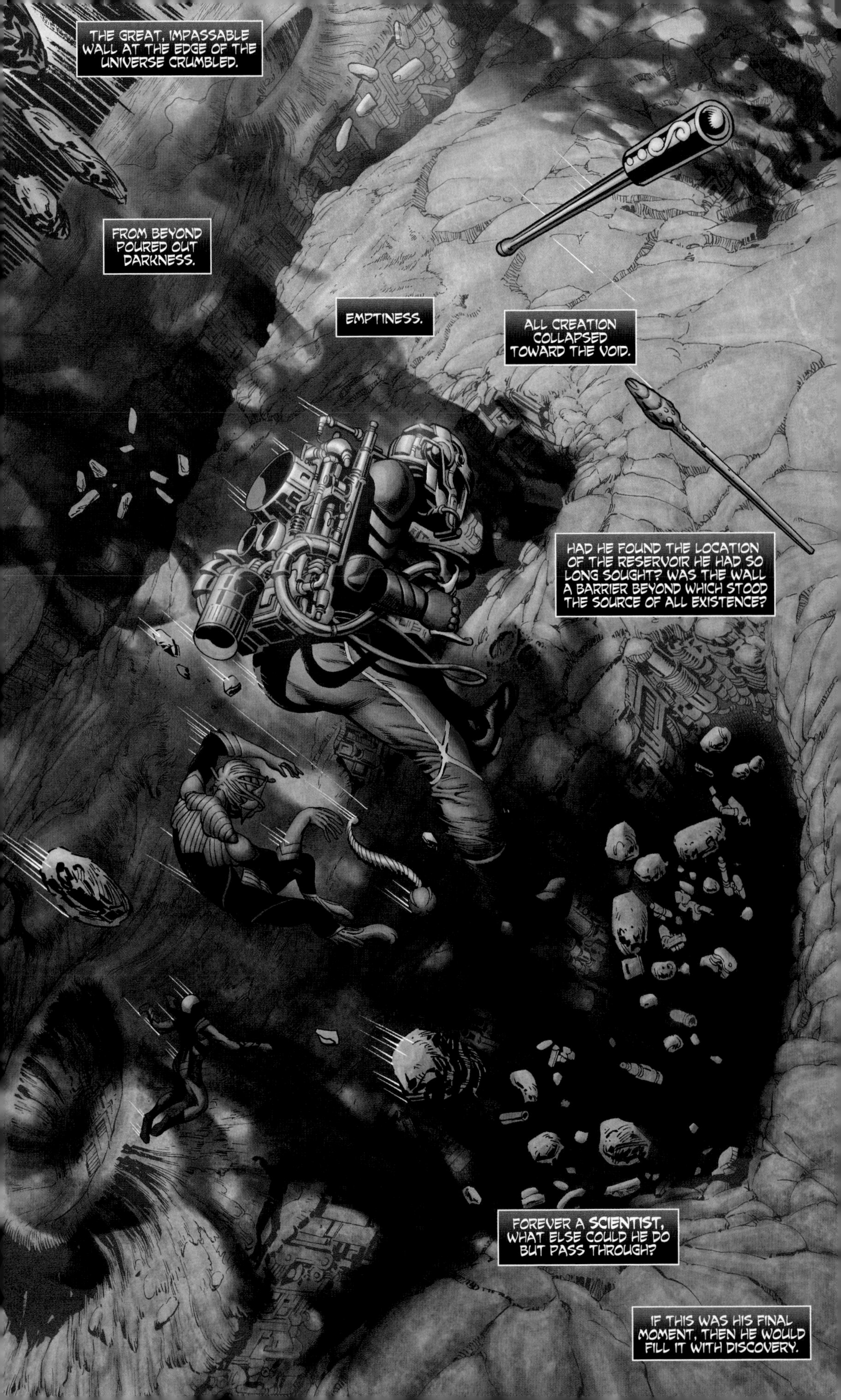
THE GREAT, IMPASSABLE WALL AT THE EDGE OF THE UNIVERSE CRUMBLED.
FROM BEYOND POURED OUT DARKNESS.
EMPTINESS.
ALL CREATION COLLAPSED TOWARD THE VOID.
HAD HE FOUND THE LOCATION OF THE RESERVOIR HE HAD SO LONG SOUGHT? WAS THE WALL A BARRIER BEYOND WHICH STOOD THE SOURCE OF ALL EXISTENCE?
FOREVER A SCIENTIST, WHAT ELSE COULD HE DO BUT PASS THROUGH?
IF THIS WAS HIS FINAL MOMENT, THEN HE WOULD FILL IT WITH DISCOVERY.

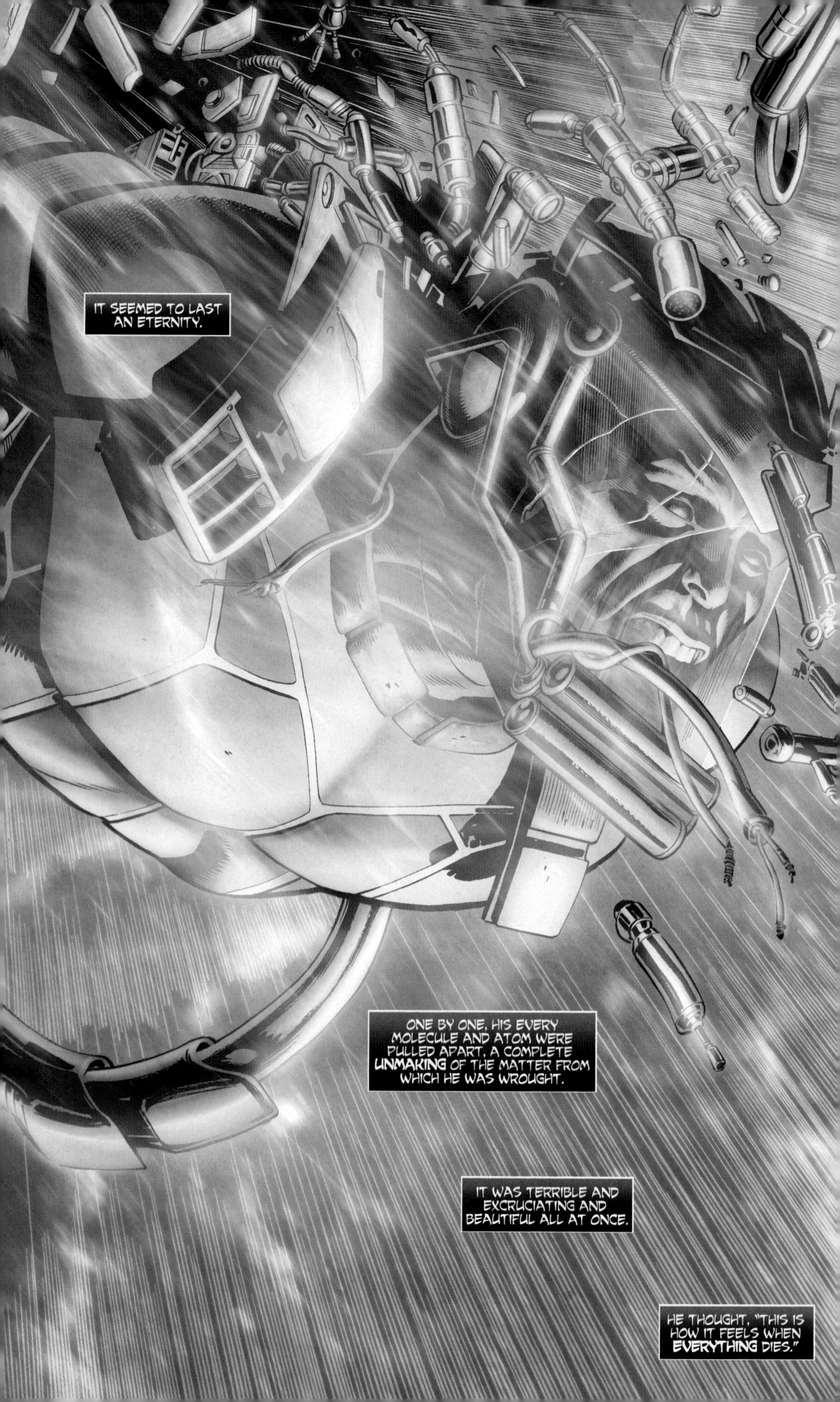

IT SEEMED TO LAST AN ETERNITY.
ONE BY ONE, HIS EVERY MOLECULE AND ATOM WERE PULLED APART, A COMPLETE **UNMAKING** OF THE MATTER FROM WHICH HE WAS WROUGHT.
IT WAS TERRIBLE AND EXCRUCIATING AND BEAUTIFUL ALL AT ONCE.
HE THOUGHT, "THIS IS HOW IT FEELS WHEN **EVERYTHING** DIES."

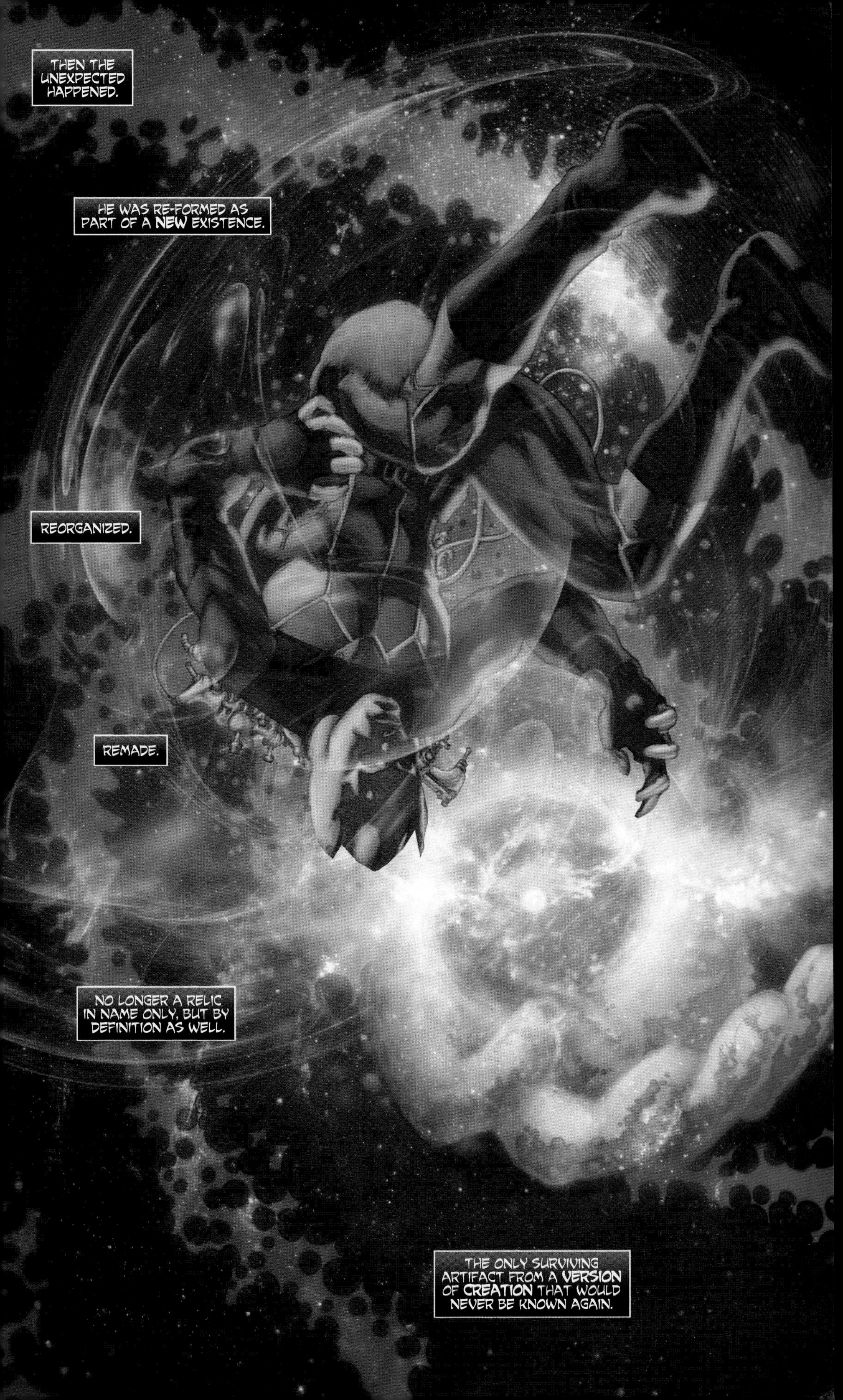
THEN THE UNEXPECTED HAPPENED.
HE WAS RE-FORMED AS PART OF A NEW EXISTENCE.
REORGANIZED.
REMADE.
NO LONGER A RELIC IN NAME ONLY, BUT BY DEFINITION AS WELL.
THE ONLY SURVIVING ARTIFACT FROM A VERSION OF CREATION THAT WOULD NEVER BE KNOWN AGAIN.

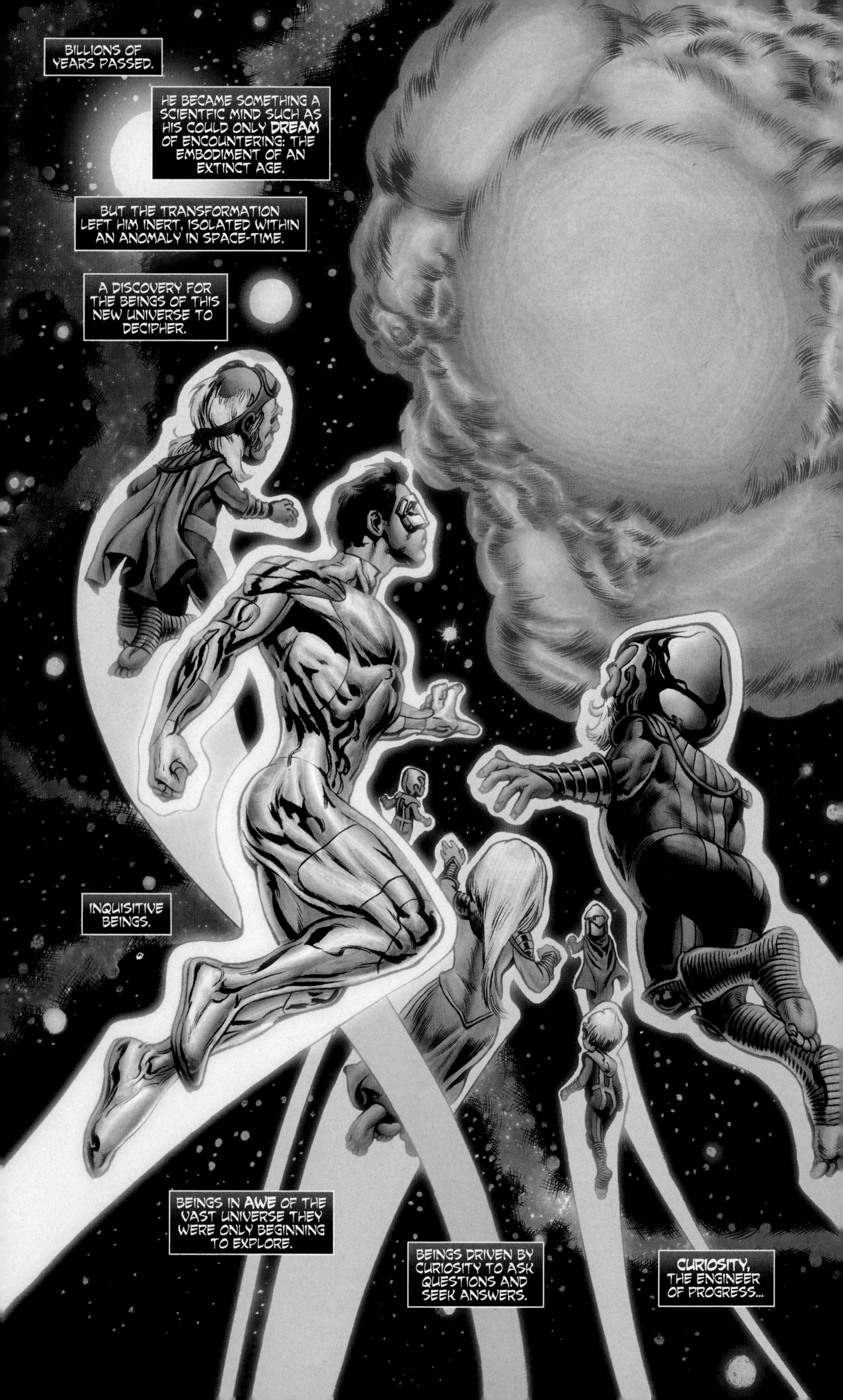
BILLIONS OF YEARS PASSED.
HE BECAME SOMETHING A SCIENTFIC MIND SUCH AS HIS COULD ONLY **DREAM** OF ENCOUNTERING: THE EMBODIMENT OF AN EXTINCT AGE.
BUT THE TRANSFORMATION LEFT HIM INERT, ISOLATED WITHIN AN ANOMALY IN SPACE-TIME.
A DISCOVERY FOR THE BEINGS OF THIS NEW UNIVERSE TO DECIPHER.
INQUISITIVE BEINGS.
BEINGS IN **AWE** OF THE VAST UNIVERSE THEY WERE ONLY BEGINNING TO EXPLORE.
BEINGS DRIVEN BY CURIOSITY TO ASK QUESTIONS AND SEEK ANSWERS.
CURIOSITY, THE ENGINEER OF PROGRESS...

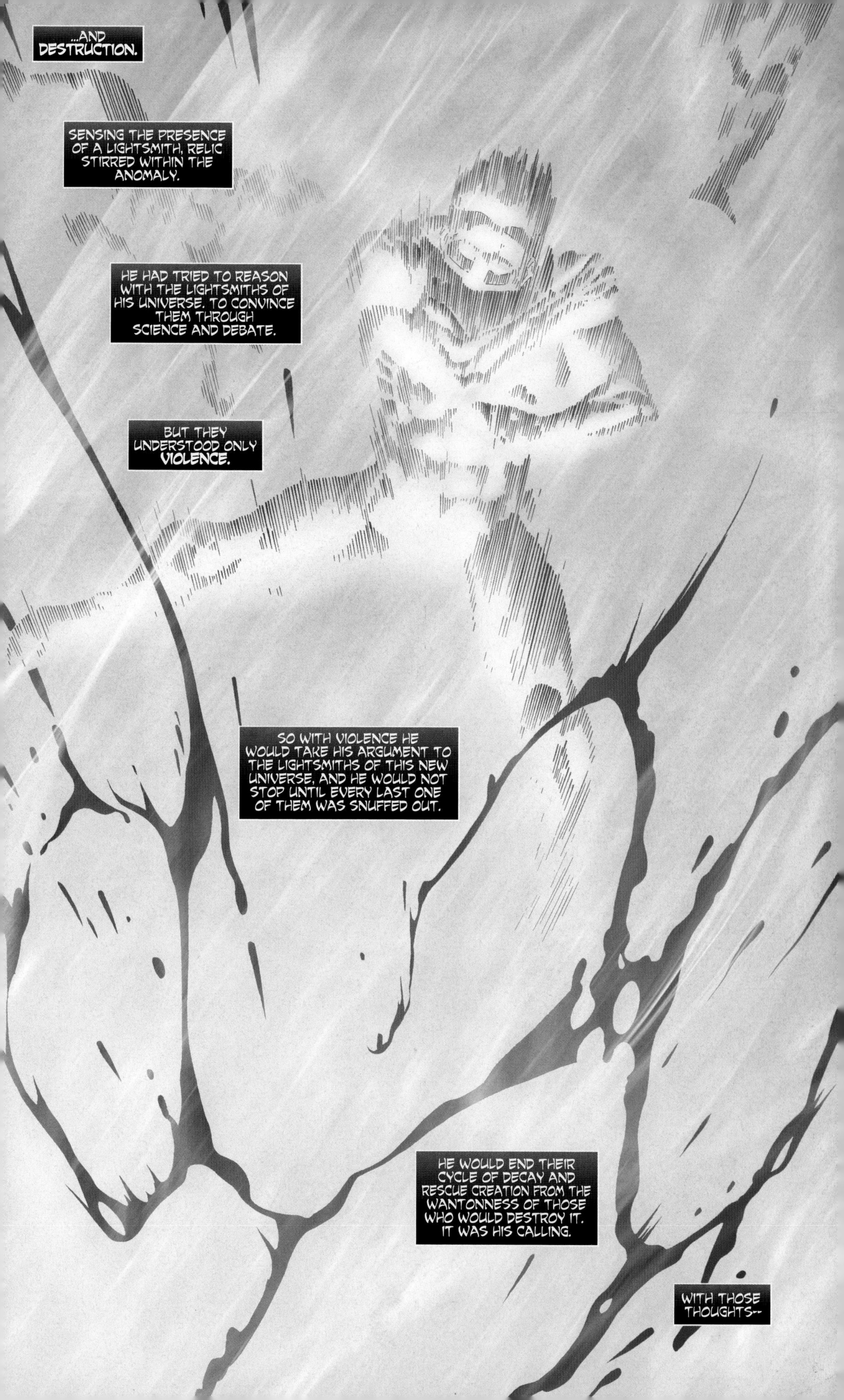
...AND DESTRUCTION.
SENSING THE PRESENCE OF A LIGHTSMITH, RELIC STIRRED WITHIN THE ANOMALY.
HE HAD TRIED TO REASON WITH THE LIGHTSMITHS OF HIS UNIVERSE. TO CONVINCE THEM THROUGH SCIENCE AND DEBATE.
BUT THEY UNDERSTOOD ONLY VIOLENCE.
SO WITH VIOLENCE HE WOULD TAKE HIS ARGUMENT TO THE LIGHTSMITHS OF THIS NEW UNIVERSE, AND HE WOULD NOT STOP UNTIL EVERY LAST ONE OF THEM WAS SNUFFED OUT.
HE WOULD END THEIR CYCLE OF DECAY AND RESCUE CREATION FROM THE WANTONNESS OF THOSE WHO WOULD DESTROY IT. IT WAS HIS CALLING.
WITH THOSE THOUGHTS--

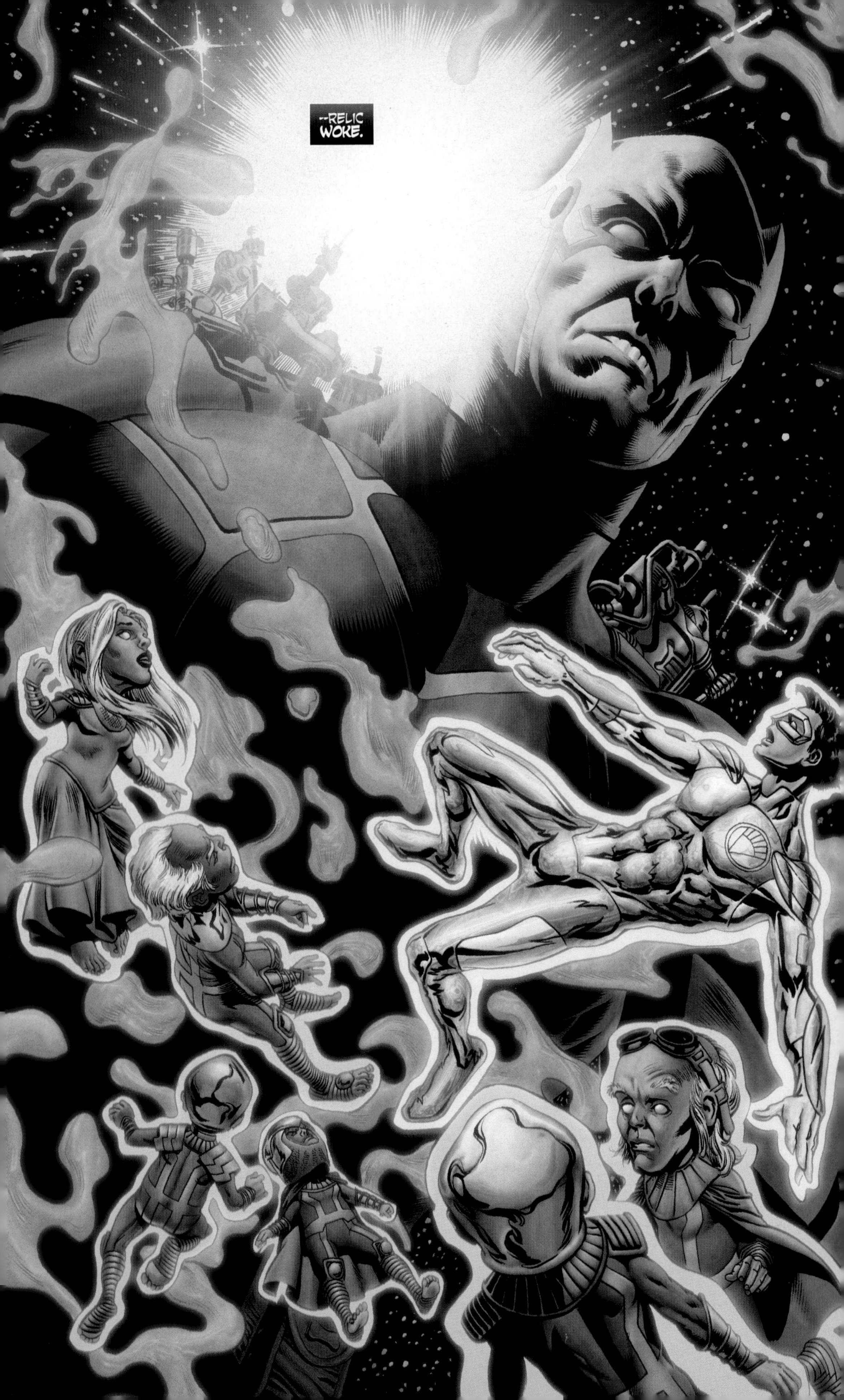
--RELIC
WOKE.

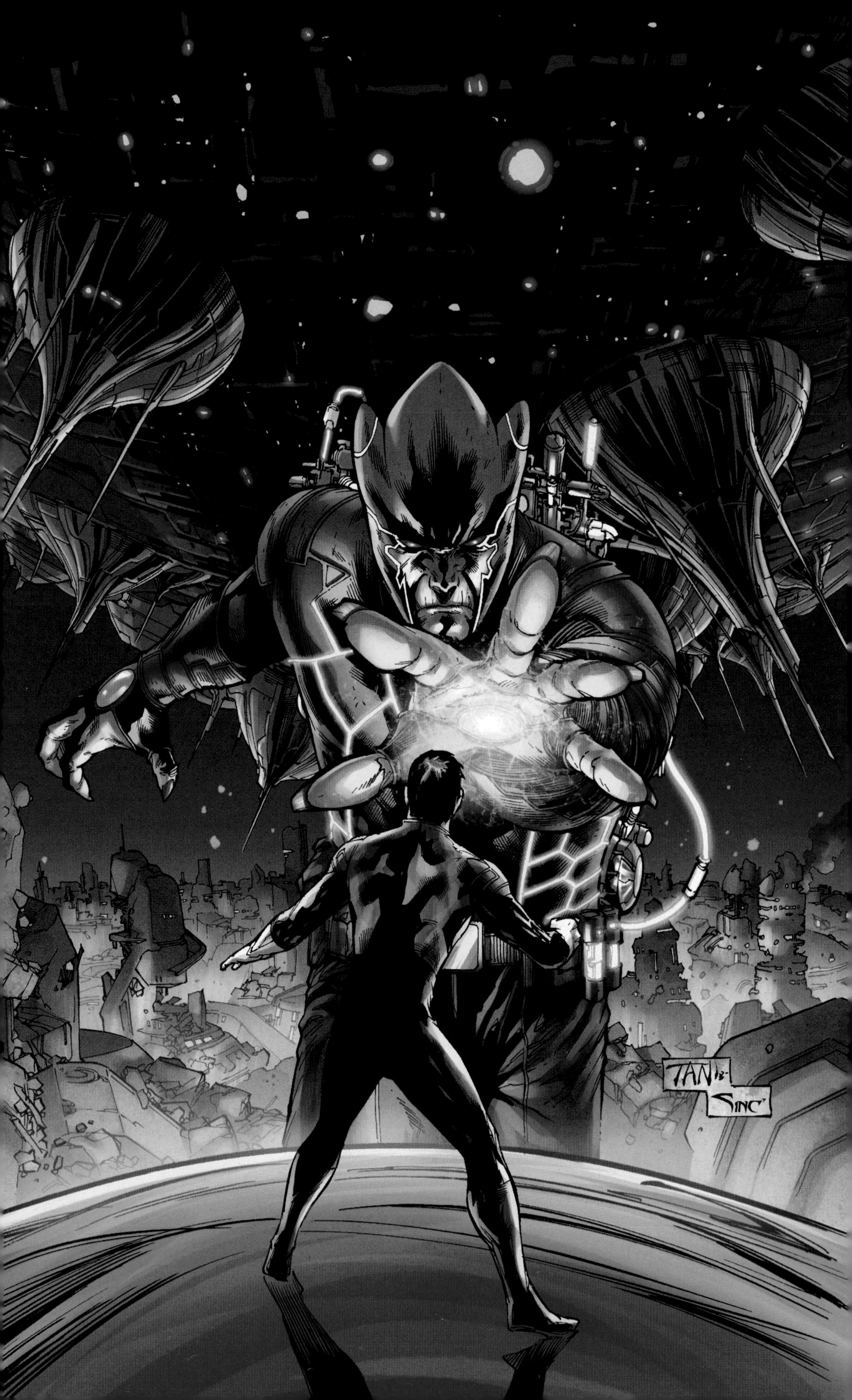

ROBERT VENDITTI writer BILLY TAN penciller ROB HUNTER inker
cover art by BILLY TAN & ALEX SINCLAIR

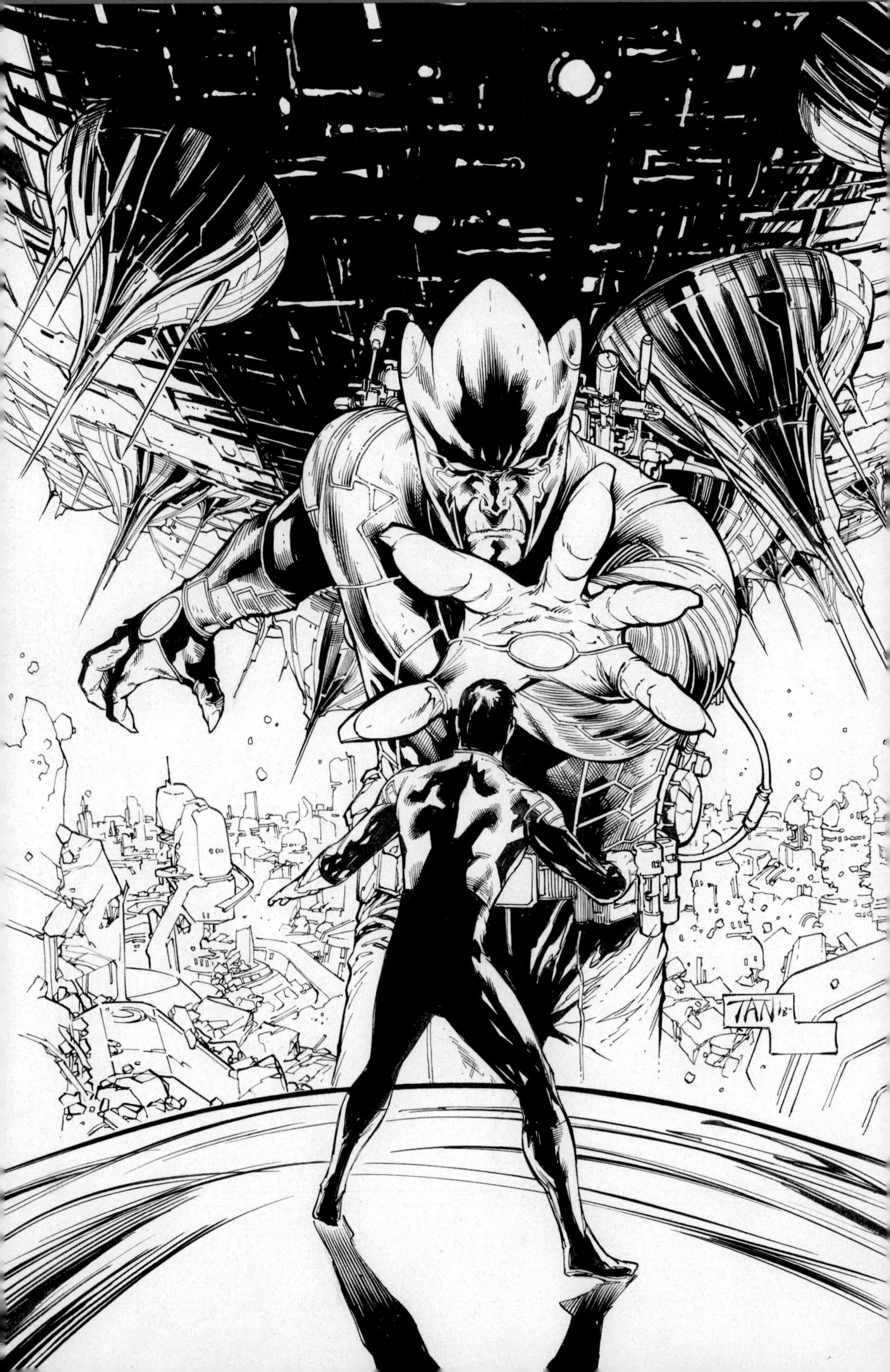
TAN '13

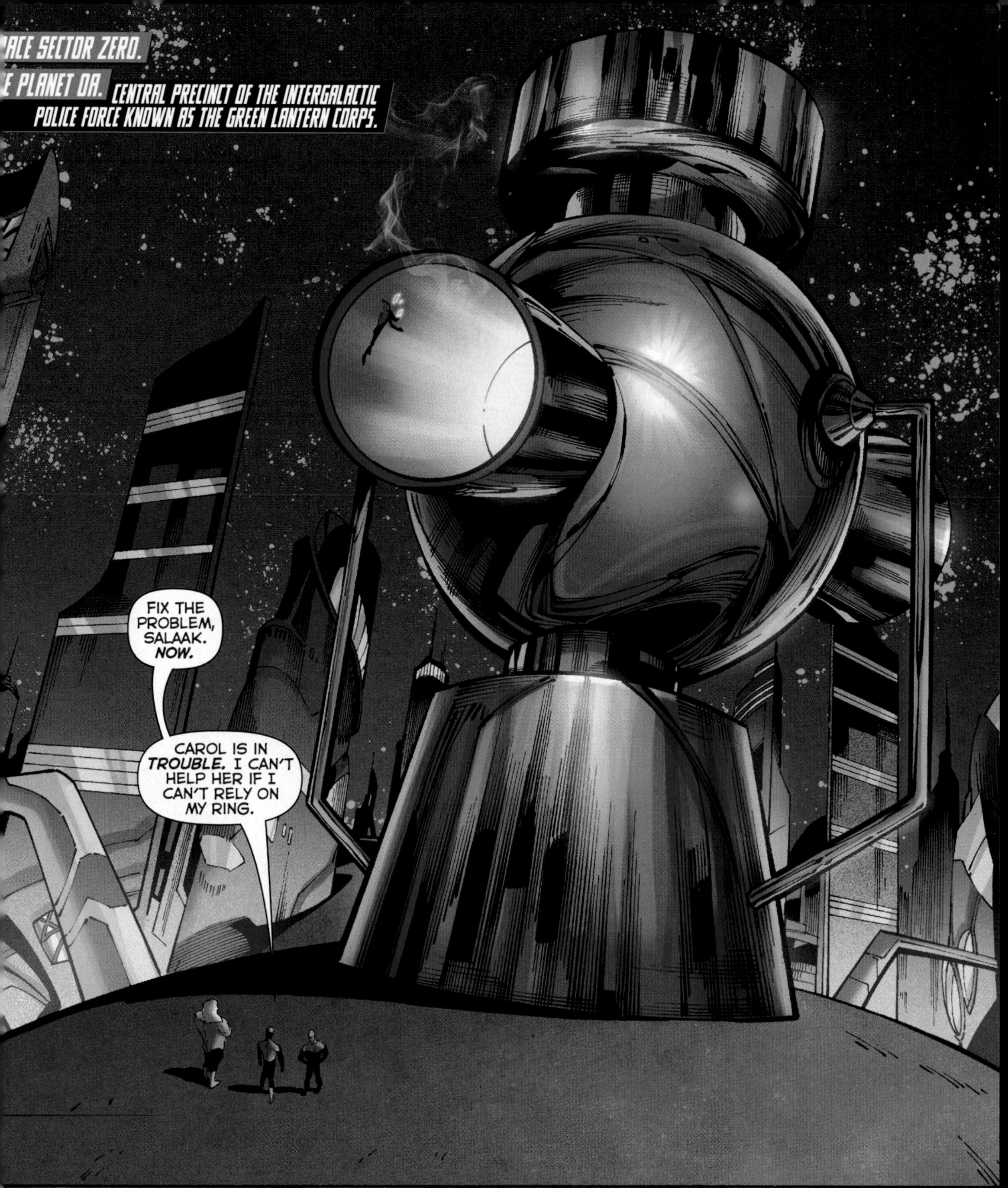

ACE SECTOR ZERO.
E PLANET OA.
CENTRAL PRECINCT OF THE INTERGALACTIC POLICE FORCE KNOWN AS THE GREEN LANTERN CORPS.
FIX THE PROBLEM, SALAAK. NOW.
CAROL IS IN TROUBLE. I CAN'T HELP HER IF I CAN'T RELY ON MY RING.

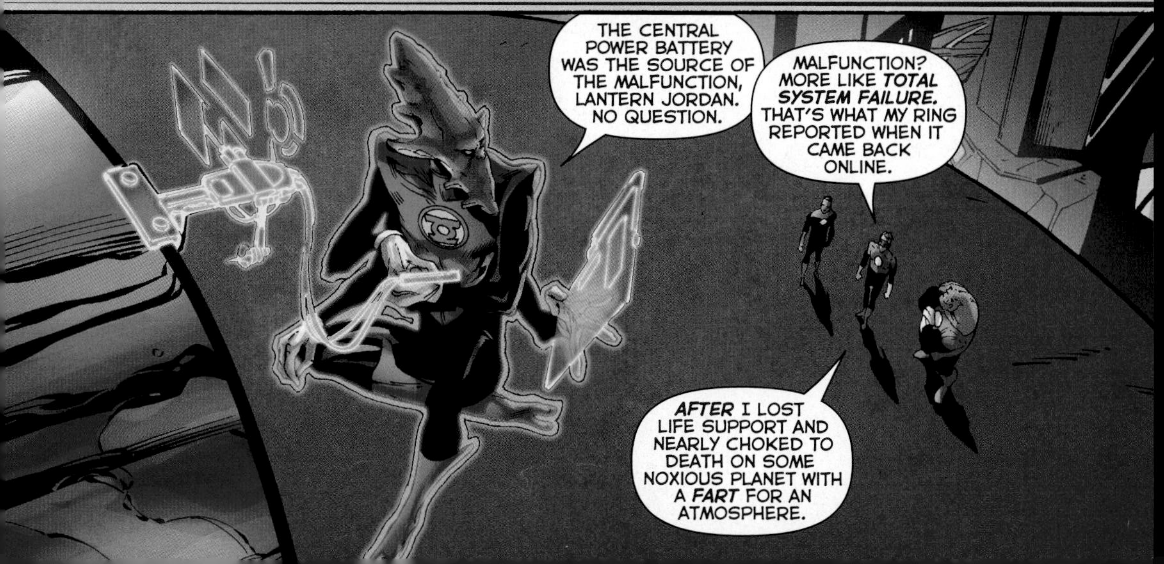

THE CENTRAL POWER BATTERY WAS THE SOURCE OF THE MALFUNCTION, LANTERN JORDAN. NO QUESTION.
MALFUNCTION? MORE LIKE TOTAL SYSTEM FAILURE. THAT'S WHAT MY RING REPORTED WHEN IT CAME BACK ONLINE.
AFTER I LOST LIFE SUPPORT AND NEARLY CHOKED TO DEATH ON SOME NOXIOUS PLANET WITH A FART FOR AN ATMOSPHERE.

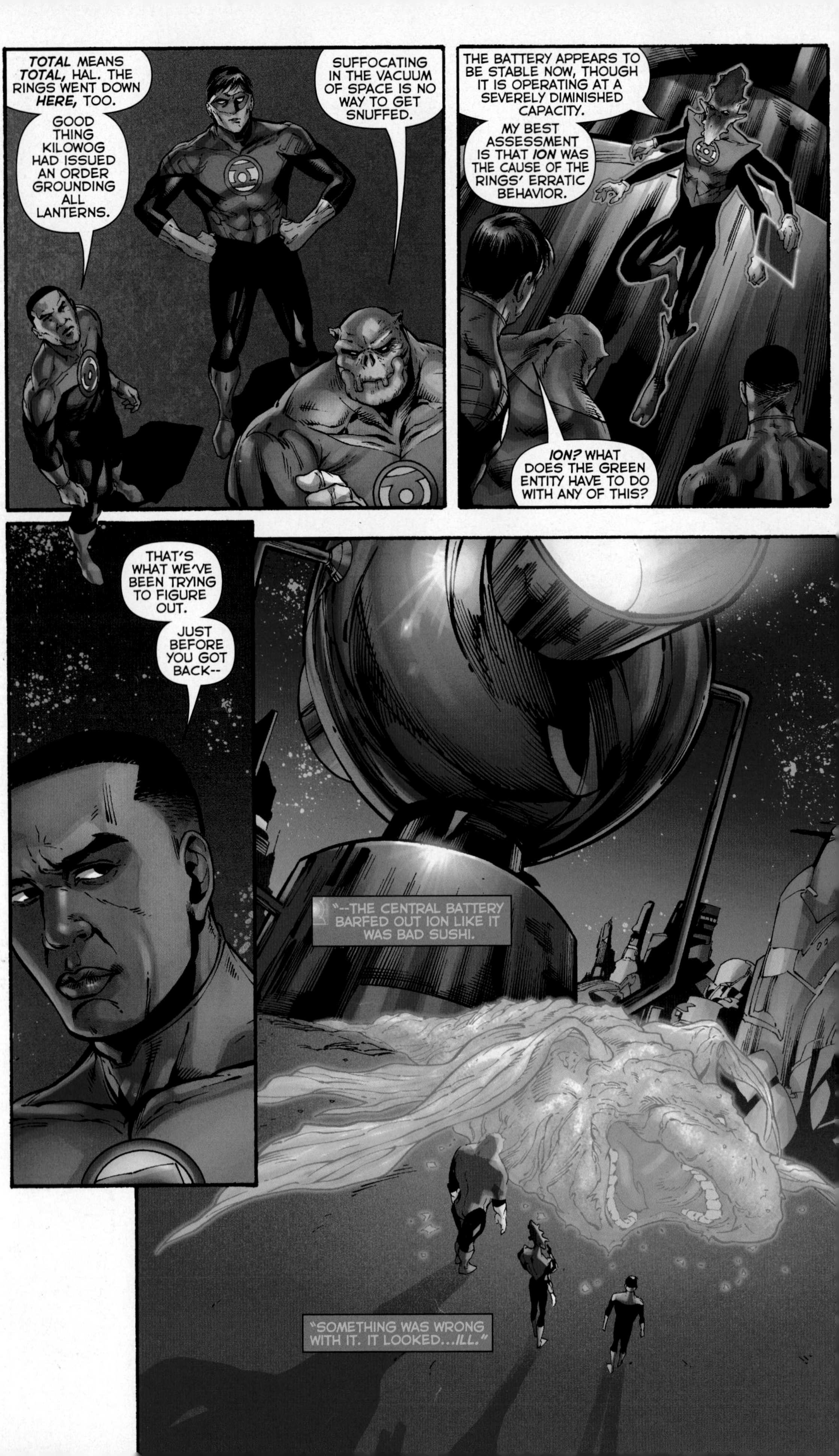
TOTAL MEANS TOTAL, HAL. THE RINGS WENT DOWN HERE, TOO.
GOOD THING KILOWOG HAD ISSUED AN ORDER GROUNDING ALL LANTERNS.
SUFFOCATING IN THE VACUUM OF SPACE IS NO WAY TO GET SNUFFED.
THE BATTERY APPEARS TO BE STABLE NOW, THOUGH IT IS OPERATING AT A SEVERELY DIMINISHED CAPACITY.
MY BEST ASSESSMENT IS THAT ION WAS THE CAUSE OF THE RINGS' ERRATIC BEHAVIOR.
ION? WHAT DOES THE GREEN ENTITY HAVE TO DO WITH ANY OF THIS?
THAT'S WHAT WE'VE BEEN TRYING TO FIGURE OUT.
JUST BEFORE YOU GOT BACK--
"--THE CENTRAL BATTERY BARFED OUT ION LIKE IT WAS BAD SUSHI.
"SOMETHING WAS WRONG WITH IT. IT LOOKED...ILL."

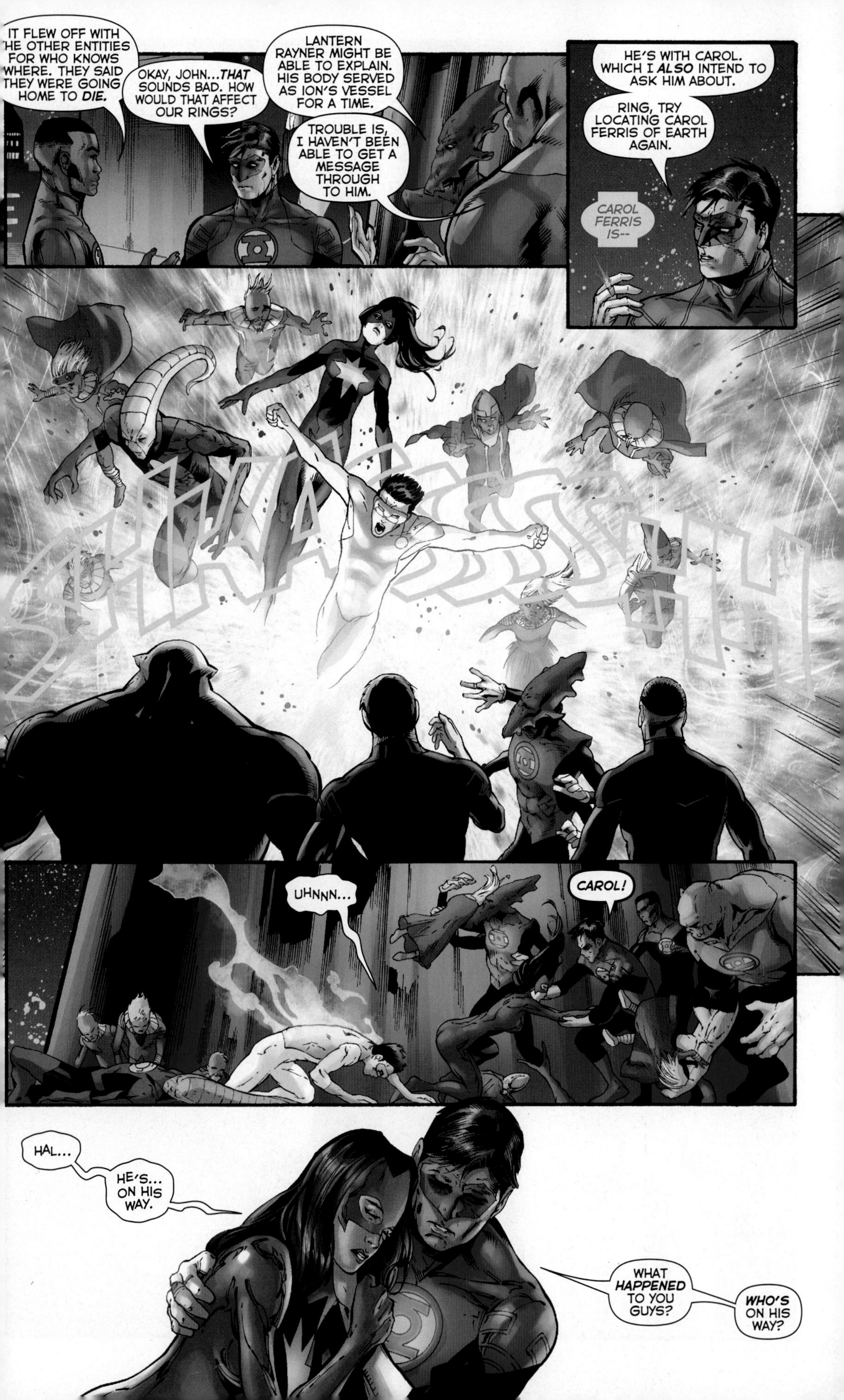
IT FLEW OFF WITH THE OTHER ENTITIES FOR WHO KNOWS WHERE. THEY SAID THEY WERE GOING HOME TO DIE.
OKAY, JOHN...THAT SOUNDS BAD. HOW WOULD THAT AFFECT OUR RINGS?
LANTERN RAYNER MIGHT BE ABLE TO EXPLAIN. HIS BODY SERVED AS ION'S VESSEL FOR A TIME.
TROUBLE IS, I HAVEN'T BEEN ABLE TO GET A MESSAGE THROUGH TO HIM.
HE'S WITH CAROL. WHICH I ALSO INTEND TO ASK HIM ABOUT.
RING, TRY LOCATING CAROL FERRIS OF EARTH AGAIN.
CAROL FERRIS IS--
SHWASHH
UHNNN...
CAROL!
HAL...
HE'S... ON HIS WAY.
WHAT HAPPENED TO YOU GUYS?
WHO'S ON HIS WAY?

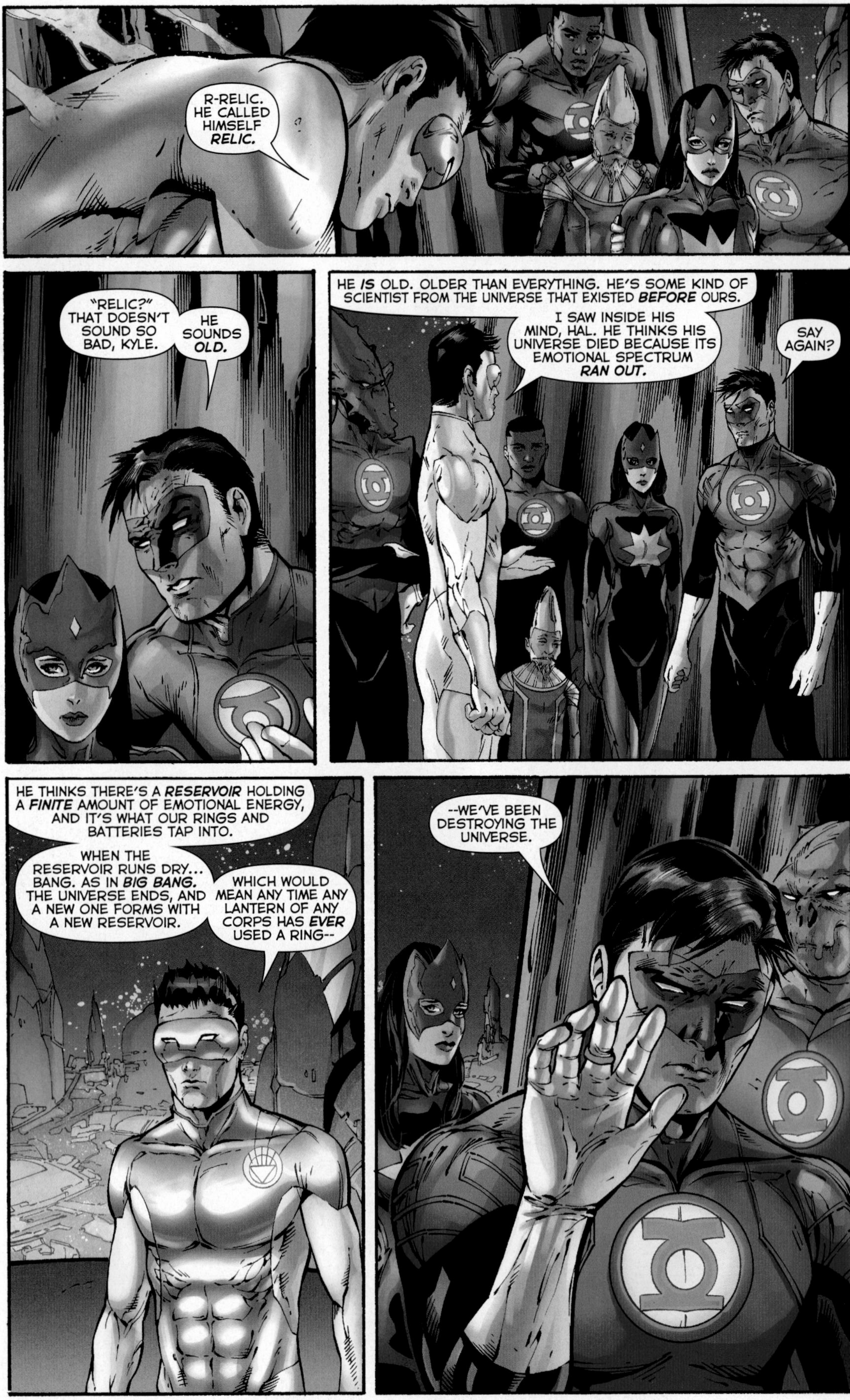
R-RELIC. HE CALLED HIMSELF RELIC.
"RELIC?" THAT DOESN'T SOUND SO BAD, KYLE.
HE SOUNDS OLD.
HE IS OLD. OLDER THAN EVERYTHING. HE'S SOME KIND OF SCIENTIST FROM THE UNIVERSE THAT EXISTED BEFORE OURS.
I SAW INSIDE HIS MIND, HAL. HE THINKS HIS UNIVERSE DIED BECAUSE ITS EMOTIONAL SPECTRUM RAN OUT.
SAY AGAIN?
HE THINKS THERE'S A RESERVOIR HOLDING A FINITE AMOUNT OF EMOTIONAL ENERGY, AND IT'S WHAT OUR RINGS AND BATTERIES TAP INTO.
WHEN THE RESERVOIR RUNS DRY... BANG. AS IN BIG BANG. THE UNIVERSE ENDS, AND A NEW ONE FORMS WITH A NEW RESERVOIR.
WHICH WOULD MEAN ANY TIME ANY LANTERN OF ANY CORPS HAS EVER USED A RING--
--WE'VE BEEN DESTROYING THE UNIVERSE.

PRETTY MUCH SUCKS TO THINK ABOUT, DOESN'T IT?

THE GREEN LANTERN CORPS HAS MAINTAINED ORDER THROUGHOUT THE UNIVERSE FOR MILLENNIA. WE'RE *PROTECTORS*, NOT DESTROYERS.

I WON'T BELIEVE OTHERWISE JUST BECAUSE SOME *LAB COAT* SAYS SO.

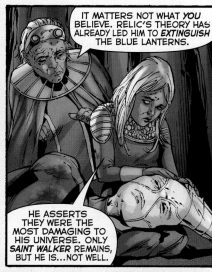

IT MATTERS NOT WHAT *YOU* BELIEVE. RELIC'S THEORY HAS ALREADY LED HIM TO *EXTINGUISH* THE BLUE LANTERNS.

HE ASSERTS THEY WERE THE MOST DAMAGING TO HIS UNIVERSE. ONLY *SAINT WALKER* REMAINS, BUT HE IS...NOT WELL.

THE BLUE LANTERNS ARE *GONE?*

I TRIED HEALING WALKER, BUT MY RING DOESN'T SEEM ABLE TO.

RELIC *INVADED* MY THOUGHTS, HAL. HE KNOWS WHAT I KNOW ABOUT THIS UNIVERSE'S USE OF THE EMOTIONAL SPECTRUM.

AND AS THE ONLY BEING TO EVER MASTER ALL SEVEN COLORS, I KNOW *A LOT.*

GUY...

WHAT *ABOUT* GUY?

HAL, THE GREEN LANTERNS ARE THE BIGGEST OF ALL THE CORPS. WE THINK RELIC HAS HIS SIGHTS SET ON OA NEXT. YOU NEED TO BE READY.

ONE GEEZER BEAT ALL OF YOU *AND* THE BLUE LANTERNS?

BY HIMSELF?

JUST ONE.

KKK-KK-KK-KKKLL

IN OUR DEFENSE--

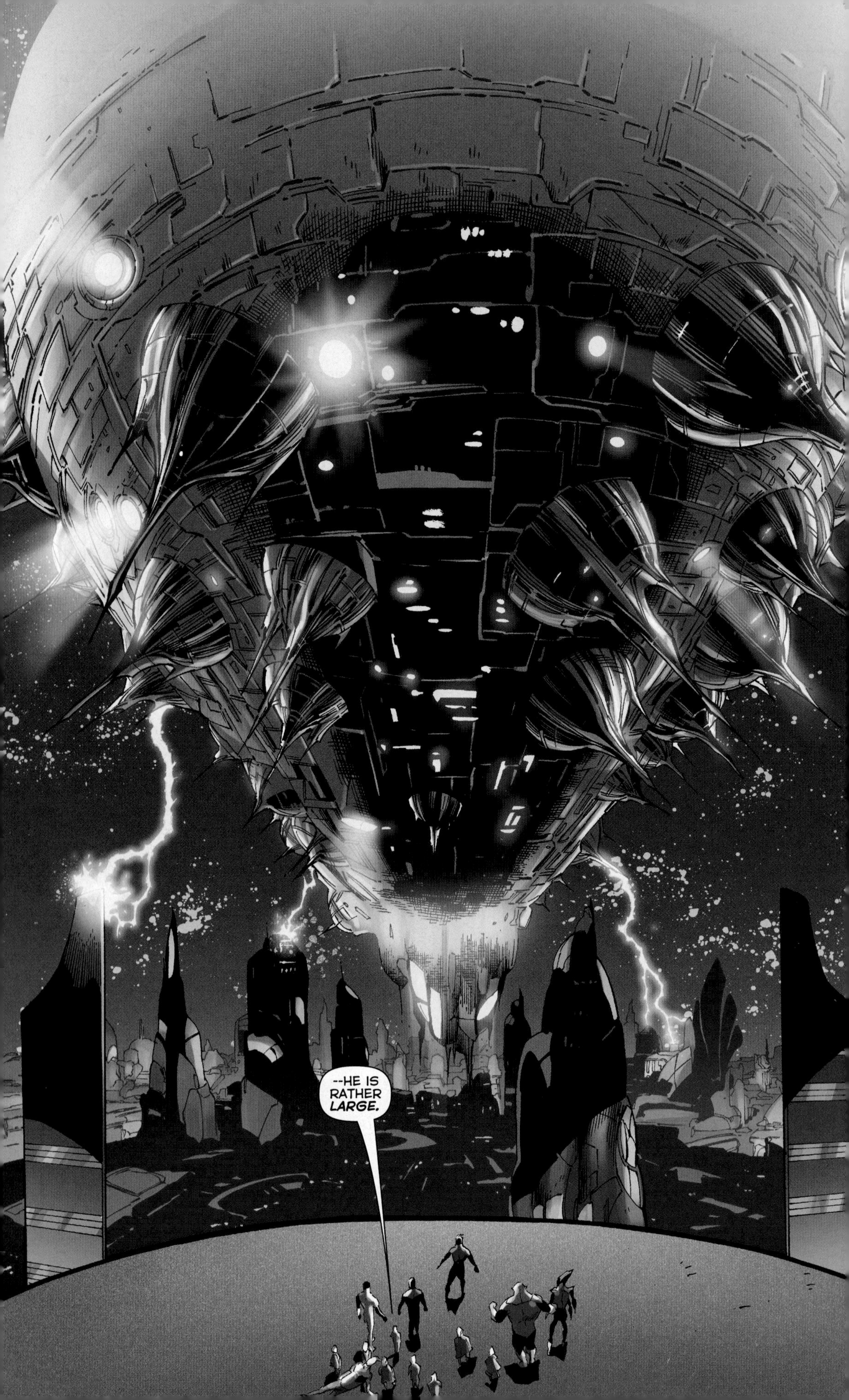
--HE IS RATHER LARGE.

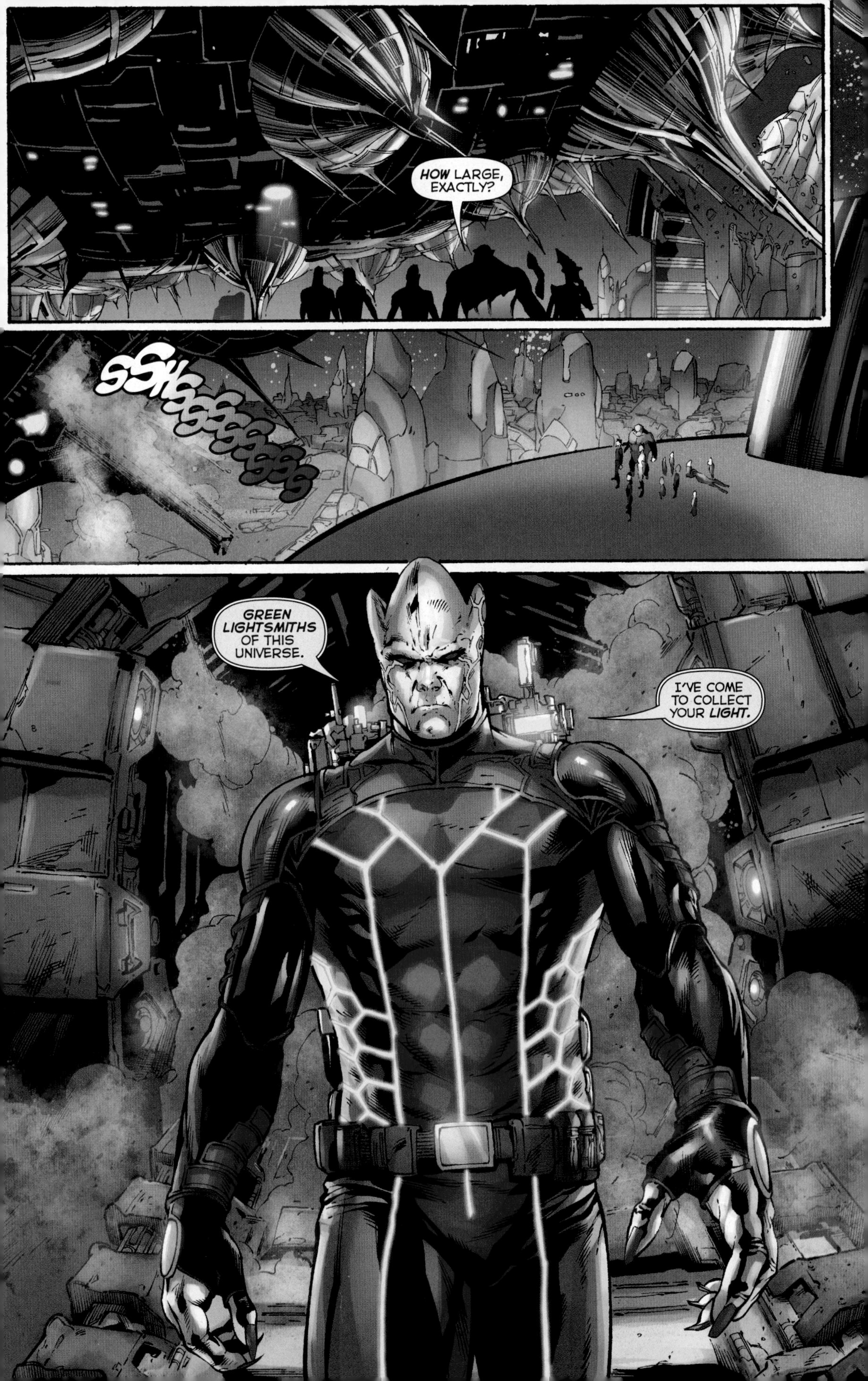
HOW LARGE, EXACTLY?
SSHSSSSSSSS
GREEN LIGHTSMITHS OF THIS UNIVERSE.
I'VE COME TO COLLECT YOUR LIGHT.

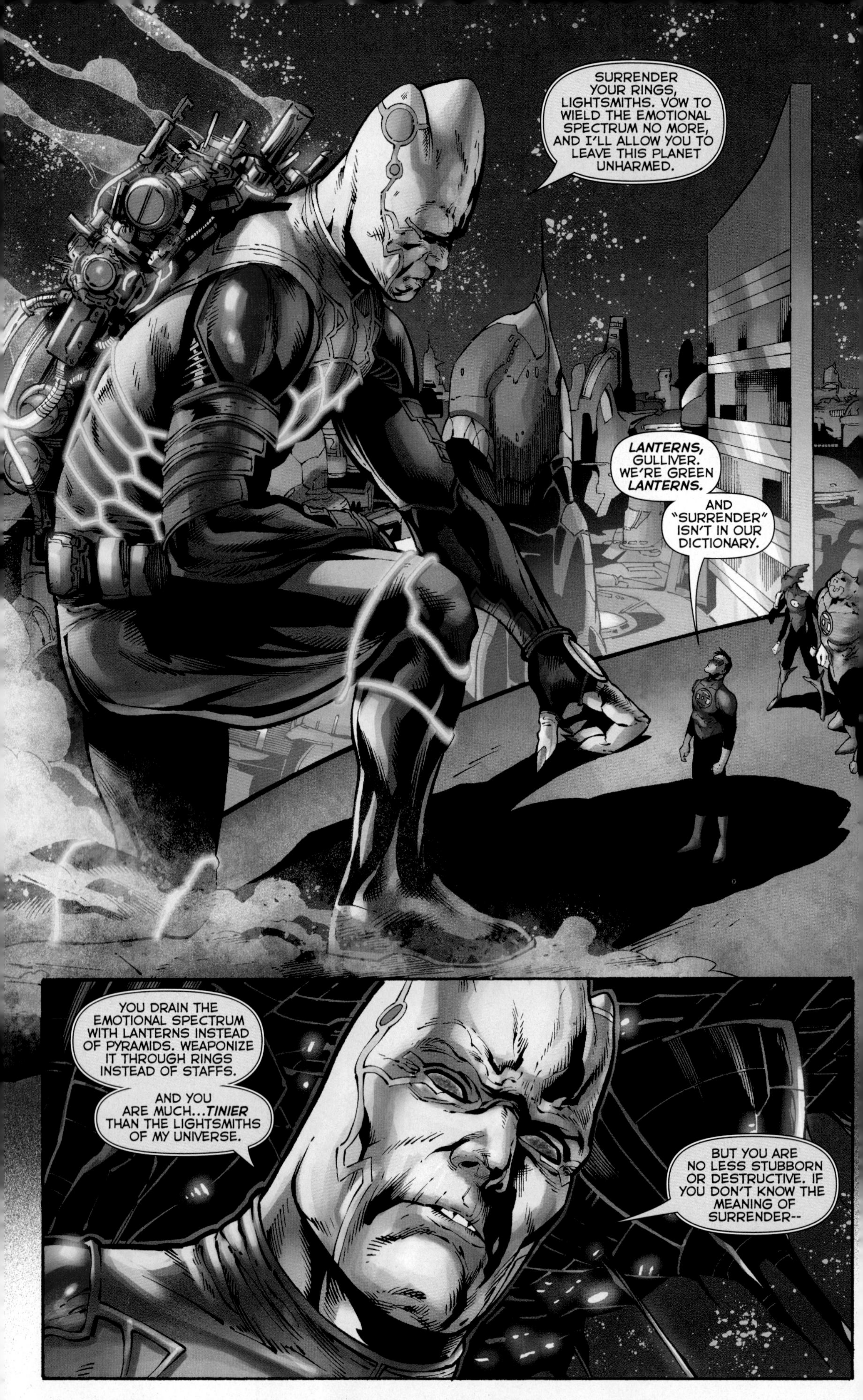
SURRENDER YOUR RINGS, LIGHTSMITHS. VOW TO WIELD THE EMOTIONAL SPECTRUM NO MORE, AND I'LL ALLOW YOU TO LEAVE THIS PLANET UNHARMED.
LANTERNS, GULLIVER. WE'RE GREEN *LANTERNS.*
AND "SURRENDER" ISN'T IN OUR DICTIONARY.
YOU DRAIN THE EMOTIONAL SPECTRUM WITH LANTERNS INSTEAD OF PYRAMIDS. WEAPONIZE IT THROUGH RINGS INSTEAD OF STAFFS.
AND YOU ARE MUCH...*TINIER* THAN THE LIGHTSMITHS OF MY UNIVERSE.
BUT YOU ARE NO LESS STUBBORN OR DESTRUCTIVE. IF YOU DON'T KNOW THE MEANING OF SURRENDER--

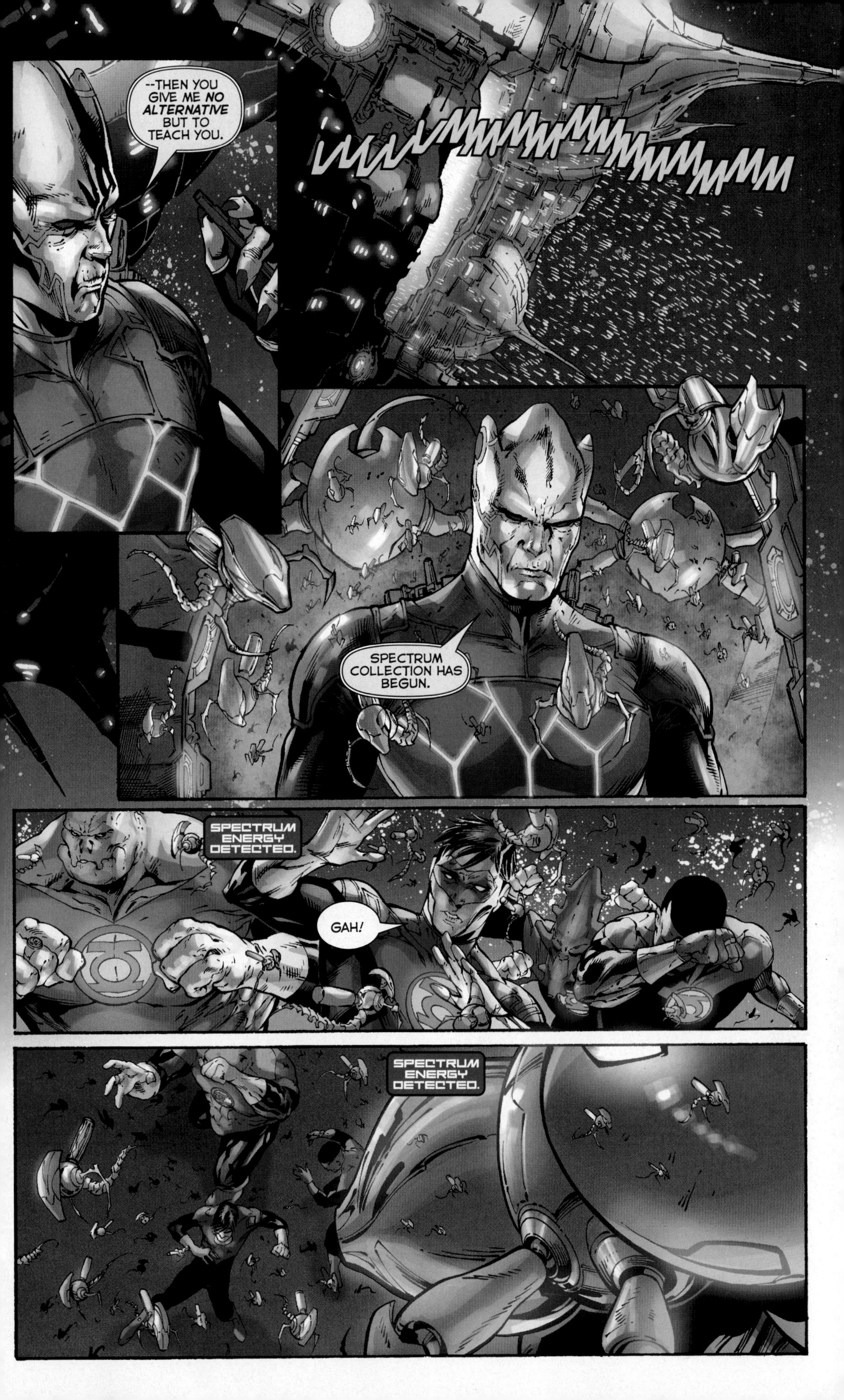
--THEN YOU GIVE ME NO ALTERNATIVE BUT TO TEACH YOU.
VVVVVVMMMMMMMMMMMMMMMMMMMM
SPECTRUM COLLECTION HAS BEGUN.
SPECTRUM ENERGY DETECTED.
GAH!
SPECTRUM ENERGY DETECTED.

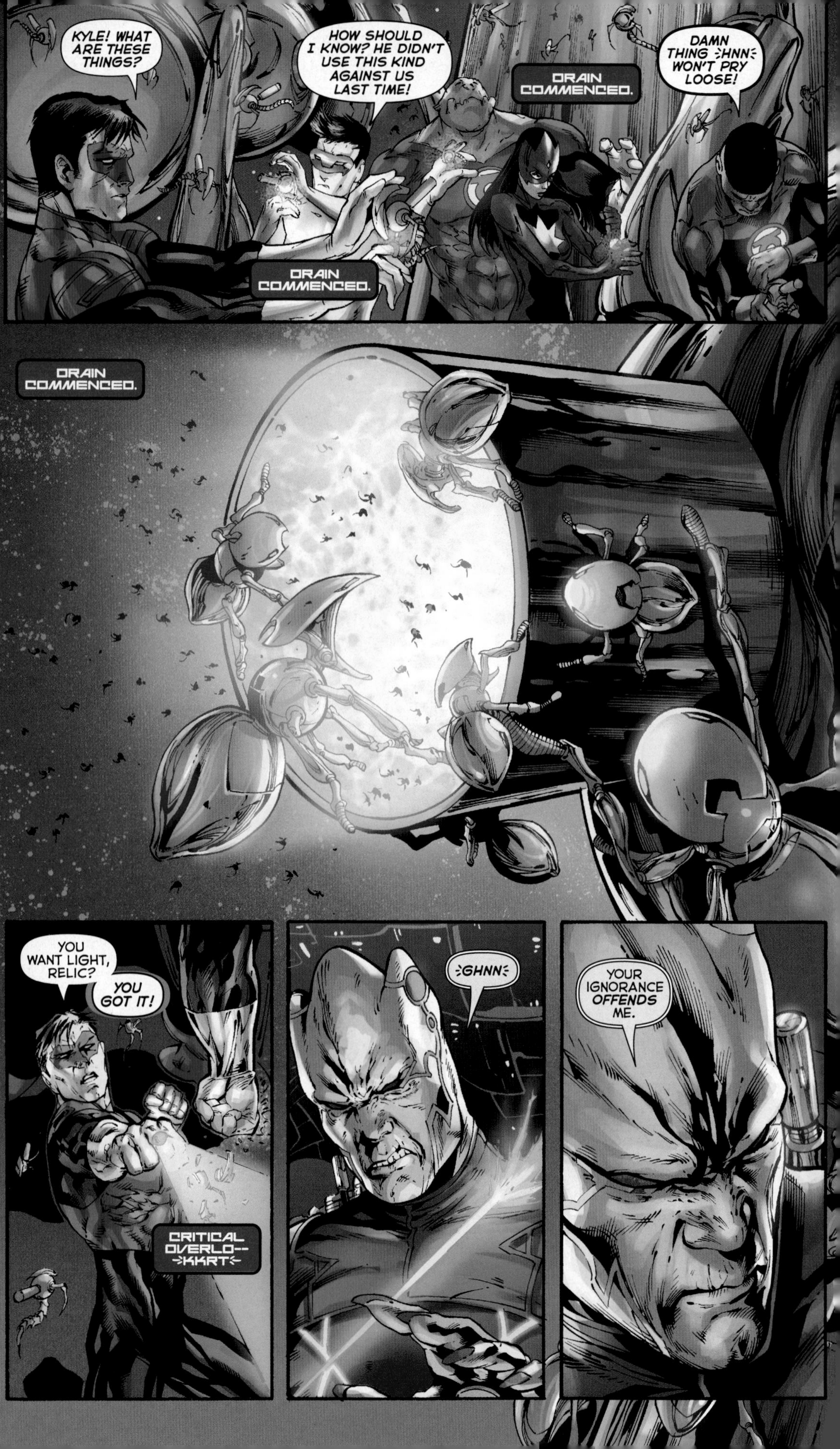
KYLE! WHAT ARE THESE THINGS?
HOW SHOULD I KNOW? HE DIDN'T USE THIS KIND AGAINST US LAST TIME!
DRAIN COMMENCED.
DAMN THING -HNN- WON'T PRY LOOSE!
DRAIN COMMENCED.
DRAIN COMMENCED.
YOU WANT LIGHT, RELIC?
YOU GOT IT!
CRITICAL OVERLO-- -KKRT-
-GHNN-
YOUR IGNORANCE OFFENDS ME.

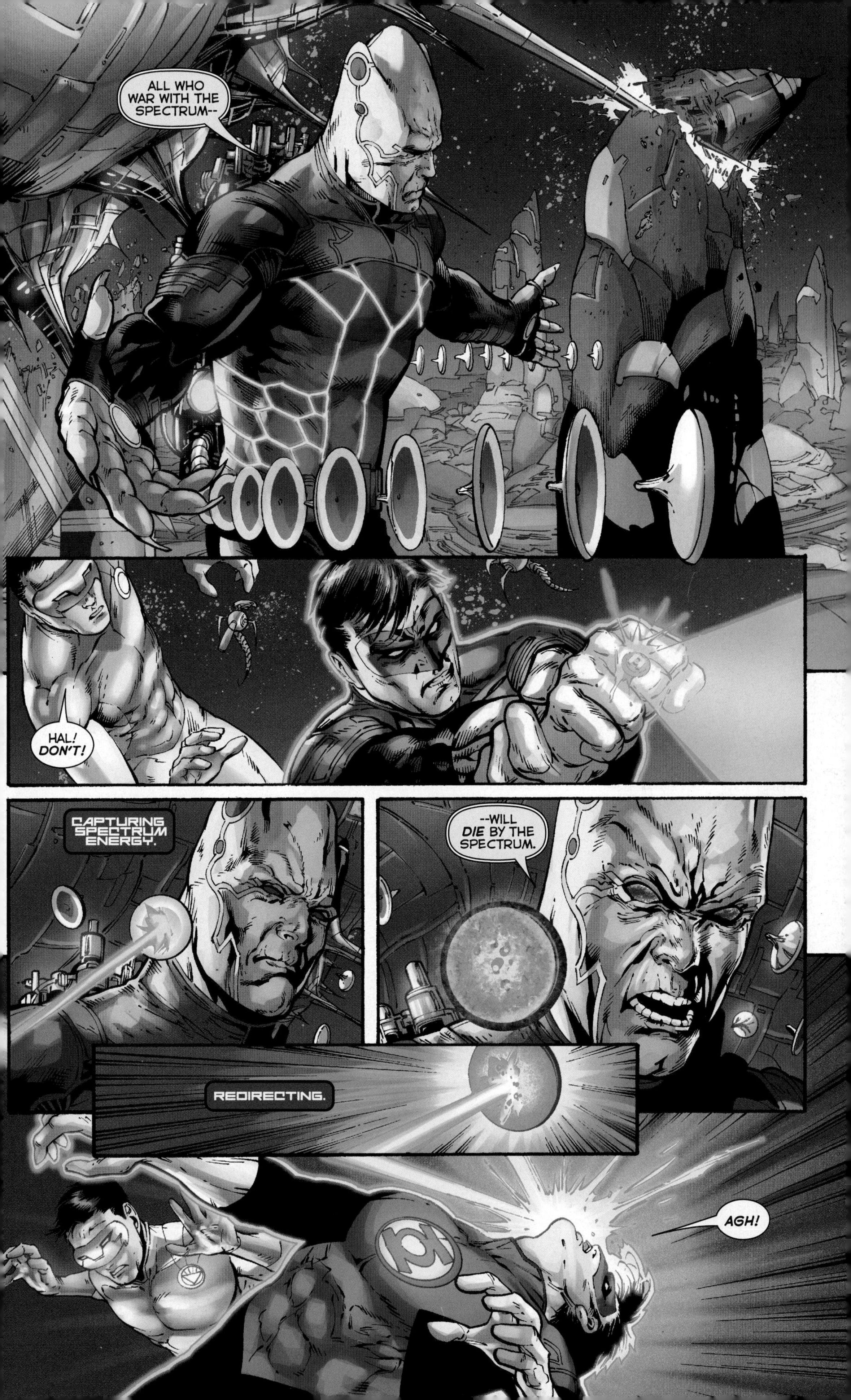
ALL WHO WAR WITH THE SPECTRUM--
HAL! DON'T!
CAPTURING SPECTRUM ENERGY.
--WILL DIE BY THE SPECTRUM.
REDIRECTING.
AGH!

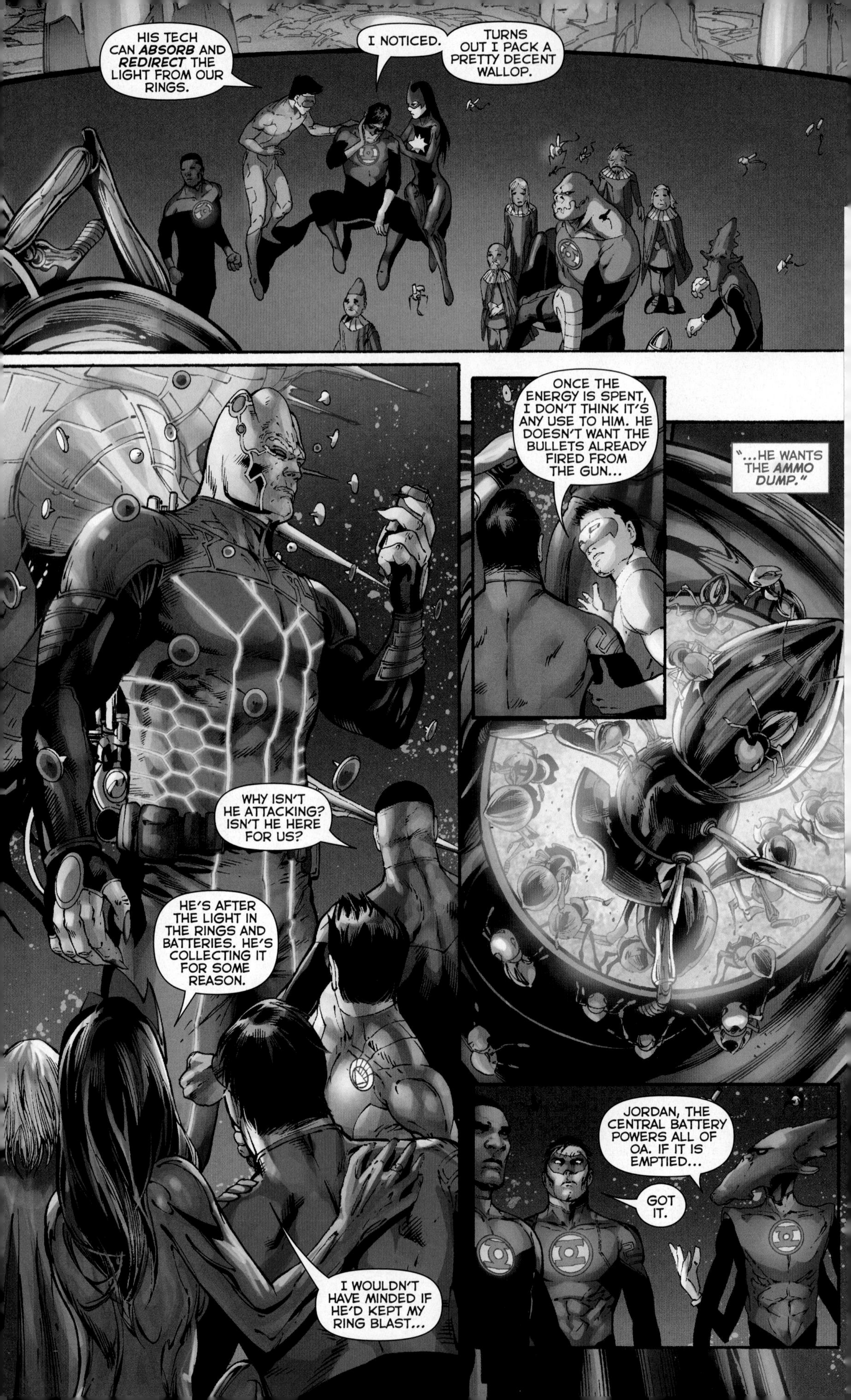
HIS TECH CAN ABSORB AND REDIRECT THE LIGHT FROM OUR RINGS.
I NOTICED.
TURNS OUT I PACK A PRETTY DECENT WALLOP.
WHY ISN'T HE ATTACKING? ISN'T HE HERE FOR US?
HE'S AFTER THE LIGHT IN THE RINGS AND BATTERIES. HE'S COLLECTING IT FOR SOME REASON.
I WOULDN'T HAVE MINDED IF HE'D KEPT MY RING BLAST...
ONCE THE ENERGY IS SPENT, I DON'T THINK IT'S ANY USE TO HIM. HE DOESN'T WANT THE BULLETS ALREADY FIRED FROM THE GUN...
"...HE WANTS THE AMMO DUMP."
JORDAN, THE CENTRAL BATTERY POWERS ALL OF OA. IF IT IS EMPTIED...
GOT IT.

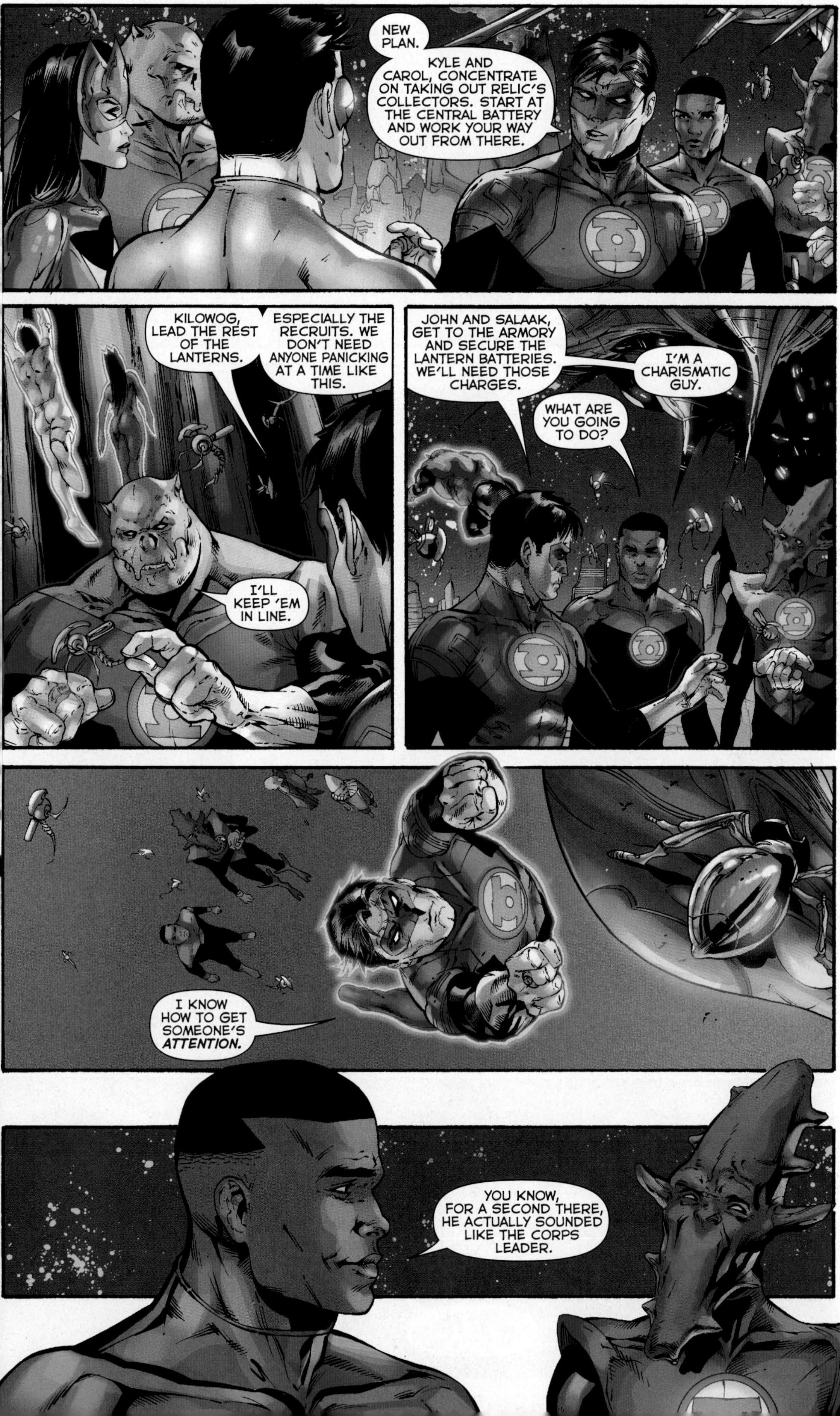
NEW PLAN.
KYLE AND CAROL, CONCENTRATE ON TAKING OUT RELIC'S COLLECTORS. START AT THE CENTRAL BATTERY AND WORK YOUR WAY OUT FROM THERE.
KILOWOG, LEAD THE REST OF THE LANTERNS.
ESPECIALLY THE RECRUITS. WE DON'T NEED ANYONE PANICKING AT A TIME LIKE THIS.
I'LL KEEP 'EM IN LINE.
JOHN AND SALAAK, GET TO THE ARMORY AND SECURE THE LANTERN BATTERIES. WE'LL NEED THOSE CHARGES.
WHAT ARE YOU GOING TO DO?
I'M A CHARISMATIC GUY.
I KNOW HOW TO GET SOMEONE'S *ATTENTION.*
YOU KNOW, FOR A SECOND THERE, HE ACTUALLY SOUNDED LIKE THE CORPS LEADER.

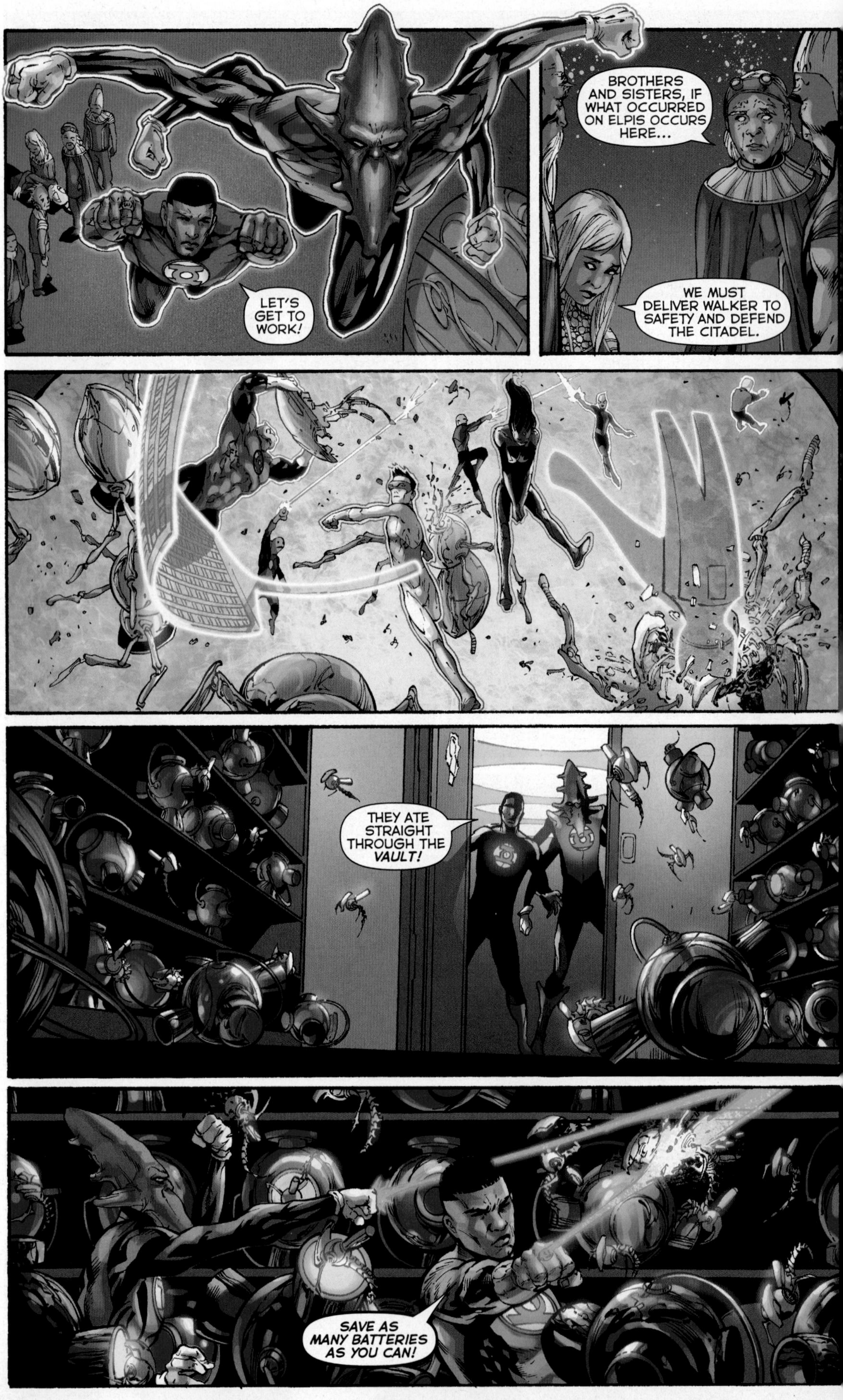
LET'S GET TO WORK!
BROTHERS AND SISTERS, IF WHAT OCCURRED ON ELPIS OCCURS HERE...
WE MUST DELIVER WALKER TO SAFETY AND DEFEND THE CITADEL.
THEY ATE STRAIGHT THROUGH THE *VAULT!*
SAVE AS MANY BATTERIES AS YOU CAN!

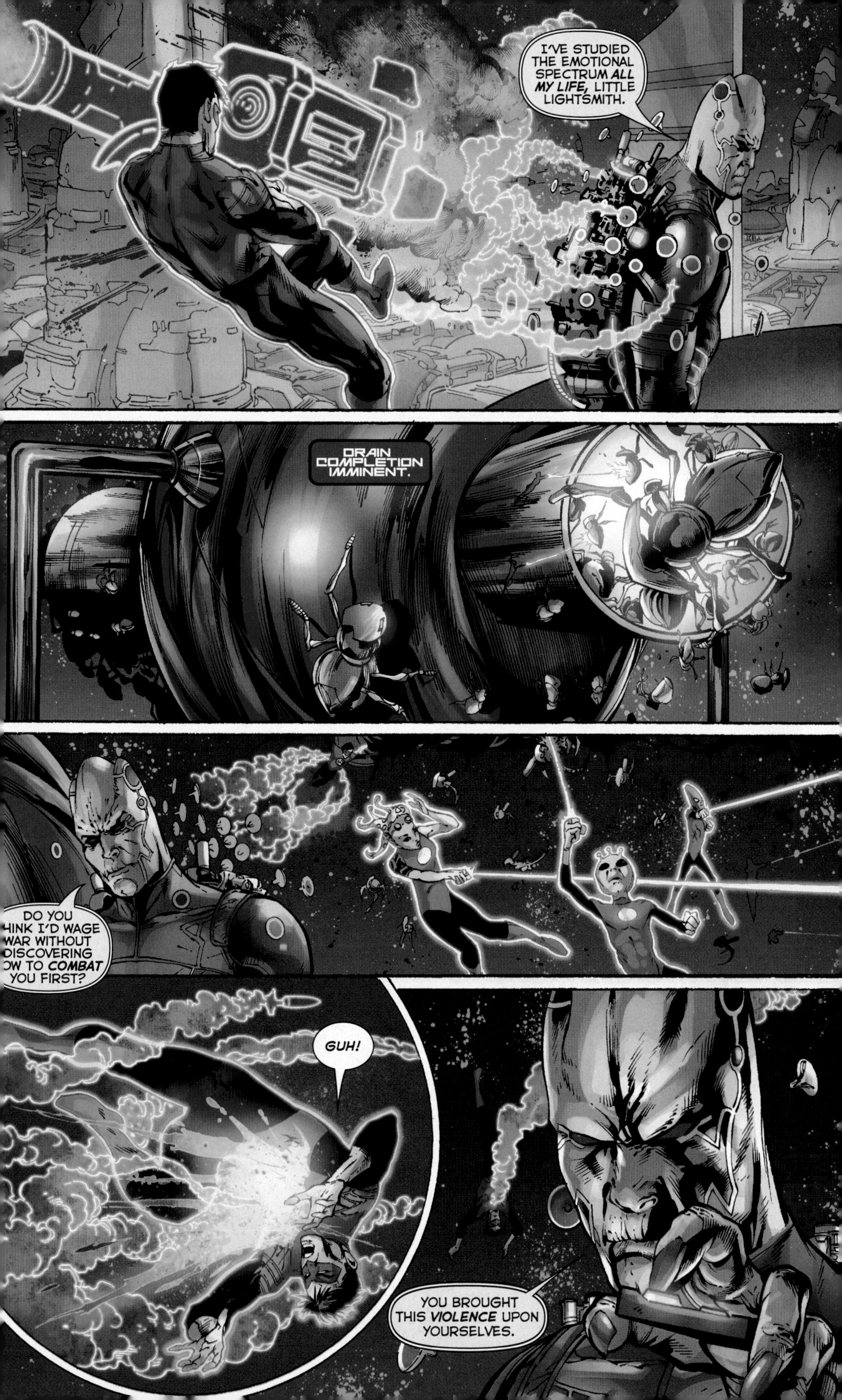

I'VE STUDIED THE EMOTIONAL SPECTRUM ALL MY LIFE, LITTLE LIGHTSMITH.
DRAIN COMPLETION IMMINENT.
DO YOU THINK I'D WAGE WAR WITHOUT DISCOVERING HOW TO COMBAT YOU FIRST?
GUH!
YOU BROUGHT THIS VIOLENCE UPON YOURSELVES.

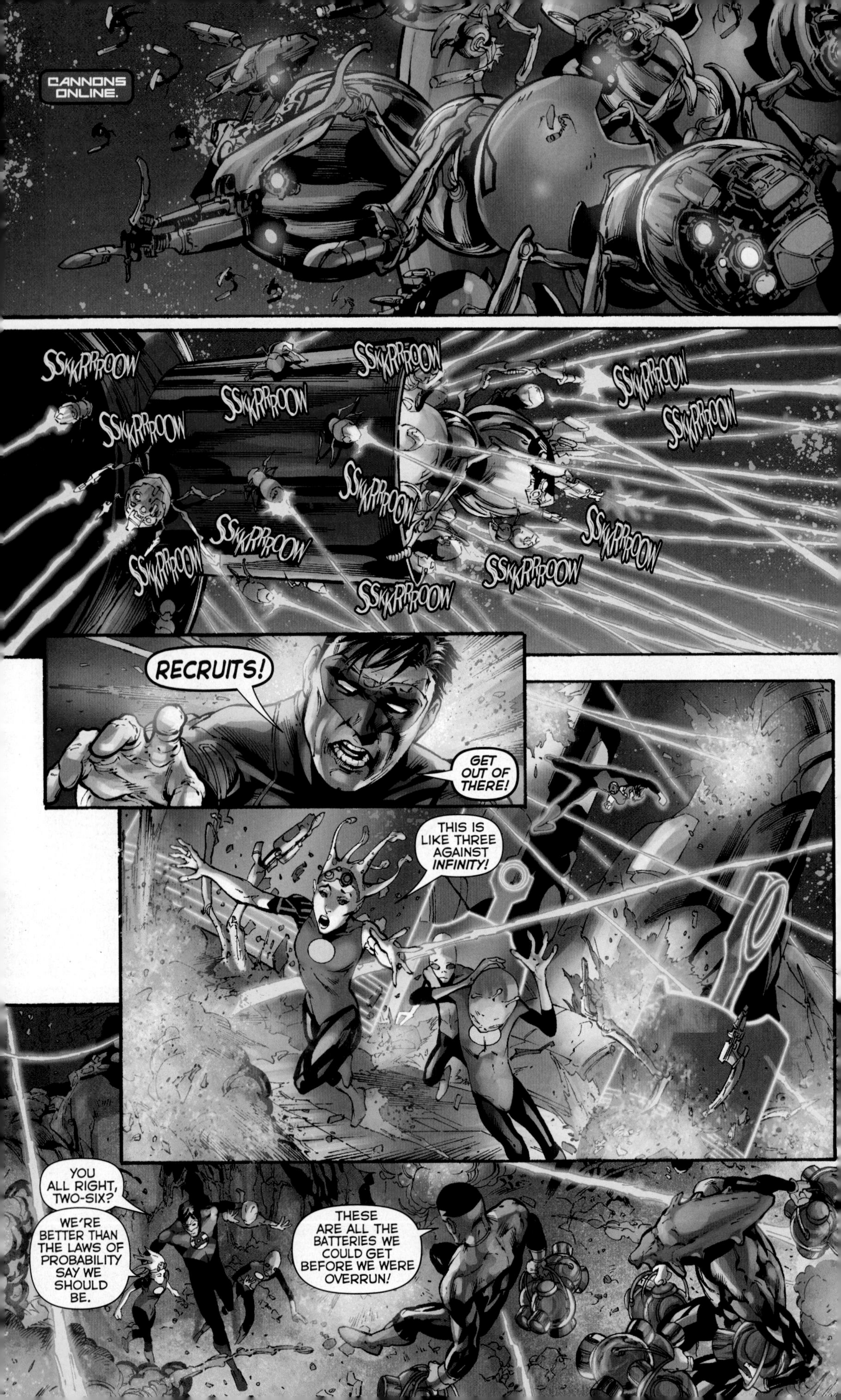
CANNONS ONLINE.
SSKKRRROOW
SSKKRRROOW
SSKKRRROOW
SSKKRRROOW
SSKKRRROOW
SSKKRRROOW
SSKKRRROOW
SSKKRRROOW
SSKKRRROOW
SSKKRRROOW
SSKKRRROOW
SSKKRRROOW
RECRUITS!
GET OUT OF THERE!
THIS IS LIKE THREE AGAINST INFINITY!
YOU ALL RIGHT, TWO-SIX?
WE'RE BETTER THAN THE LAWS OF PROBABILITY SAY WE SHOULD BE.
THESE ARE ALL THE BATTERIES WE COULD GET BEFORE WE WERE OVERRUN!

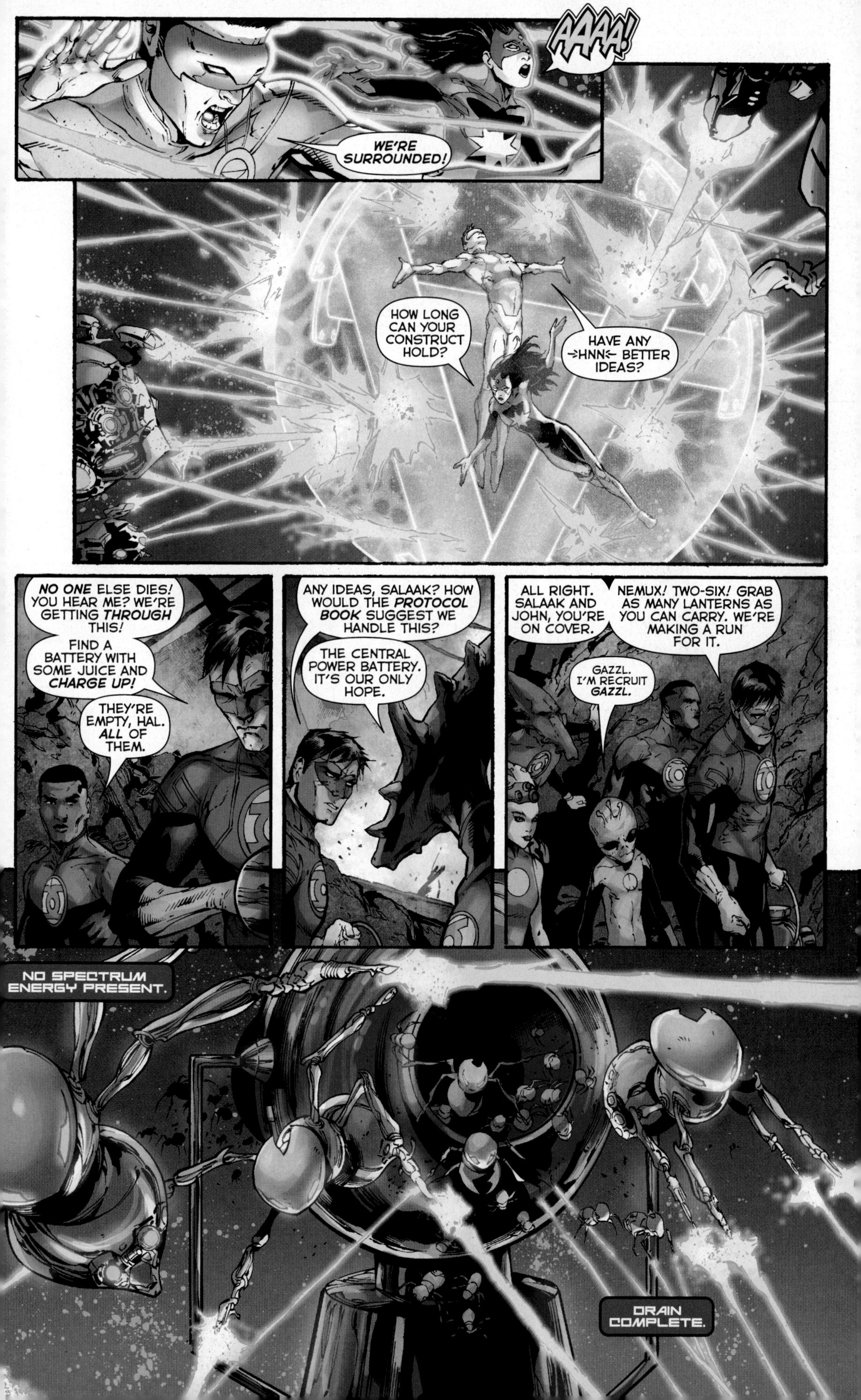
AAAA!
WE'RE SURROUNDED!
HOW LONG CAN YOUR CONSTRUCT HOLD?
HAVE ANY ~HNN~ BETTER IDEAS?
NO ONE ELSE DIES! YOU HEAR ME? WE'RE GETTING THROUGH THIS!
FIND A BATTERY WITH SOME JUICE AND CHARGE UP!
THEY'RE EMPTY, HAL. ALL OF THEM.
ANY IDEAS, SALAAK? HOW WOULD THE PROTOCOL BOOK SUGGEST WE HANDLE THIS?
THE CENTRAL POWER BATTERY. IT'S OUR ONLY HOPE.
ALL RIGHT. SALAAK AND JOHN, YOU'RE ON COVER.
NEMUX! TWO-SIX! GRAB AS MANY LANTERNS AS YOU CAN CARRY. WE'RE MAKING A RUN FOR IT.
GAZZL. I'M RECRUIT GAZZL.
NO SPECTRUM ENERGY PRESENT.
DRAIN COMPLETE.

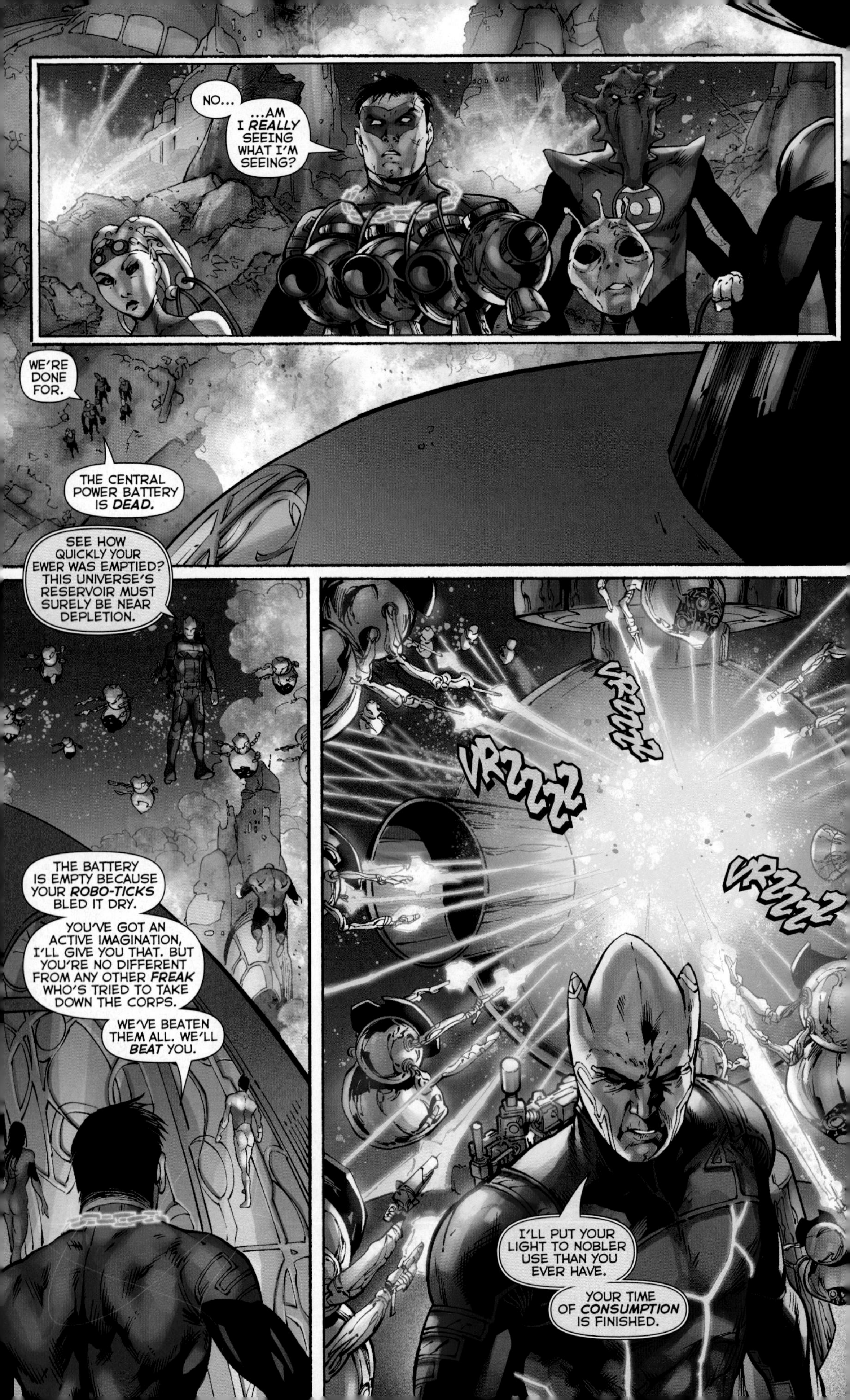
NO...
...AM I REALLY SEEING WHAT I'M SEEING?
WE'RE DONE FOR.
THE CENTRAL POWER BATTERY IS DEAD.
SEE HOW QUICKLY YOUR EWER WAS EMPTIED? THIS UNIVERSE'S RESERVOIR MUST SURELY BE NEAR DEPLETION.
THE BATTERY IS EMPTY BECAUSE YOUR ROBO-TICKS BLED IT DRY.
YOU'VE GOT AN ACTIVE IMAGINATION, I'LL GIVE YOU THAT. BUT YOU'RE NO DIFFERENT FROM ANY OTHER FREAK WHO'S TRIED TO TAKE DOWN THE CORPS.
WE'VE BEATEN THEM ALL. WE'LL BEAT YOU.
VRZZZZ
VRZZZZ
VRZZZZ
I'LL PUT YOUR LIGHT TO NOBLER USE THAN YOU EVER HAVE.
YOUR TIME OF CONSUMPTION IS FINISHED.

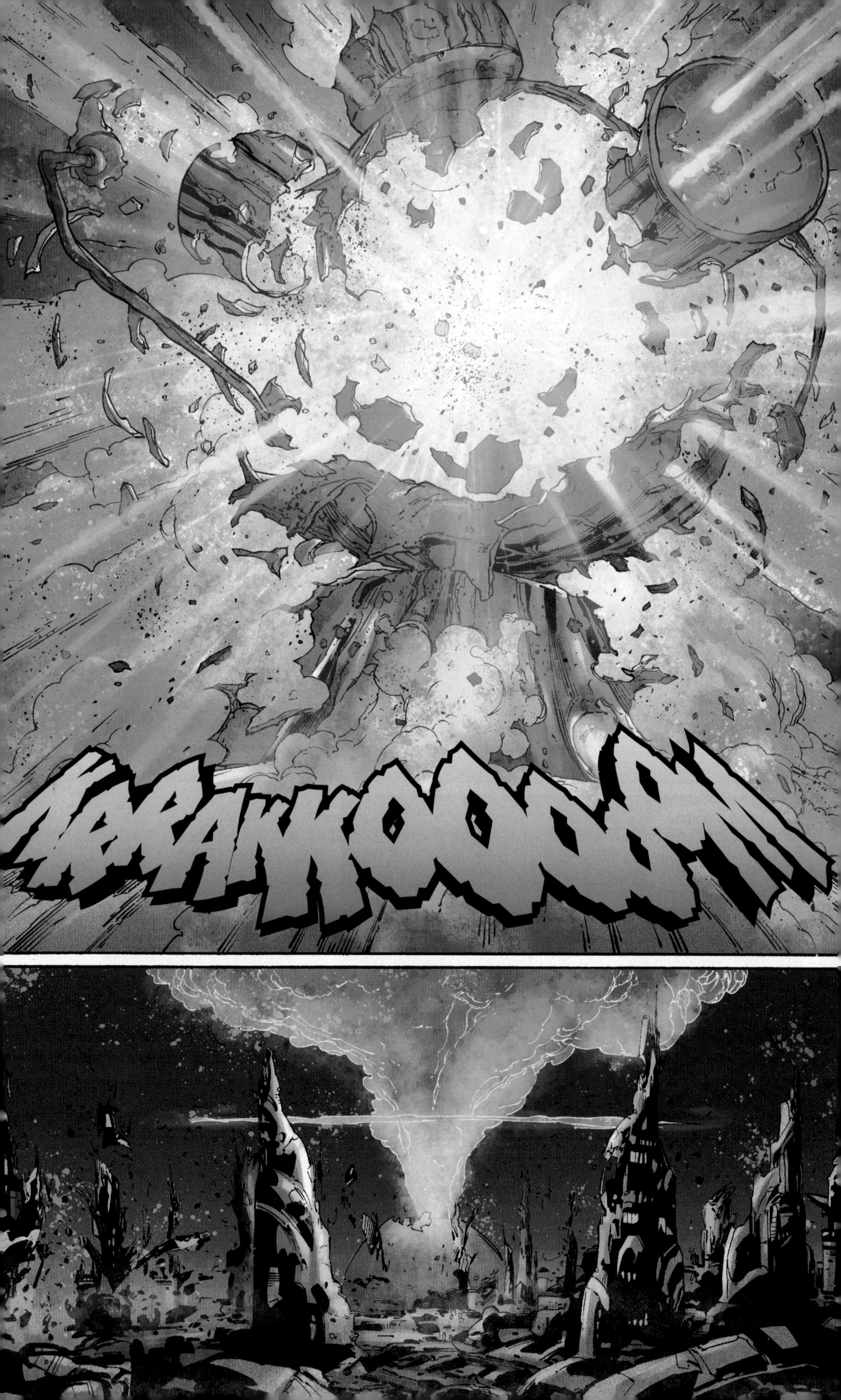
KRAKOOOM!!

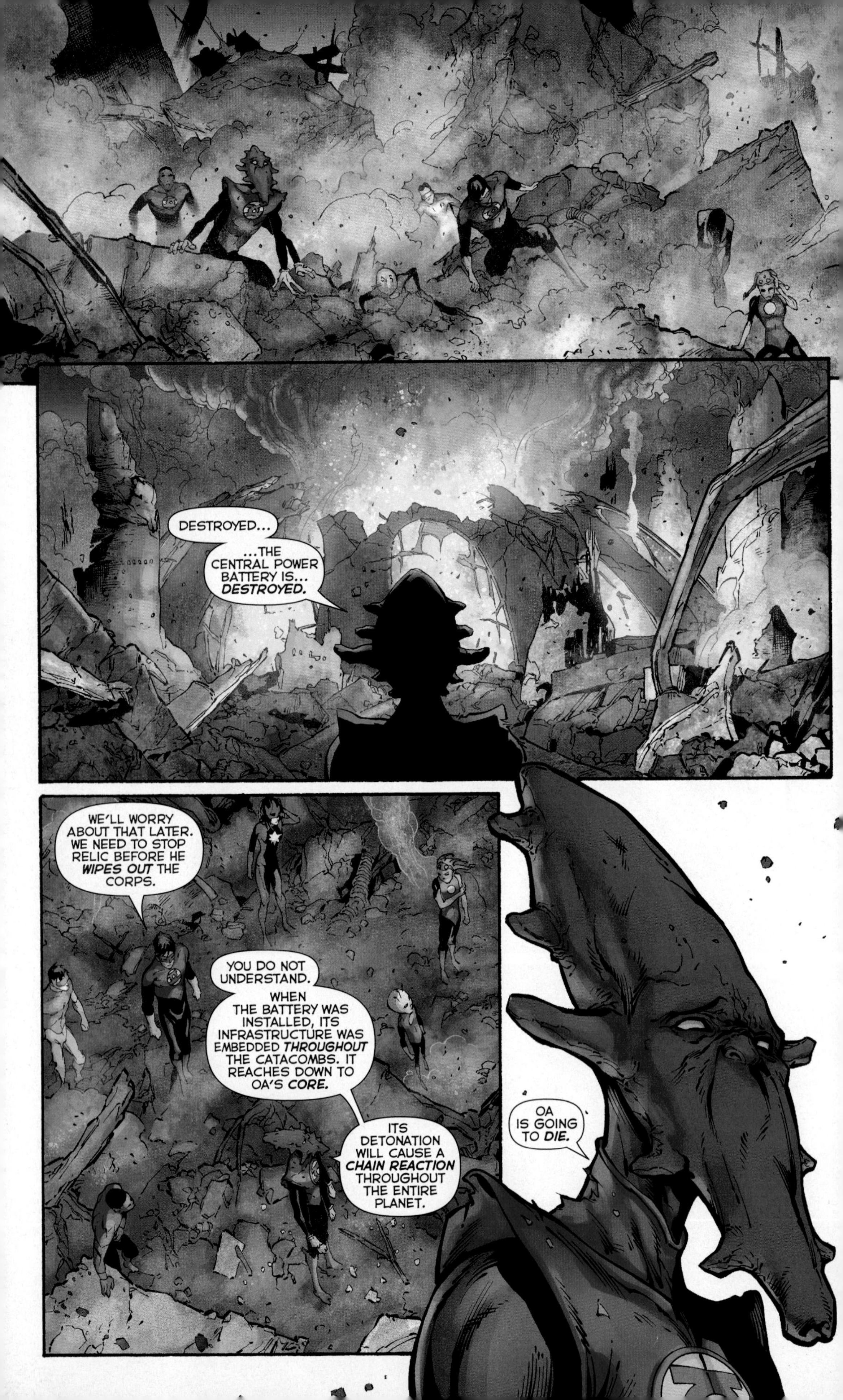

DESTROYED...
...THE CENTRAL POWER BATTERY IS... DESTROYED.
WE'LL WORRY ABOUT THAT LATER. WE NEED TO STOP RELIC BEFORE HE WIPES OUT THE CORPS.
YOU DO NOT UNDERSTAND.
WHEN THE BATTERY WAS INSTALLED, ITS INFRASTRUCTURE WAS EMBEDDED THROUGHOUT THE CATACOMBS. IT REACHES DOWN TO OA'S CORE.
ITS DETONATION WILL CAUSE A CHAIN REACTION THROUGHOUT THE ENTIRE PLANET.
OA IS GOING TO DIE.

ELSEWHERE IN "LIGHTS OUT"...

Salaak's unbelievable prediction came true: the destruction of the Central Power Battery destabilized the very core of Oa. As the planet shook itself apart, Hal Jordan led a massive evacuation of the Green Lantern homeworld — and John Stewart and his untested new recruits covered their getaway by distracting Relic with an all-out assault. Ergann, the nomadic new Lantern of Sector 1234, gave his life to hold Relic back as Oa exploded... but Relic, unfortunately, survived. The rest of the Lanterns believed John's team to be lost as well — but instead of rejoining their comrades, John had taken his squad to Nok, the home of the mysterious Indigo Tribe.

Shaken by their loss, Hal Jordan decided to lead the Corps into the arms of the enemy: they would travel to Ysmault and seek help from the Red Lanterns, the dangerous maniacs that Hal had just sent Guy Gardner to infiltrate. But the universe had one more setback in store, as the fantastically powerful Entities, the living avatars of the emotional spectrum, suddenly arrived and possessed Kyle Rayner, sweeping the Green Lantern Corps away to Ysmault and taking Kyle away for their own purposes. It took the intervention of the New Guardians to break the Entities' control over Kyle, but with the Entities inside him, he now saw the conflict the way they did: Relic was right. The emotional spectrum was being depleted, and the universe would surely die as a result. Relic had taken up a post at the Source Wall, attempting to break through the barrier and into the reservoir beyond, with the intent of replenishing it... and Kyle and the Guardians would have to help him.

And on Ysmault, Hal Jordan and the Corps didn't receive the welcome they expected from Guy Gardner, who in his short time with the Red Lanterns had quickly gotten in over his head. His first spectacular outburst of rage had led to his beating their leader, Atrocitus, to the brink of death, and taking his red ring. Guy's influence on the Reds was uncertain, and he could only stay alive if they believed he was one of them and not still a Green Lantern in disguise — so an armada of Greens asking for help was the last thing he needed! To get the help of the Red Lanterns, Hal Jordan would have to offer them something in return — their own space sector to patrol, free of the influence of Green Lanterns. With that deal in place, the Red and Green Lanterns were tenuously united against Relic — but first, they had to find him...

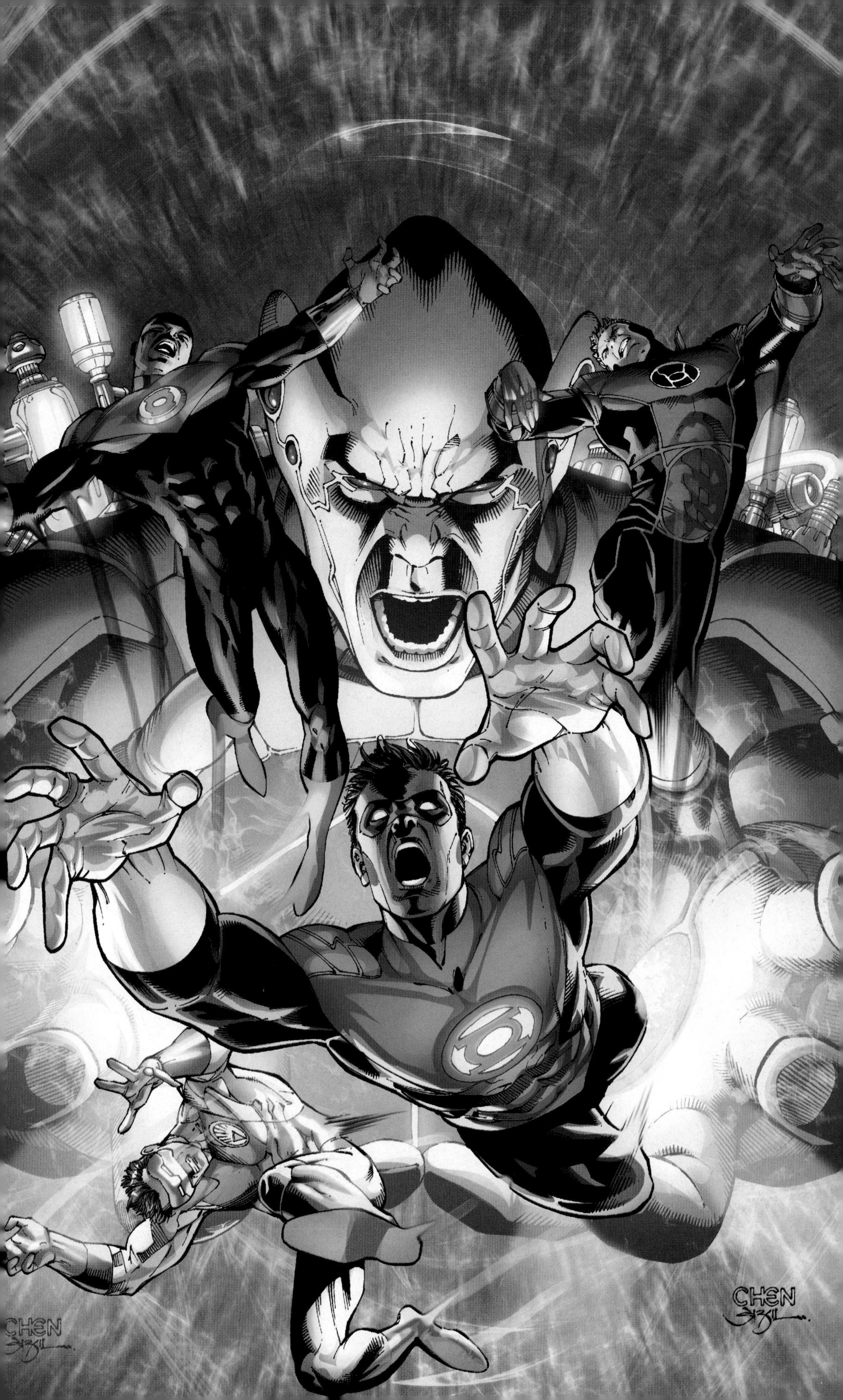
CHEN
CHEN

ROBERT VENDITTI writer SEAN CHEN penciller JON SIBAL & WALDEN WONG inkers
cover art by SEAN CHEN, JON SIBAL & ALEX SINCLAIR

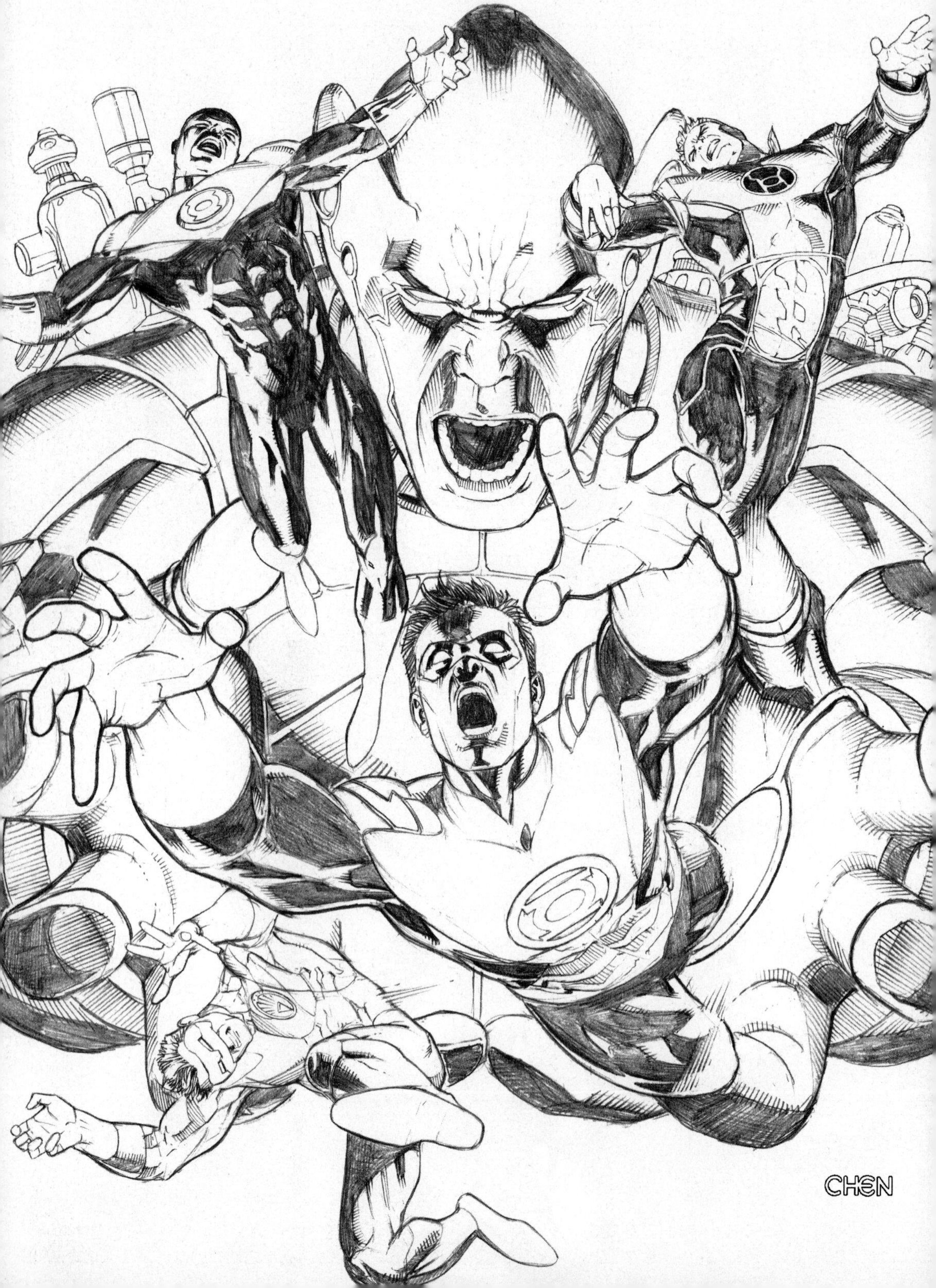
CHEN

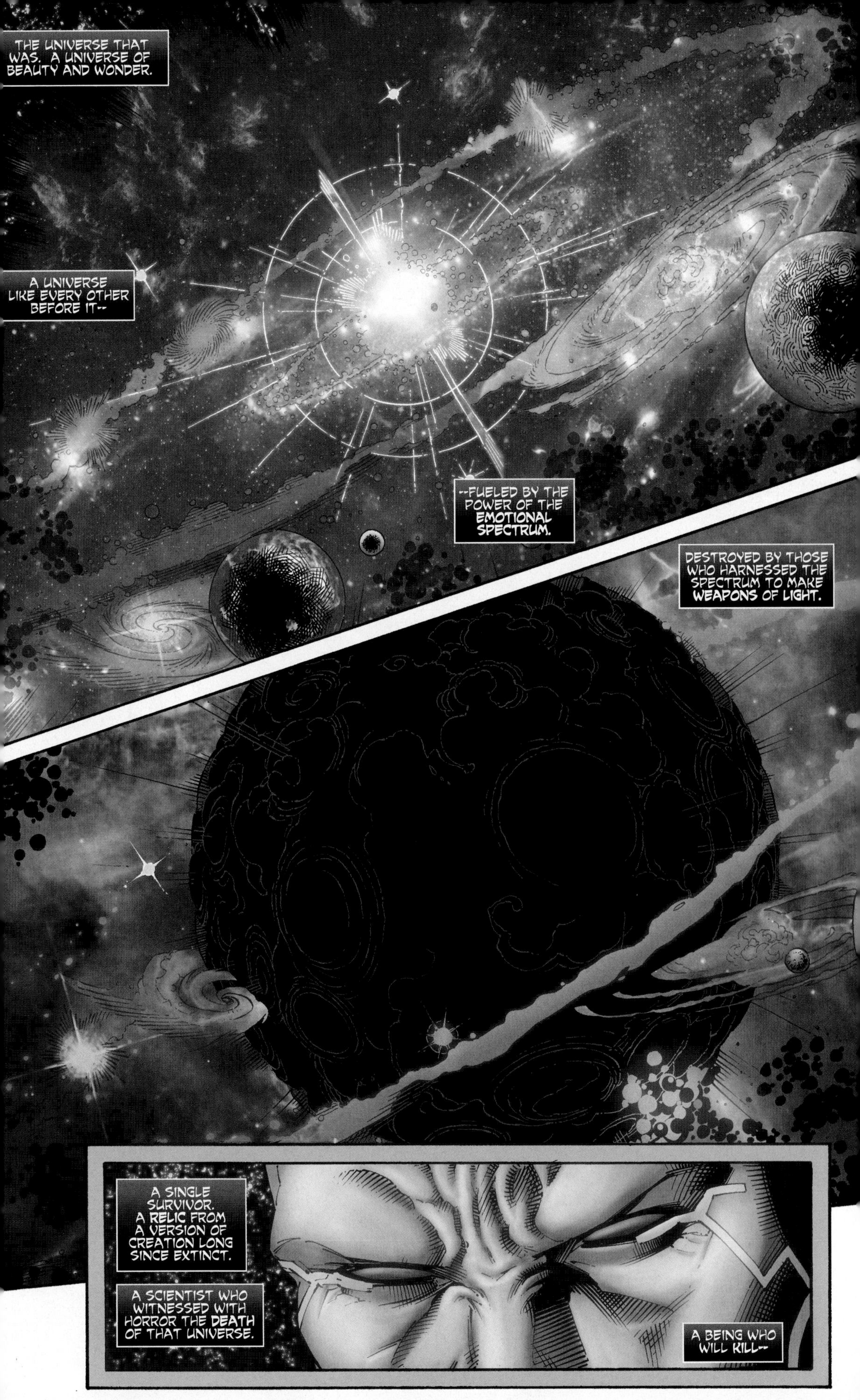
THE UNIVERSE THAT WAS. A UNIVERSE OF BEAUTY AND WONDER.
A UNIVERSE LIKE EVERY OTHER BEFORE IT--
--FUELED BY THE POWER OF THE EMOTIONAL SPECTRUM.
DESTROYED BY THOSE WHO HARNESSED THE SPECTRUM TO MAKE WEAPONS OF LIGHT.
A SINGLE SURVIVOR. A RELIC FROM A VERSION OF CREATION LONG SINCE EXTINCT.
A SCIENTIST WHO WITNESSED WITH HORROR THE DEATH OF THAT UNIVERSE.
A BEING WHO WILL KILL--

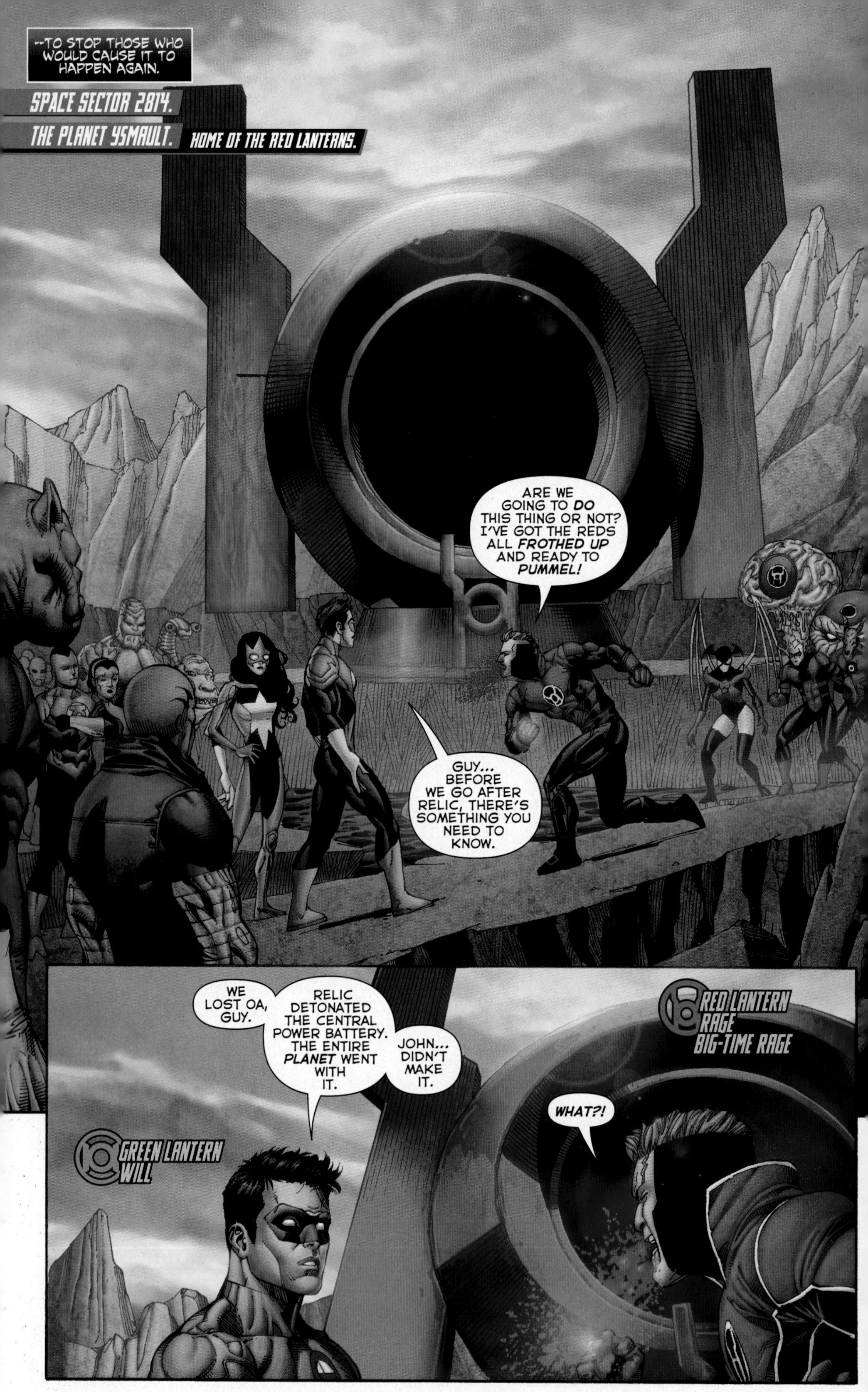
--TO STOP THOSE WHO WOULD CAUSE IT TO HAPPEN AGAIN.
SPACE SECTOR 2814.
THE PLANET YSMAULT.
HOME OF THE RED LANTERNS.
ARE WE GOING TO DO THIS THING OR NOT? I'VE GOT THE REDS ALL FROTHED UP AND READY TO PUMMEL!
GUY... BEFORE WE GO AFTER RELIC, THERE'S SOMETHING YOU NEED TO KNOW.
WE LOST OA, GUY.
RELIC DETONATED THE CENTRAL POWER BATTERY. THE ENTIRE PLANET WENT WITH IT.
JOHN... DIDN'T MAKE IT.
RED LANTERN RAGE BIG-TIME RAGE
WHAT?!
GREEN LANTERN WILL

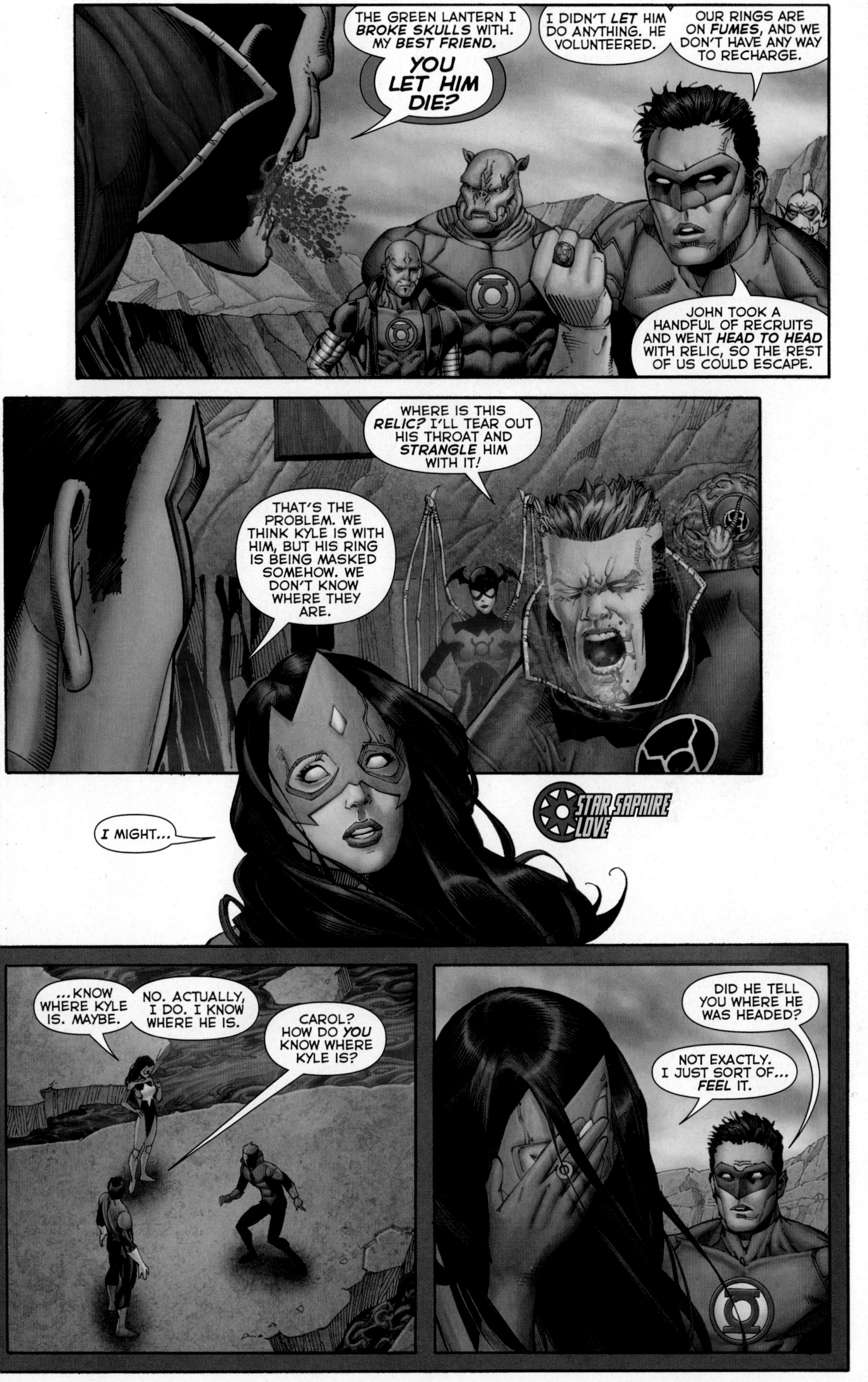

THE GREEN LANTERN I BROKE SKULLS WITH. MY BEST FRIEND.
YOU LET HIM DIE?
I DIDN'T LET HIM DO ANYTHING. HE VOLUNTEERED.
OUR RINGS ARE ON FUMES, AND WE DON'T HAVE ANY WAY TO RECHARGE.
JOHN TOOK A HANDFUL OF RECRUITS AND WENT HEAD TO HEAD WITH RELIC, SO THE REST OF US COULD ESCAPE.
WHERE IS THIS RELIC? I'LL TEAR OUT HIS THROAT AND STRANGLE HIM WITH IT!
THAT'S THE PROBLEM. WE THINK KYLE IS WITH HIM, BUT HIS RING IS BEING MASKED SOMEHOW. WE DON'T KNOW WHERE THEY ARE.
STAR SAPHIRE LOVE
I MIGHT...
...KNOW WHERE KYLE IS. MAYBE.
NO. ACTUALLY, I DO. I KNOW WHERE HE IS.
CAROL? HOW DO YOU KNOW WHERE KYLE IS?
DID HE TELL YOU WHERE HE WAS HEADED?
NOT EXACTLY. I JUST SORT OF... FEEL IT.

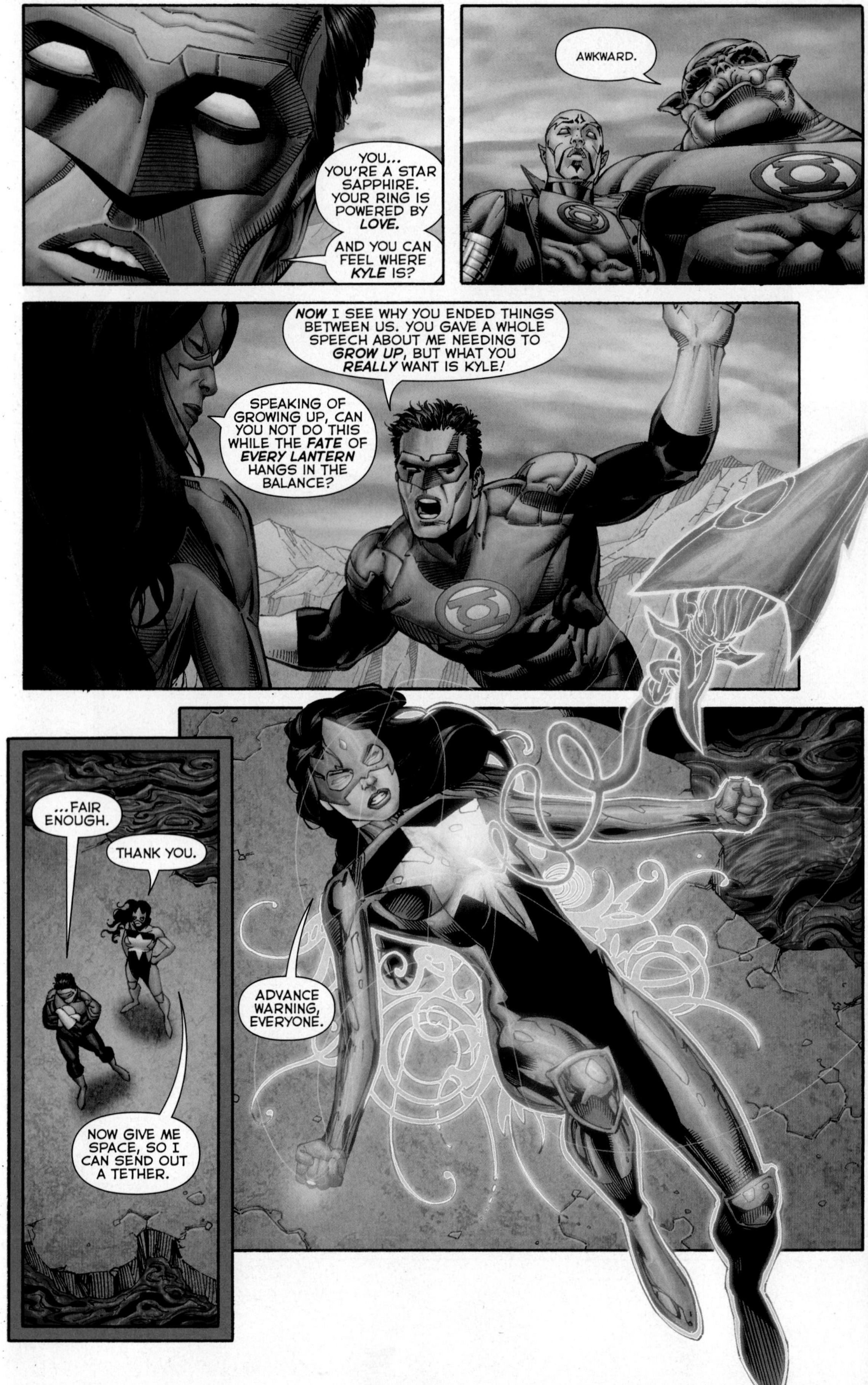
YOU... YOU'RE A STAR SAPPHIRE. YOUR RING IS POWERED BY LOVE.
AND YOU CAN FEEL WHERE KYLE IS?
AWKWARD.
NOW I SEE WHY YOU ENDED THINGS BETWEEN US. YOU GAVE A WHOLE SPEECH ABOUT ME NEEDING TO GROW UP, BUT WHAT YOU REALLY WANT IS KYLE!
SPEAKING OF GROWING UP, CAN YOU NOT DO THIS WHILE THE FATE OF EVERY LANTERN HANGS IN THE BALANCE?
...FAIR ENOUGH.
THANK YOU.
NOW GIVE ME SPACE, SO I CAN SEND OUT A TETHER.
ADVANCE WARNING, EVERYONE.

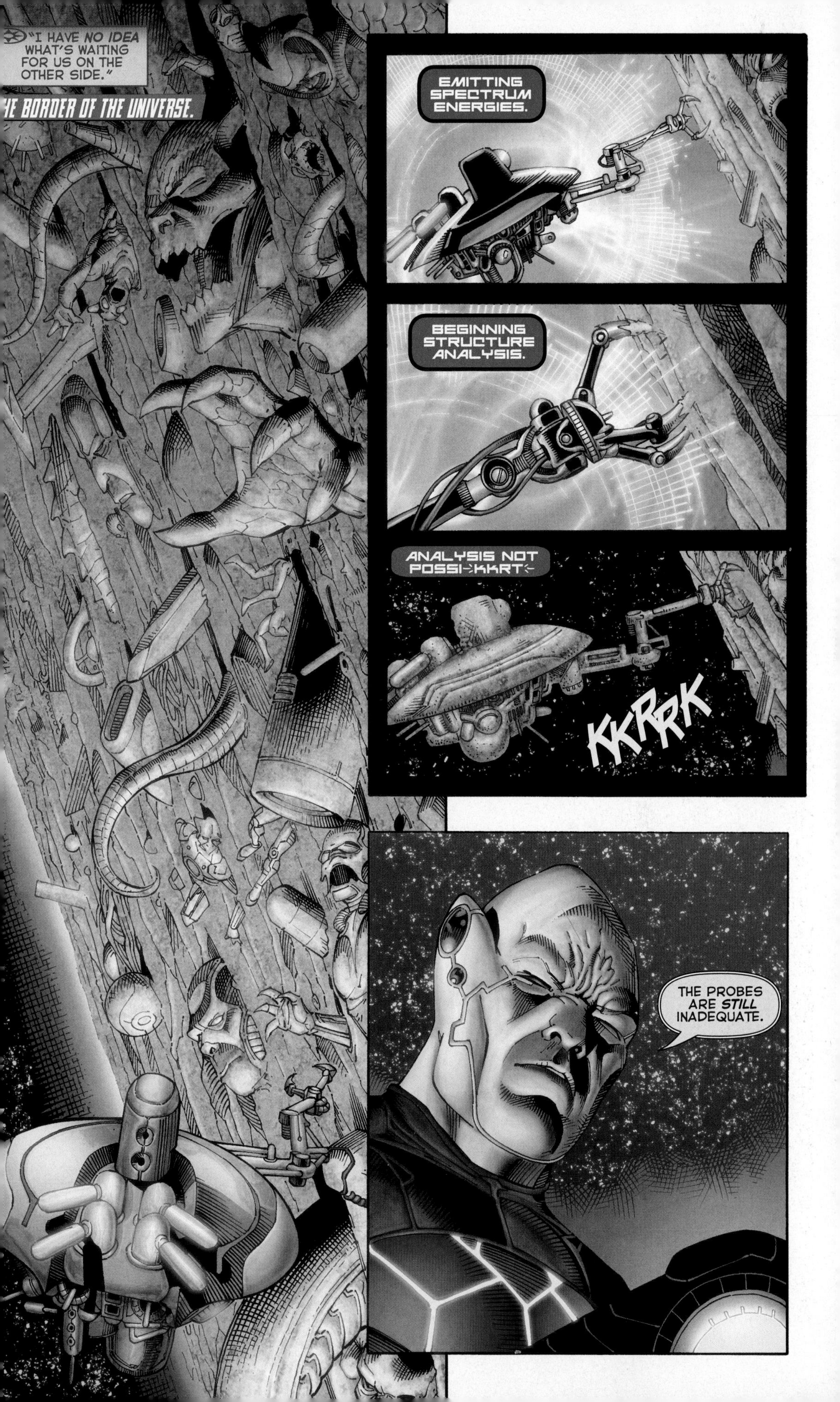
"I HAVE NO IDEA WHAT'S WAITING FOR US ON THE OTHER SIDE."
HE BORDER OF THE UNIVERSE.
EMITTING SPECTRUM ENERGIES.
BEGINNING STRUCTURE ANALYSIS.
ANALYSIS NOT POSSI-KKRT-
KKRRK
THE PROBES ARE STILL INADEQUATE.

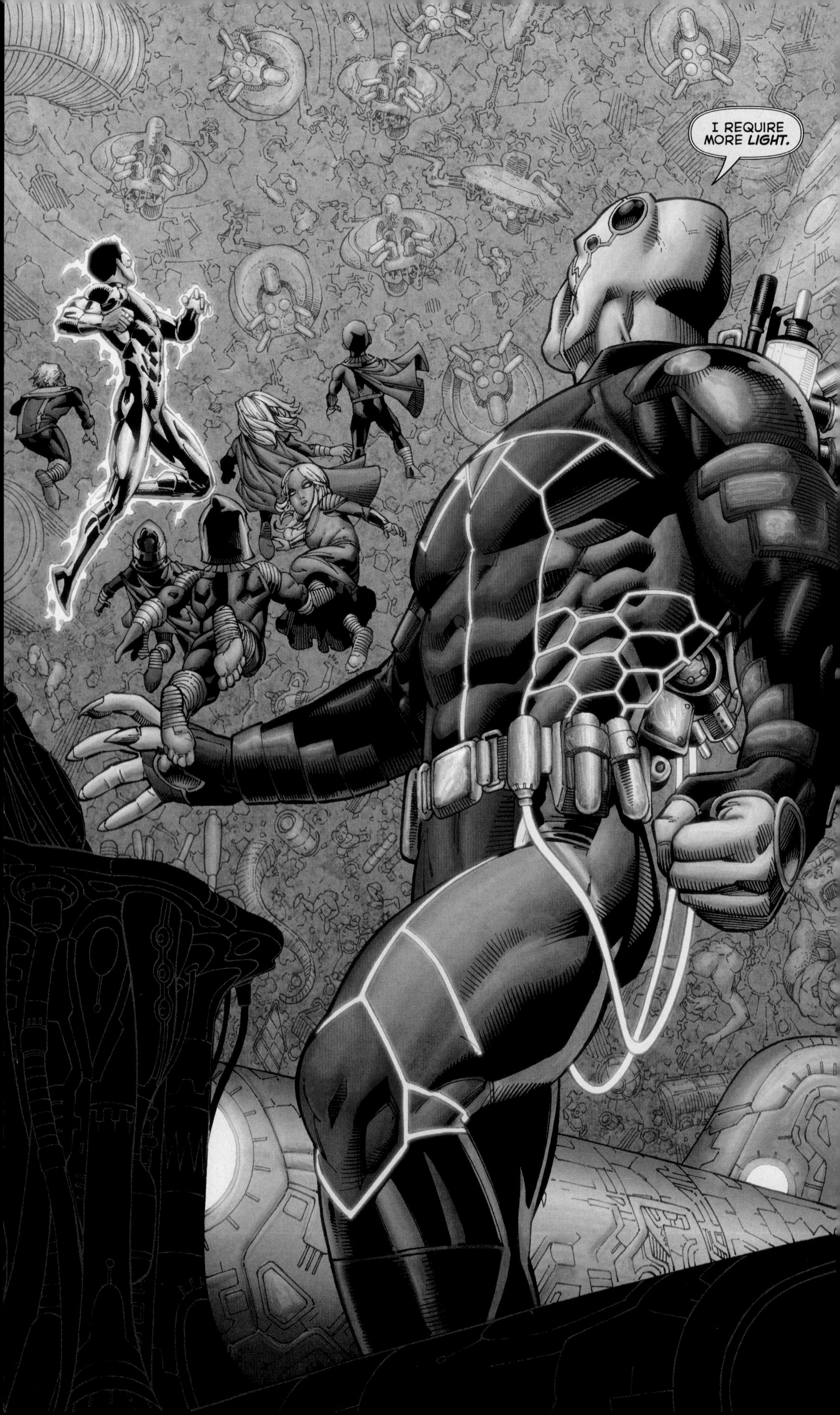
I REQUIRE MORE LIGHT.

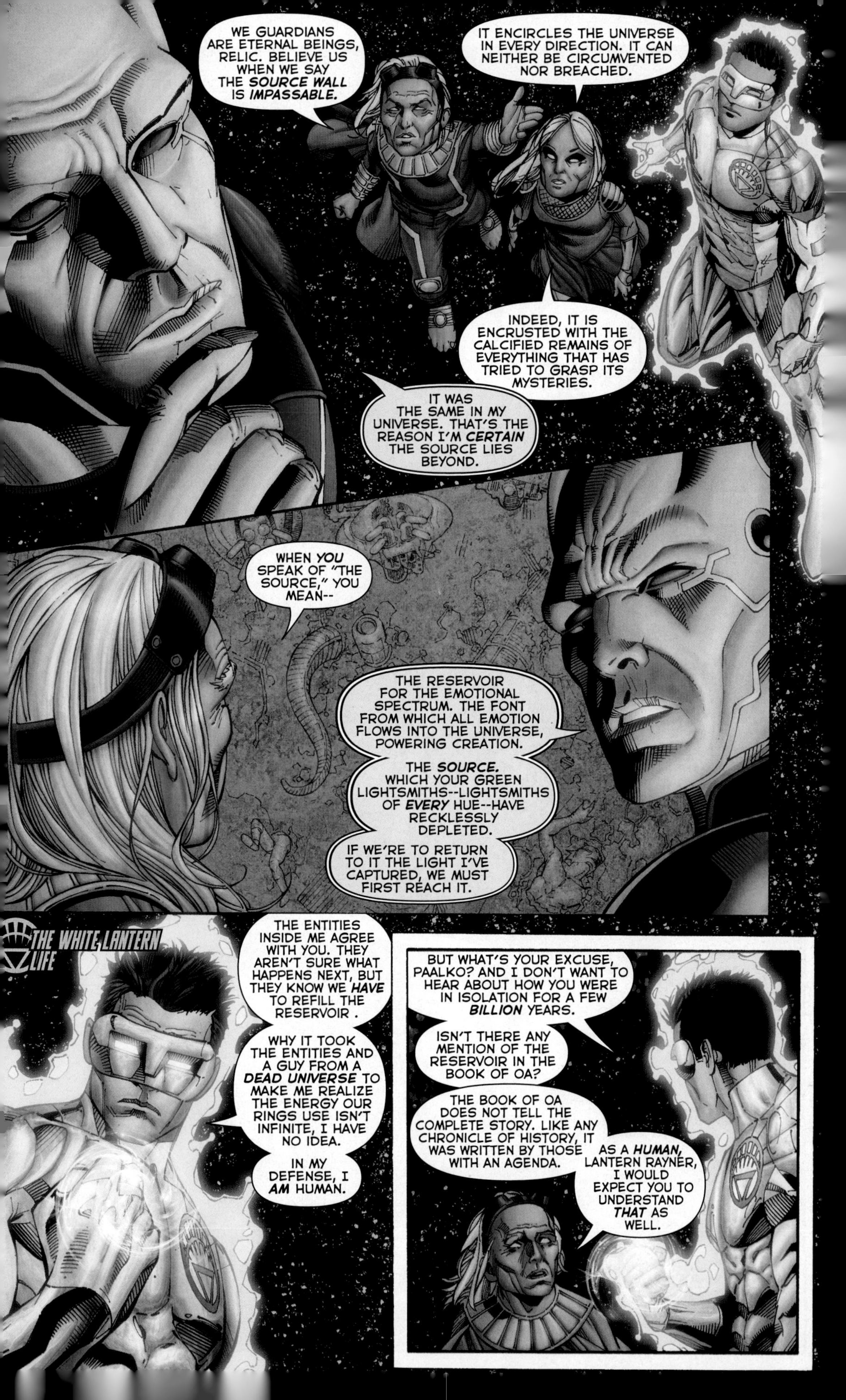
WE GUARDIANS ARE ETERNAL BEINGS, RELIC. BELIEVE US WHEN WE SAY THE SOURCE WALL IS IMPASSABLE.
IT ENCIRCLES THE UNIVERSE IN EVERY DIRECTION. IT CAN NEITHER BE CIRCUMVENTED NOR BREACHED.
INDEED, IT IS ENCRUSTED WITH THE CALCIFIED REMAINS OF EVERYTHING THAT HAS TRIED TO GRASP ITS MYSTERIES.
IT WAS THE SAME IN MY UNIVERSE. THAT'S THE REASON I'M CERTAIN THE SOURCE LIES BEYOND.
WHEN YOU SPEAK OF "THE SOURCE," YOU MEAN--
THE RESERVOIR FOR THE EMOTIONAL SPECTRUM. THE FONT FROM WHICH ALL EMOTION FLOWS INTO THE UNIVERSE, POWERING CREATION.
THE SOURCE. WHICH YOUR GREEN LIGHTSMITHS--LIGHTSMITHS OF EVERY HUE--HAVE RECKLESSLY DEPLETED.
IF WE'RE TO RETURN TO IT THE LIGHT I'VE CAPTURED, WE MUST FIRST REACH IT.
THE WHITE LANTERN LIFE
THE ENTITIES INSIDE ME AGREE WITH YOU. THEY AREN'T SURE WHAT HAPPENS NEXT, BUT THEY KNOW WE HAVE TO REFILL THE RESERVOIR .
WHY IT TOOK THE ENTITIES AND A GUY FROM A DEAD UNIVERSE TO MAKE ME REALIZE THE ENERGY OUR RINGS USE ISN'T INFINITE, I HAVE NO IDEA.
IN MY DEFENSE, I AM HUMAN.
BUT WHAT'S YOUR EXCUSE, PAALKO? AND I DON'T WANT TO HEAR ABOUT HOW YOU WERE IN ISOLATION FOR A FEW BILLION YEARS.
ISN'T THERE ANY MENTION OF THE RESERVOIR IN THE BOOK OF OA?
THE BOOK OF OA DOES NOT TELL THE COMPLETE STORY. LIKE ANY CHRONICLE OF HISTORY, IT WAS WRITTEN BY THOSE WITH AN AGENDA.
AS A HUMAN, LANTERN RAYNER, I WOULD EXPECT YOU TO UNDERSTAND THAT AS WELL.

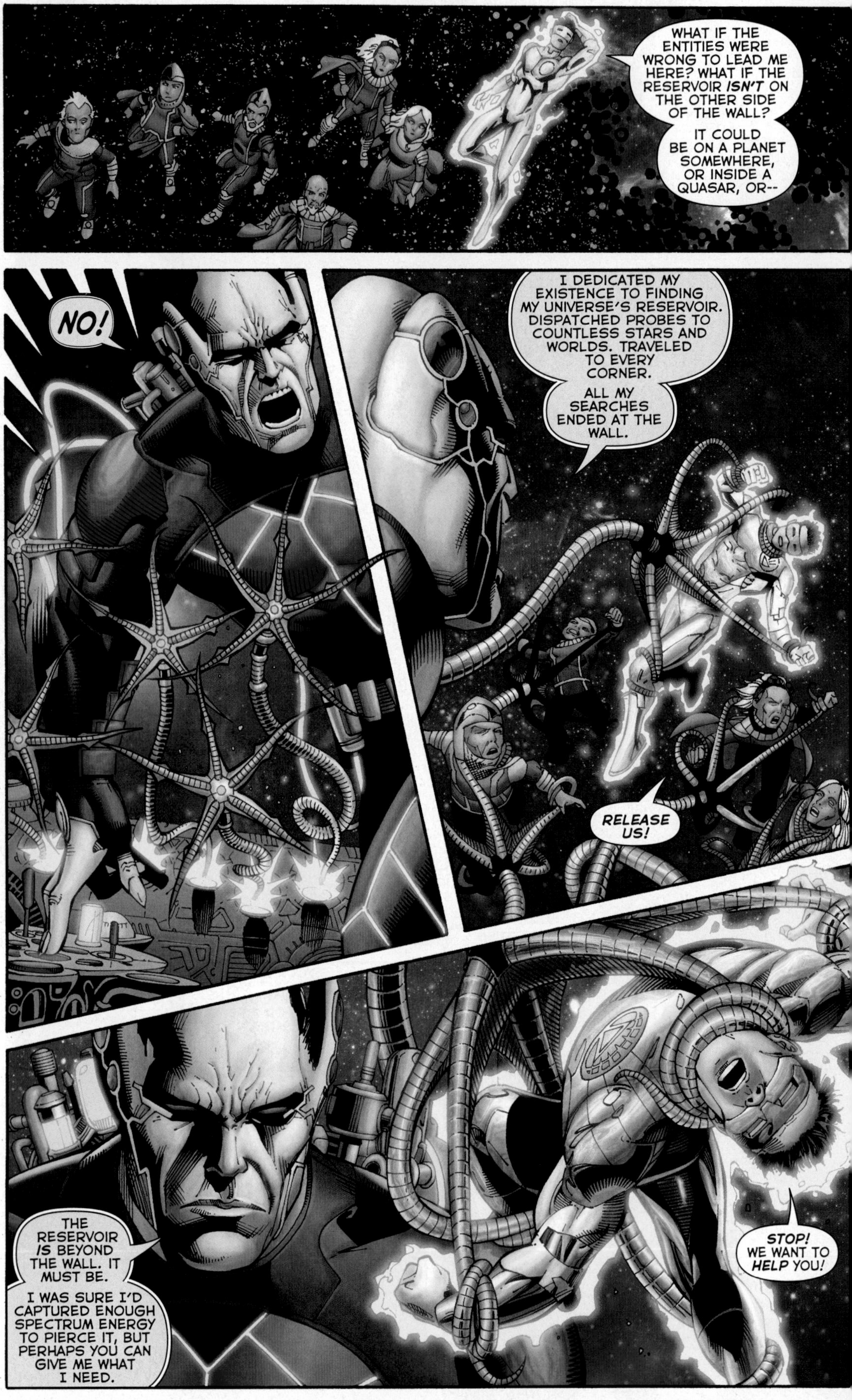
WHAT IF THE ENTITIES WERE WRONG TO LEAD ME HERE? WHAT IF THE RESERVOIR ISN'T ON THE OTHER SIDE OF THE WALL?
IT COULD BE ON A PLANET SOMEWHERE, OR INSIDE A QUASAR, OR--
NO!
I DEDICATED MY EXISTENCE TO FINDING MY UNIVERSE'S RESERVOIR. DISPATCHED PROBES TO COUNTLESS STARS AND WORLDS. TRAVELED TO EVERY CORNER.
ALL MY SEARCHES ENDED AT THE WALL.
RELEASE US!
THE RESERVOIR IS BEYOND THE WALL. IT MUST BE.
I WAS SURE I'D CAPTURED ENOUGH SPECTRUM ENERGY TO PIERCE IT, BUT PERHAPS YOU CAN GIVE ME WHAT I NEED.
STOP! WE WANT TO HELP YOU!

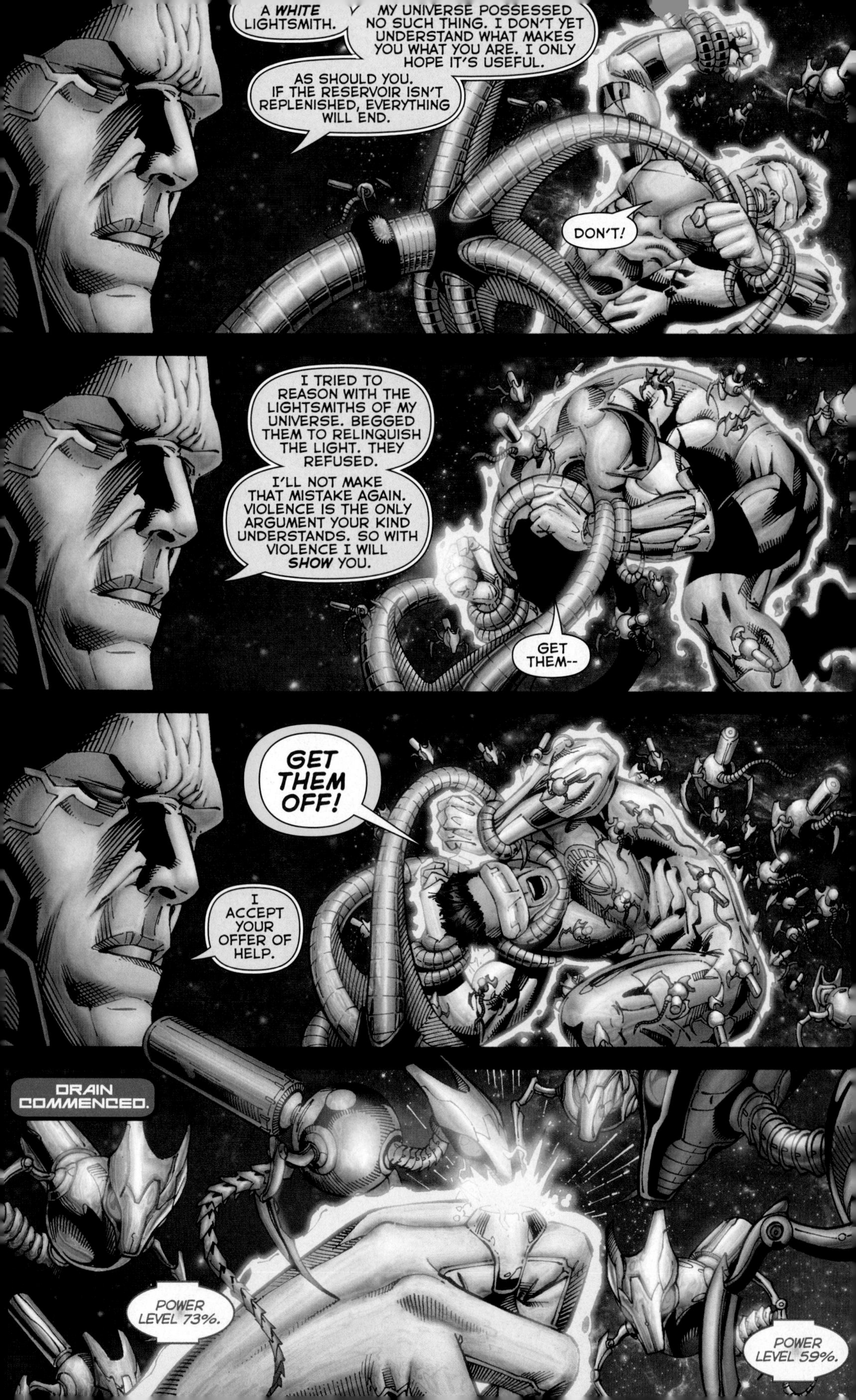

A *WHITE* LIGHTSMITH.
MY UNIVERSE POSSESSED NO SUCH THING. I DON'T YET UNDERSTAND WHAT MAKES YOU WHAT YOU ARE. I ONLY HOPE IT'S USEFUL.
AS SHOULD YOU. IF THE RESERVOIR ISN'T REPLENISHED, EVERYTHING WILL END.
DON'T!
I TRIED TO REASON WITH THE LIGHTSMITHS OF MY UNIVERSE. BEGGED THEM TO RELINQUISH THE LIGHT. THEY REFUSED.
I'LL NOT MAKE THAT MISTAKE AGAIN. VIOLENCE IS THE ONLY ARGUMENT YOUR KIND UNDERSTANDS. SO WITH VIOLENCE I WILL *SHOW* YOU.
GET THEM--
GET THEM OFF!
I ACCEPT YOUR OFFER OF HELP.
DRAIN COMMENCED.
POWER LEVEL 73%.
POWER LEVEL 59%.

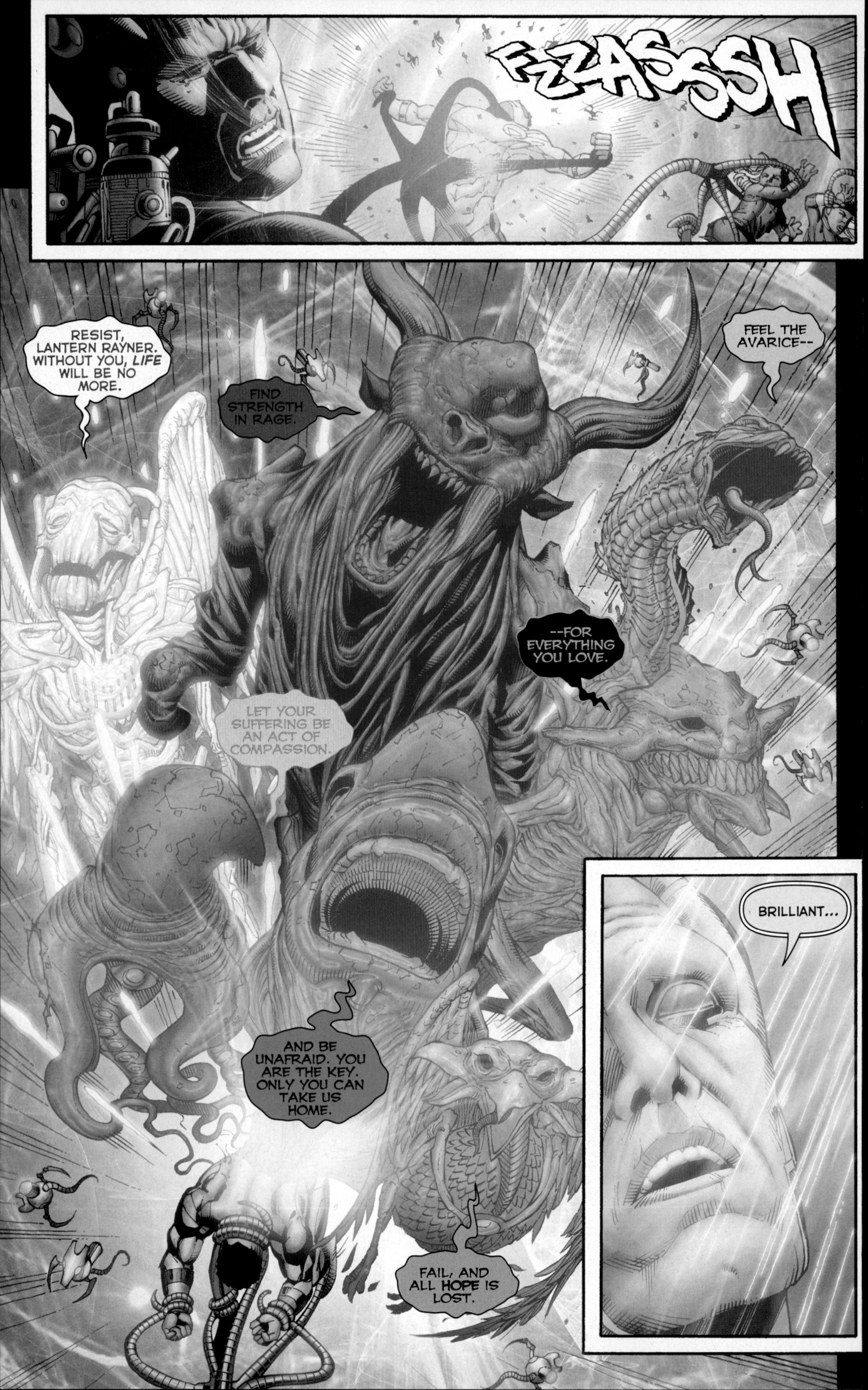
FZZASSSH
RESIST, LANTERN RAYNER. WITHOUT YOU, *LIFE* WILL BE NO MORE.
FIND STRENGTH IN RAGE.
FEEL THE AVARICE--
--FOR EVERYTHING YOU LOVE.
LET YOUR SUFFERING BE AN ACT OF COMPASSION.
AND BE UNAFRAID. YOU ARE THE KEY. ONLY YOU CAN TAKE US HOME.
FAIL, AND ALL **HOPE** IS LOST.
BRILLIANT...

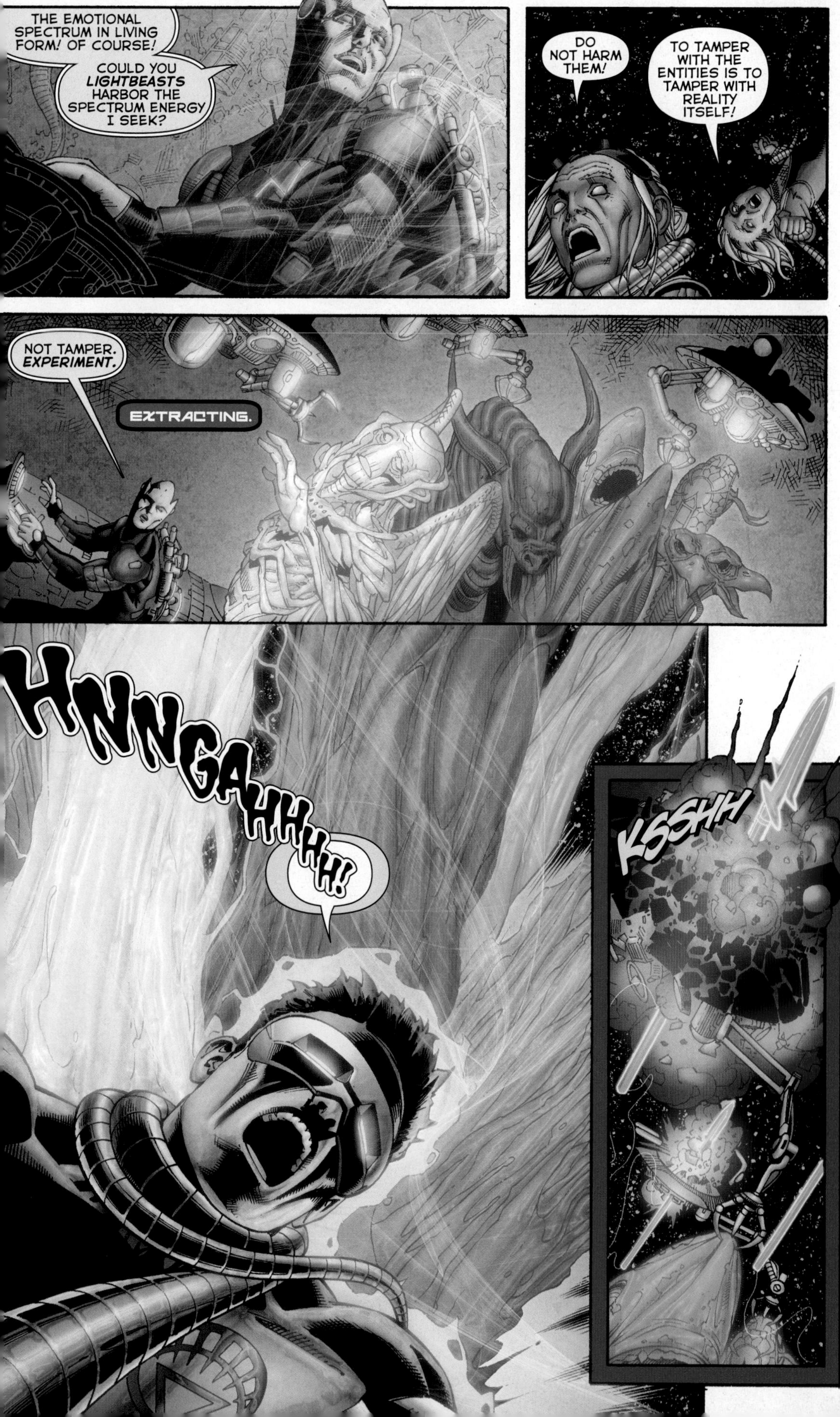

THE EMOTIONAL SPECTRUM IN LIVING FORM! OF COURSE!
COULD YOU LIGHTBEASTS HARBOR THE SPECTRUM ENERGY I SEEK?
DO NOT HARM THEM!
TO TAMPER WITH THE ENTITIES IS TO TAMPER WITH REALITY ITSELF!
NOT TAMPER. EXPERIMENT.
EXTRACTING.
HNNGAHHHHH!
KSSHH

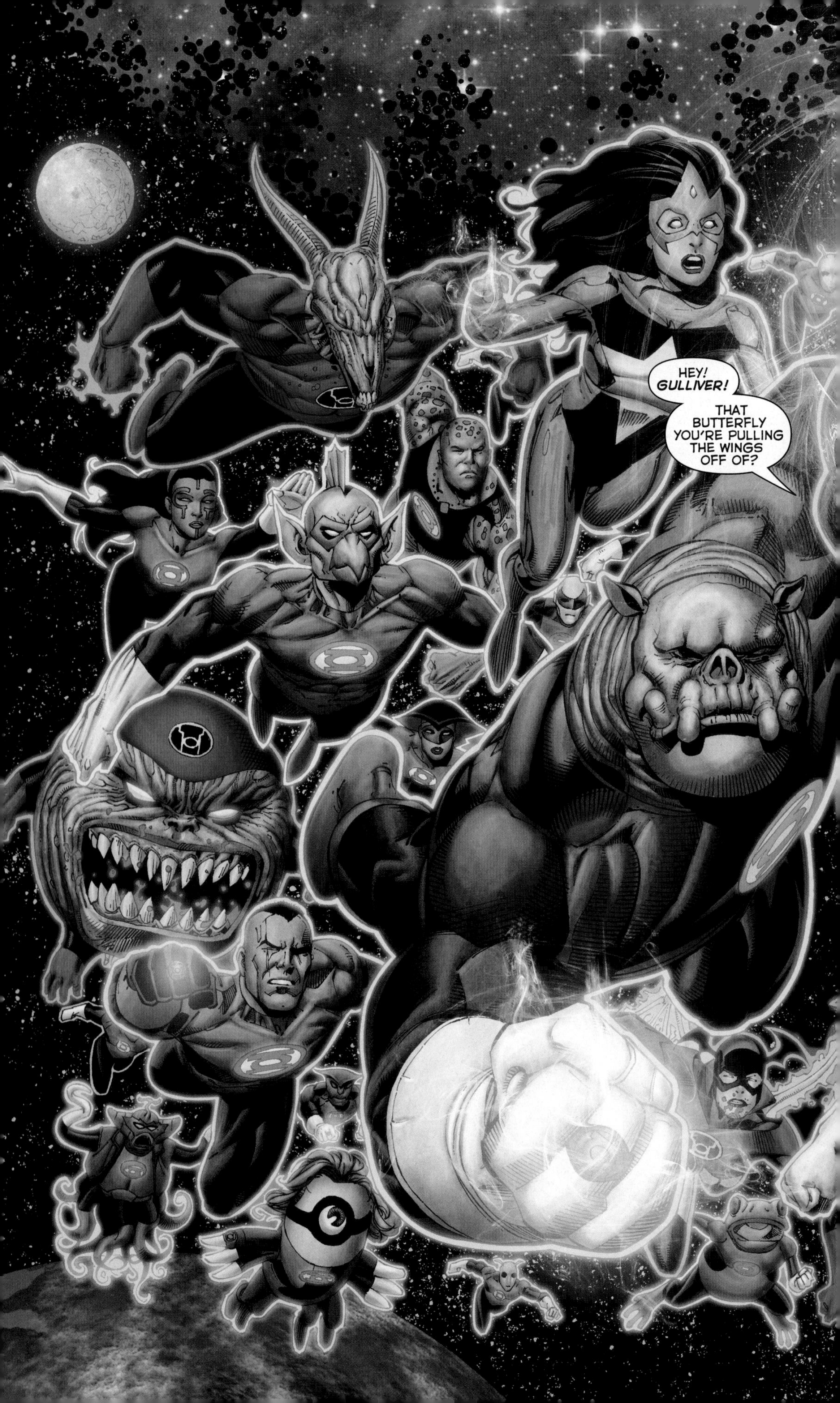
HEY! GULLIVER!
THAT BUTTERFLY YOU'RE PULLING THE WINGS OFF OF?

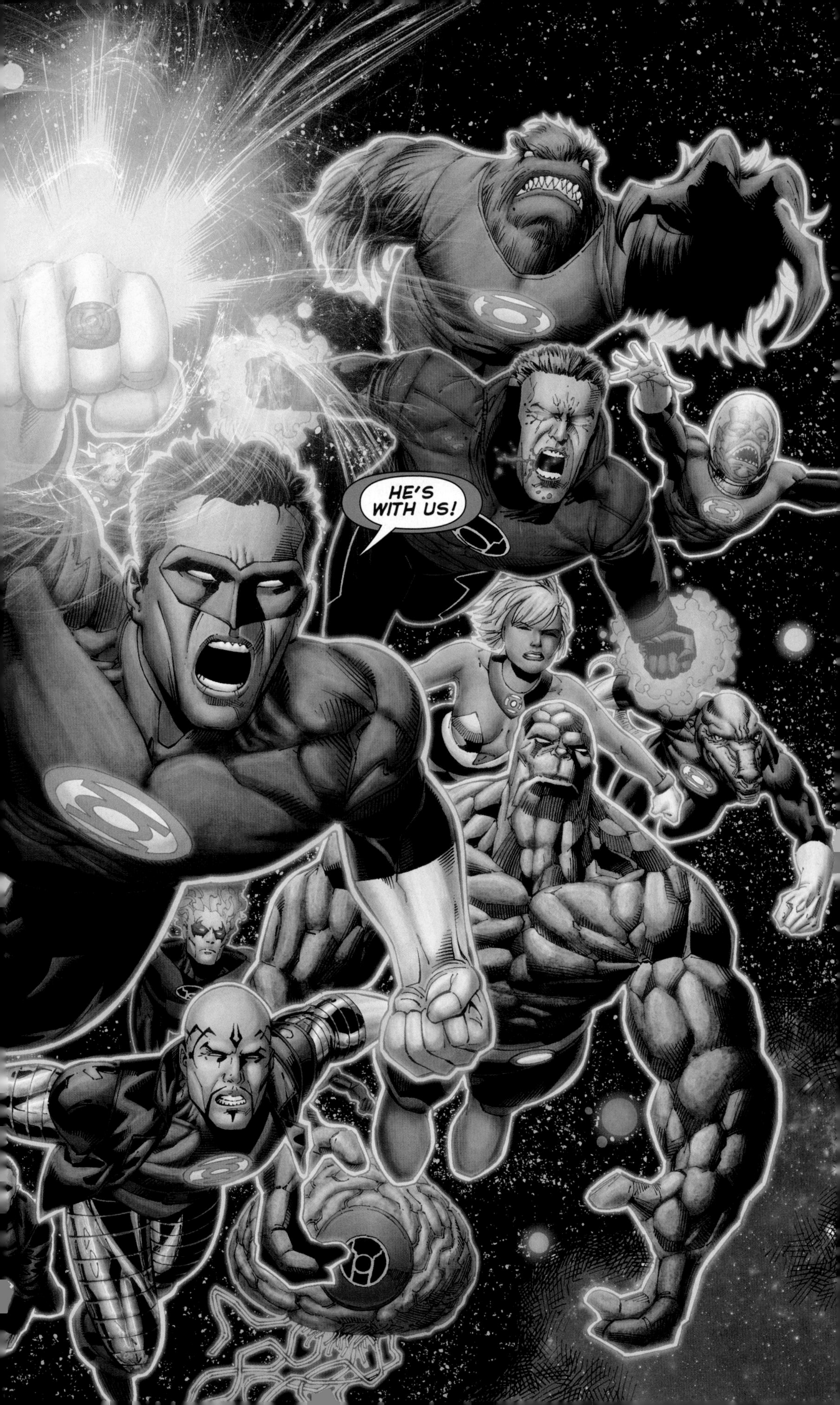
HE'S WITH US!

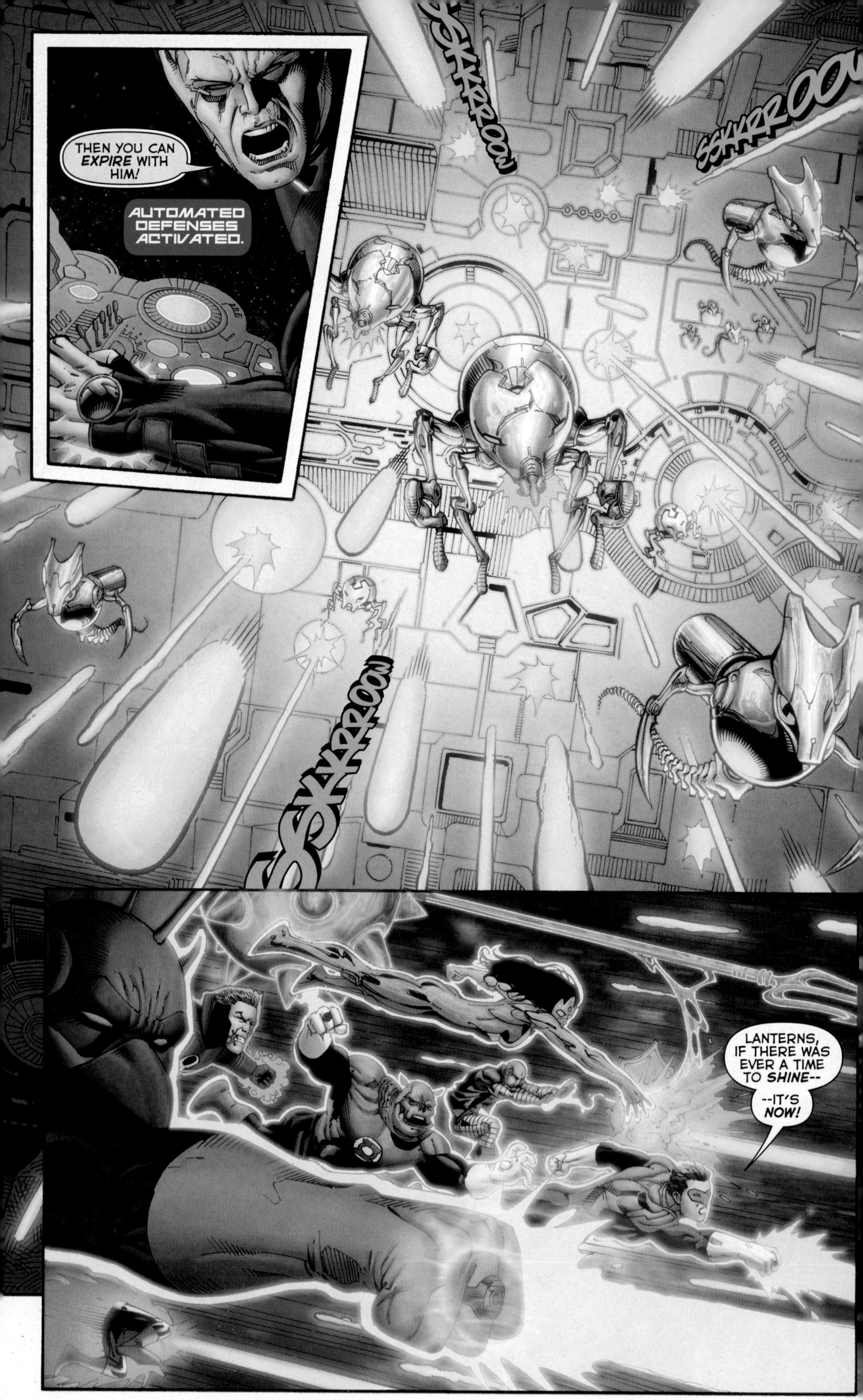

THEN YOU CAN *EXPIRE* WITH HIM!
AUTOMATED DEFENSES ACTIVATED.
SSKKRROOW
SSKKRROOOW
SSKKRROOOW
SSKKRROOW
SSKKRROOW
LANTERNS, IF THERE WAS EVER A TIME TO *SHINE*--
--IT'S *NOW!*

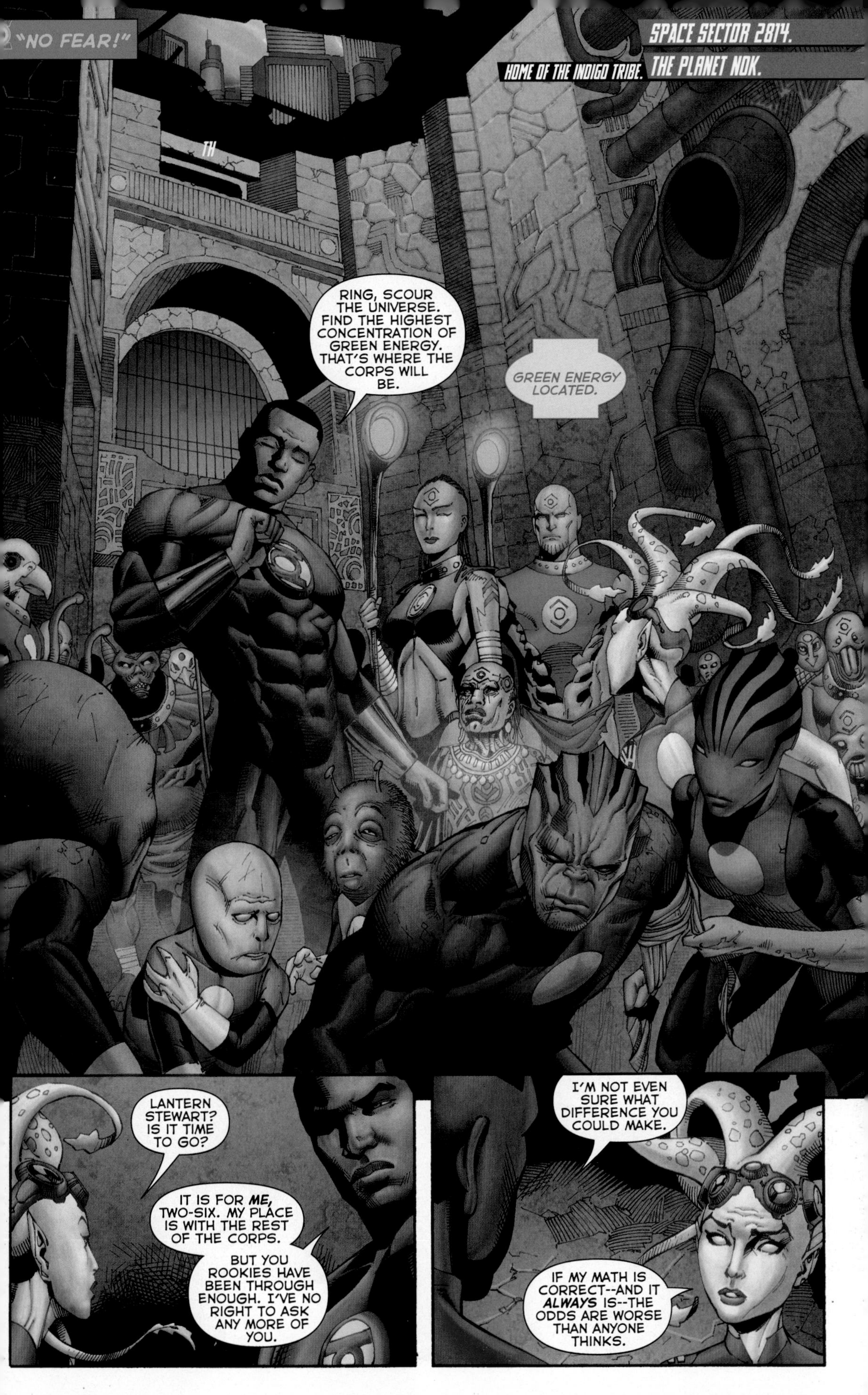

"NO FEAR!"
SPACE SECTOR 2814.
HOME OF THE INDIGO TRIBE. THE PLANET NOK.
TH
RING, SCOUR THE UNIVERSE. FIND THE HIGHEST CONCENTRATION OF GREEN ENERGY. THAT'S WHERE THE CORPS WILL BE.
GREEN ENERGY LOCATED.
LANTERN STEWART? IS IT TIME TO GO?
IT IS FOR ME, TWO-SIX. MY PLACE IS WITH THE REST OF THE CORPS.
BUT YOU ROOKIES HAVE BEEN THROUGH ENOUGH. I'VE NO RIGHT TO ASK ANY MORE OF YOU.
I'M NOT EVEN SURE WHAT DIFFERENCE YOU COULD MAKE.
IF MY MATH IS CORRECT--AND IT ALWAYS IS--THE ODDS ARE WORSE THAN ANYONE THINKS.

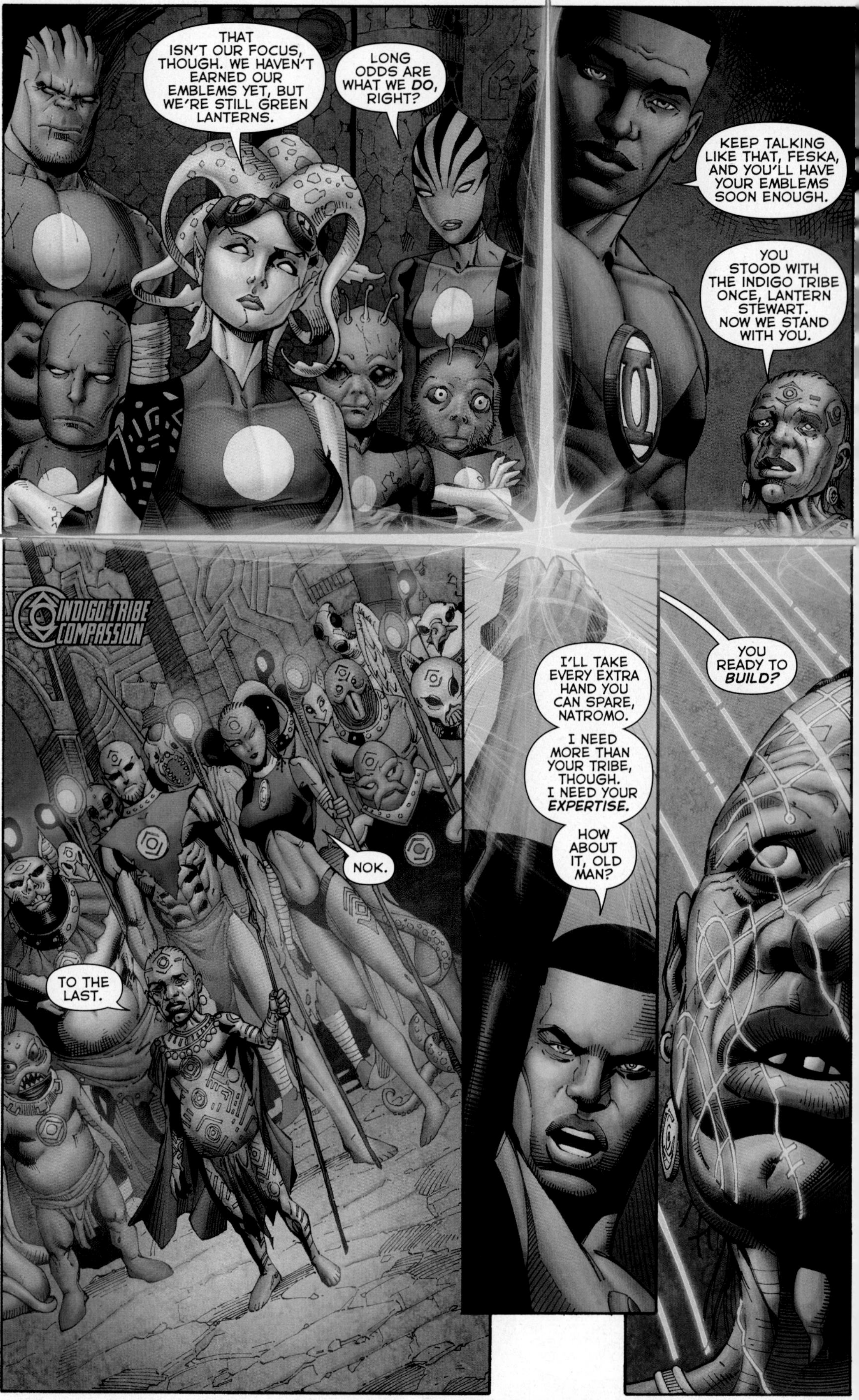
THAT ISN'T OUR FOCUS, THOUGH. WE HAVEN'T EARNED OUR EMBLEMS YET, BUT WE'RE STILL GREEN LANTERNS.
LONG ODDS ARE WHAT WE *DO*, RIGHT?
KEEP TALKING LIKE THAT, FESKA, AND YOU'LL HAVE YOUR EMBLEMS SOON ENOUGH.
YOU STOOD WITH THE INDIGO TRIBE ONCE, LANTERN STEWART. NOW WE STAND WITH YOU.
INDIGO TRIBE
COMPASSION
NOK.
TO THE LAST.
I'LL TAKE EVERY EXTRA HAND YOU CAN SPARE, NATROMO.
I NEED MORE THAN YOUR TRIBE, THOUGH. I NEED YOUR *EXPERTISE.*
HOW ABOUT IT, OLD MAN?
YOU READY TO *BUILD?*

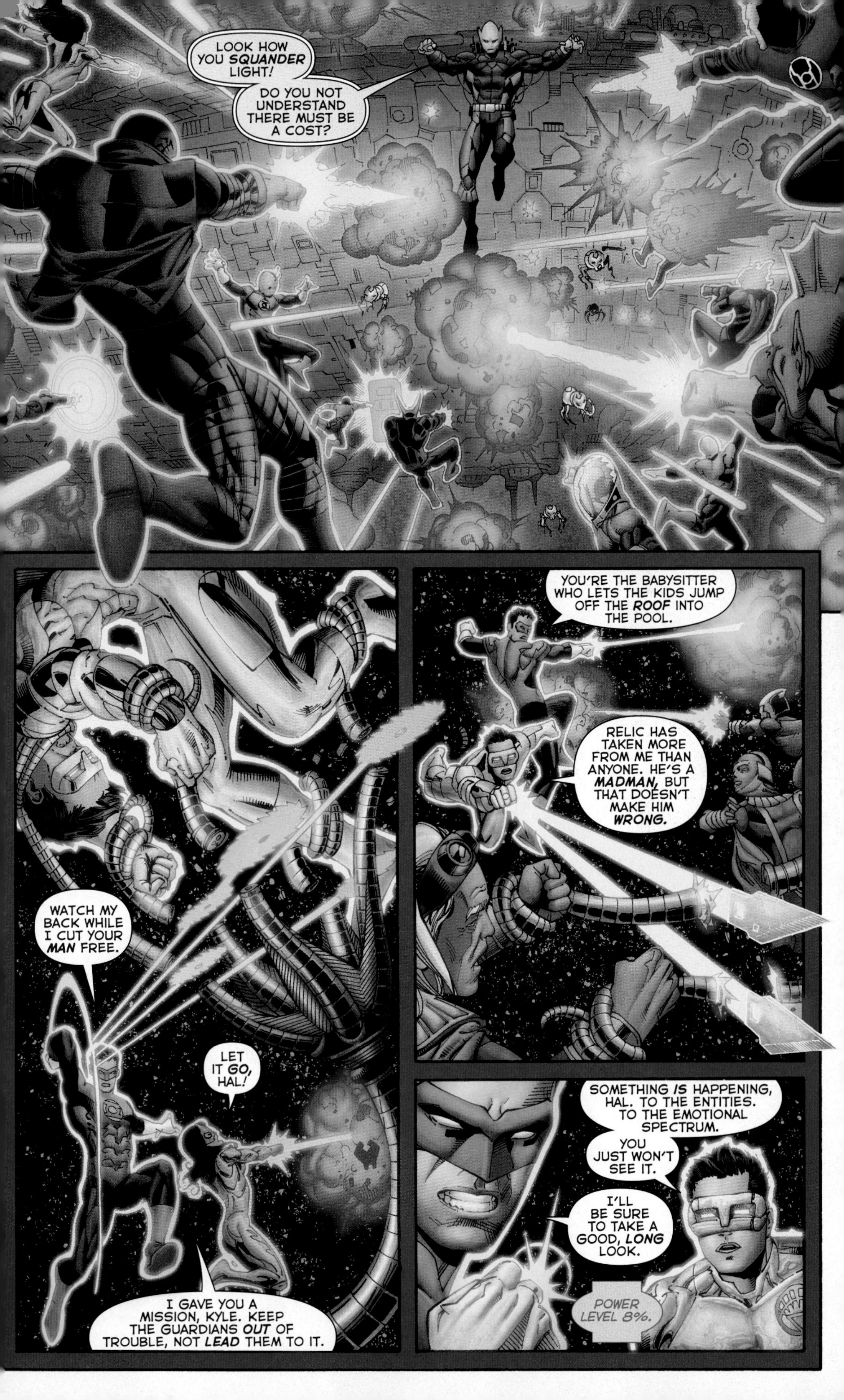
LOOK HOW YOU SQUANDER LIGHT!
DO YOU NOT UNDERSTAND THERE MUST BE A COST?
WATCH MY BACK WHILE I CUT YOUR MAN FREE.
LET IT GO, HAL!
I GAVE YOU A MISSION, KYLE. KEEP THE GUARDIANS OUT OF TROUBLE, NOT LEAD THEM TO IT.
YOU'RE THE BABYSITTER WHO LETS THE KIDS JUMP OFF THE ROOF INTO THE POOL.
RELIC HAS TAKEN MORE FROM ME THAN ANYONE. HE'S A MADMAN, BUT THAT DOESN'T MAKE HIM WRONG.
SOMETHING IS HAPPENING, HAL. TO THE ENTITIES. TO THE EMOTIONAL SPECTRUM.
YOU JUST WON'T SEE IT.
I'LL BE SURE TO TAKE A GOOD, LONG LOOK.
POWER LEVEL 8%.

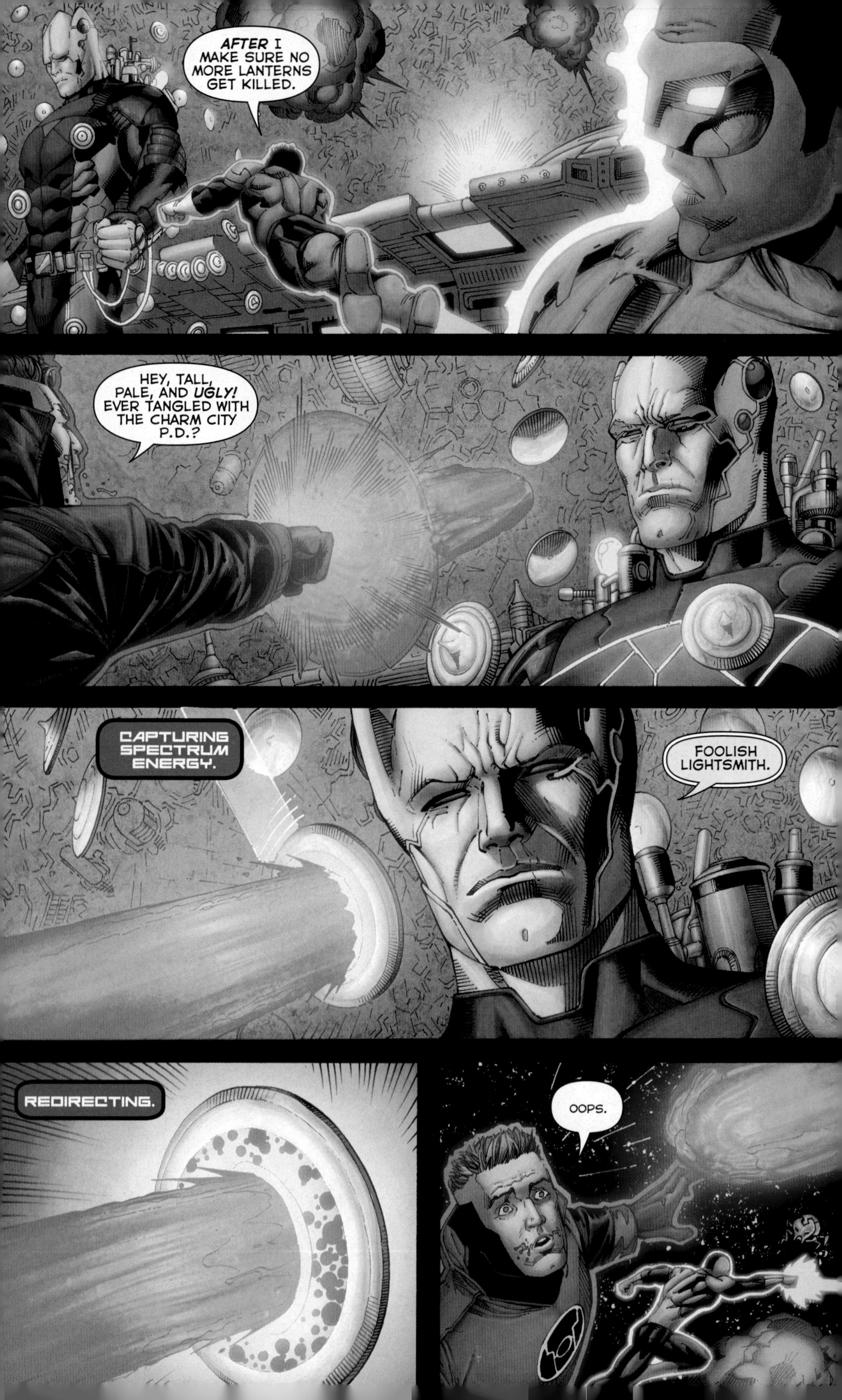

AFTER I MAKE SURE NO MORE LANTERNS GET KILLED.
HEY, TALL, PALE, AND UGLY! EVER TANGLED WITH THE CHARM CITY P.D.?
CAPTURING SPECTRUM ENERGY.
FOOLISH LIGHTSMITH.
REDIRECTING.
OOPS.

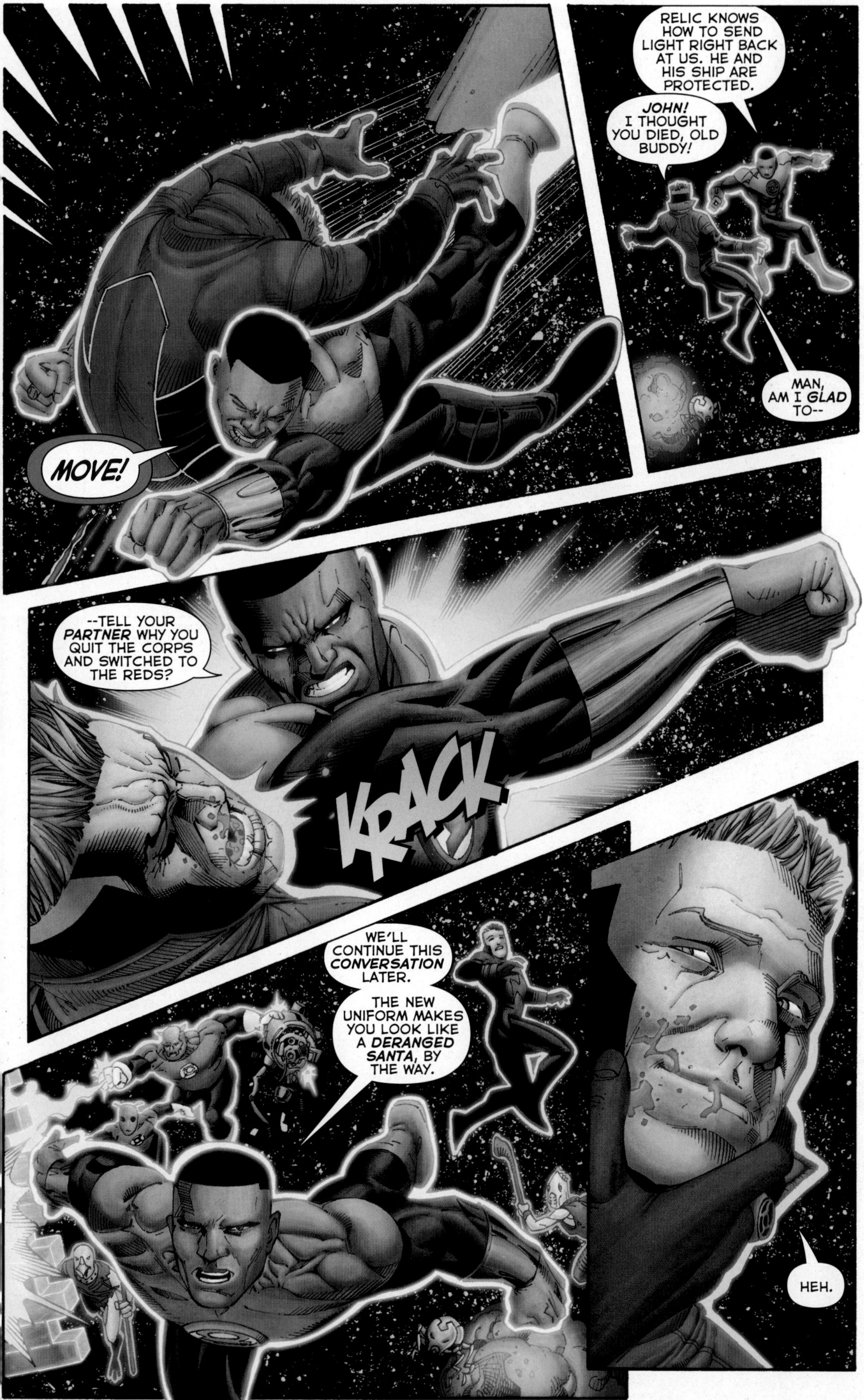
RELIC KNOWS HOW TO SEND LIGHT RIGHT BACK AT US. HE AND HIS SHIP ARE PROTECTED.
JOHN! I THOUGHT YOU DIED, OLD BUDDY!
MAN, AM I GLAD TO--
MOVE!
--TELL YOUR PARTNER WHY YOU QUIT THE CORPS AND SWITCHED TO THE REDS?
KRACK
WE'LL CONTINUE THIS CONVERSATION LATER.
THE NEW UNIFORM MAKES YOU LOOK LIKE A DERANGED SANTA, BY THE WAY.
HEH.

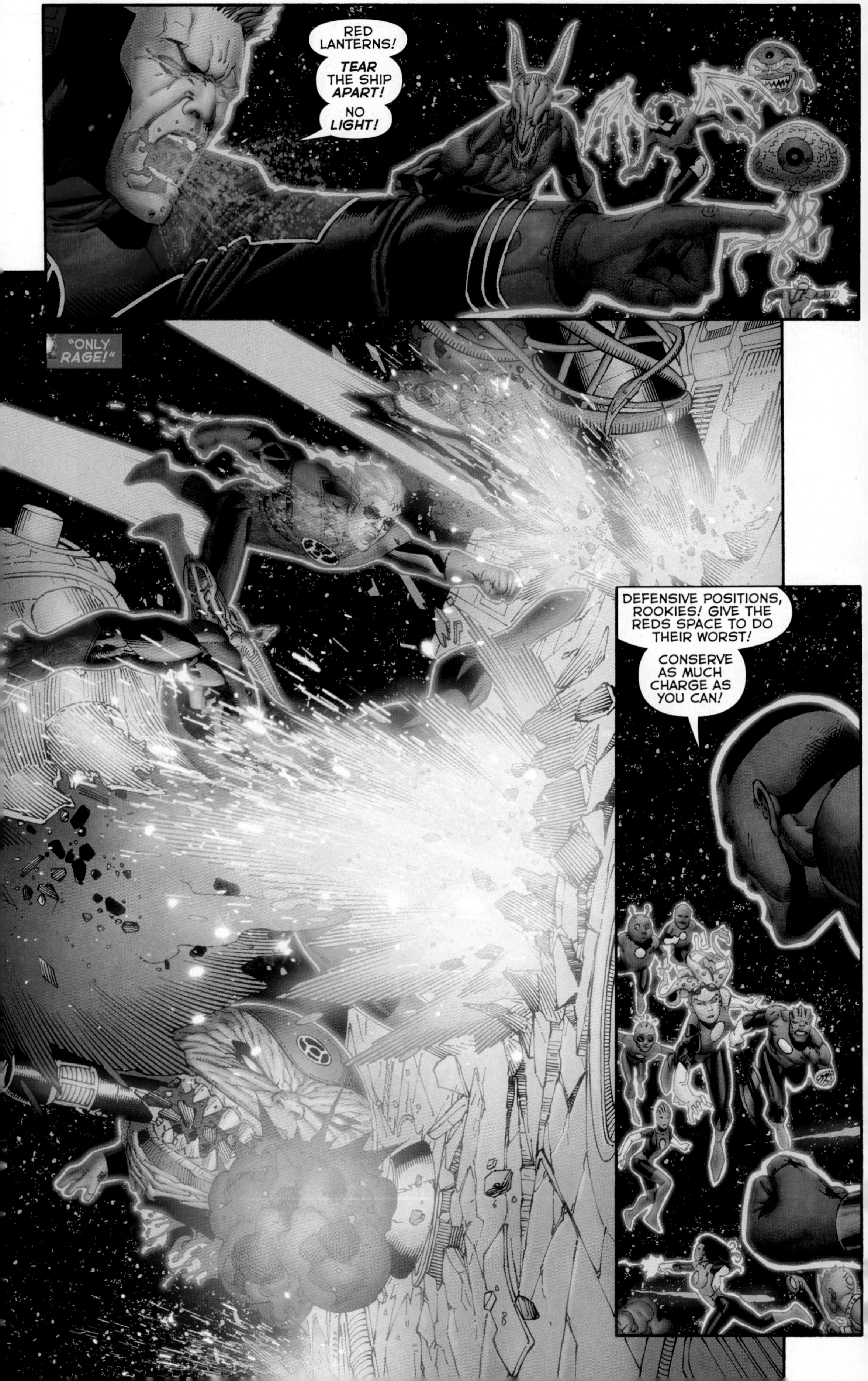
RED LANTERNS!
TEAR THE SHIP APART!
NO LIGHT!
"ONLY RAGE!"
DEFENSIVE POSITIONS, ROOKIES! GIVE THE REDS SPACE TO DO THEIR WORST!
CONSERVE AS MUCH CHARGE AS YOU CAN!

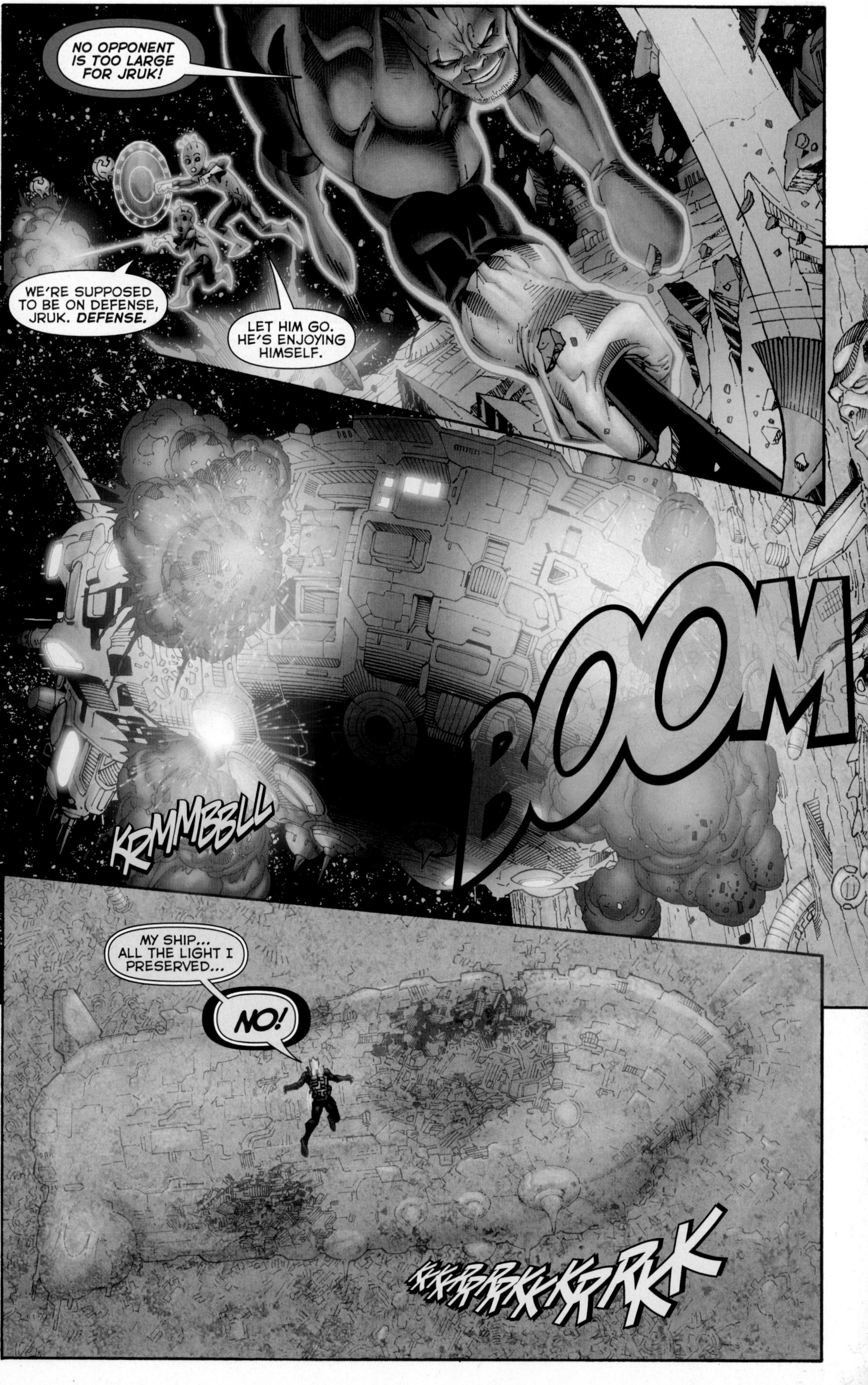
NO OPPONENT IS TOO LARGE FOR JRUK!
WE'RE SUPPOSED TO BE ON DEFENSE, JRUK. DEFENSE.
LET HIM GO. HE'S ENJOYING HIMSELF.
BOOM
KRMMMBBLL
MY SHIP... ALL THE LIGHT I PRESERVED...
NO!
KKKKRRRKKKKRRRKK

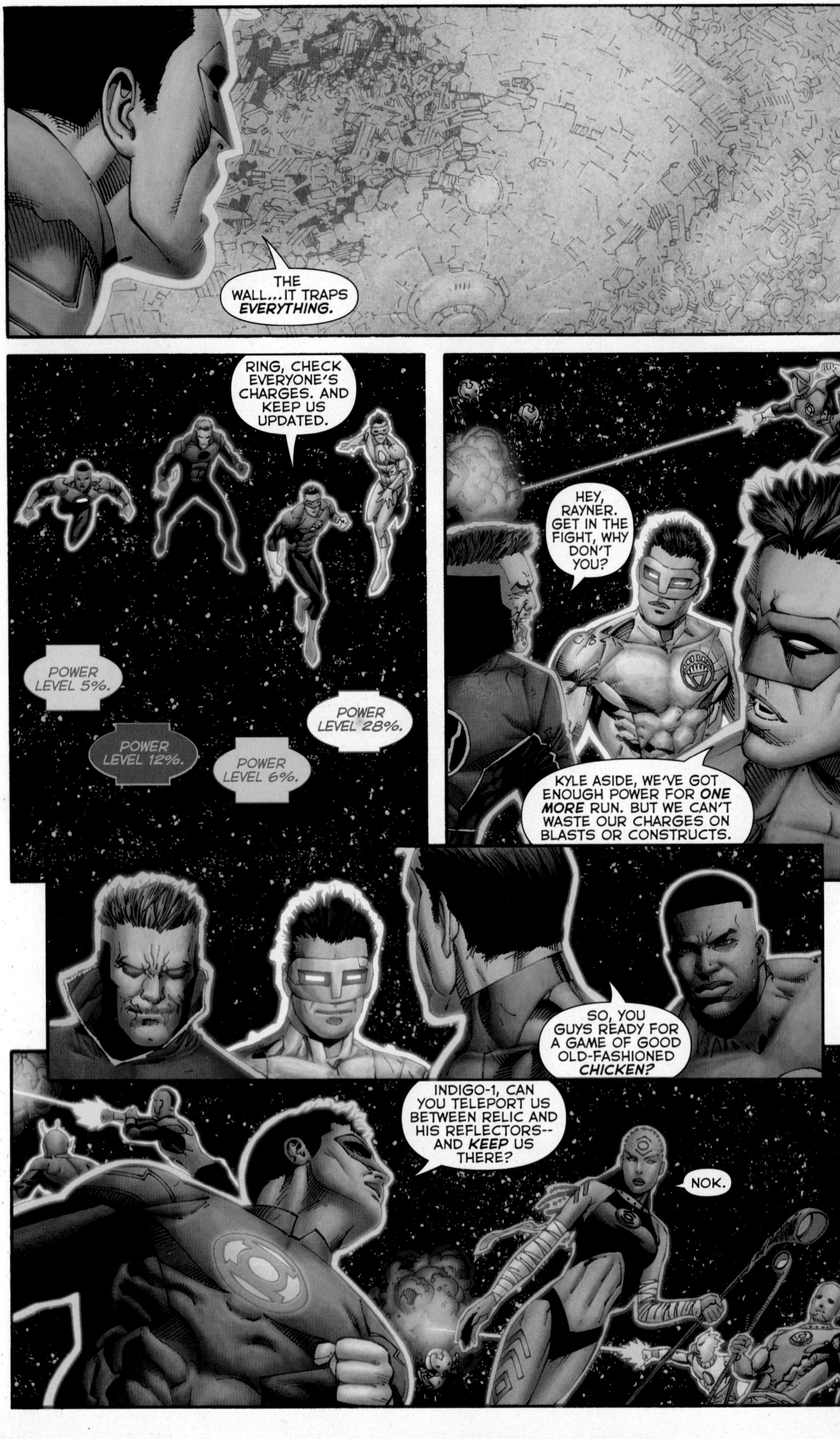

THE WALL...IT TRAPS EVERYTHING.
RING, CHECK EVERYONE'S CHARGES. AND KEEP US UPDATED.
POWER LEVEL 5%.
POWER LEVEL 12%.
POWER LEVEL 6%.
POWER LEVEL 28%.
HEY, RAYNER. GET IN THE FIGHT, WHY DON'T YOU?
KYLE ASIDE, WE'VE GOT ENOUGH POWER FOR ONE MORE RUN. BUT WE CAN'T WASTE OUR CHARGES ON BLASTS OR CONSTRUCTS.
SO, YOU GUYS READY FOR A GAME OF GOOD OLD-FASHIONED CHICKEN?
INDIGO-1, CAN YOU TELEPORT US BETWEEN RELIC AND HIS REFLECTORS--AND KEEP US THERE?
NOK.

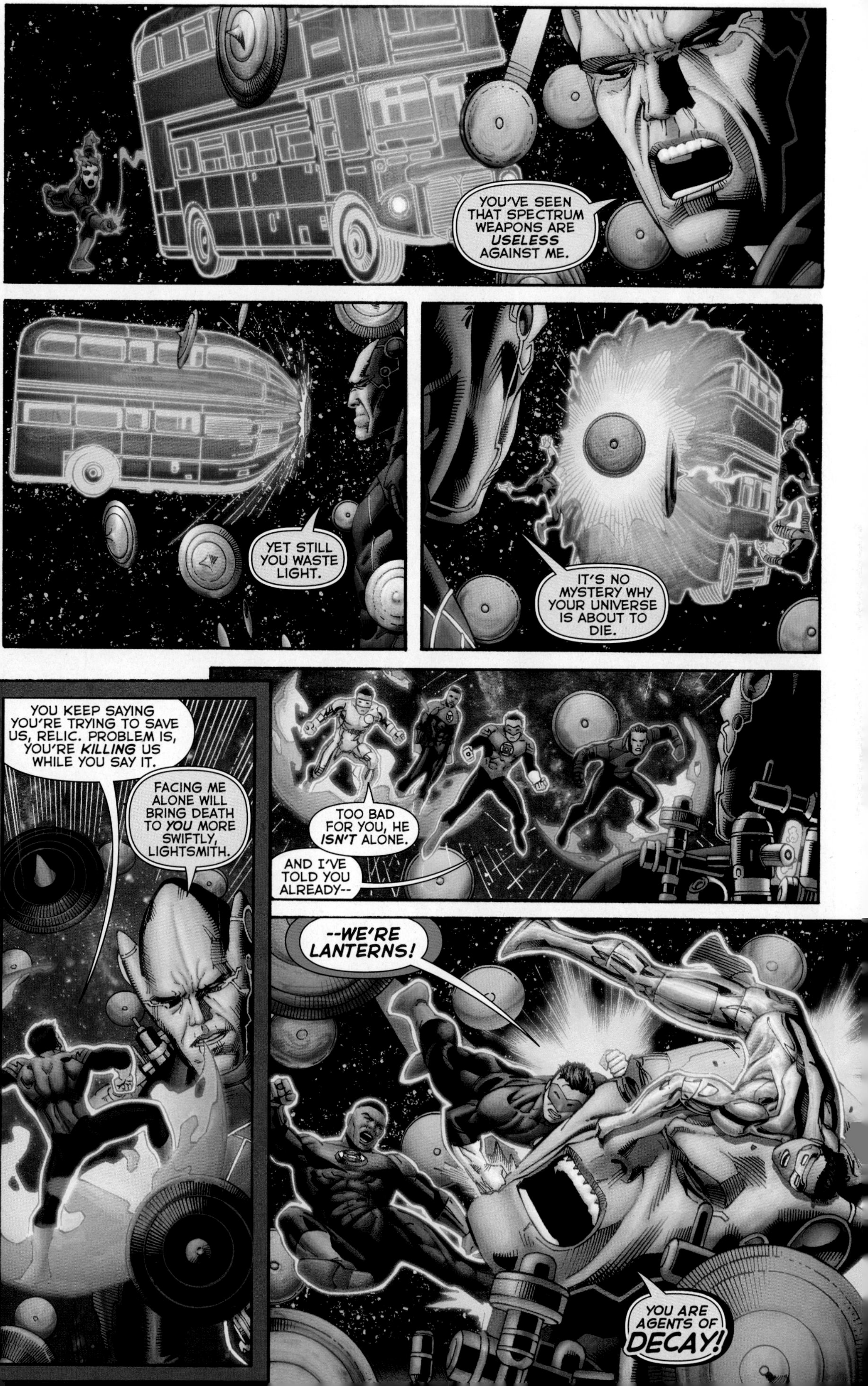

YOU'VE SEEN THAT SPECTRUM WEAPONS ARE *USELESS* AGAINST ME.
YET STILL YOU WASTE LIGHT.
IT'S NO MYSTERY WHY YOUR UNIVERSE IS ABOUT TO DIE.
YOU KEEP SAYING YOU'RE TRYING TO SAVE US, RELIC. PROBLEM IS, YOU'RE *KILLING* US WHILE YOU SAY IT.
FACING ME ALONE WILL BRING DEATH TO *YOU* MORE SWIFTLY, LIGHTSMITH.
TOO BAD FOR YOU, HE *ISN'T* ALONE.
AND I'VE TOLD YOU ALREADY--
--*WE'RE LANTERNS!*
YOU ARE AGENTS OF *DECAY!*

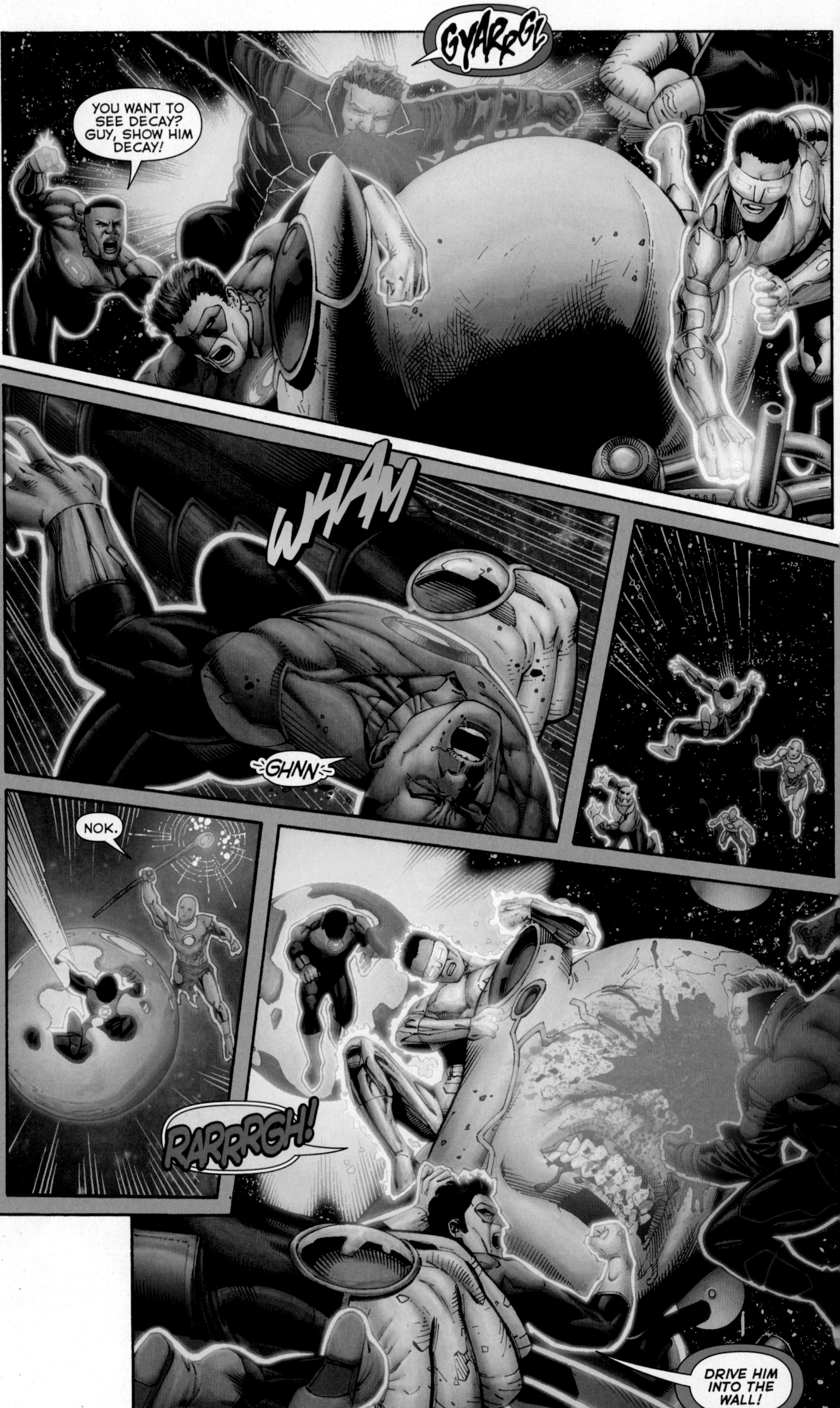
GYARRGL
YOU WANT TO SEE DECAY? GUY, SHOW HIM DECAY!
WHAM
GHNN
NOK.
RARRRGH!
DRIVE HIM INTO THE WALL!

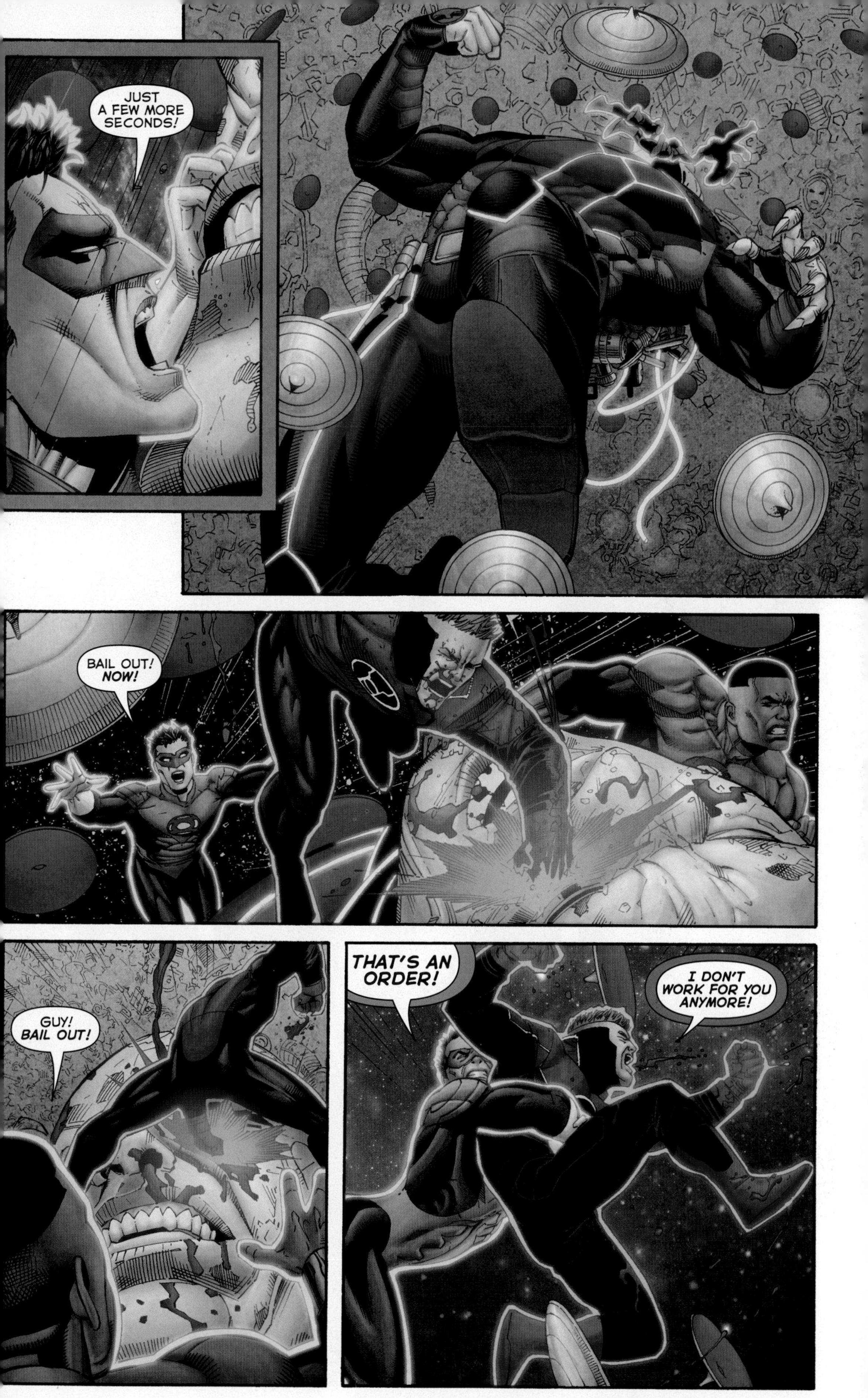

JUST A FEW MORE SECONDS!
BAIL OUT! NOW!
GUY! BAIL OUT!
THAT'S AN ORDER!
I DON'T WORK FOR YOU ANYMORE!

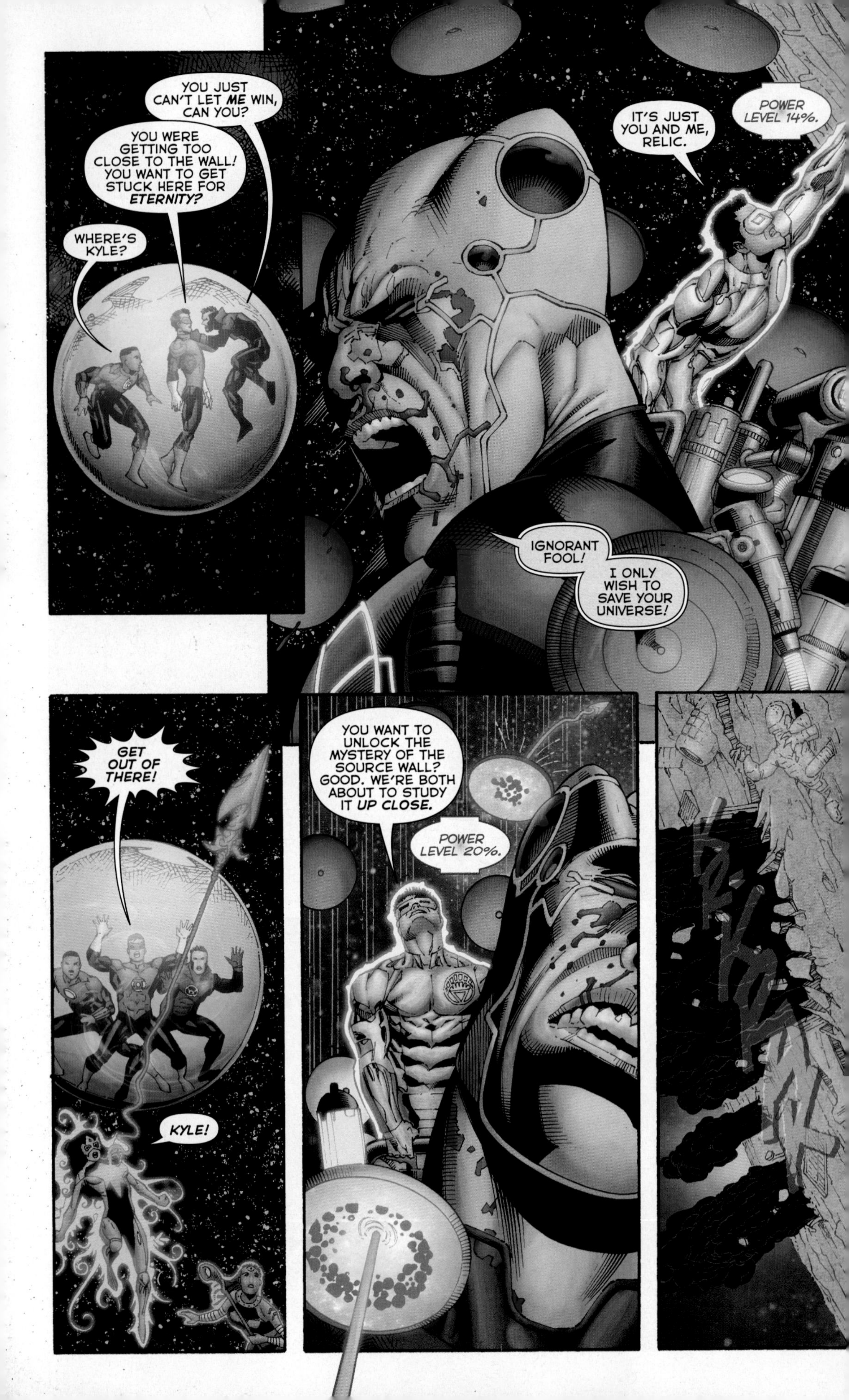

YOU JUST CAN'T LET ME WIN, CAN YOU?
YOU WERE GETTING TOO CLOSE TO THE WALL! YOU WANT TO GET STUCK HERE FOR ETERNITY?
WHERE'S KYLE?
IT'S JUST YOU AND ME, RELIC.
POWER LEVEL 14%.
IGNORANT FOOL!
I ONLY WISH TO SAVE YOUR UNIVERSE!
GET OUT OF THERE!
KYLE!
YOU WANT TO UNLOCK THE MYSTERY OF THE SOURCE WALL? GOOD. WE'RE BOTH ABOUT TO STUDY IT UP CLOSE.
POWER LEVEL 20%.

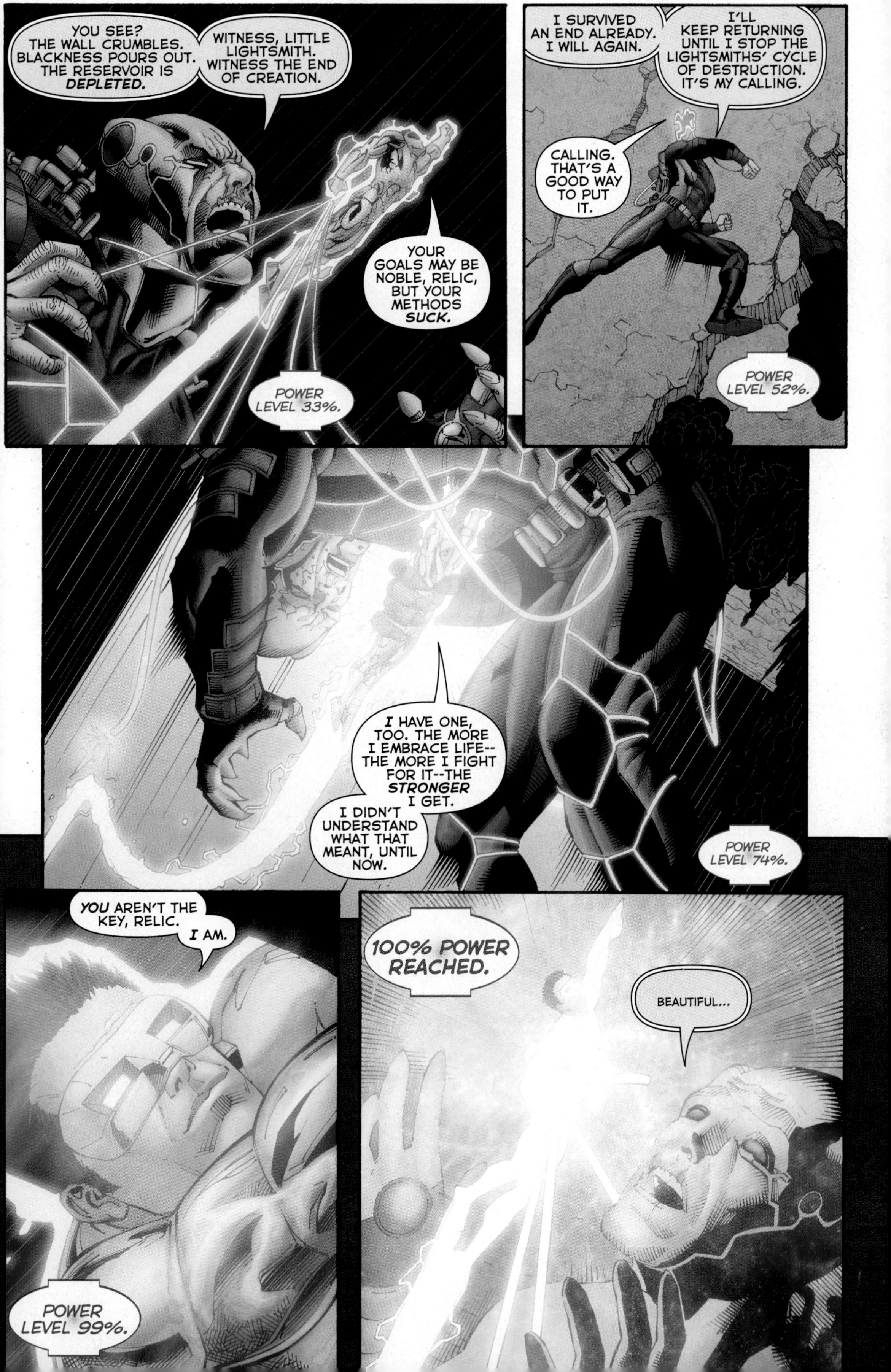
YOU SEE? THE WALL CRUMBLES. BLACKNESS POURS OUT. THE RESERVOIR IS DEPLETED.
WITNESS, LITTLE LIGHTSMITH. WITNESS THE END OF CREATION.
YOUR GOALS MAY BE NOBLE, RELIC, BUT YOUR METHODS SUCK.
POWER LEVEL 33%.
I SURVIVED AN END ALREADY. I WILL AGAIN.
I'LL KEEP RETURNING UNTIL I STOP THE LIGHTSMITHS' CYCLE OF DESTRUCTION. IT'S MY CALLING.
CALLING. THAT'S A GOOD WAY TO PUT IT.
POWER LEVEL 52%.
I HAVE ONE, TOO. THE MORE I EMBRACE LIFE-- THE MORE I FIGHT FOR IT--THE STRONGER I GET.
I DIDN'T UNDERSTAND WHAT THAT MEANT, UNTIL NOW.
POWER LEVEL 74%.
YOU AREN'T THE KEY, RELIC.
I AM.
POWER LEVEL 99%.
100% POWER REACHED.
BEAUTIFUL...

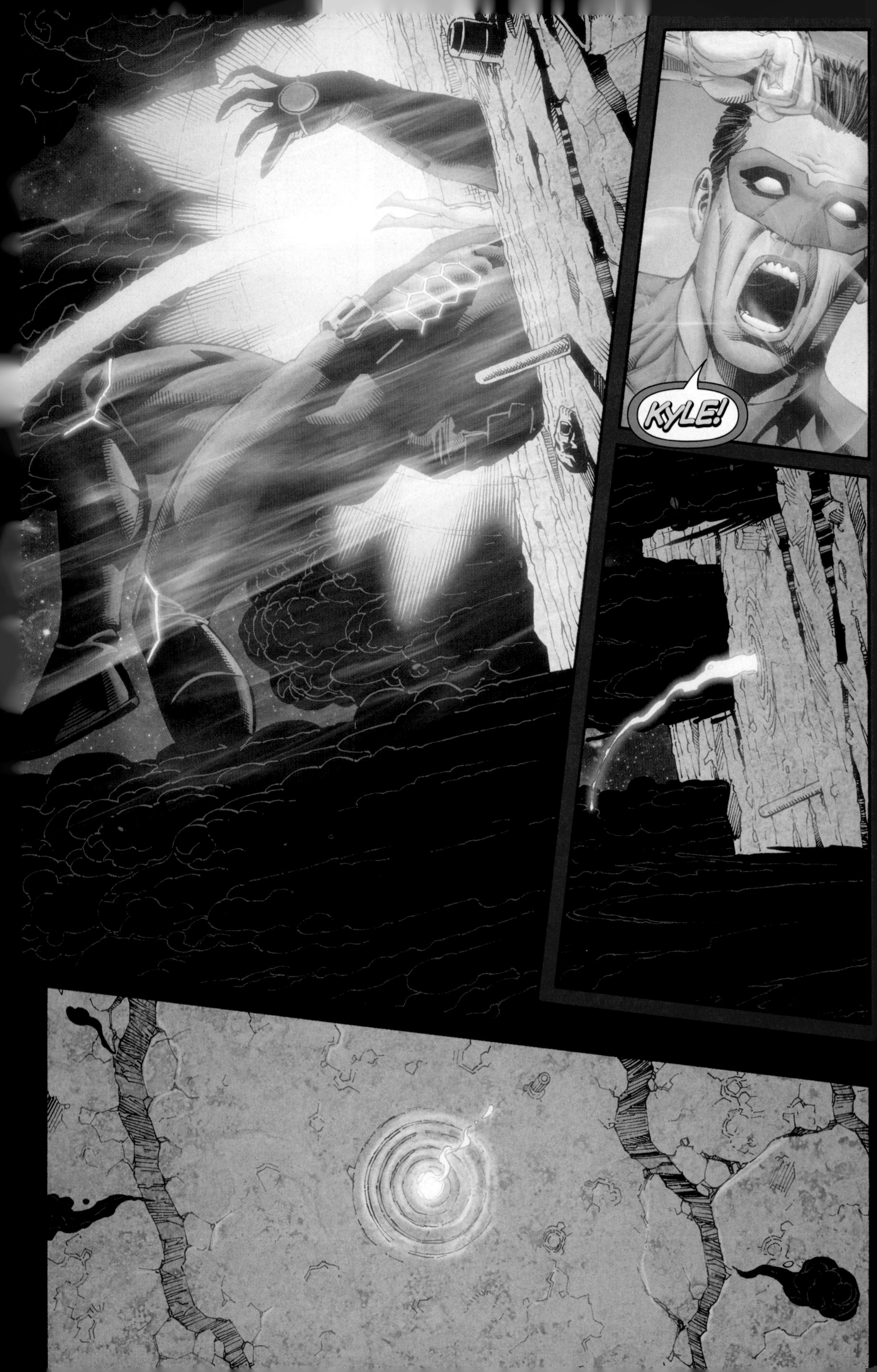
KYLE!

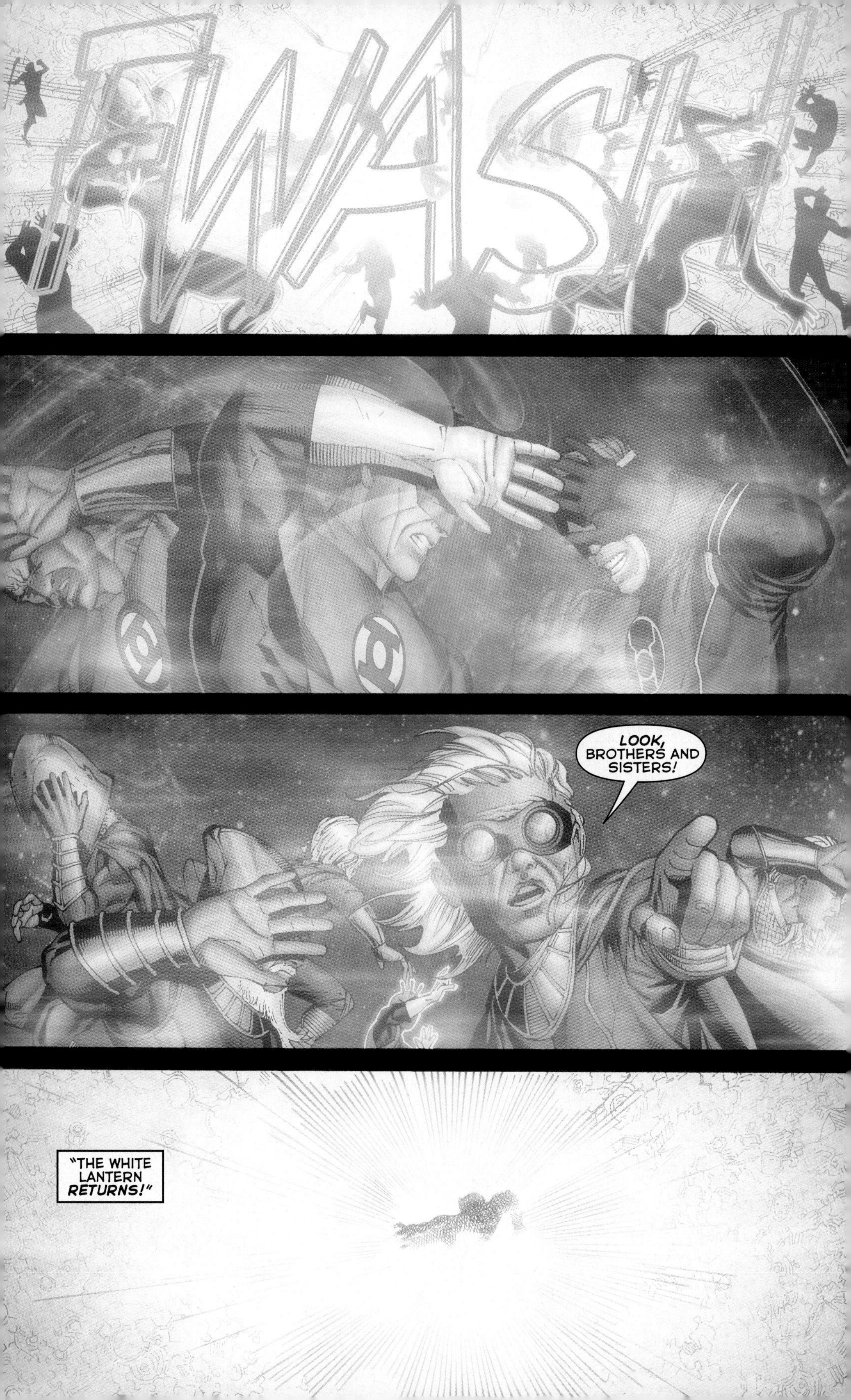
FWASH!
LOOK, BROTHERS AND SISTERS!
"THE WHITE LANTERN RETURNS!"

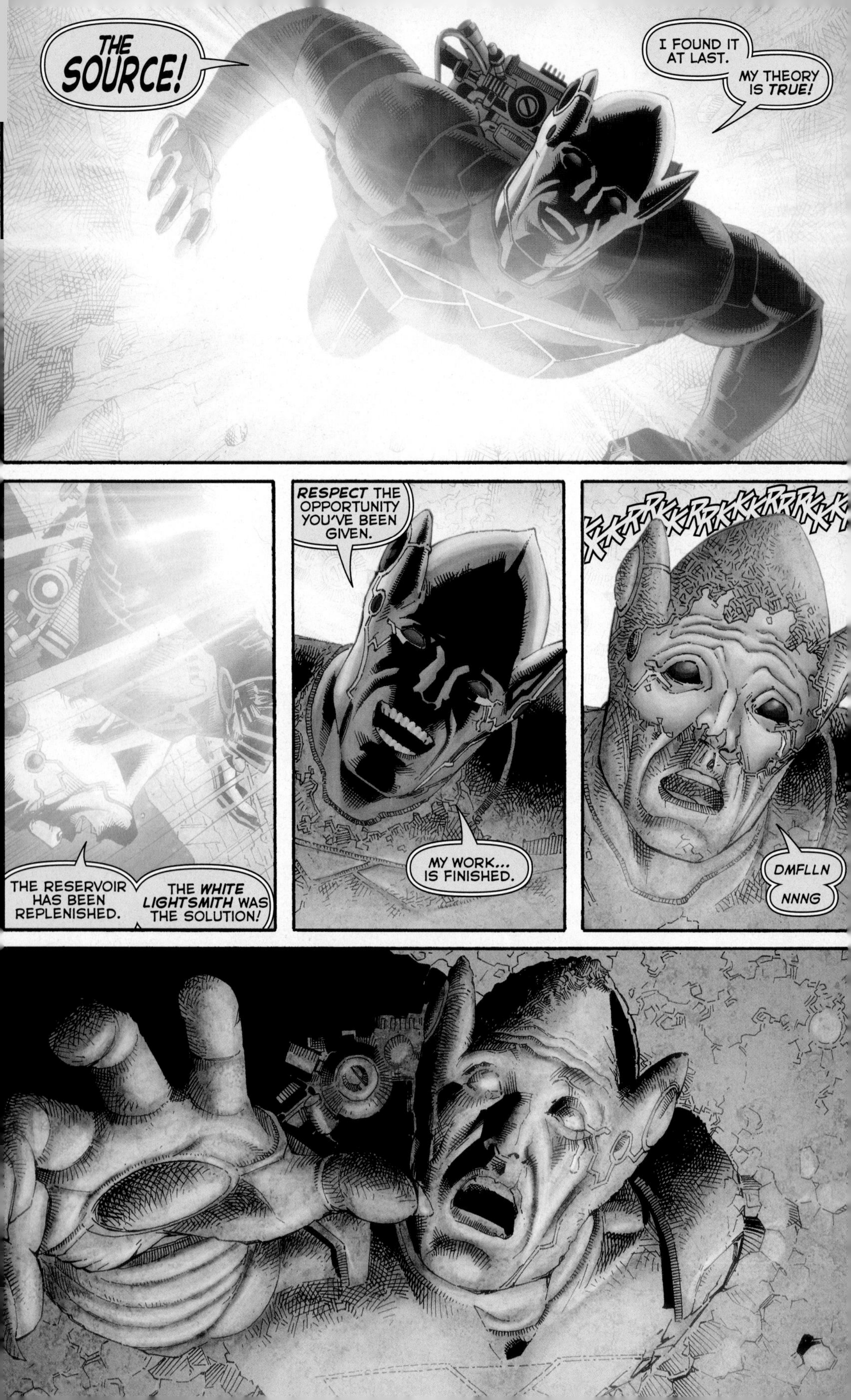
THE SOURCE!
I FOUND IT AT LAST.
MY THEORY IS TRUE!
THE RESERVOIR HAS BEEN REPLENISHED.
THE WHITE LIGHTSMITH WAS THE SOLUTION!
RESPECT THE OPPORTUNITY YOU'VE BEEN GIVEN.
MY WORK... IS FINISHED.
DMFLLN
NNNG

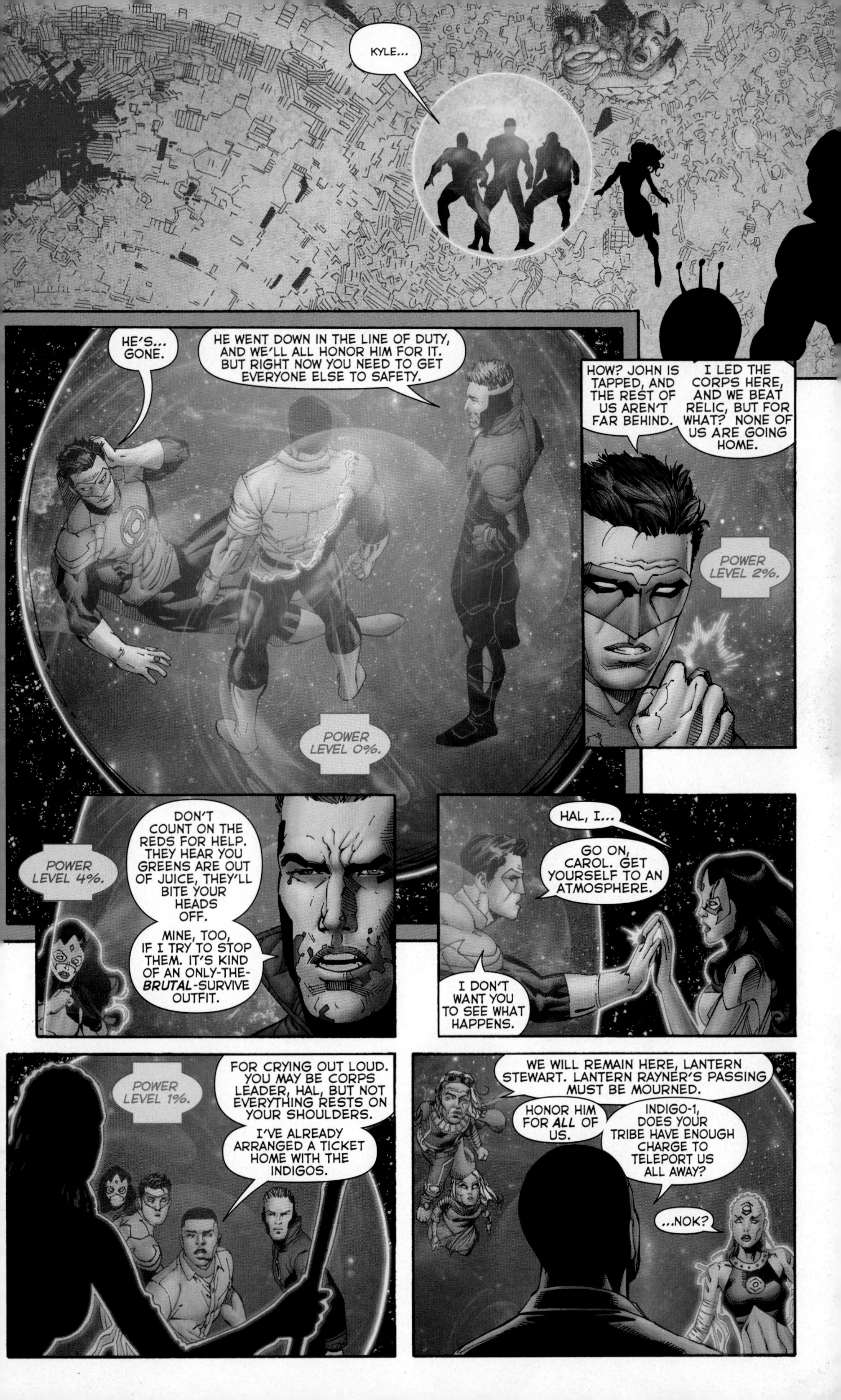
KYLE...
HE'S... GONE.
HE WENT DOWN IN THE LINE OF DUTY, AND WE'LL ALL HONOR HIM FOR IT. BUT RIGHT NOW YOU NEED TO GET EVERYONE ELSE TO SAFETY.
POWER LEVEL 0%.
HOW? JOHN IS TAPPED, AND THE REST OF US AREN'T FAR BEHIND.
I LED THE CORPS HERE, AND WE BEAT RELIC, BUT FOR WHAT? NONE OF US ARE GOING HOME.
POWER LEVEL 2%.
POWER LEVEL 4%.
DON'T COUNT ON THE REDS FOR HELP. THEY HEAR YOU GREENS ARE OUT OF JUICE, THEY'LL BITE YOUR HEADS OFF.
MINE, TOO, IF I TRY TO STOP THEM. IT'S KIND OF AN ONLY-THE-BRUTAL-SURVIVE OUTFIT.
HAL, I...
GO ON, CAROL. GET YOURSELF TO AN ATMOSPHERE.
I DON'T WANT YOU TO SEE WHAT HAPPENS.
POWER LEVEL 1%.
FOR CRYING OUT LOUD. YOU MAY BE CORPS LEADER, HAL, BUT NOT EVERYTHING RESTS ON YOUR SHOULDERS.
I'VE ALREADY ARRANGED A TICKET HOME WITH THE INDIGOS.
WE WILL REMAIN HERE, LANTERN STEWART. LANTERN RAYNER'S PASSING MUST BE MOURNED.
HONOR HIM FOR ALL OF US.
INDIGO-1, DOES YOUR TRIBE HAVE ENOUGH CHARGE TO TELEPORT US ALL AWAY?
...NOK?

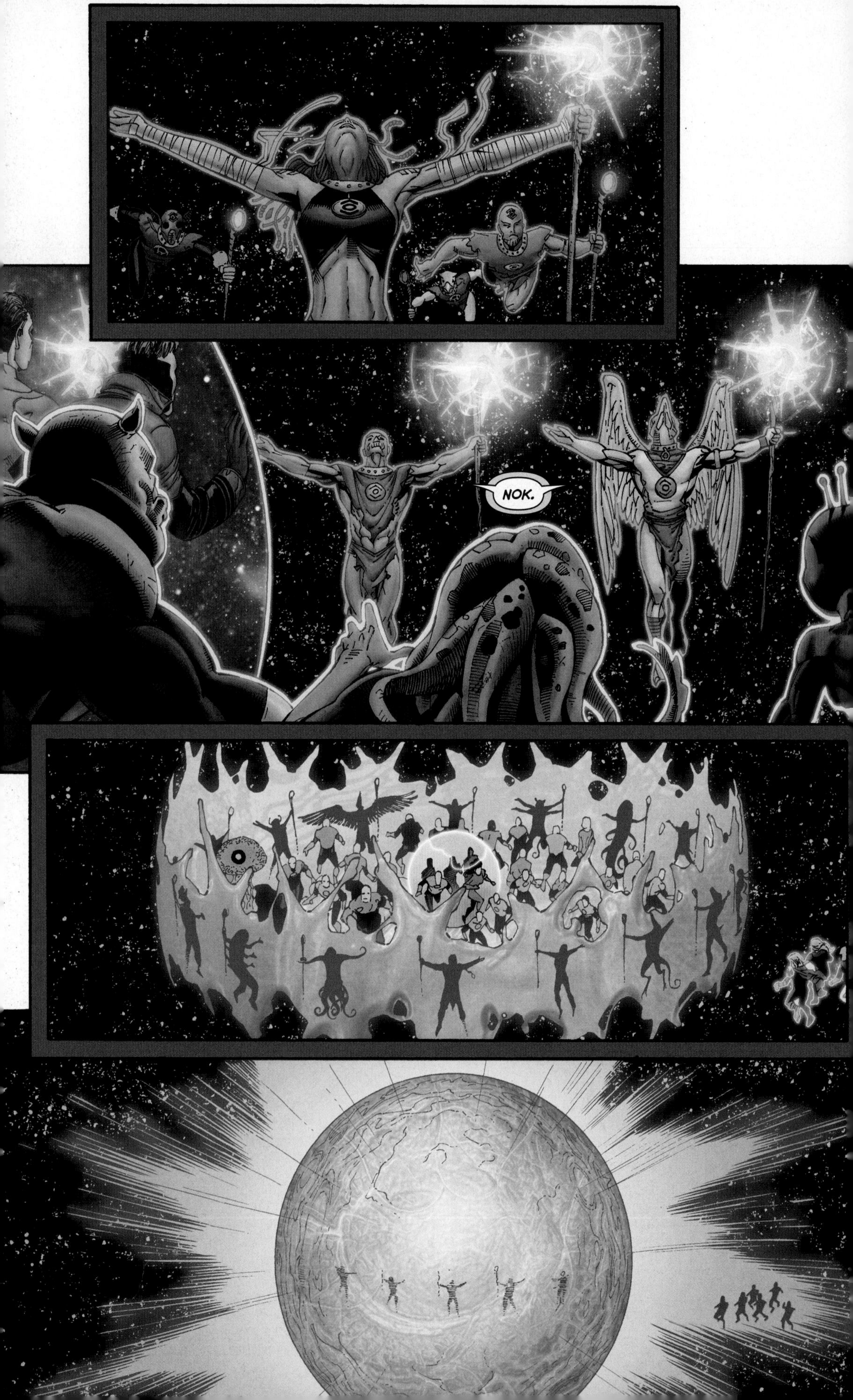
NOK.

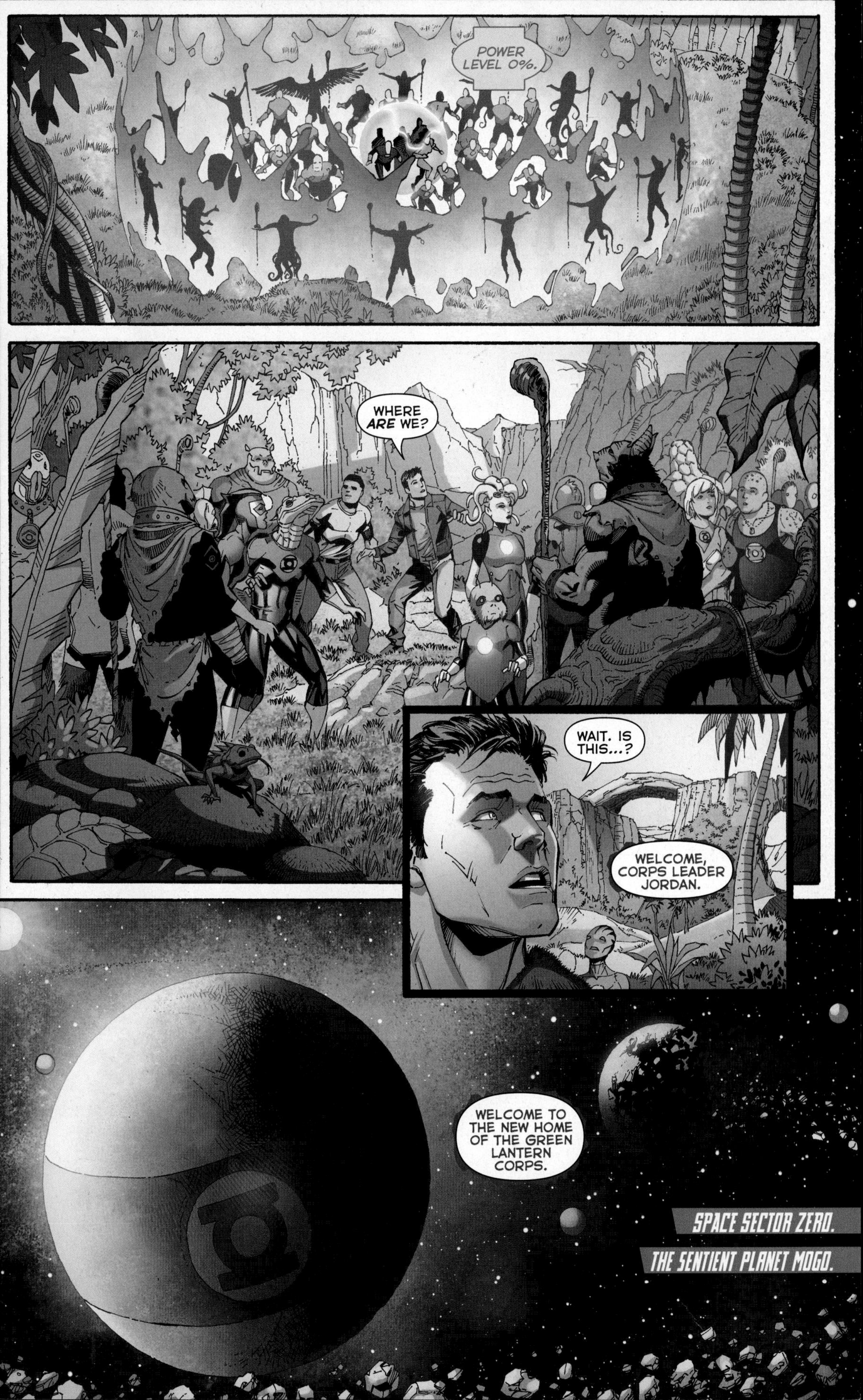
POWER LEVEL 0%.
WHERE ARE WE?
WAIT. IS THIS...?
WELCOME, CORPS LEADER JORDAN.
WELCOME TO THE NEW HOME OF THE GREEN LANTERN CORPS.
SPACE SECTOR ZERO.
THE SENTIENT PLANET MOGO.

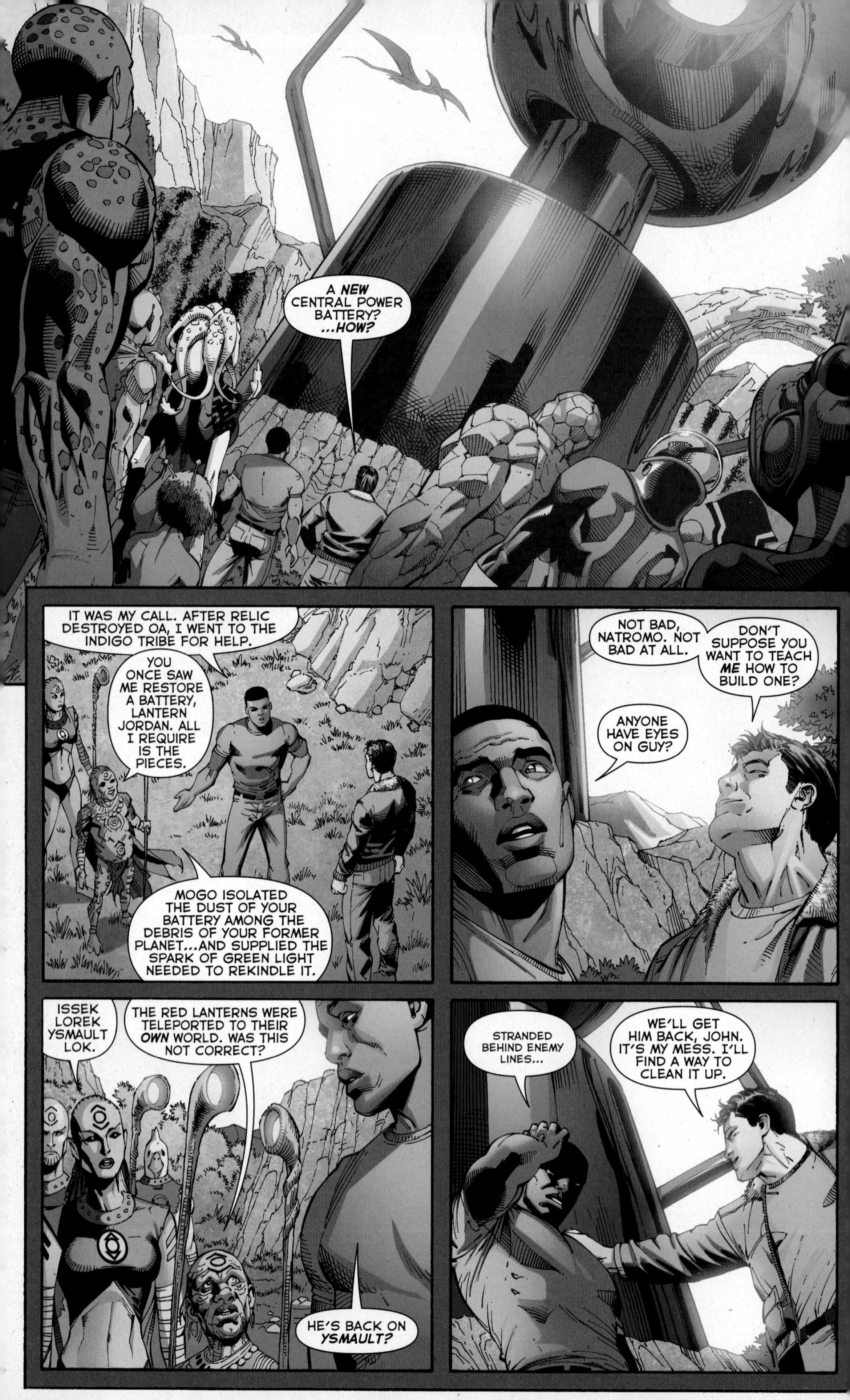

A NEW CENTRAL POWER BATTERY? ...HOW?
IT WAS MY CALL. AFTER RELIC DESTROYED OA, I WENT TO THE INDIGO TRIBE FOR HELP.
YOU ONCE SAW ME RESTORE A BATTERY, LANTERN JORDAN. ALL I REQUIRE IS THE PIECES.
MOGO ISOLATED THE DUST OF YOUR BATTERY AMONG THE DEBRIS OF YOUR FORMER PLANET...AND SUPPLIED THE SPARK OF GREEN LIGHT NEEDED TO REKINDLE IT.
NOT BAD, NATROMO. NOT BAD AT ALL.
DON'T SUPPOSE YOU WANT TO TEACH ME HOW TO BUILD ONE?
ANYONE HAVE EYES ON GUY?
ISSEK LOREK YSMAULT LOK.
THE RED LANTERNS WERE TELEPORTED TO THEIR OWN WORLD. WAS THIS NOT CORRECT?
HE'S BACK ON YSMAULT?
STRANDED BEHIND ENEMY LINES...
WE'LL GET HIM BACK, JOHN. IT'S MY MESS. I'LL FIND A WAY TO CLEAN IT UP.

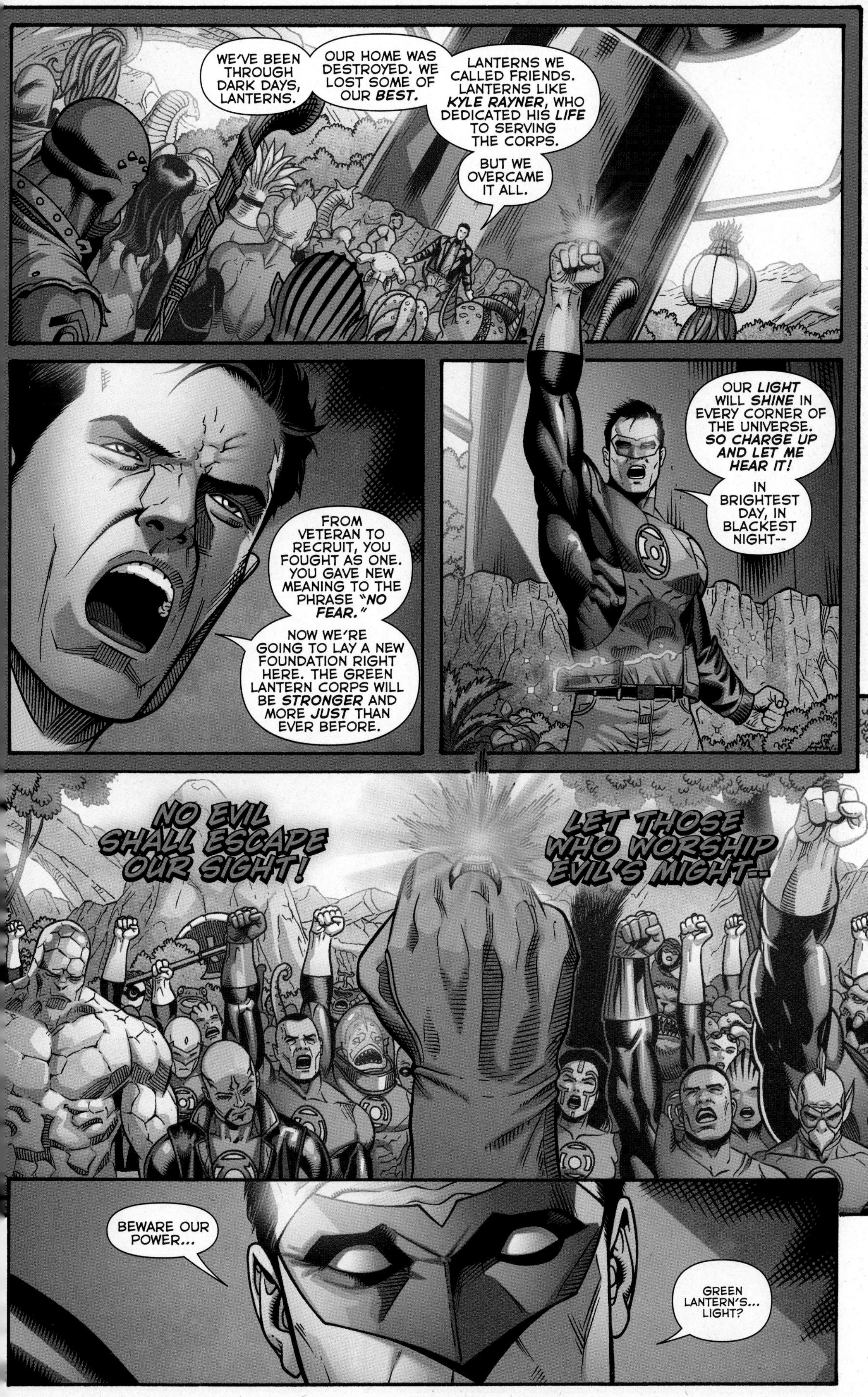

WE'VE BEEN THROUGH DARK DAYS, LANTERNS.
OUR HOME WAS DESTROYED. WE LOST SOME OF OUR BEST.
LANTERNS WE CALLED FRIENDS. LANTERNS LIKE KYLE RAYNER, WHO DEDICATED HIS LIFE TO SERVING THE CORPS.
BUT WE OVERCAME IT ALL.
FROM VETERAN TO RECRUIT, YOU FOUGHT AS ONE. YOU GAVE NEW MEANING TO THE PHRASE "NO FEAR."
NOW WE'RE GOING TO LAY A NEW FOUNDATION RIGHT HERE. THE GREEN LANTERN CORPS WILL BE STRONGER AND MORE JUST THAN EVER BEFORE.
OUR LIGHT WILL SHINE IN EVERY CORNER OF THE UNIVERSE. SO CHARGE UP AND LET ME HEAR IT!
IN BRIGHTEST DAY, IN BLACKEST NIGHT--
NO EVIL SHALL ESCAPE OUR SIGHT!
LET THOSE WHO WORSHIP EVIL'S MIGHT--
BEWARE OUR POWER...
GREEN LANTERN'S... LIGHT?

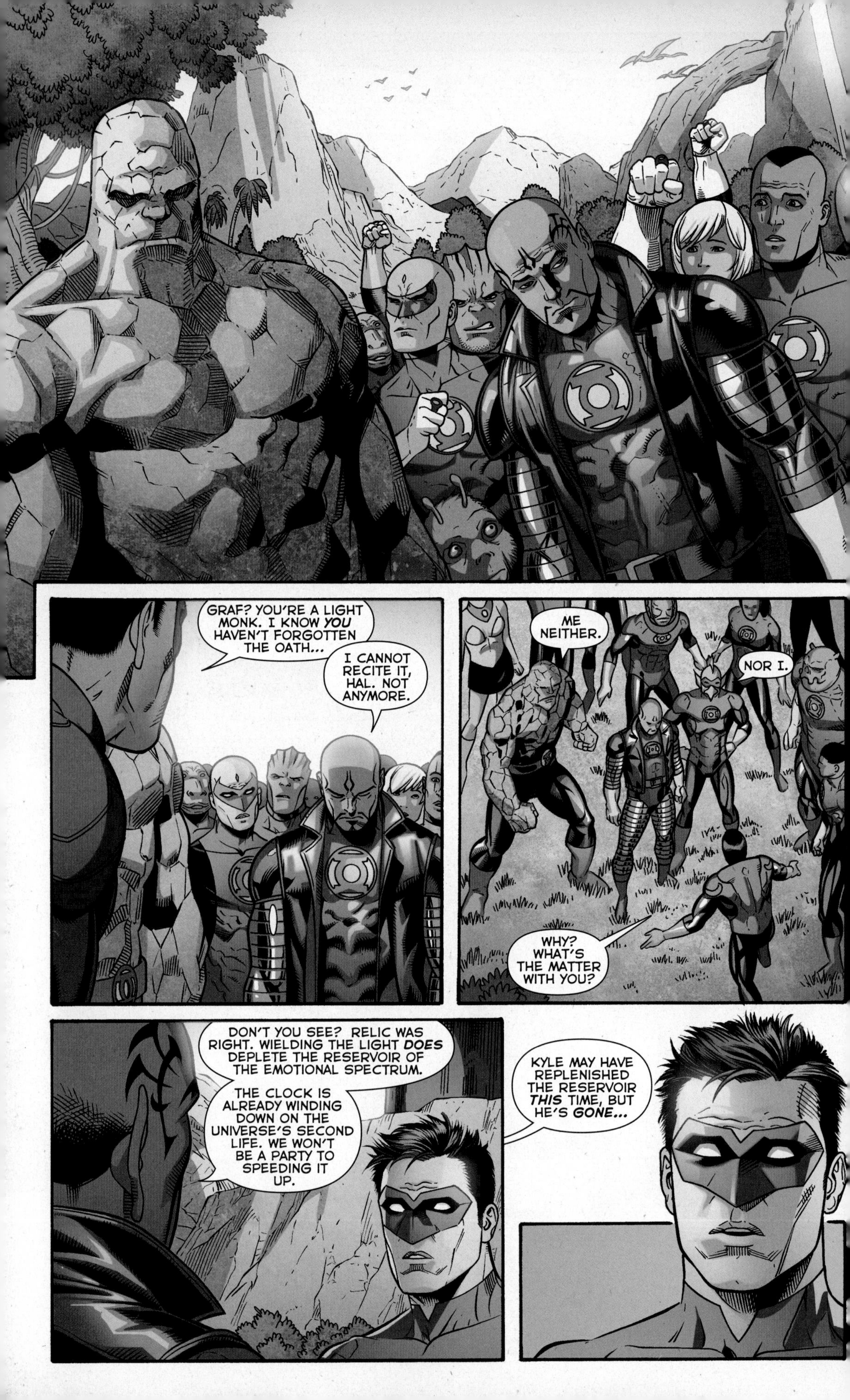
GRAF? YOU'RE A LIGHT MONK. I KNOW *YOU* HAVEN'T FORGOTTEN THE OATH...
I CANNOT RECITE IT, HAL. NOT ANYMORE.
ME NEITHER.
NOR I.
WHY? WHAT'S THE MATTER WITH YOU?
DON'T YOU SEE? RELIC WAS RIGHT. WIELDING THE LIGHT *DOES* DEPLETE THE RESERVOIR OF THE EMOTIONAL SPECTRUM.
THE CLOCK IS ALREADY WINDING DOWN ON THE UNIVERSE'S SECOND LIFE. WE WON'T BE A PARTY TO SPEEDING IT UP.
KYLE MAY HAVE REPLENISHED THE RESERVOIR *THIS* TIME, BUT HE'S *GONE*...

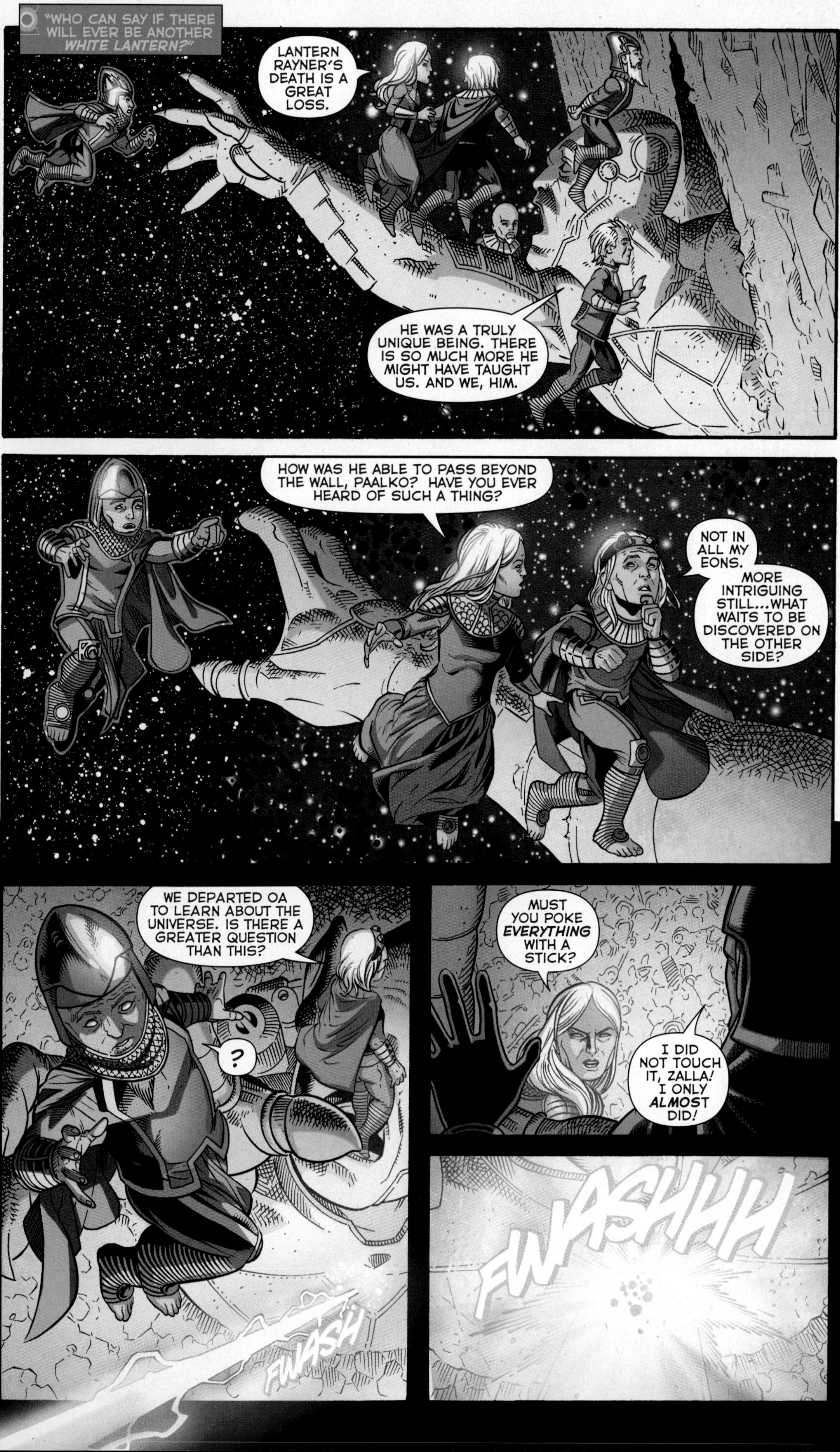

"WHO CAN SAY IF THERE WILL EVER BE ANOTHER *WHITE LANTERN?*"
LANTERN RAYNER'S DEATH IS A GREAT LOSS.
HE WAS A TRULY UNIQUE BEING. THERE IS SO MUCH MORE HE MIGHT HAVE TAUGHT US. AND WE, HIM.
HOW WAS HE ABLE TO PASS BEYOND THE WALL, PAALKO? HAVE YOU EVER HEARD OF SUCH A THING?
NOT IN ALL MY EONS.
MORE INTRIGUING STILL...WHAT WAITS TO BE DISCOVERED ON THE OTHER SIDE?
WE DEPARTED OA TO LEARN ABOUT THE UNIVERSE. IS THERE A GREATER QUESTION THAN THIS?
?
FWASH
MUST YOU POKE *EVERYTHING* WITH A STICK?
I DID NOT TOUCH IT, ZALLA! I ONLY *ALMOST* DID!
FWASHHH

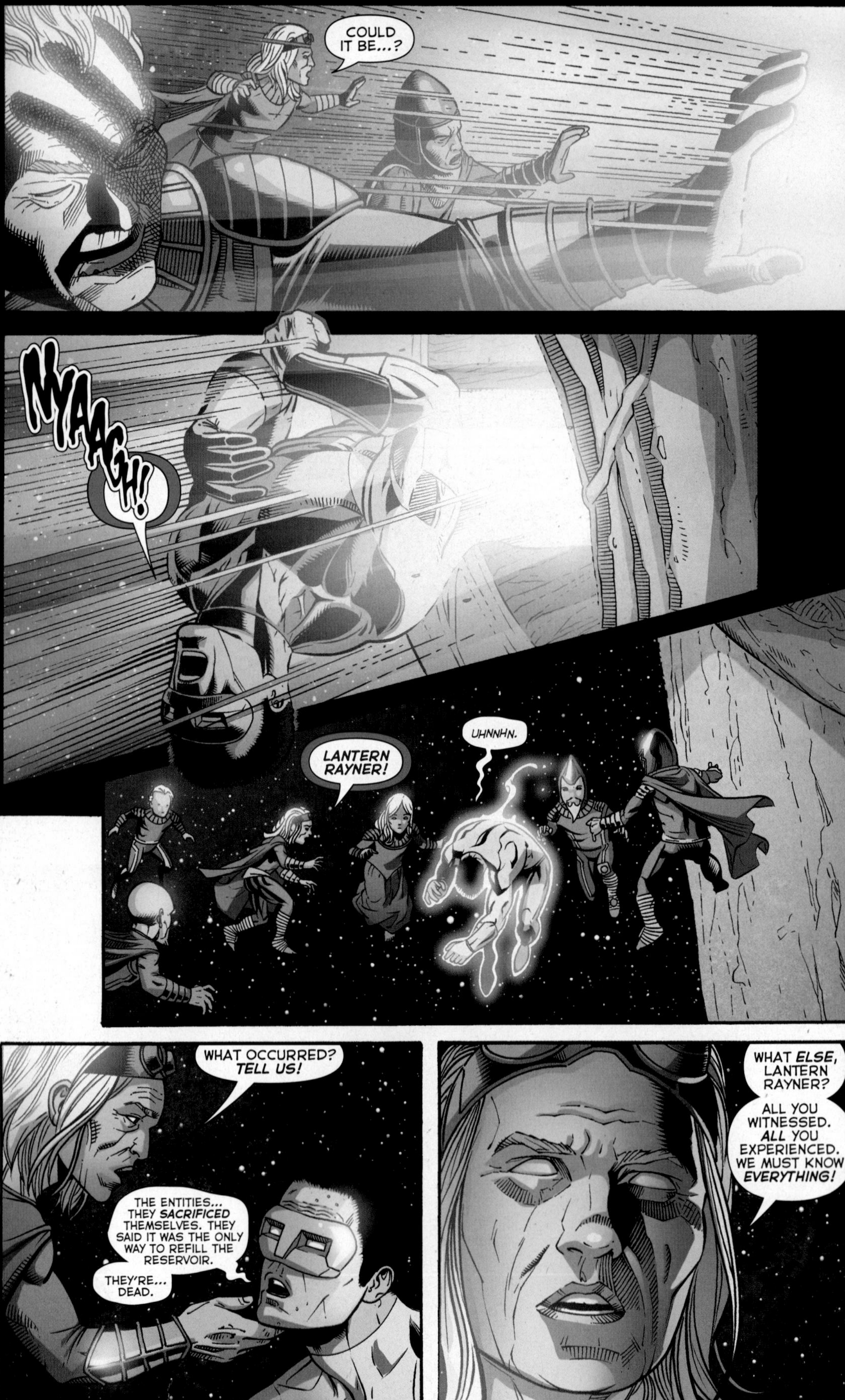
COULD IT BE...?
NYAAAGH!
LANTERN RAYNER!
UHNNHN.
WHAT OCCURRED? TELL US!
THE ENTITIES... THEY SACRIFICED THEMSELVES. THEY SAID IT WAS THE ONLY WAY TO REFILL THE RESERVOIR.
THEY'RE... DEAD.
WHAT ELSE, LANTERN RAYNER?
ALL YOU WITNESSED. ALL YOU EXPERIENCED. WE MUST KNOW EVERYTHING!

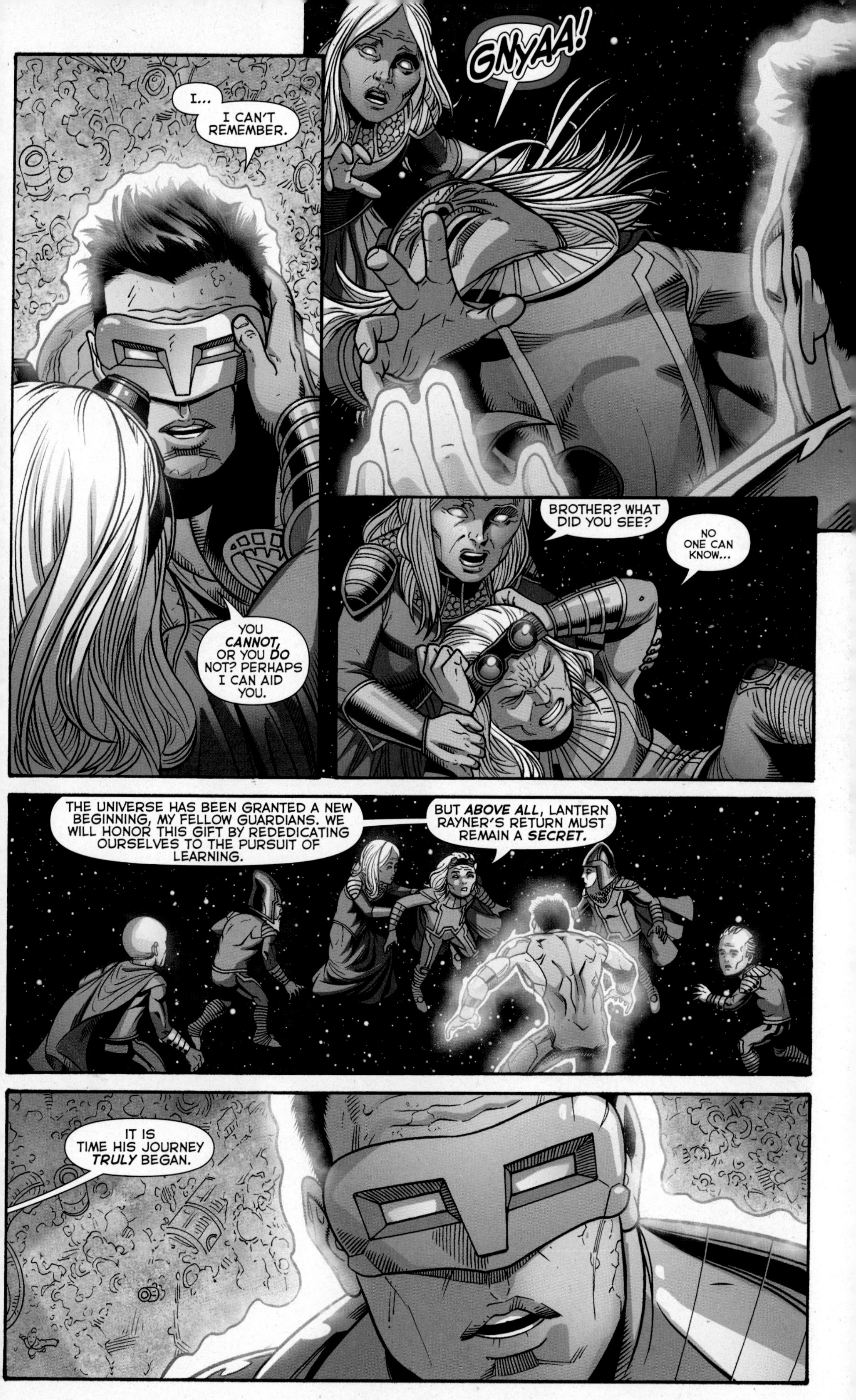
I... I CAN'T REMEMBER.
GNYAA!
YOU CANNOT, OR YOU DO NOT? PERHAPS I CAN AID YOU.
BROTHER? WHAT DID YOU SEE?
NO ONE CAN KNOW...
THE UNIVERSE HAS BEEN GRANTED A NEW BEGINNING, MY FELLOW GUARDIANS. WE WILL HONOR THIS GIFT BY REDEDICATING OURSELVES TO THE PURSUIT OF LEARNING.
BUT ABOVE ALL, LANTERN RAYNER'S RETURN MUST REMAIN A SECRET.
IT IS TIME HIS JOURNEY TRULY BEGAN.

ROBERT VENDITTI writer **BILLY TAN** penciller **ROB HUNTER** inker
cover art by **BILLY TAN & ALEX SINCLAIR**

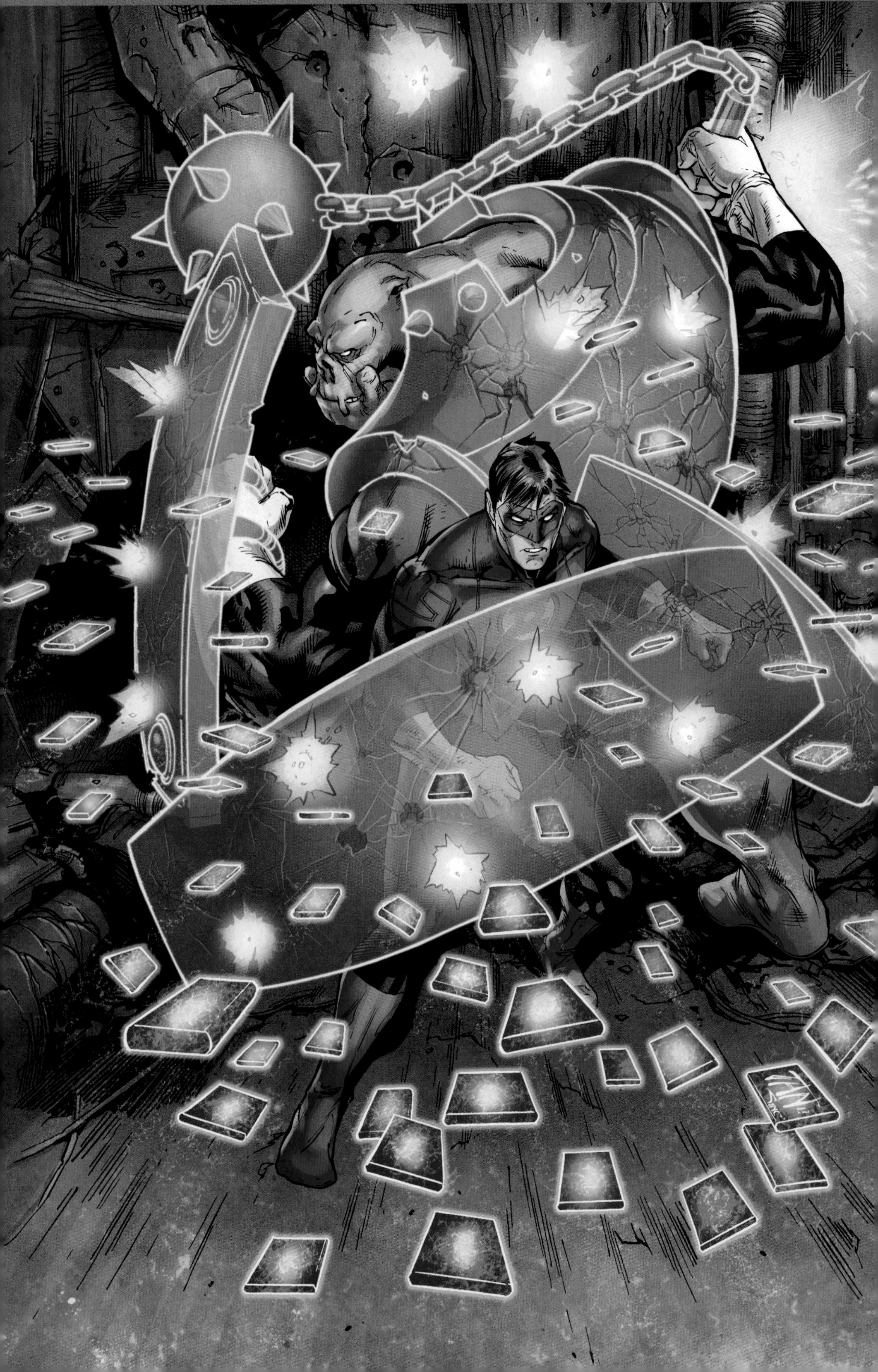

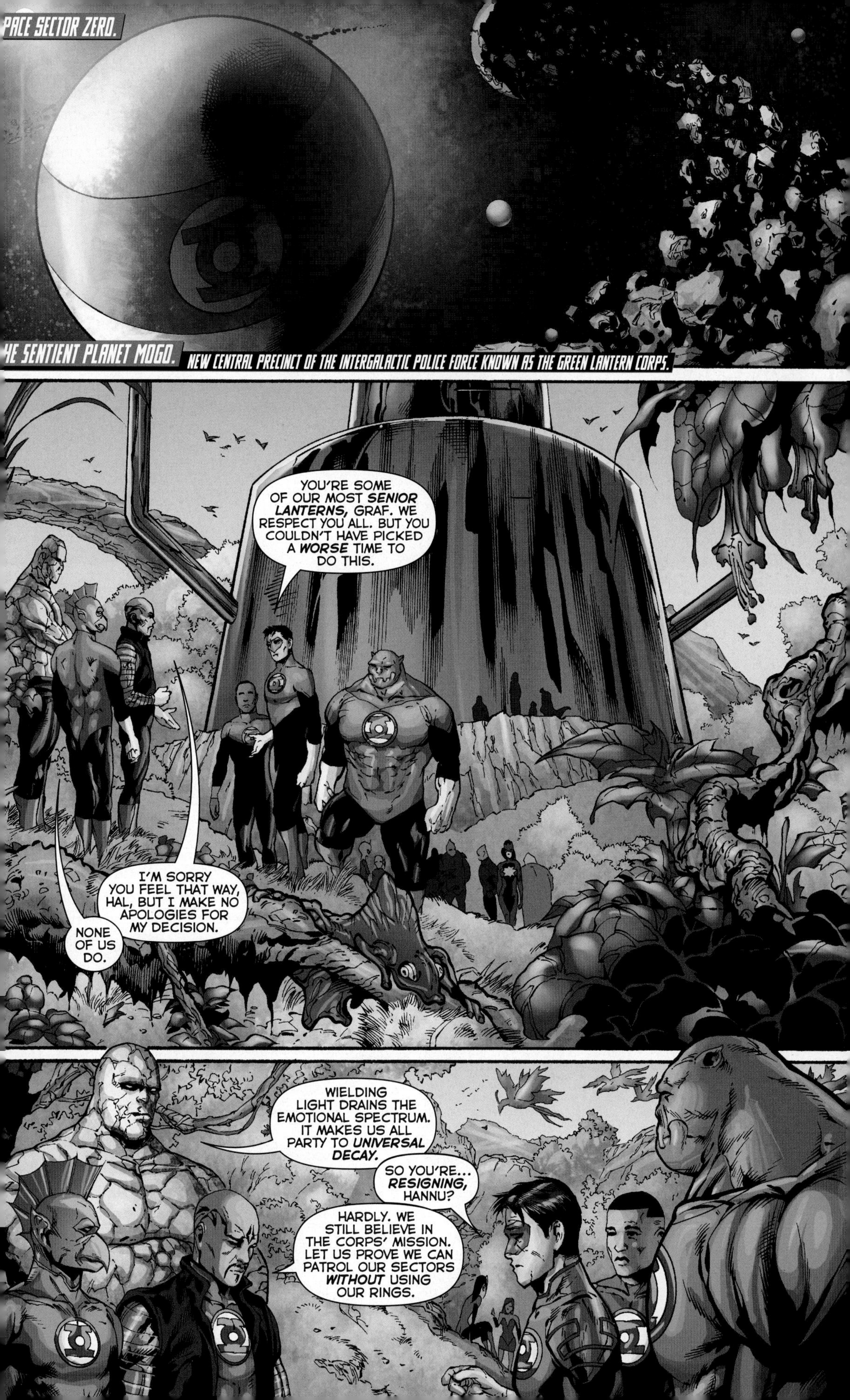
PACE SECTOR ZERO.
HE SENTIENT PLANET MOGO.
NEW CENTRAL PRECINCT OF THE INTERGALACTIC POLICE FORCE KNOWN AS THE GREEN LANTERN CORPS.
YOU'RE SOME OF OUR MOST SENIOR LANTERNS, GRAF. WE RESPECT YOU ALL. BUT YOU COULDN'T HAVE PICKED A WORSE TIME TO DO THIS.
I'M SORRY YOU FEEL THAT WAY, HAL, BUT I MAKE NO APOLOGIES FOR MY DECISION.
NONE OF US DO.
WIELDING LIGHT DRAINS THE EMOTIONAL SPECTRUM. IT MAKES US ALL PARTY TO UNIVERSAL DECAY.
SO YOU'RE... RESIGNING, HANNU?
HARDLY. WE STILL BELIEVE IN THE CORPS' MISSION. LET US PROVE WE CAN PATROL OUR SECTORS WITHOUT USING OUR RINGS.

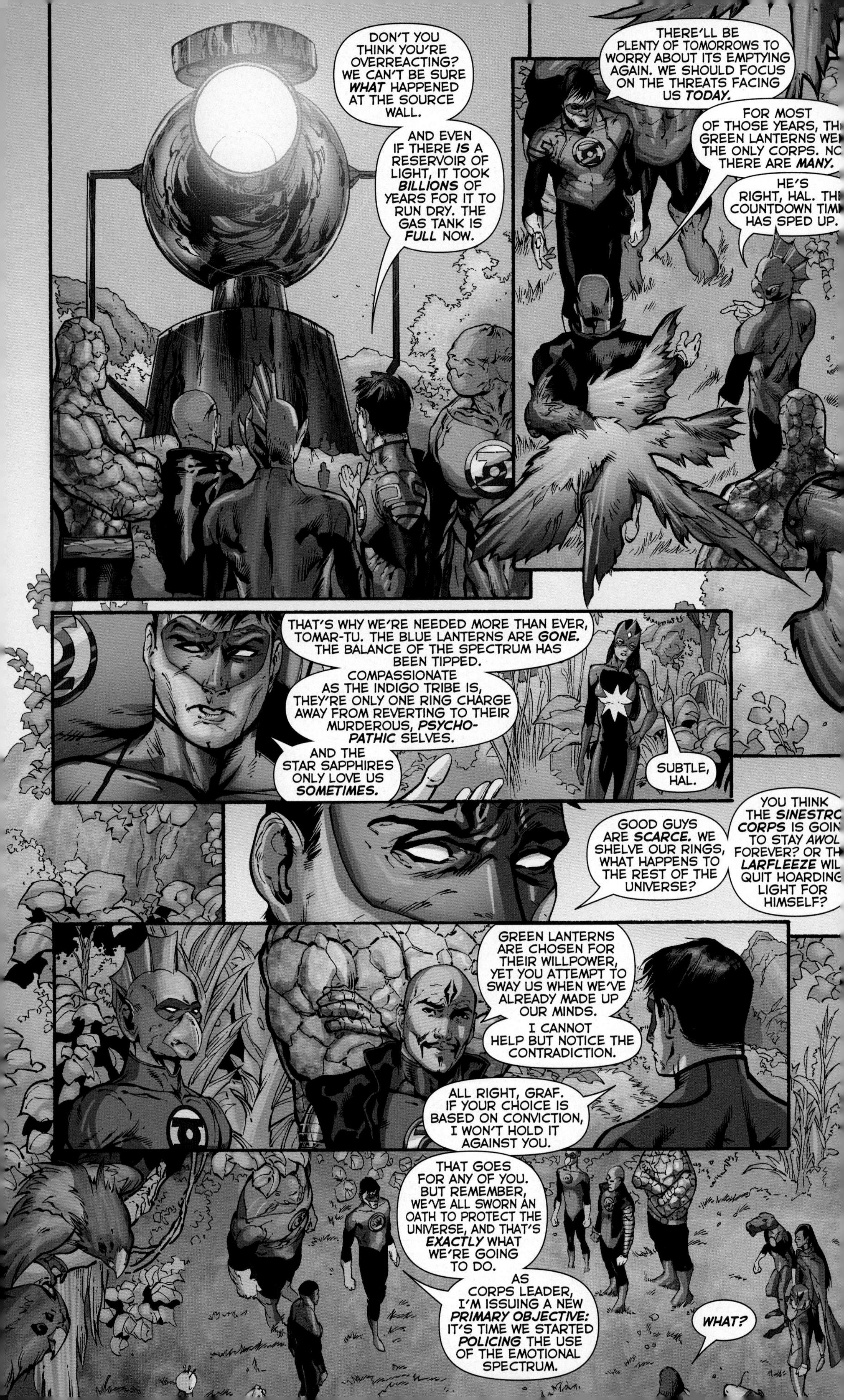
DON'T YOU THINK YOU'RE OVERREACTING? WE CAN'T BE SURE *WHAT* HAPPENED AT THE SOURCE WALL.
AND EVEN IF THERE *IS* A RESERVOIR OF LIGHT, IT TOOK *BILLIONS* OF YEARS FOR IT TO RUN DRY. THE GAS TANK IS *FULL* NOW.
THERE'LL BE PLENTY OF TOMORROWS TO WORRY ABOUT ITS EMPTYING AGAIN. WE SHOULD FOCUS ON THE THREATS FACING US *TODAY.*
FOR MOST OF THOSE YEARS, TH GREEN LANTERNS WE THE ONLY CORPS. NO THERE ARE *MANY.*
HE'S RIGHT, HAL. TH COUNTDOWN TIM HAS SPED UP.
THAT'S WHY WE'RE NEEDED MORE THAN EVER, TOMAR-TU. THE BLUE LANTERNS ARE *GONE.* THE BALANCE OF THE SPECTRUM HAS BEEN TIPPED.
COMPASSIONATE AS THE INDIGO TRIBE IS, THEY'RE ONLY ONE RING CHARGE AWAY FROM REVERTING TO THEIR MURDEROUS, *PSYCHO-PATHIC* SELVES.
AND THE STAR SAPPHIRES ONLY LOVE US *SOMETIMES.*
SUBTLE, HAL.
GOOD GUYS ARE *SCARCE.* WE SHELVE OUR RINGS, WHAT HAPPENS TO THE REST OF THE UNIVERSE?
YOU THINK THE *SINESTRO CORPS* IS GOIN TO STAY *AWOL* FOREVER? OR TH *LARFLEEZE* WIL QUIT HOARDING LIGHT FOR HIMSELF?
GREEN LANTERNS ARE CHOSEN FOR THEIR WILLPOWER, YET YOU ATTEMPT TO SWAY US WHEN WE'VE ALREADY MADE UP OUR MINDS.
I CANNOT HELP BUT NOTICE THE CONTRADICTION.
ALL RIGHT, GRAF. IF YOUR CHOICE IS BASED ON CONVICTION, I WON'T HOLD IT AGAINST YOU.
THAT GOES FOR ANY OF YOU. BUT REMEMBER, WE'VE ALL SWORN AN OATH TO PROTECT THE UNIVERSE, AND THAT'S *EXACTLY* WHAT WE'RE GOING TO DO.
AS CORPS LEADER, I'M ISSUING A NEW *PRIMARY OBJECTIVE:* IT'S TIME WE STARTED *POLICING* THE USE OF THE EMOTIONAL SPECTRUM.
WHAT?

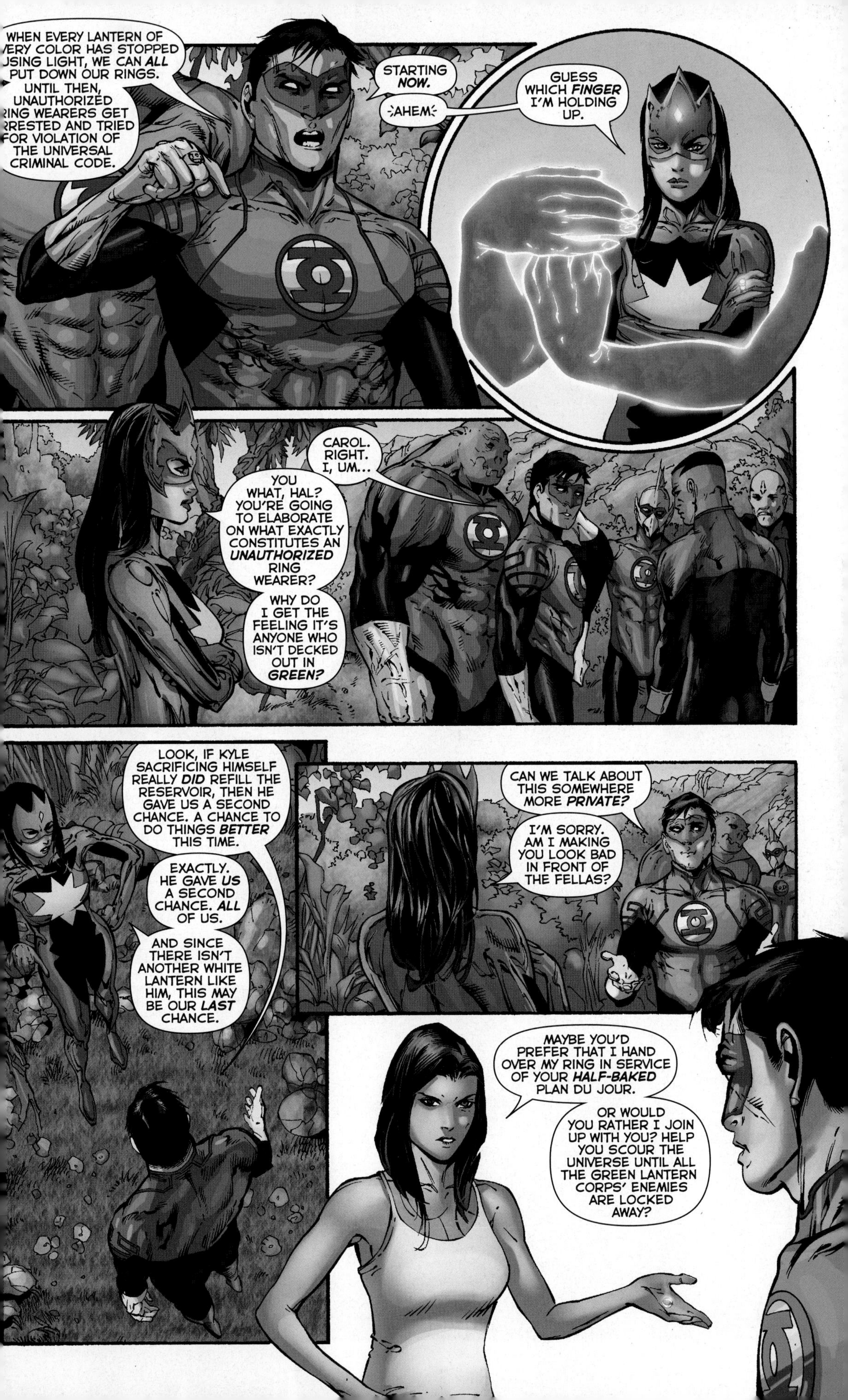
WHEN EVERY LANTERN OF VERY COLOR HAS STOPPED USING LIGHT, WE CAN ALL PUT DOWN OUR RINGS.
UNTIL THEN, UNAUTHORIZED RING WEARERS GET RRESTED AND TRIED FOR VIOLATION OF THE UNIVERSAL CRIMINAL CODE.
STARTING NOW.
AHEM
GUESS WHICH FINGER I'M HOLDING UP.
CAROL. RIGHT. I, UM...
YOU WHAT, HAL? YOU'RE GOING TO ELABORATE ON WHAT EXACTLY CONSTITUTES AN UNAUTHORIZED RING WEARER?
WHY DO I GET THE FEELING IT'S ANYONE WHO ISN'T DECKED OUT IN GREEN?
LOOK, IF KYLE SACRIFICING HIMSELF REALLY DID REFILL THE RESERVOIR, THEN HE GAVE US A SECOND CHANCE. A CHANCE TO DO THINGS BETTER THIS TIME.
EXACTLY. HE GAVE US A SECOND CHANCE. ALL OF US.
AND SINCE THERE ISN'T ANOTHER WHITE LANTERN LIKE HIM, THIS MAY BE OUR LAST CHANCE.
CAN WE TALK ABOUT THIS SOMEWHERE MORE PRIVATE?
I'M SORRY. AM I MAKING YOU LOOK BAD IN FRONT OF THE FELLAS?
MAYBE YOU'D PREFER THAT I HAND OVER MY RING IN SERVICE OF YOUR HALF-BAKED PLAN DU JOUR.
OR WOULD YOU RATHER I JOIN UP WITH YOU? HELP YOU SCOUR THE UNIVERSE UNTIL ALL THE GREEN LANTERN CORPS' ENEMIES ARE LOCKED AWAY?

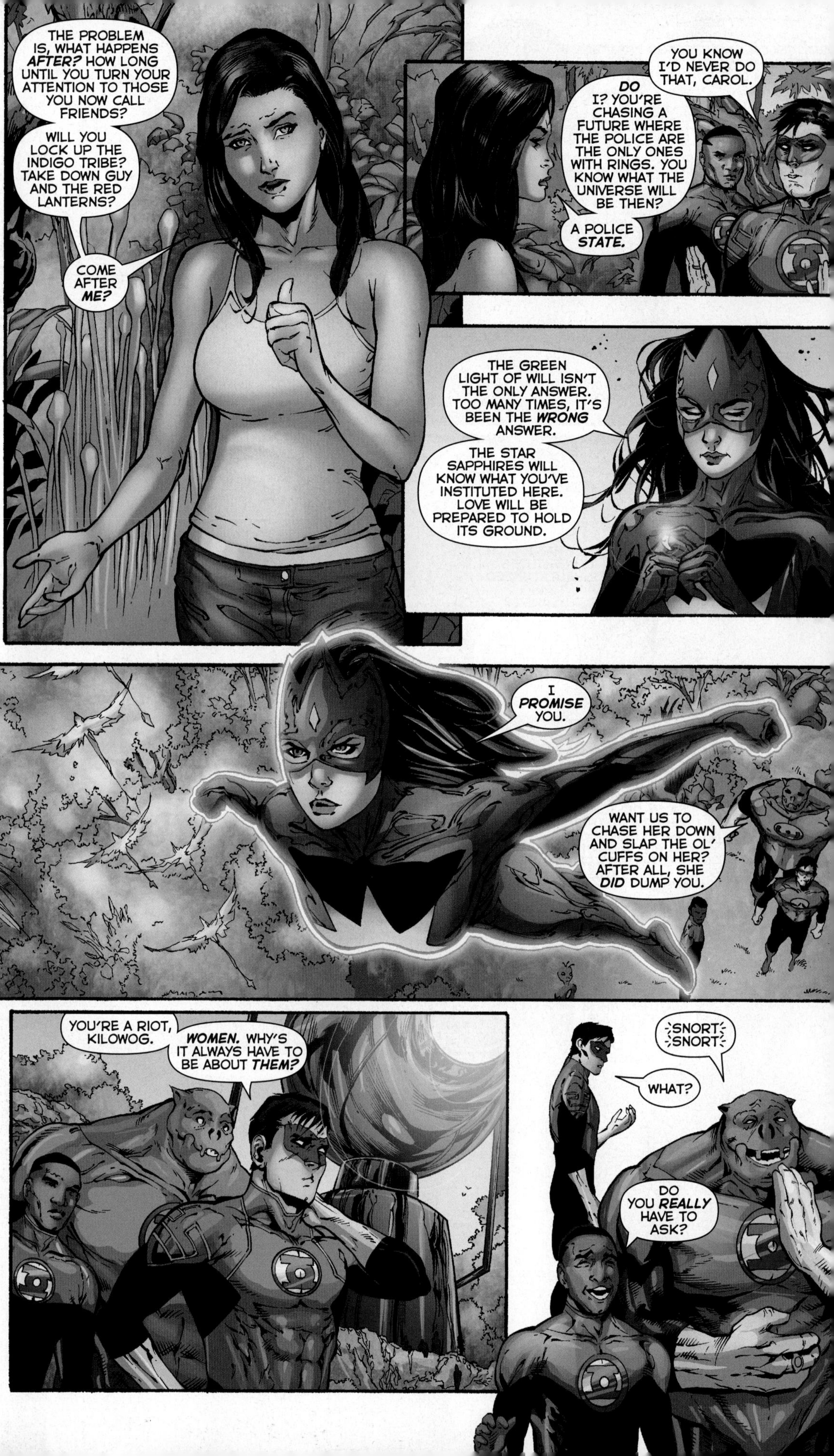
THE PROBLEM IS, WHAT HAPPENS *AFTER?* HOW LONG UNTIL YOU TURN YOUR ATTENTION TO THOSE YOU NOW CALL FRIENDS?
WILL YOU LOCK UP THE INDIGO TRIBE? TAKE DOWN GUY AND THE RED LANTERNS?
COME AFTER *ME?*
YOU KNOW I'D NEVER DO THAT, CAROL.
DO I? YOU'RE CHASING A FUTURE WHERE THE POLICE ARE THE ONLY ONES WITH RINGS. YOU KNOW WHAT THE UNIVERSE WILL BE THEN?
A POLICE *STATE.*
THE GREEN LIGHT OF WILL ISN'T THE ONLY ANSWER. TOO MANY TIMES, IT'S BEEN THE *WRONG* ANSWER.
THE STAR SAPPHIRES WILL KNOW WHAT YOU'VE INSTITUTED HERE. LOVE WILL BE PREPARED TO HOLD ITS GROUND.
I *PROMISE* YOU.
WANT US TO CHASE HER DOWN AND SLAP THE OL' CUFFS ON HER? AFTER ALL, SHE *DID* DUMP YOU.
YOU'RE A RIOT, KILOWOG.
WOMEN. WHY'S IT ALWAYS HAVE TO BE ABOUT *THEM?*
SNORT SNORT
WHAT?
DO YOU *REALLY* HAVE TO ASK?

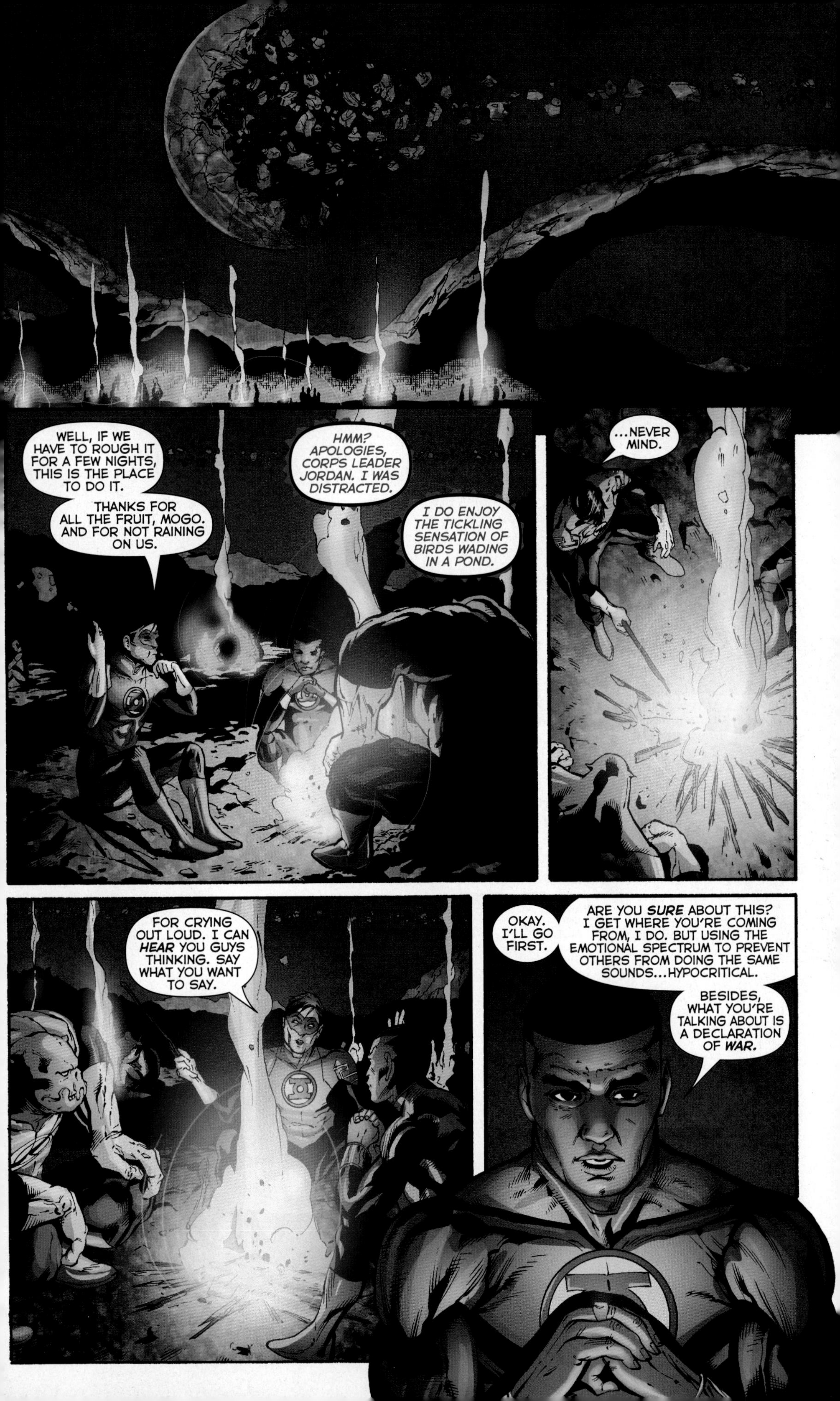
WELL, IF WE HAVE TO ROUGH IT FOR A FEW NIGHTS, THIS IS THE PLACE TO DO IT.
THANKS FOR ALL THE FRUIT, MOGO. AND FOR NOT RAINING ON US.
HMM? APOLOGIES, CORPS LEADER JORDAN. I WAS DISTRACTED.
I DO ENJOY THE TICKLING SENSATION OF BIRDS WADING IN A POND.
...NEVER MIND.
FOR CRYING OUT LOUD. I CAN HEAR YOU GUYS THINKING. SAY WHAT YOU WANT TO SAY.
OKAY. I'LL GO FIRST.
ARE YOU SURE ABOUT THIS? I GET WHERE YOU'RE COMING FROM, I DO. BUT USING THE EMOTIONAL SPECTRUM TO PREVENT OTHERS FROM DOING THE SAME SOUNDS...HYPOCRITICAL.
BESIDES, WHAT YOU'RE TALKING ABOUT IS A DECLARATION OF WAR.

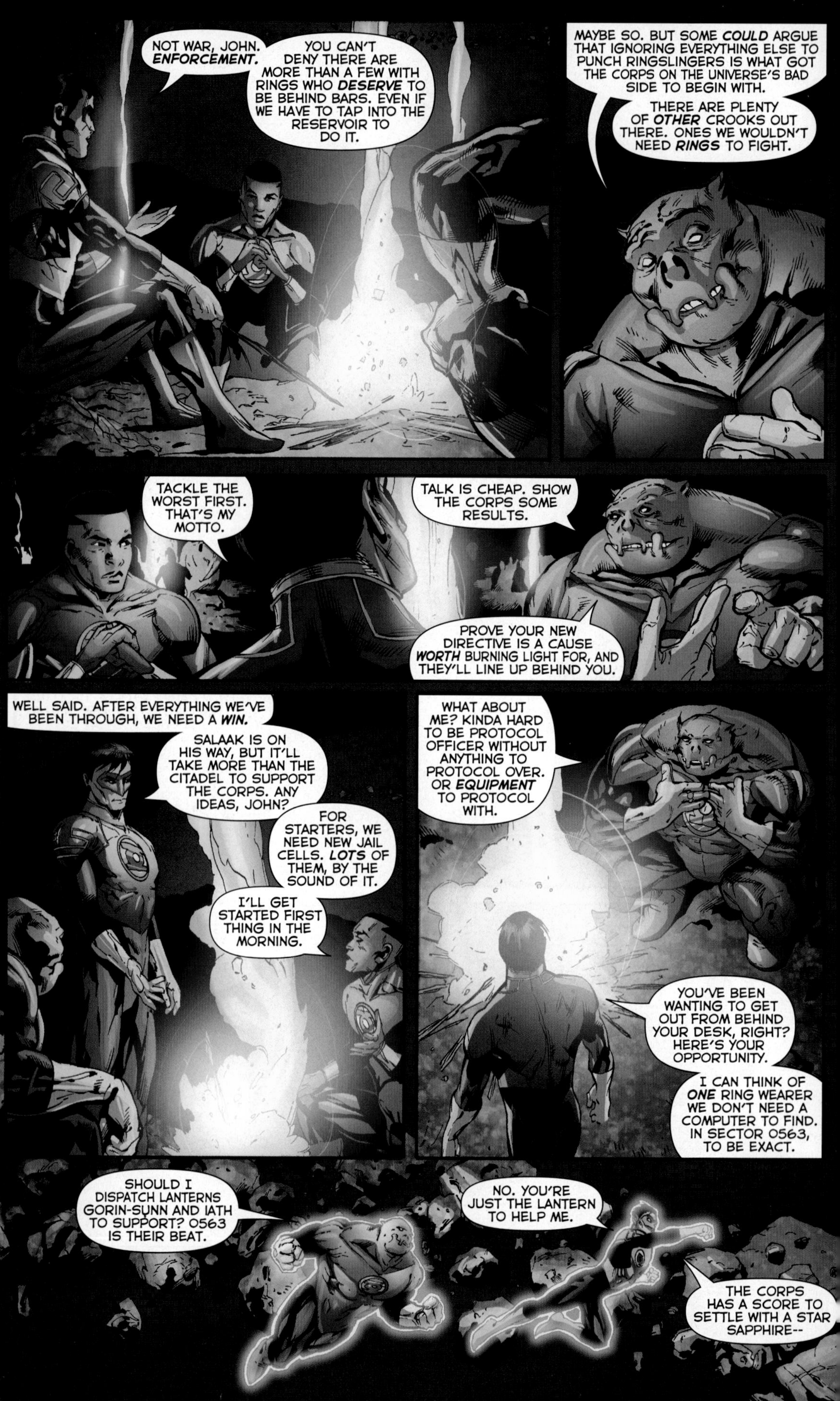
NOT WAR, JOHN. ENFORCEMENT.
YOU CAN'T DENY THERE ARE MORE THAN A FEW WITH RINGS WHO DESERVE TO BE BEHIND BARS. EVEN IF WE HAVE TO TAP INTO THE RESERVOIR TO DO IT.
MAYBE SO. BUT SOME COULD ARGUE THAT IGNORING EVERYTHING ELSE TO PUNCH RINGSLINGERS IS WHAT GOT THE CORPS ON THE UNIVERSE'S BAD SIDE TO BEGIN WITH.
THERE ARE PLENTY OF OTHER CROOKS OUT THERE. ONES WE WOULDN'T NEED RINGS TO FIGHT.
TACKLE THE WORST FIRST. THAT'S MY MOTTO.
TALK IS CHEAP. SHOW THE CORPS SOME RESULTS.
PROVE YOUR NEW DIRECTIVE IS A CAUSE WORTH BURNING LIGHT FOR, AND THEY'LL LINE UP BEHIND YOU.
WELL SAID. AFTER EVERYTHING WE'VE BEEN THROUGH, WE NEED A WIN.
SALAAK IS ON HIS WAY, BUT IT'LL TAKE MORE THAN THE CITADEL TO SUPPORT THE CORPS. ANY IDEAS, JOHN?
FOR STARTERS, WE NEED NEW JAIL CELLS. LOTS OF THEM, BY THE SOUND OF IT.
I'LL GET STARTED FIRST THING IN THE MORNING.
WHAT ABOUT ME? KINDA HARD TO BE PROTOCOL OFFICER WITHOUT ANYTHING TO PROTOCOL OVER. OR EQUIPMENT TO PROTOCOL WITH.
YOU'VE BEEN WANTING TO GET OUT FROM BEHIND YOUR DESK, RIGHT? HERE'S YOUR OPPORTUNITY.
I CAN THINK OF ONE RING WEARER WE DON'T NEED A COMPUTER TO FIND. IN SECTOR 0563, TO BE EXACT.
SHOULD I DISPATCH LANTERNS GORIN-SUNN AND IATH TO SUPPORT? 0563 IS THEIR BEAT.
NO. YOU'RE JUST THE LANTERN TO HELP ME.
THE CORPS HAS A SCORE TO SETTLE WITH A STAR SAPPHIRE--

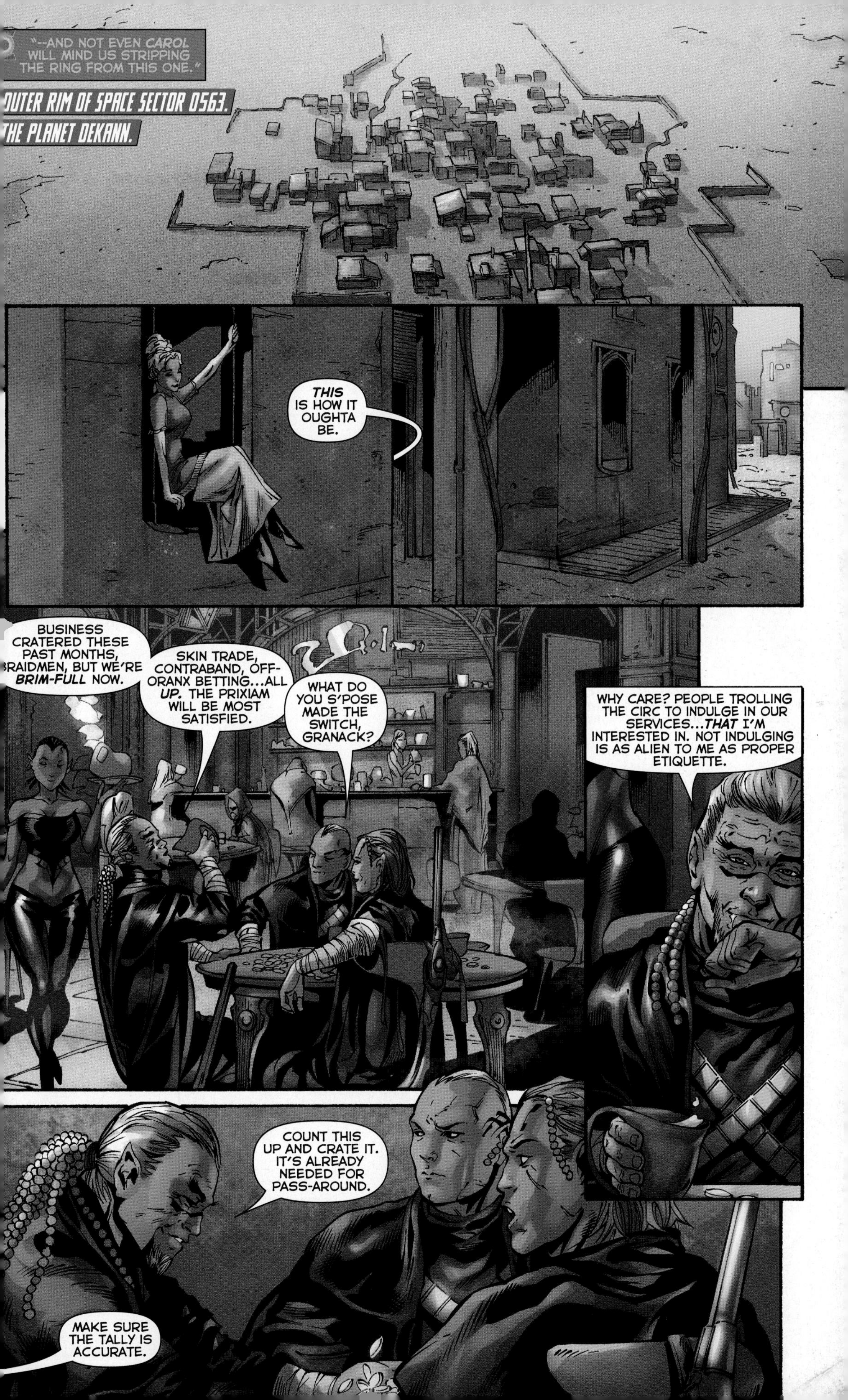
"--AND NOT EVEN CAROL WILL MIND US STRIPPING THE RING FROM THIS ONE."
OUTER RIM OF SPACE SECTOR 0563.
THE PLANET DEKANN.
THIS IS HOW IT OUGHTA BE.
BUSINESS CRATERED THESE PAST MONTHS, BRAIDMEN, BUT WE'RE BRIM-FULL NOW.
SKIN TRADE, CONTRABAND, OFF-ORANX BETTING...ALL UP. THE PRIXIAM WILL BE MOST SATISFIED.
WHAT DO YOU S'POSE MADE THE SWITCH, GRANACK?
WHY CARE? PEOPLE TROLLING THE CIRC TO INDULGE IN OUR SERVICES...THAT I'M INTERESTED IN. NOT INDULGING IS AS ALIEN TO ME AS PROPER ETIQUETTE.
COUNT THIS UP AND CRATE IT. IT'S ALREADY NEEDED FOR PASS-AROUND.
MAKE SURE THE TALLY IS ACCURATE.

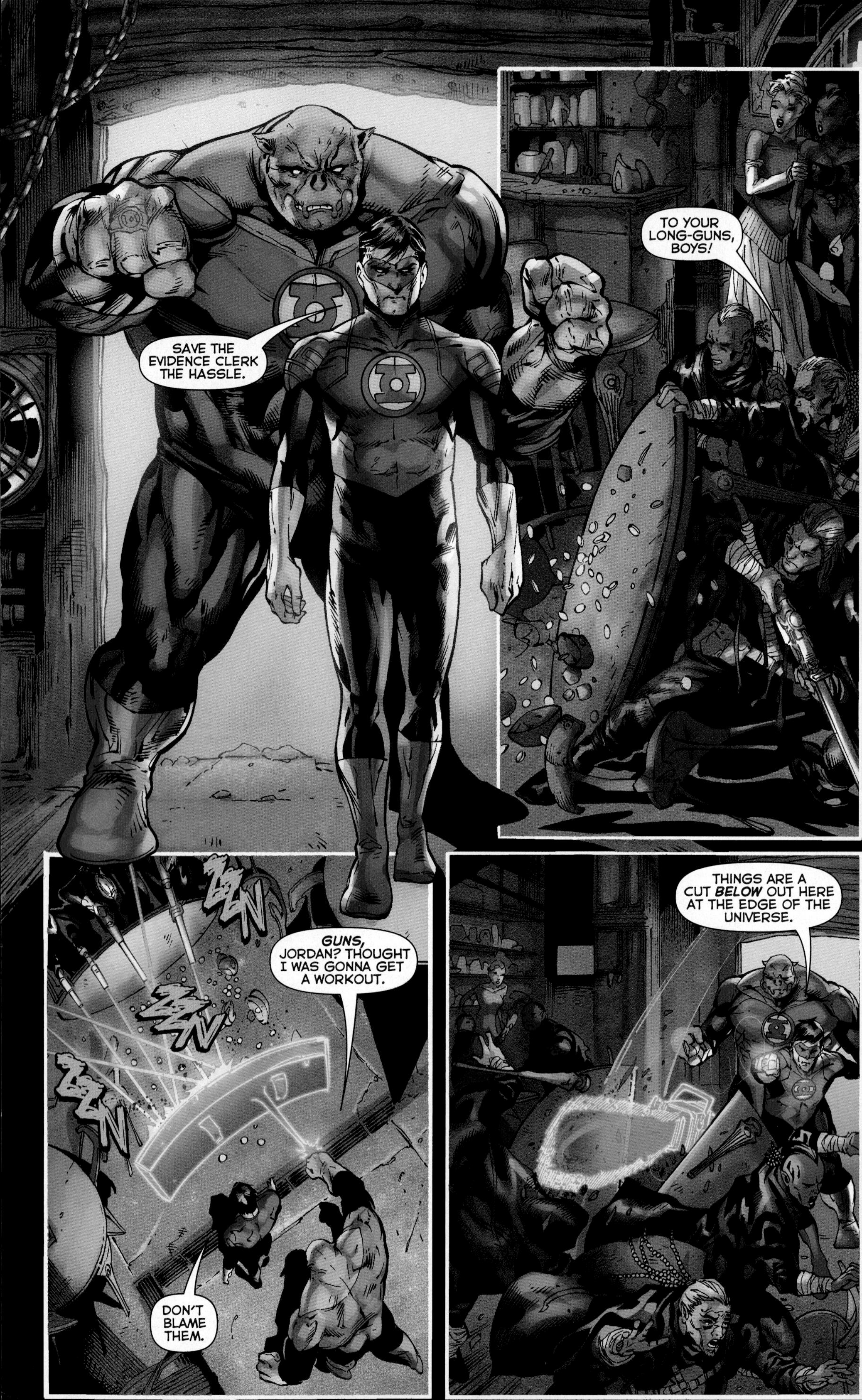
SAVE THE EVIDENCE CLERK THE HASSLE.
TO YOUR LONG-GUNS, BOYS!
ZZZN
ZZZN
ZZZN
GUNS, JORDAN? THOUGHT I WAS GONNA GET A WORKOUT.
DON'T BLAME THEM.
THINGS ARE A CUT BELOW OUT HERE AT THE EDGE OF THE UNIVERSE.

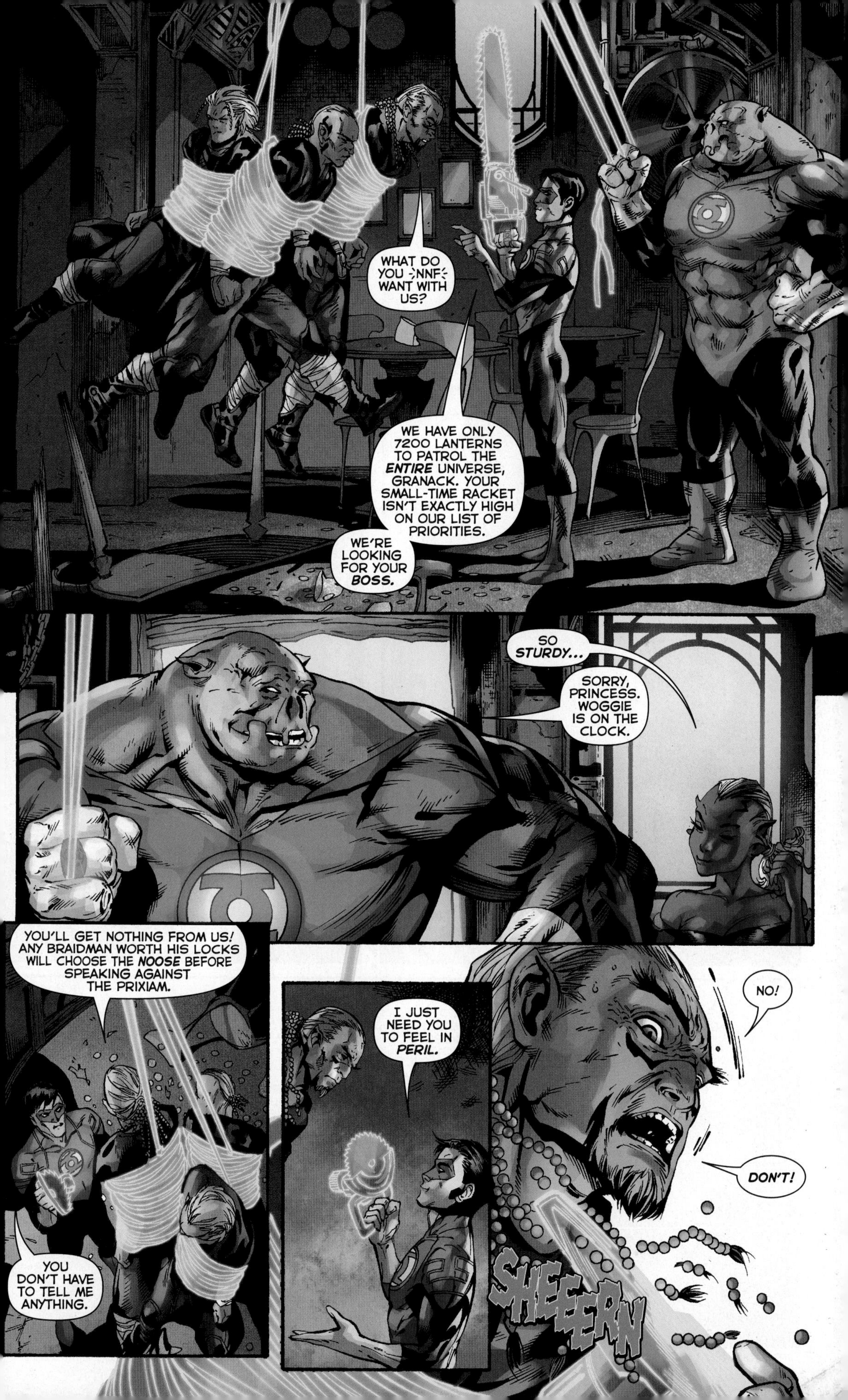
WHAT DO YOU -NNF- WANT WITH US?
WE HAVE ONLY 7200 LANTERNS TO PATROL THE ENTIRE UNIVERSE, GRANACK. YOUR SMALL-TIME RACKET ISN'T EXACTLY HIGH ON OUR LIST OF PRIORITIES.
WE'RE LOOKING FOR YOUR BOSS.
SO STURDY...
SORRY, PRINCESS. WOGGIE IS ON THE CLOCK.
YOU'LL GET NOTHING FROM US! ANY BRAIDMAN WORTH HIS LOCKS WILL CHOOSE THE NOOSE BEFORE SPEAKING AGAINST THE PRIXIAM.
YOU DON'T HAVE TO TELL ME ANYTHING.
I JUST NEED YOU TO FEEL IN PERIL.
NO!
DON'T!
SHEEERN

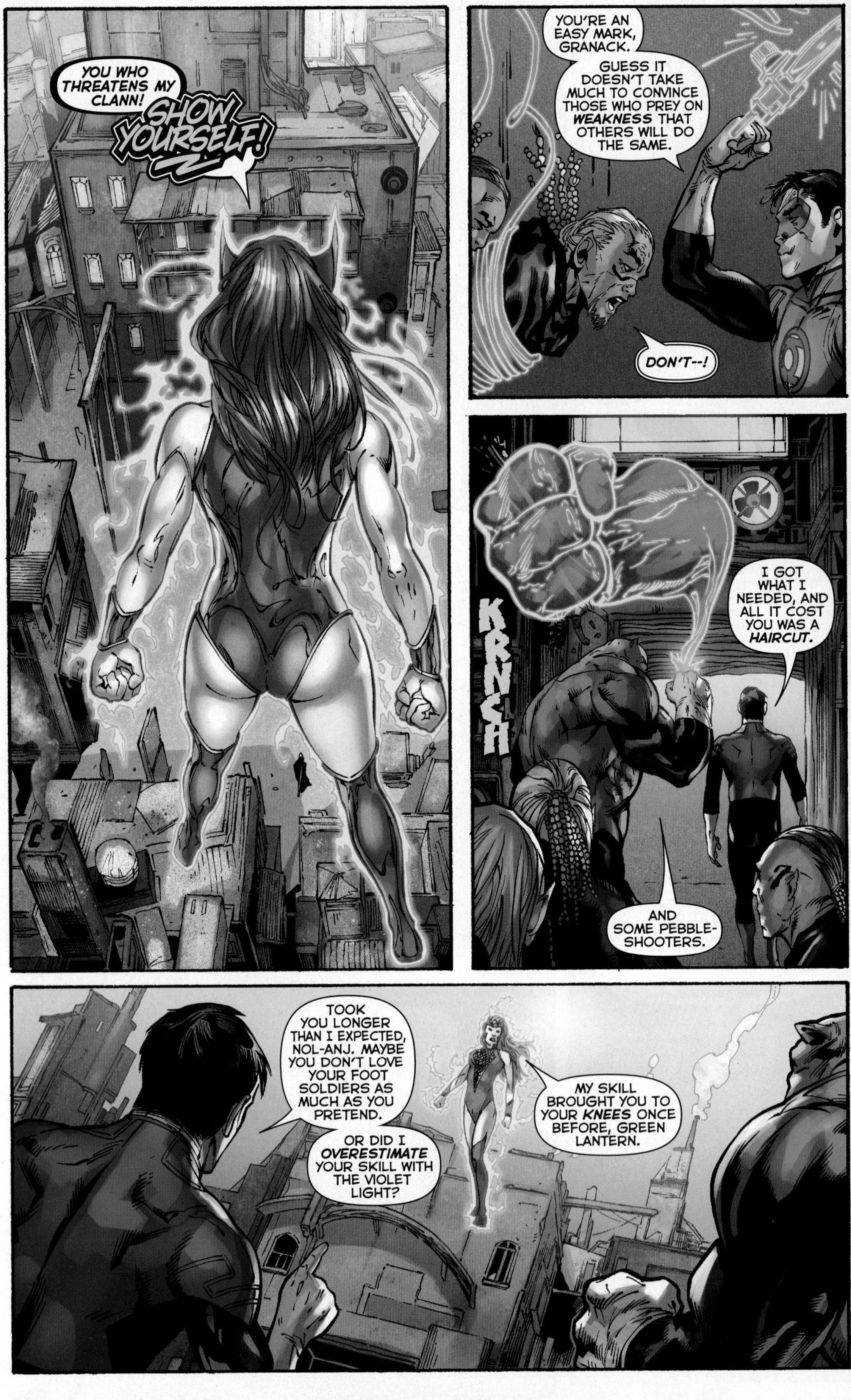
YOU WHO THREATENS MY CLANN!
SHOW YOURSELF!
YOU'RE AN EASY MARK, GRANACK.
GUESS IT DOESN'T TAKE MUCH TO CONVINCE THOSE WHO PREY ON WEAKNESS THAT OTHERS WILL DO THE SAME.
DON'T--!
KRNCH
I GOT WHAT I NEEDED, AND ALL IT COST YOU WAS A HAIRCUT.
AND SOME PEBBLE-SHOOTERS.
TOOK YOU LONGER THAN I EXPECTED, NOL-ANJ. MAYBE YOU DON'T LOVE YOUR FOOT SOLDIERS AS MUCH AS YOU PRETEND.
OR DID I OVERESTIMATE YOUR SKILL WITH THE VIOLET LIGHT?
MY SKILL BROUGHT YOU TO YOUR KNEES ONCE BEFORE, GREEN LANTERN.

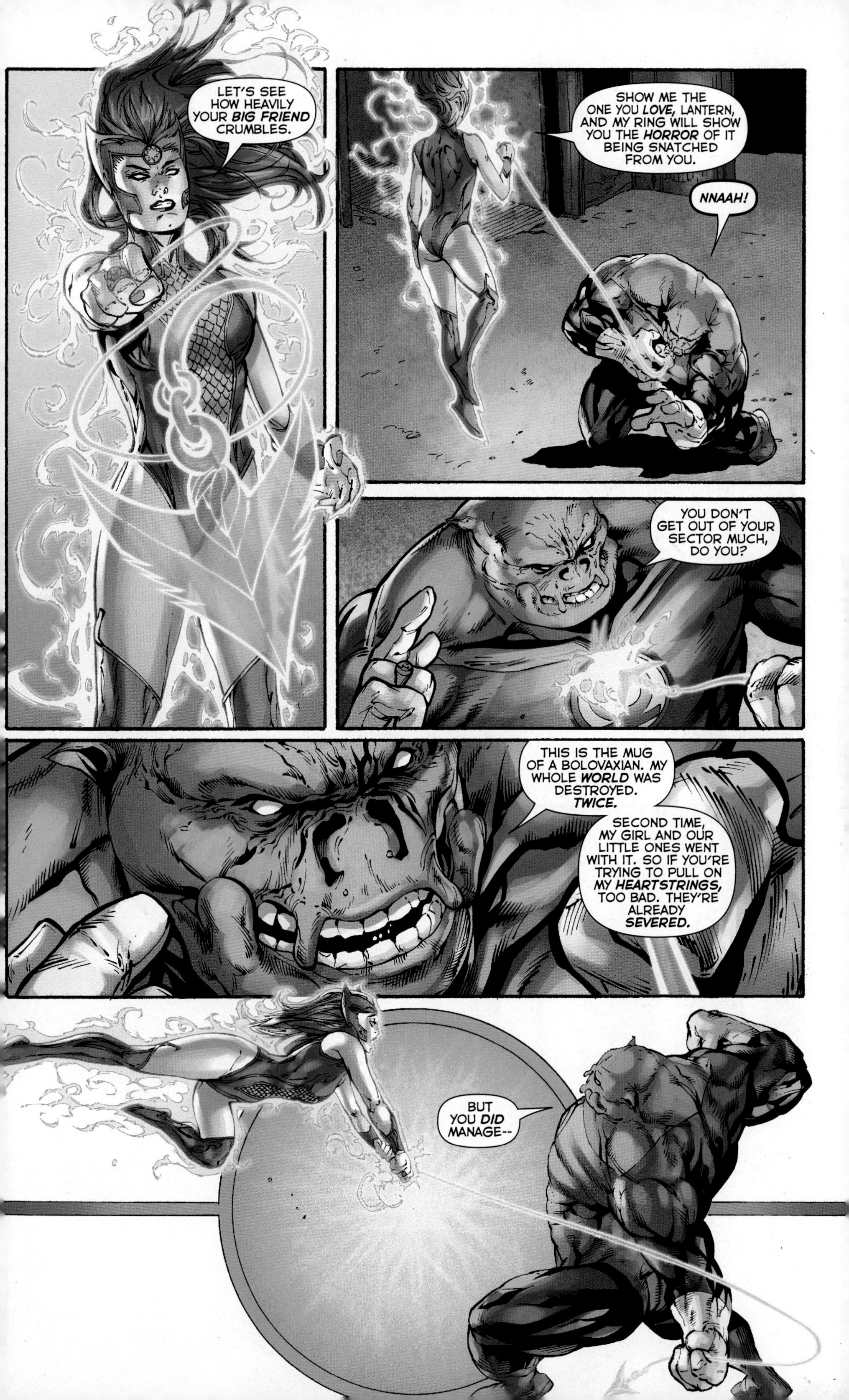
LET'S SEE HOW HEAVILY YOUR BIG FRIEND CRUMBLES.
SHOW ME THE ONE YOU LOVE, LANTERN, AND MY RING WILL SHOW YOU THE HORROR OF IT BEING SNATCHED FROM YOU.
NNAAH!
YOU DON'T GET OUT OF YOUR SECTOR MUCH, DO YOU?
THIS IS THE MUG OF A BOLOVAXIAN. MY WHOLE WORLD WAS DESTROYED. TWICE.
SECOND TIME, MY GIRL AND OUR LITTLE ONES WENT WITH IT. SO IF YOU'RE TRYING TO PULL ON MY HEARTSTRINGS, TOO BAD. THEY'RE ALREADY SEVERED.
BUT YOU DID MANAGE--

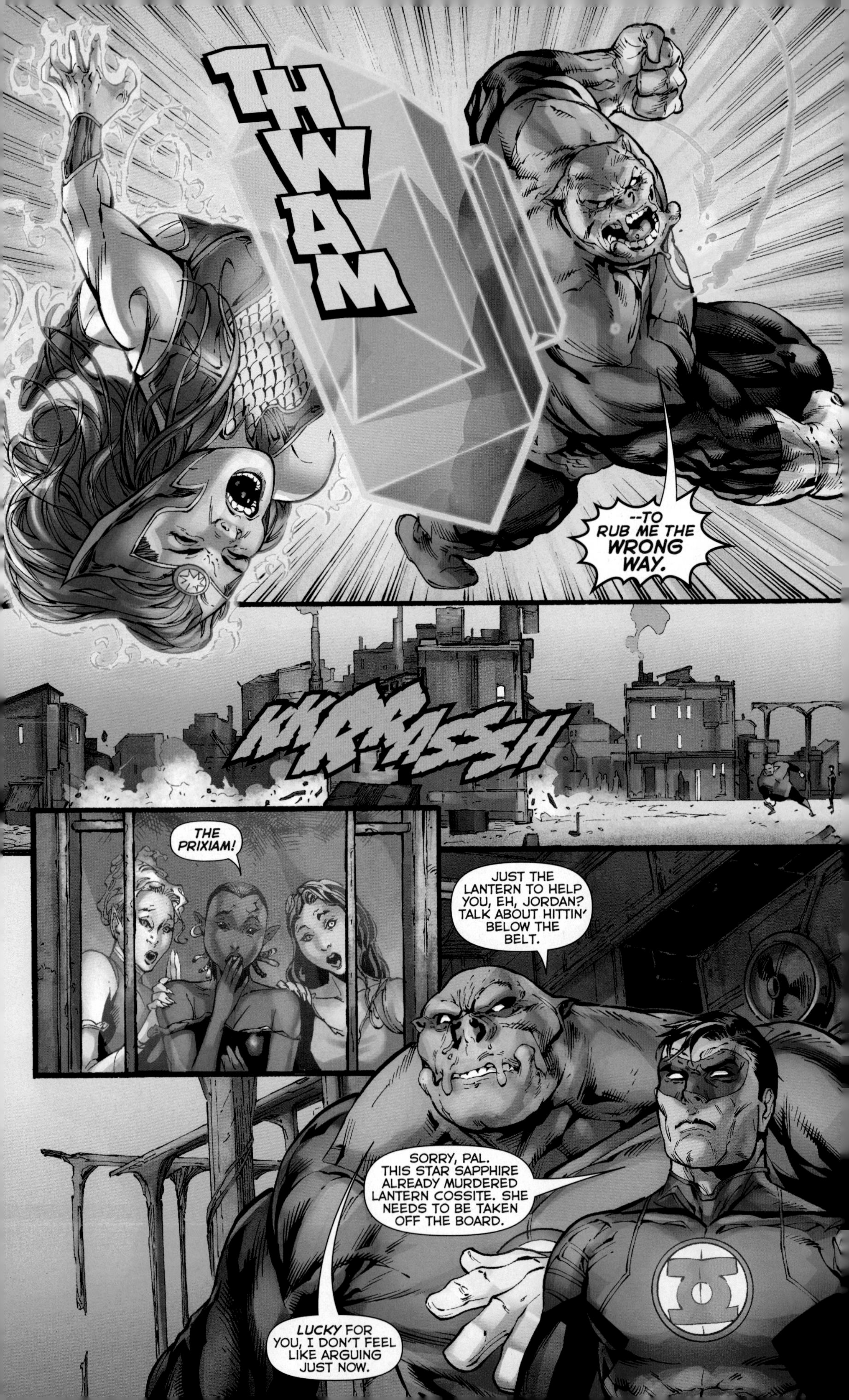

THWAM
--TO RUB ME THE WRONG WAY.
THE PRIXIAM!
JUST THE LANTERN TO HELP YOU, EH, JORDAN? TALK ABOUT HITTIN' BELOW THE BELT.
SORRY, PAL. THIS STAR SAPPHIRE ALREADY MURDERED LANTERN COSSITE. SHE NEEDS TO BE TAKEN OFF THE BOARD.
LUCKY FOR YOU, I DON'T FEEL LIKE ARGUING JUST NOW.

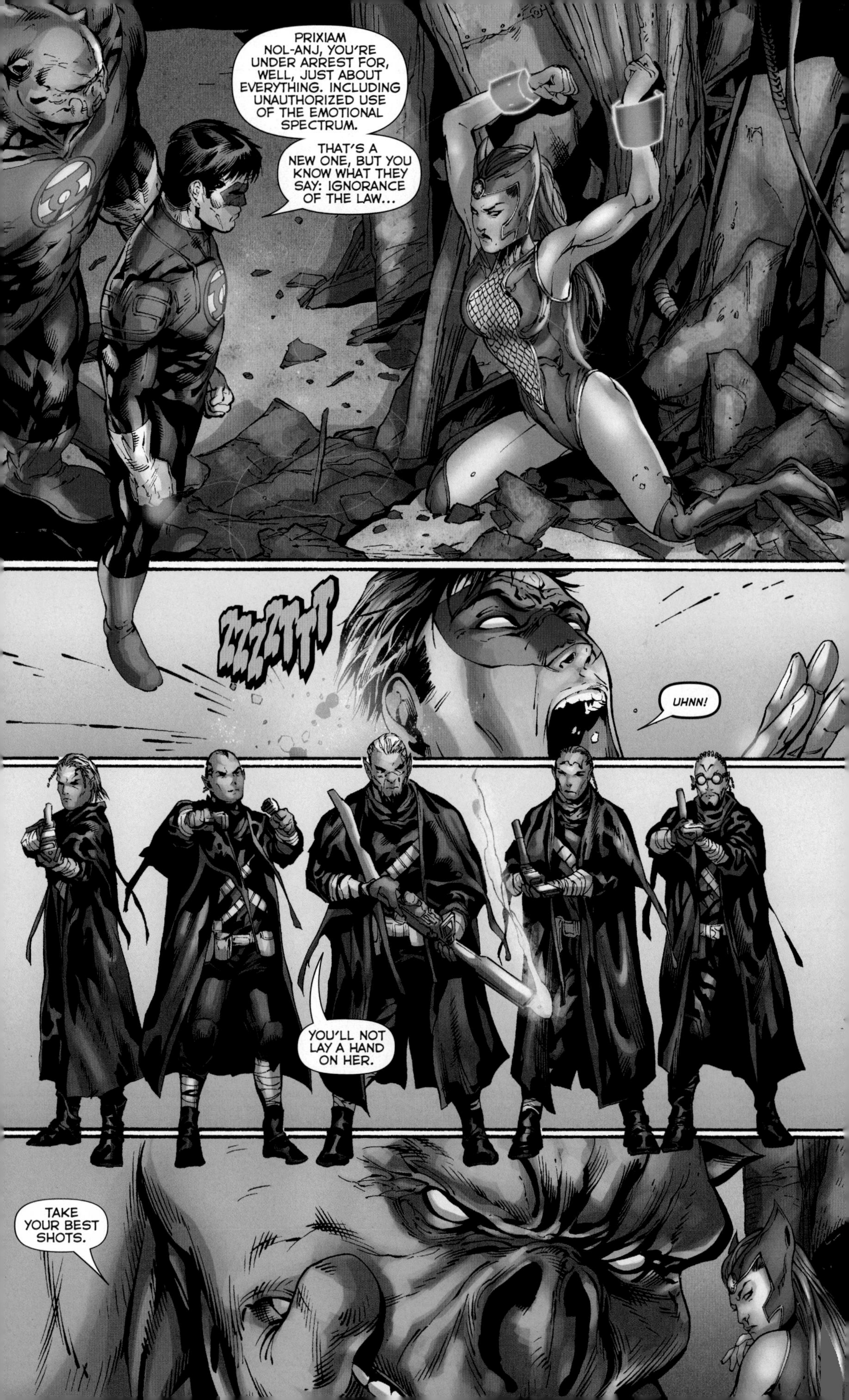
PRIXIAM NOL-ANJ, YOU'RE UNDER ARREST FOR, WELL, JUST ABOUT EVERYTHING. INCLUDING UNAUTHORIZED USE OF THE EMOTIONAL SPECTRUM.
THAT'S A NEW ONE, BUT YOU KNOW WHAT THEY SAY: IGNORANCE OF THE LAW...
ZZZZTTT
UHNN!
YOU'LL NOT LAY A HAND ON HER.
TAKE YOUR BEST SHOTS.

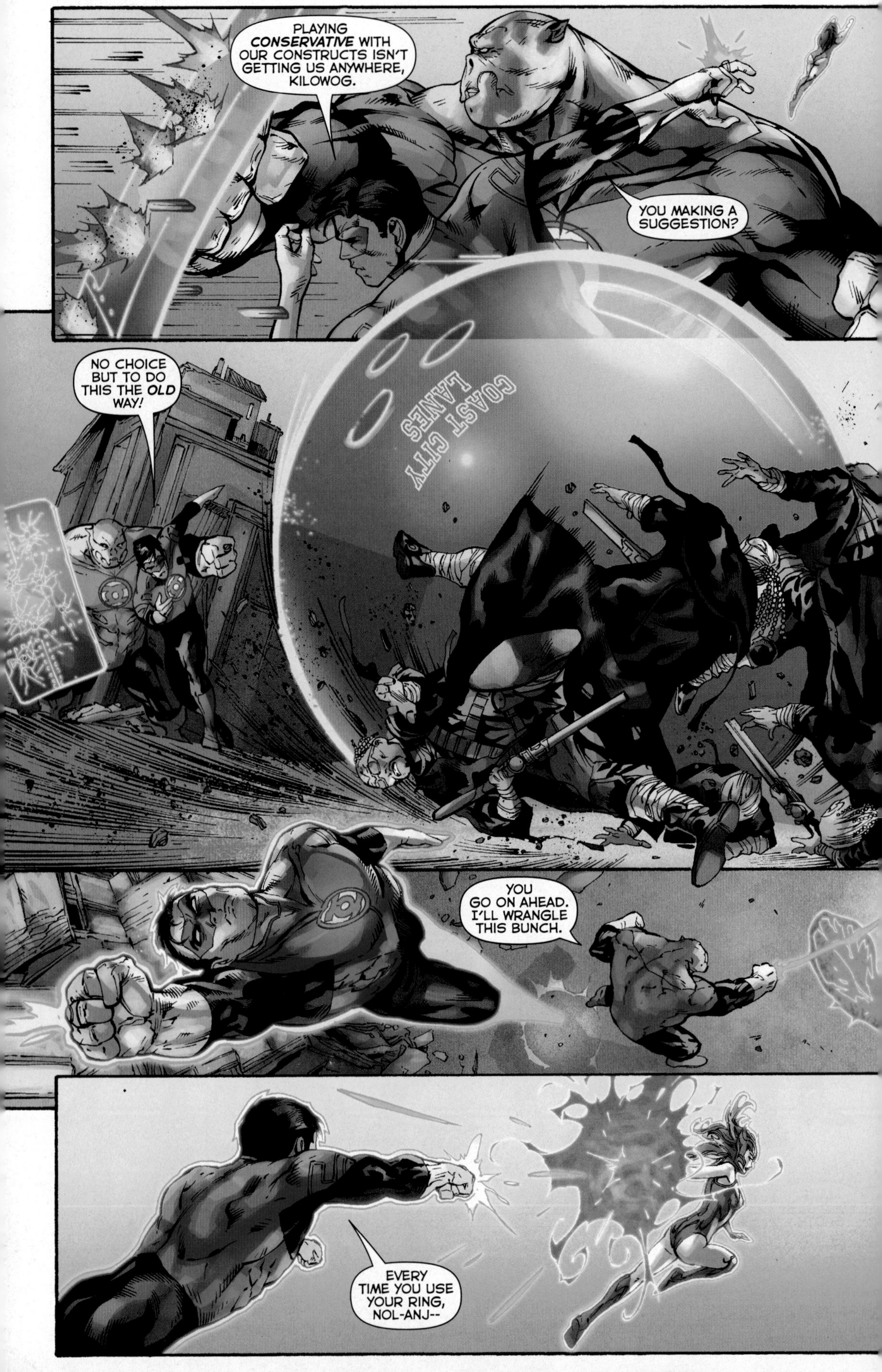

PLAYING *CONSERVATIVE* WITH OUR CONSTRUCTS ISN'T GETTING US ANYWHERE, KILOWOG.
YOU MAKING A SUGGESTION?
NO CHOICE BUT TO DO THIS THE *OLD* WAY!
COAST CITY LANES
YOU GO ON AHEAD. I'LL WRANGLE THIS BUNCH.
EVERY TIME YOU USE YOUR RING, NOL-ANJ--

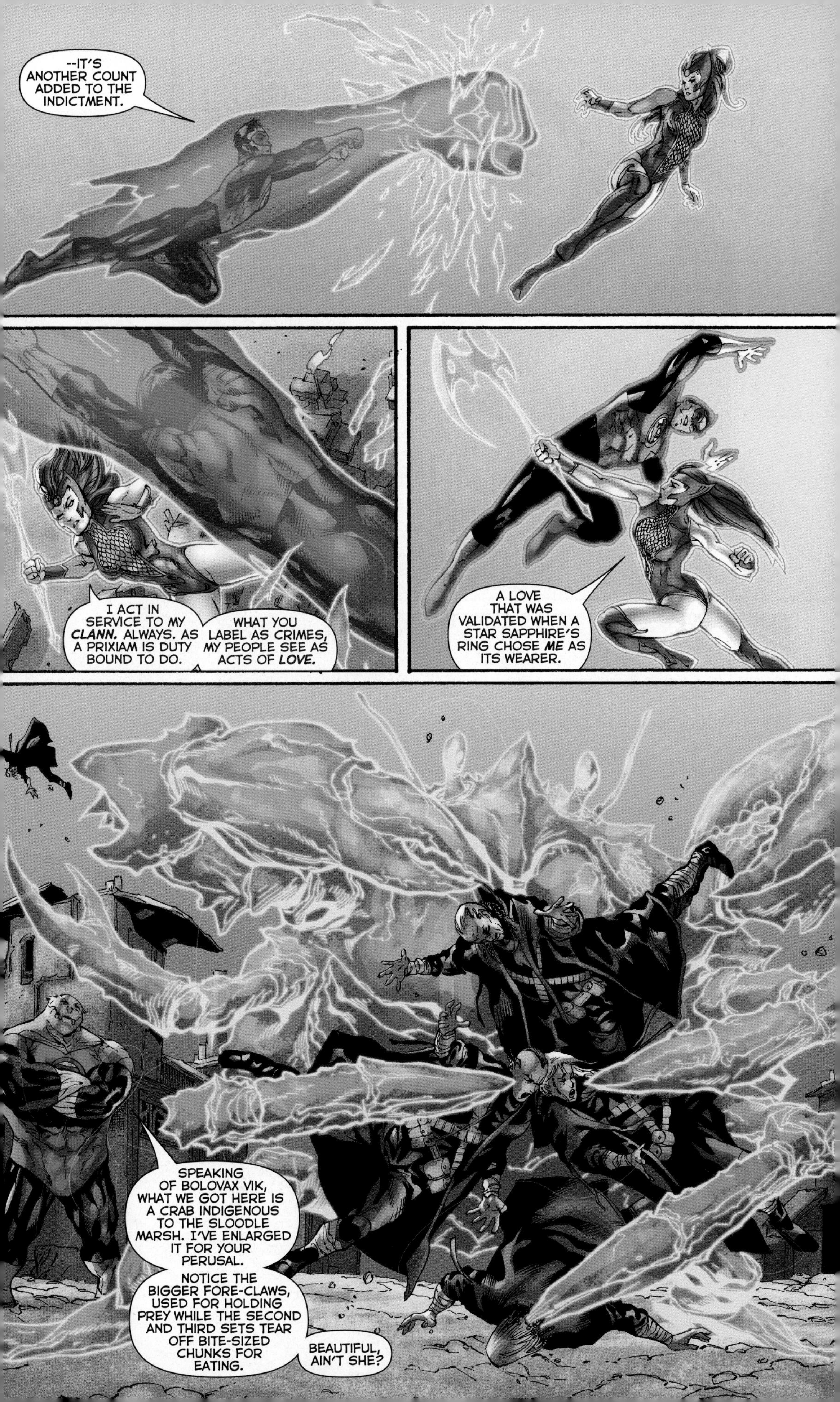
--IT'S ANOTHER COUNT ADDED TO THE INDICTMENT.
I ACT IN SERVICE TO MY CLANN. ALWAYS. AS A PRIXIAM IS DUTY BOUND TO DO.
WHAT YOU LABEL AS CRIMES, MY PEOPLE SEE AS ACTS OF LOVE.
A LOVE THAT WAS VALIDATED WHEN A STAR SAPPHIRE'S RING CHOSE ME AS ITS WEARER.
SPEAKING OF BOLOVAX VIK, WHAT WE GOT HERE IS A CRAB INDIGENOUS TO THE SLOODLE MARSH. I'VE ENLARGED IT FOR YOUR PERUSAL.
NOTICE THE BIGGER FORE-CLAWS, USED FOR HOLDING PREY WHILE THE SECOND AND THIRD SETS TEAR OFF BITE-SIZED CHUNKS FOR EATING.
BEAUTIFUL, AIN'T SHE?

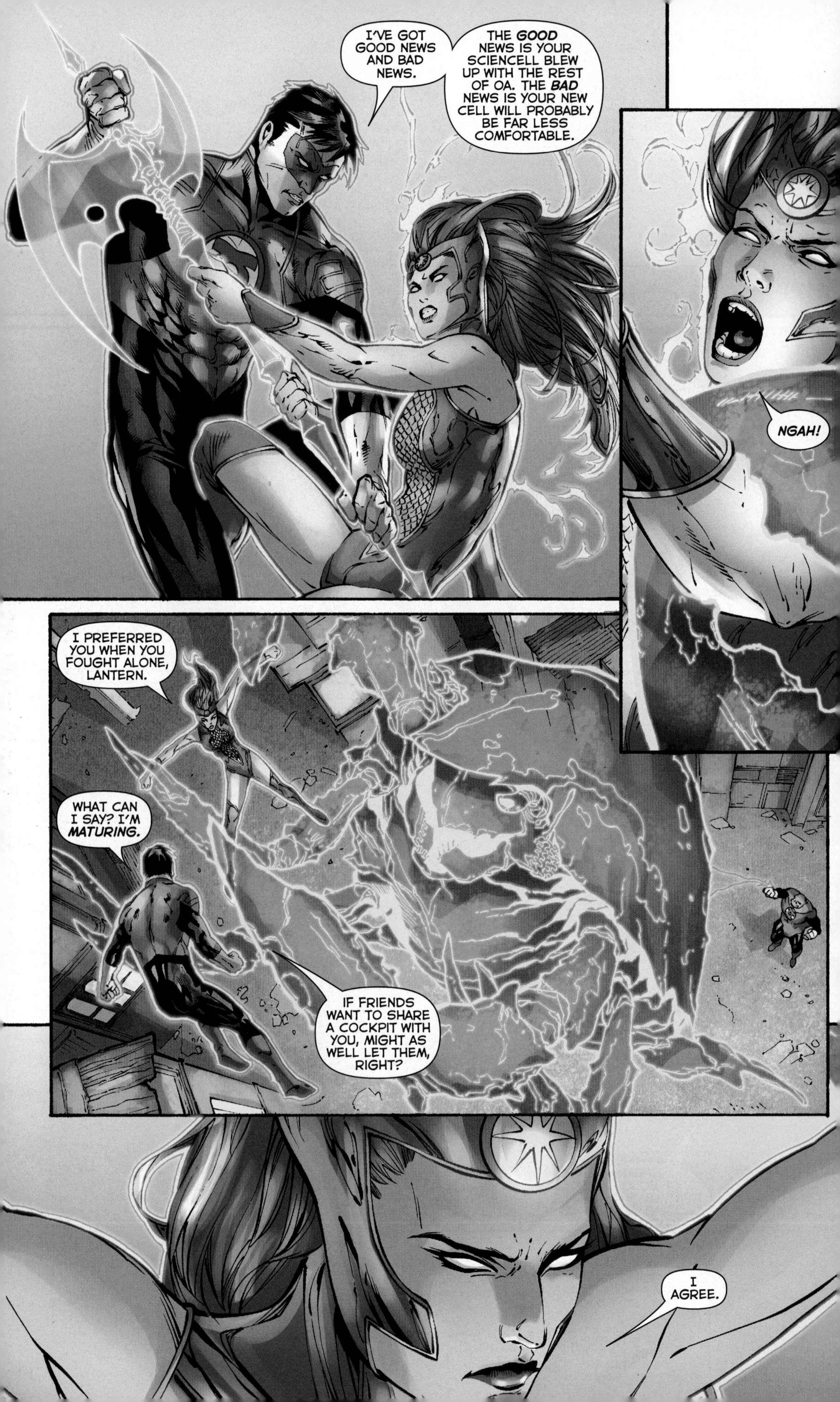

I'VE GOT GOOD NEWS AND BAD NEWS.
THE GOOD NEWS IS YOUR SCIENCELL BLEW UP WITH THE REST OF OA. THE BAD NEWS IS YOUR NEW CELL WILL PROBABLY BE FAR LESS COMFORTABLE.
NGAH!
I PREFERRED YOU WHEN YOU FOUGHT ALONE, LANTERN.
WHAT CAN I SAY? I'M MATURING.
IF FRIENDS WANT TO SHARE A COCKPIT WITH YOU, MIGHT AS WELL LET THEM, RIGHT?
I AGREE.

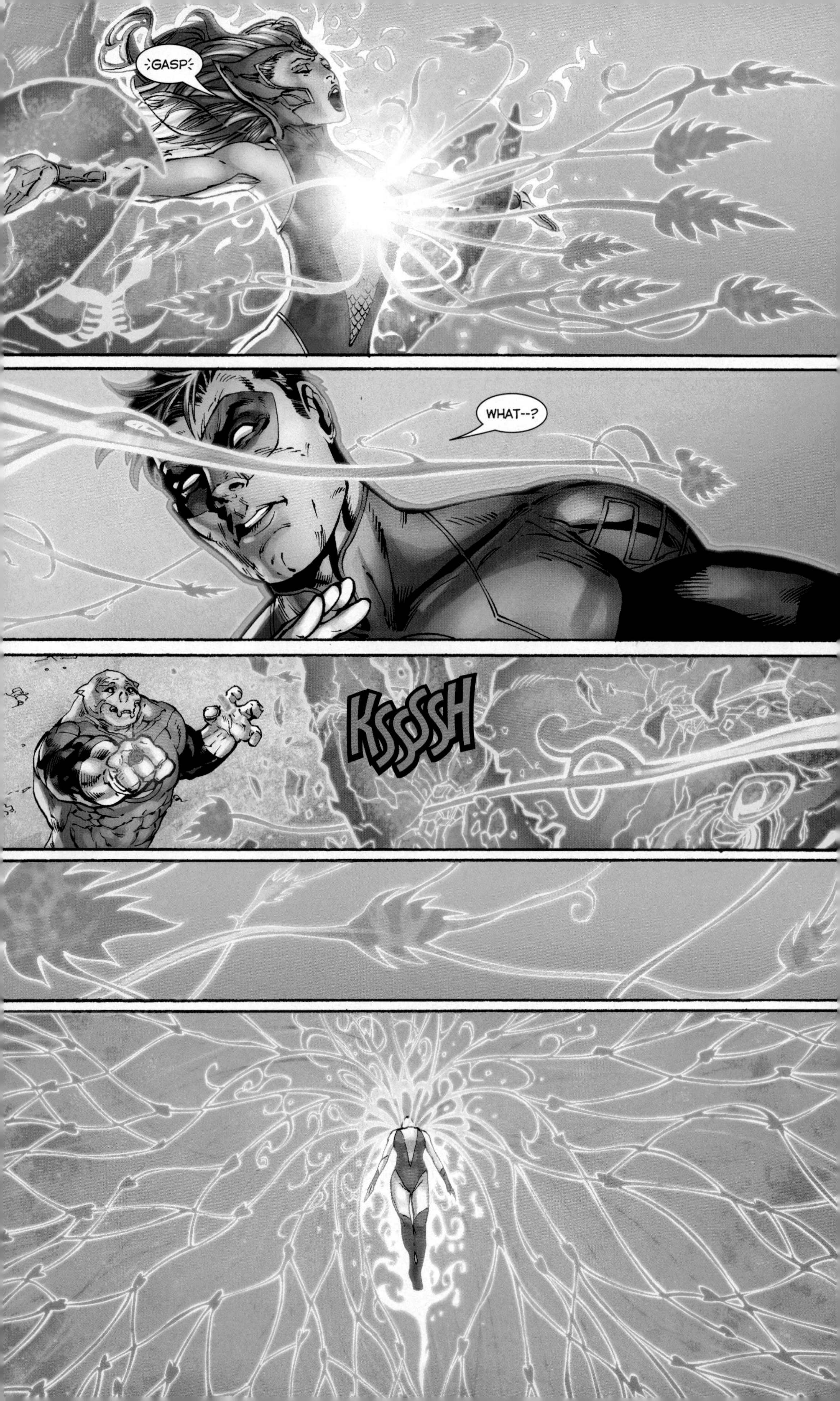
GASP
WHAT--?
KSSSSH

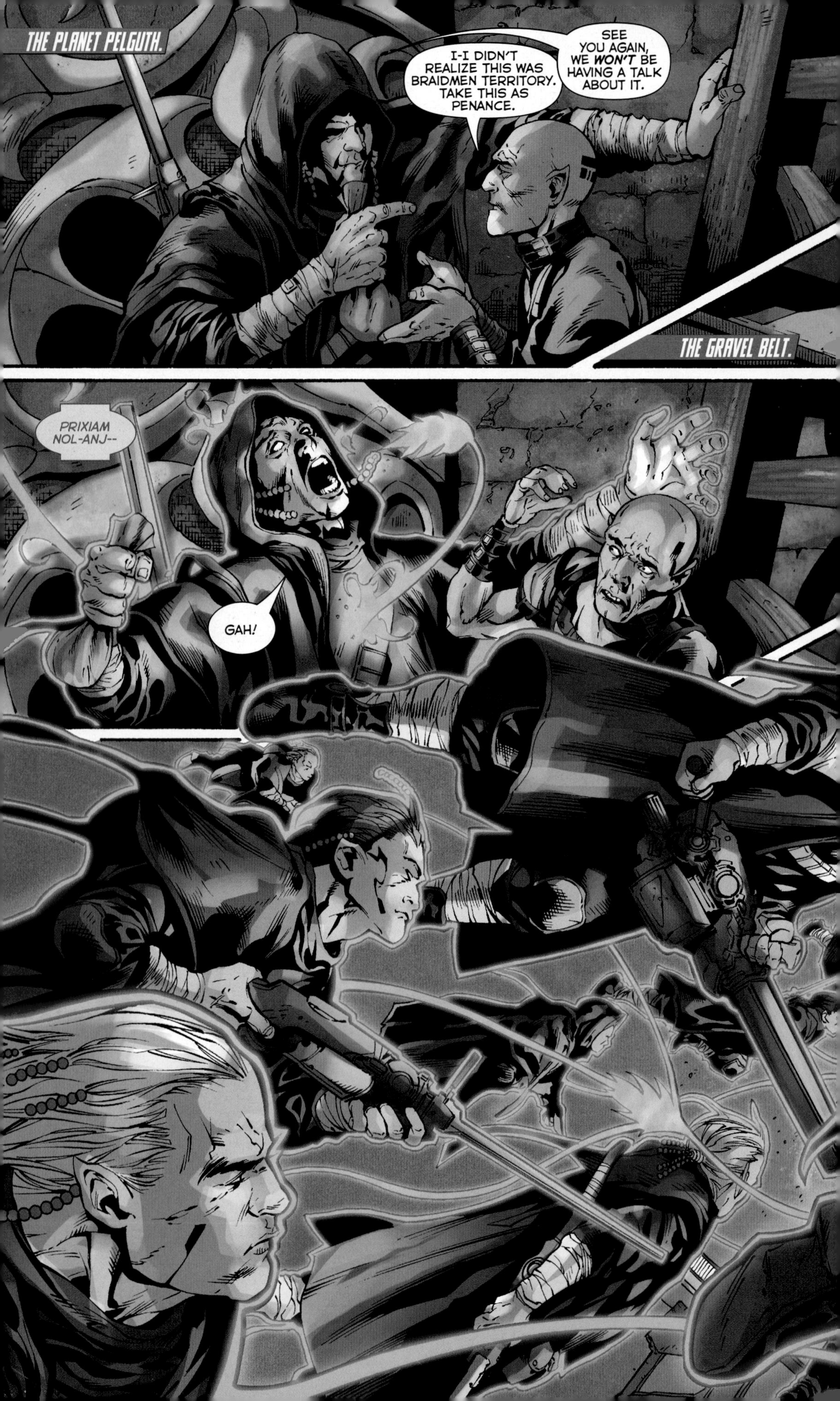
THE PLANET PELGUTH.
I-I DIDN'T REALIZE THIS WAS BRAIDMEN TERRITORY. TAKE THIS AS PENANCE.
SEE YOU AGAIN, WE WON'T BE HAVING A TALK ABOUT IT.
THE GRAVEL BELT.
PRIXIAM NOL-ANJ--
GAH!

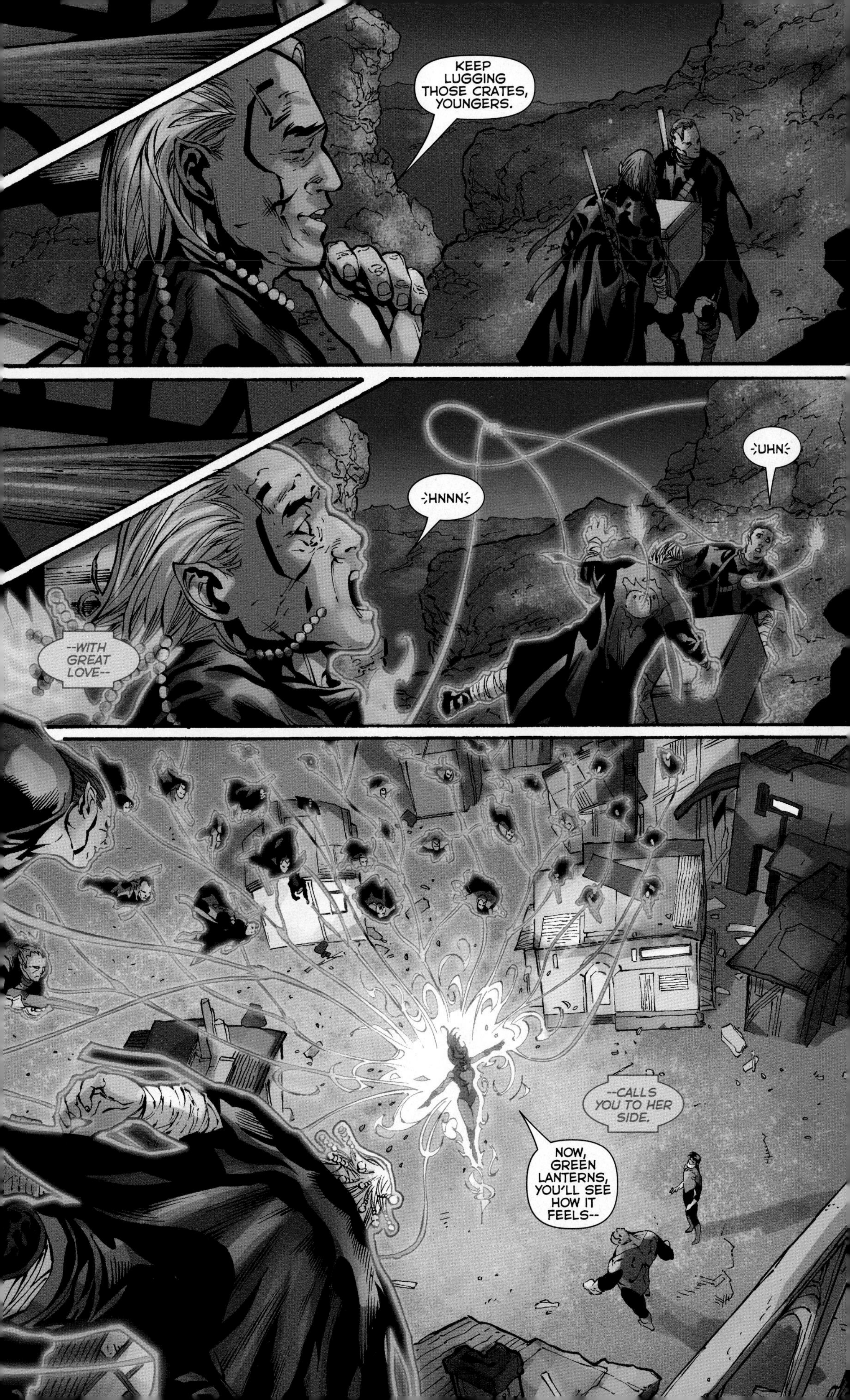
KEEP LUGGING THOSE CRATES, YOUNGERS.
HNNN
UHN
--WITH GREAT LOVE--
--CALLS YOU TO HER SIDE.
NOW, GREEN LANTERNS, YOU'LL SEE HOW IT FEELS--

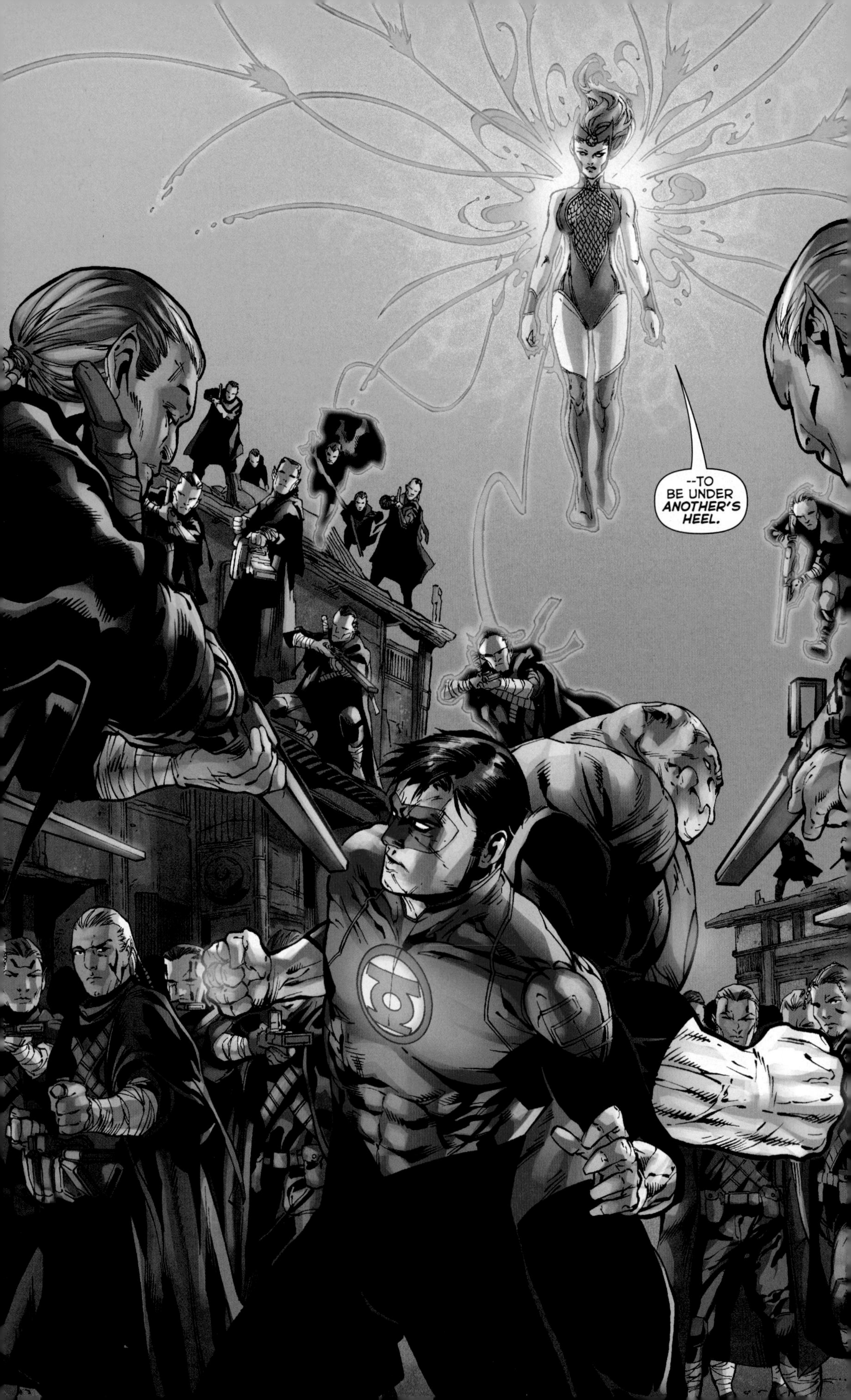
--TO BE UNDER ANOTHER'S HEEL.

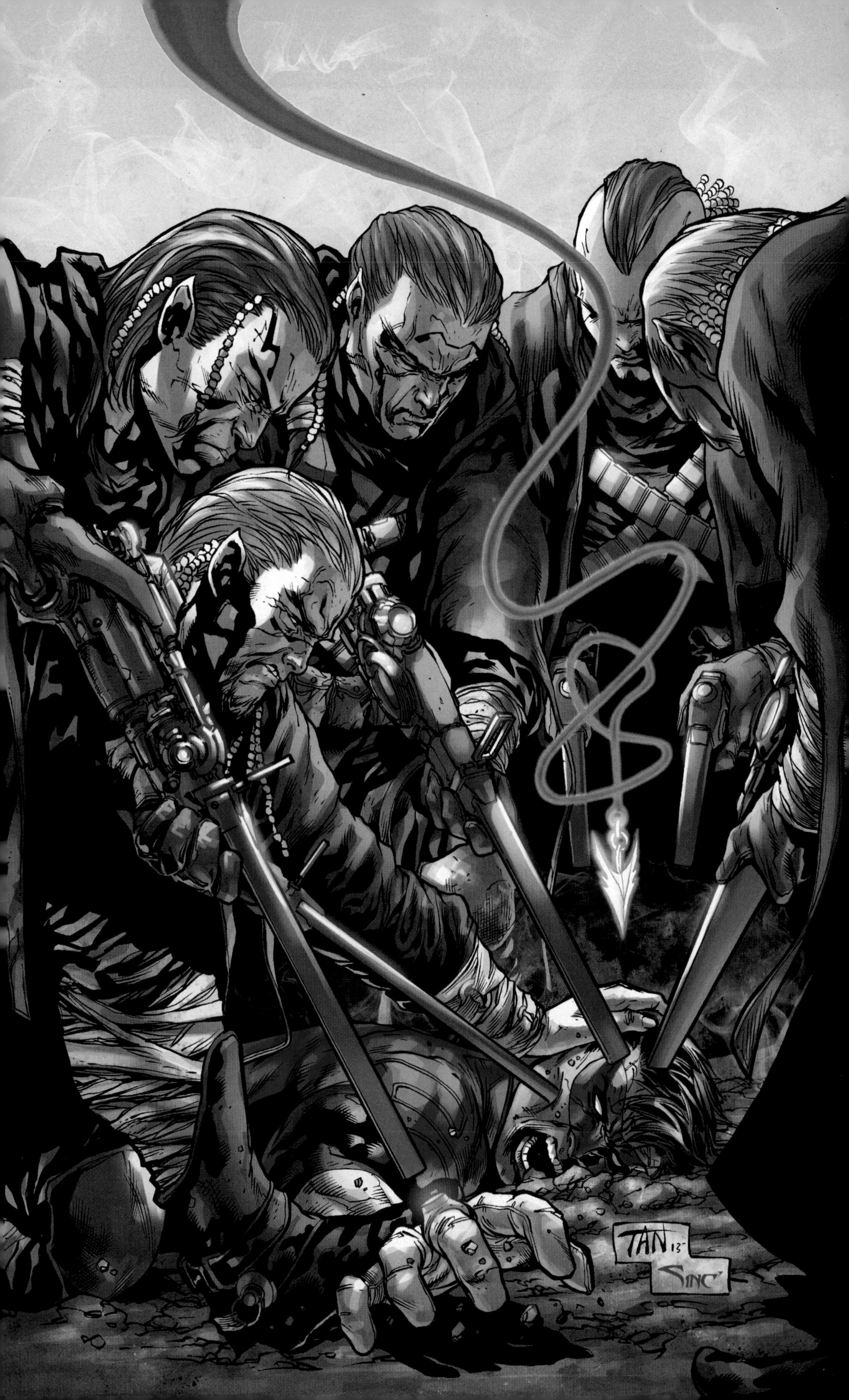
TAN 13
SINC

ROBERT VENDITTI writer **BILLY TAN** penciller **ROB HUNTER, DON HO & BILLY TAN** inkers
cover art by **BILLY TAN & ALEX SINCLAIR**

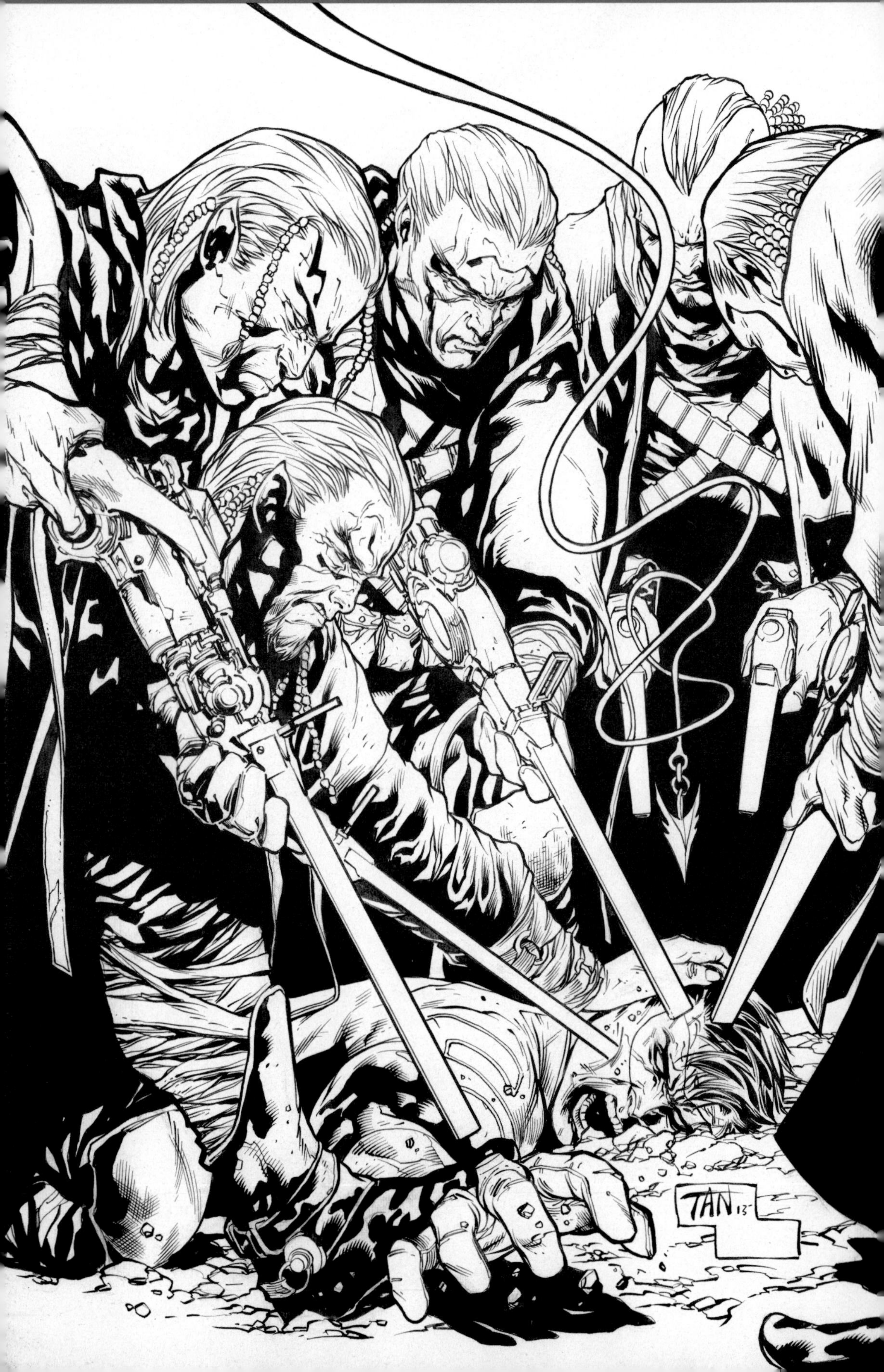
TAN 13

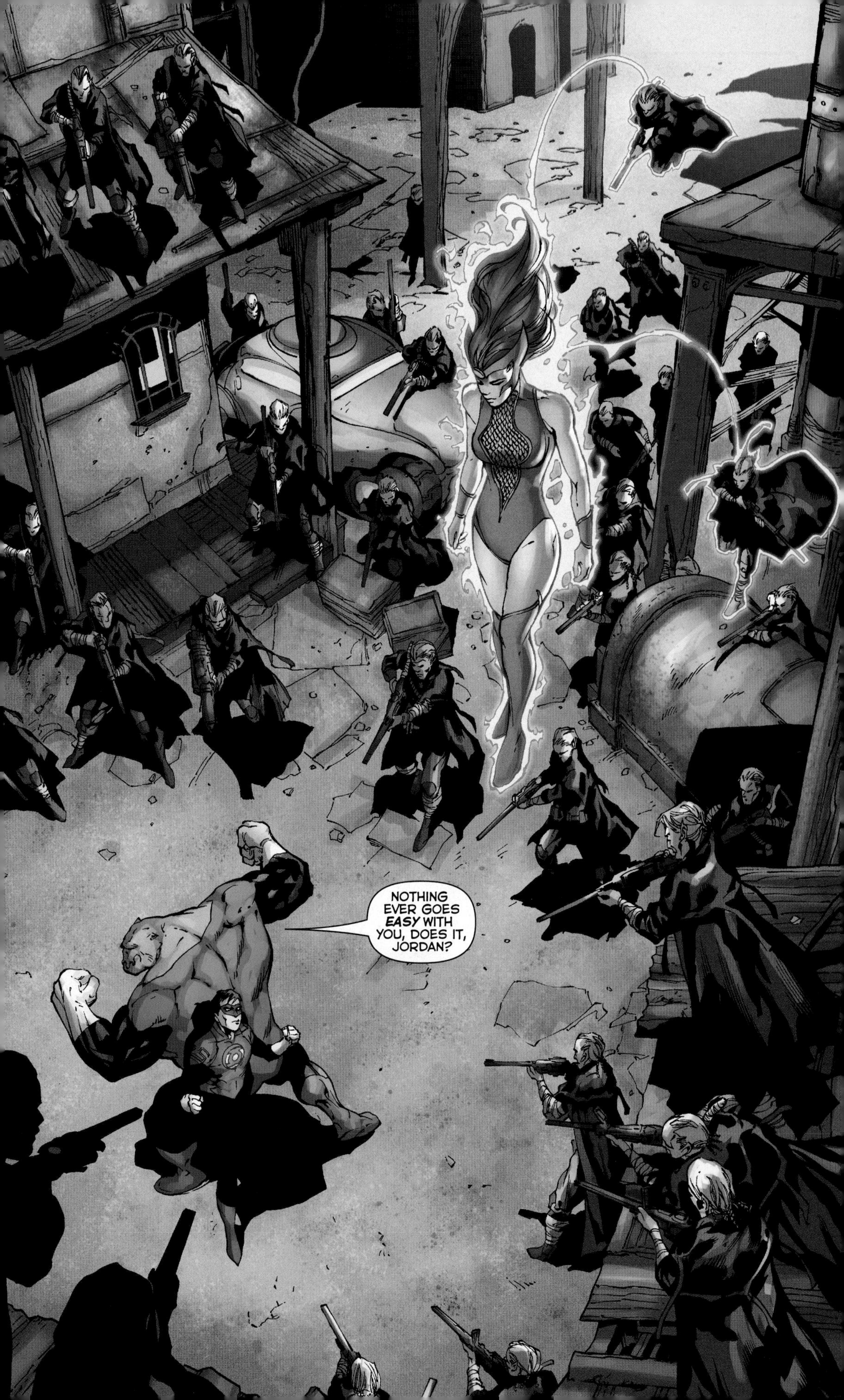
NOTHING EVER GOES EASY WITH YOU, DOES IT, JORDAN?

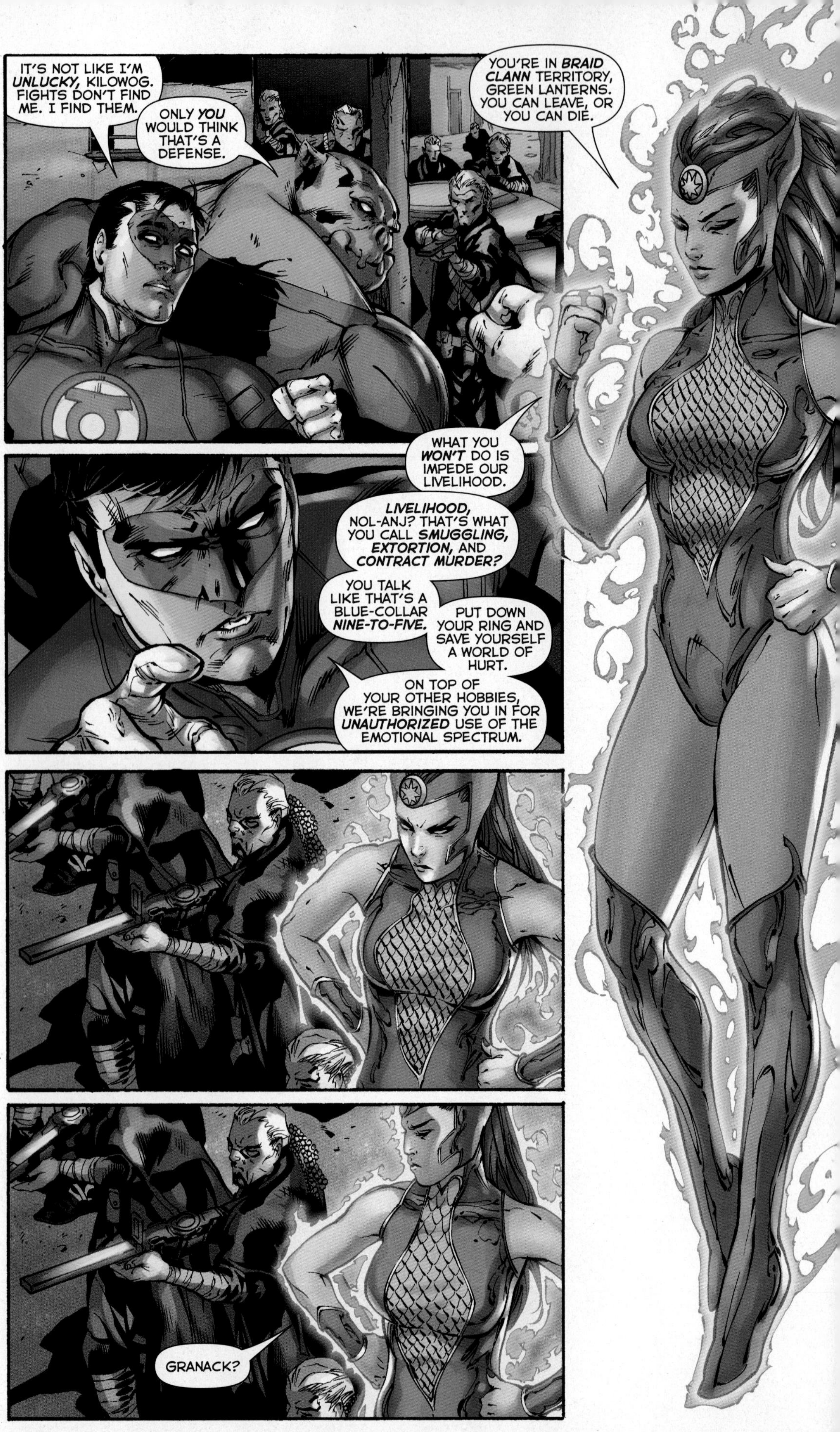
IT'S NOT LIKE I'M UNLUCKY, KILOWOG. FIGHTS DON'T FIND ME. I FIND THEM.
ONLY YOU WOULD THINK THAT'S A DEFENSE.
YOU'RE IN BRAID CLANN TERRITORY, GREEN LANTERNS. YOU CAN LEAVE, OR YOU CAN DIE.
WHAT YOU WON'T DO IS IMPEDE OUR LIVELIHOOD.
LIVELIHOOD, NOL-ANJ? THAT'S WHAT YOU CALL SMUGGLING, EXTORTION, AND CONTRACT MURDER?
YOU TALK LIKE THAT'S A BLUE-COLLAR NINE-TO-FIVE.
PUT DOWN YOUR RING AND SAVE YOURSELF A WORLD OF HURT.
ON TOP OF YOUR OTHER HOBBIES, WE'RE BRINGING YOU IN FOR UNAUTHORIZED USE OF THE EMOTIONAL SPECTRUM.
GRANACK?

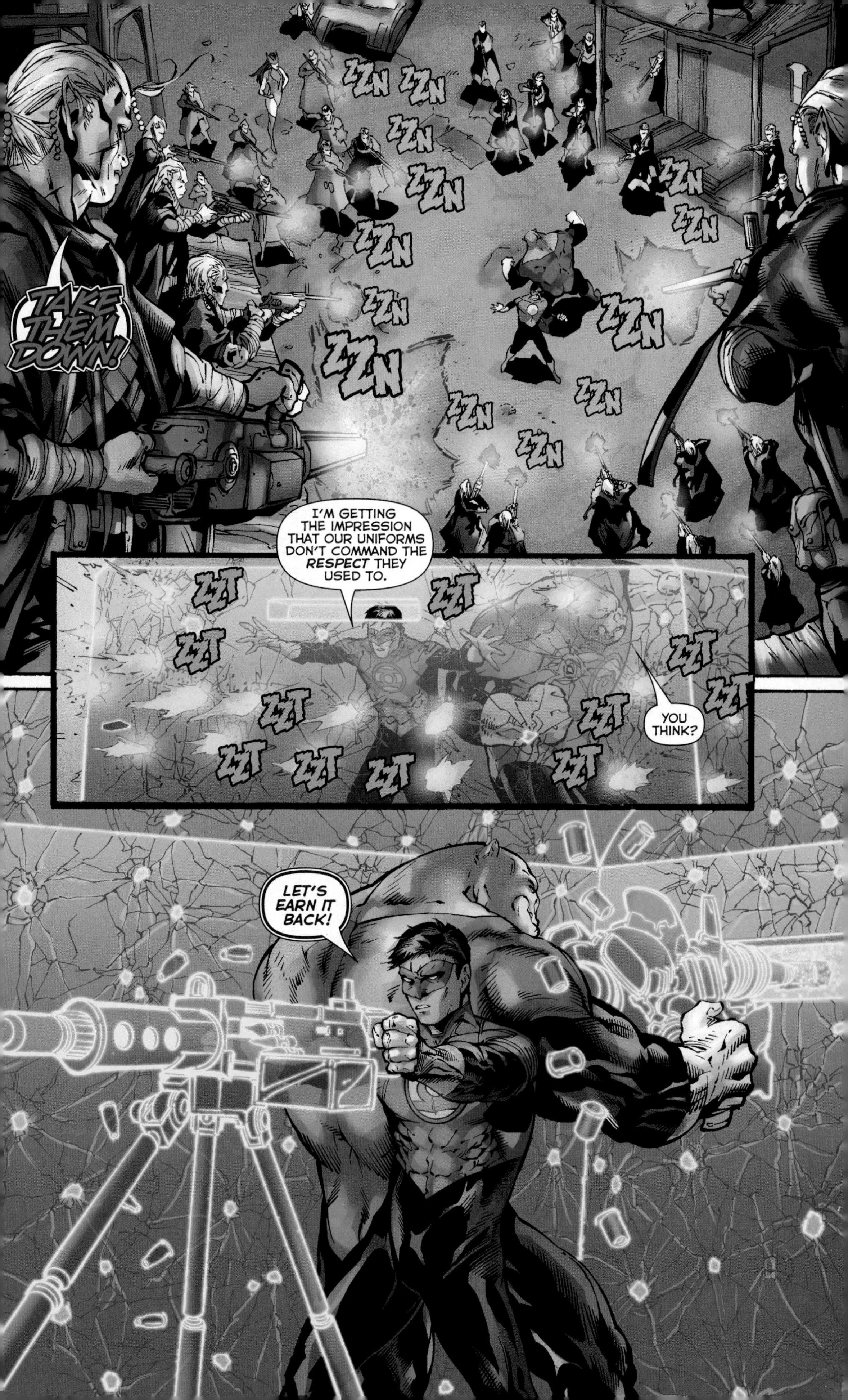
TAKE THEM DOWN!
ZZN
I'M GETTING THE IMPRESSION THAT OUR UNIFORMS DON'T COMMAND THE *RESPECT* THEY USED TO.
YOU THINK?
ZZT
LET'S EARN IT BACK!

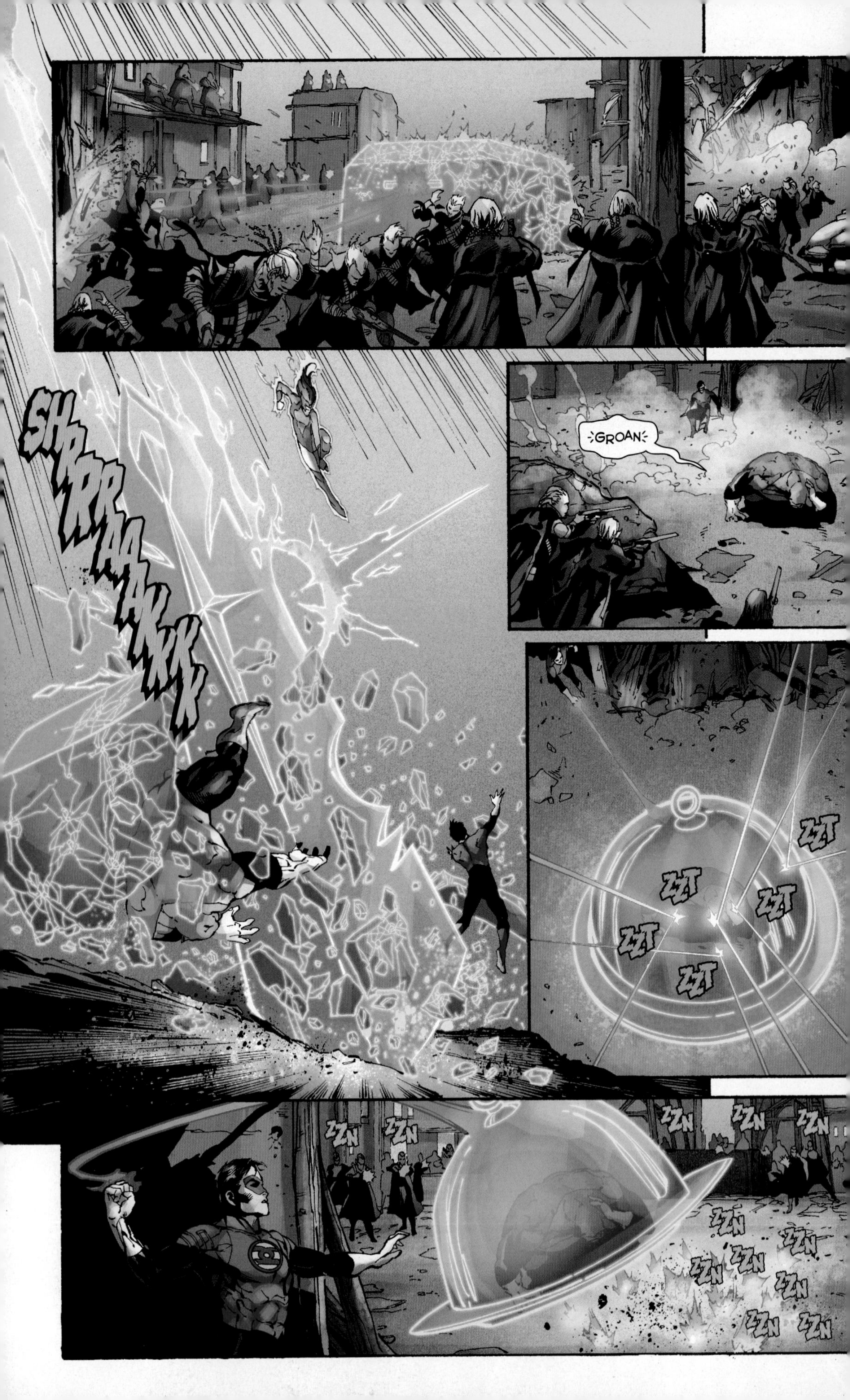
SHRRRAAAKKK
GROAN
ZZT
ZZT
ZZT
ZZT
ZZT
ZZN
ZZN
ZZN
ZZN
ZZN
ZZN
ZZN
ZZN
ZZN
ZZN
ZZN
ZZN

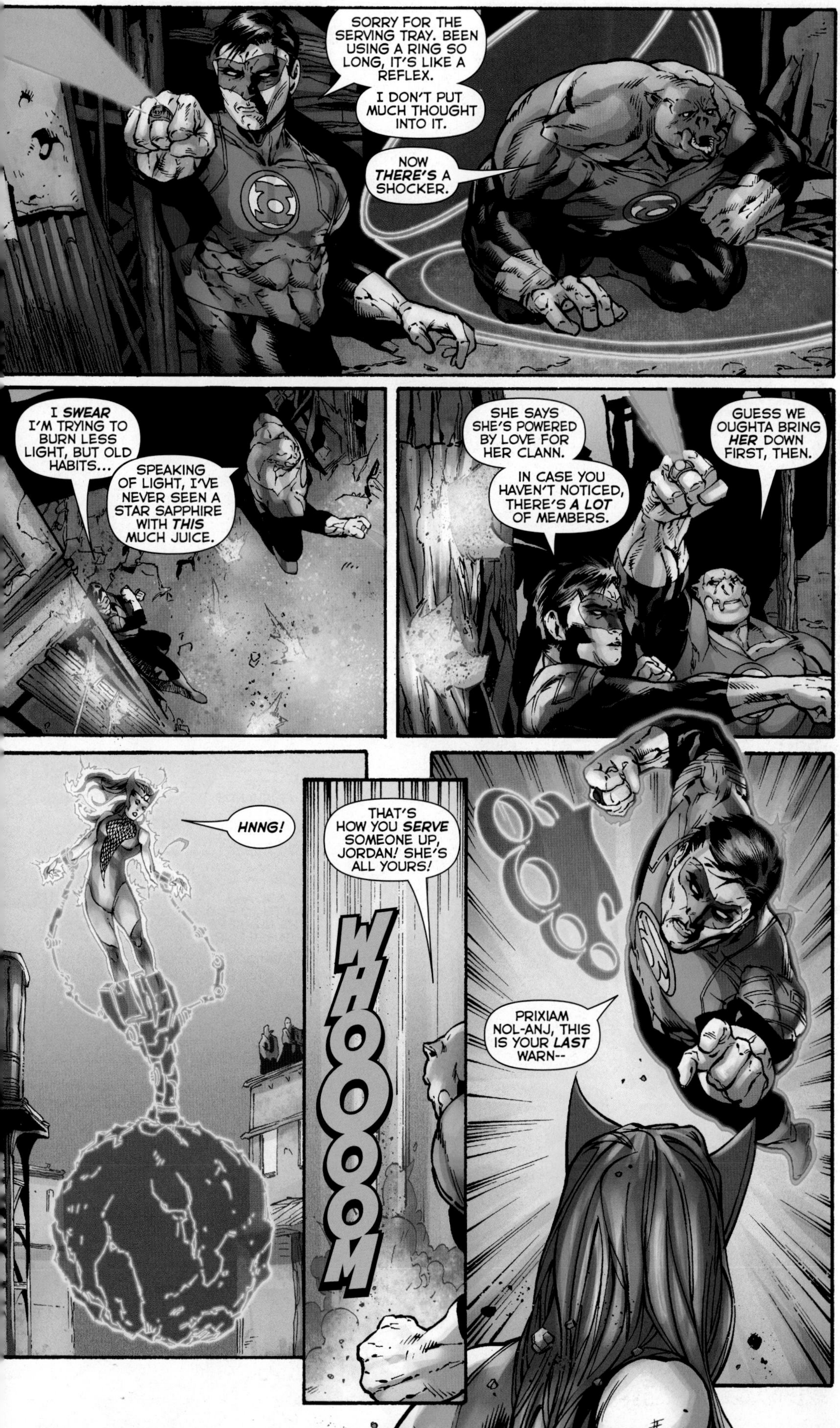
SORRY FOR THE SERVING TRAY. BEEN USING A RING SO LONG, IT'S LIKE A REFLEX.
I DON'T PUT MUCH THOUGHT INTO IT.
NOW THERE'S A SHOCKER.
I SWEAR I'M TRYING TO BURN LESS LIGHT, BUT OLD HABITS...
SPEAKING OF LIGHT, I'VE NEVER SEEN A STAR SAPPHIRE WITH THIS MUCH JUICE.
SHE SAYS SHE'S POWERED BY LOVE FOR HER CLANN.
IN CASE YOU HAVEN'T NOTICED, THERE'S A LOT OF MEMBERS.
GUESS WE OUGHTA BRING HER DOWN FIRST, THEN.
HNNG!
THAT'S HOW YOU SERVE SOMEONE UP, JORDAN! SHE'S ALL YOURS!
WHOOOOOM
PRIXIAM NOL-ANJ, THIS IS YOUR LAST WARN--

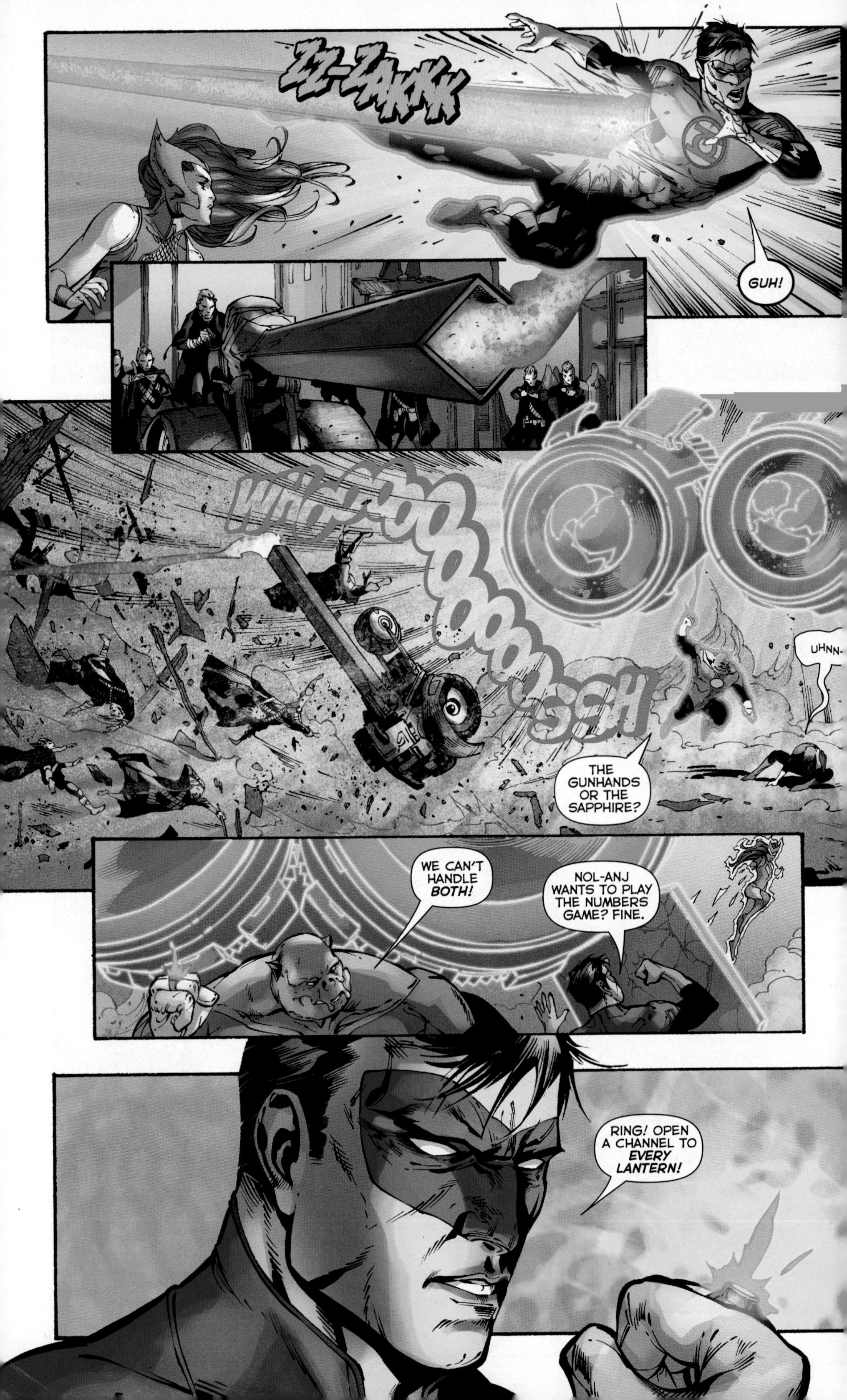
ZZ-ZAKKK
GUH!
WHOOOOOOOOSSH
UHNN-
THE GUNHANDS OR THE SAPPHIRE?
WE CAN'T HANDLE BOTH!
NOL-ANJ WANTS TO PLAY THE NUMBERS GAME? FINE.
RING! OPEN A CHANNEL TO EVERY LANTERN!

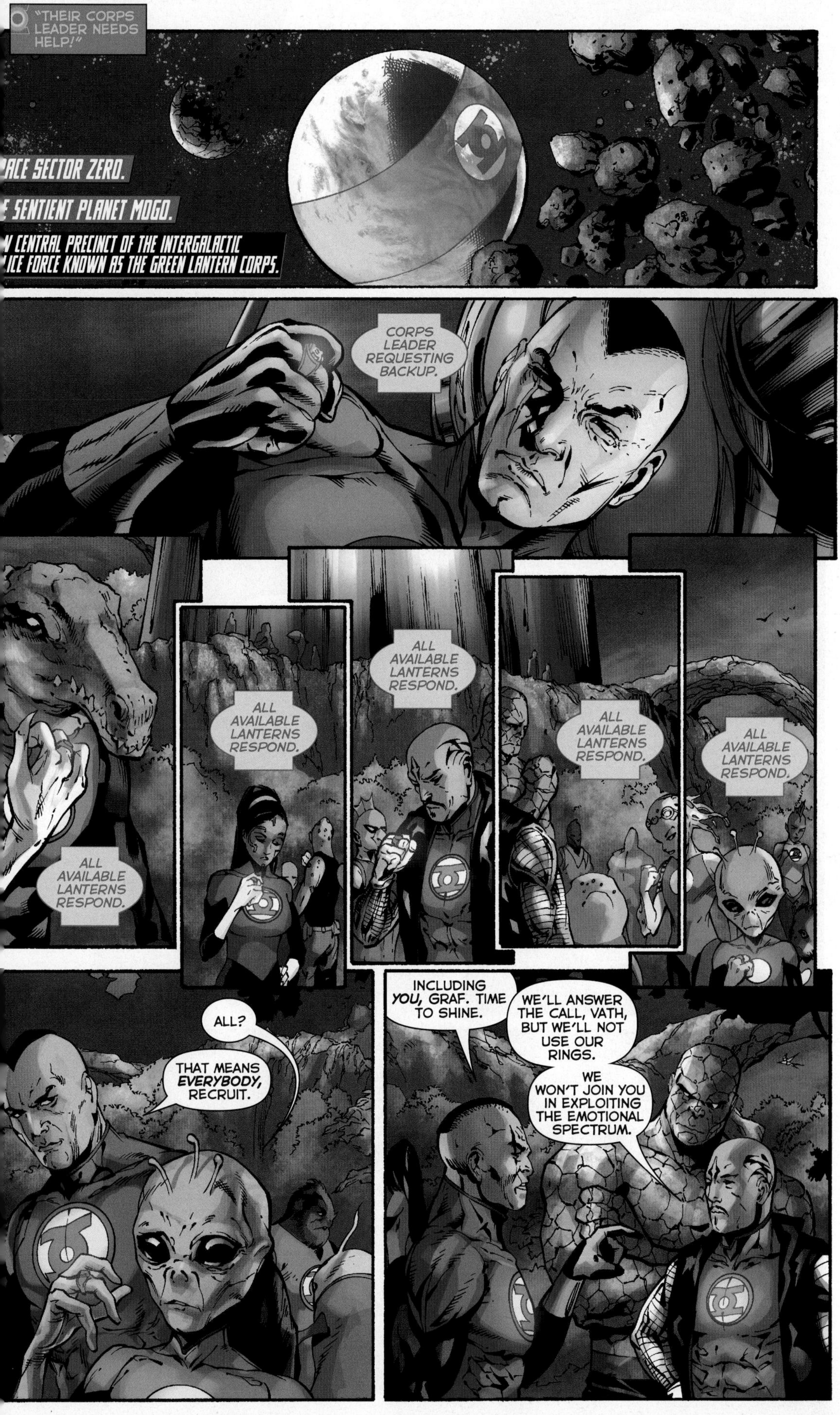
"THEIR CORPS LEADER NEEDS HELP!"
ACE SECTOR ZERO.
E SENTIENT PLANET MOGO.
V CENTRAL PRECINCT OF THE INTERGALACTIC
ICE FORCE KNOWN AS THE GREEN LANTERN CORPS.
CORPS LEADER REQUESTING BACKUP.
ALL AVAILABLE LANTERNS RESPOND.
ALL AVAILABLE LANTERNS RESPOND.
ALL AVAILABLE LANTERNS RESPOND.
ALL AVAILABLE LANTERNS RESPOND.
ALL AVAILABLE LANTERNS RESPOND.
ALL?
THAT MEANS *EVERYBODY*, RECRUIT.
INCLUDING *YOU*, GRAF. TIME TO SHINE.
WE'LL ANSWER THE CALL, VATH, BUT WE'LL NOT USE OUR RINGS.
WE WON'T JOIN YOU IN EXPLOITING THE EMOTIONAL SPECTRUM.

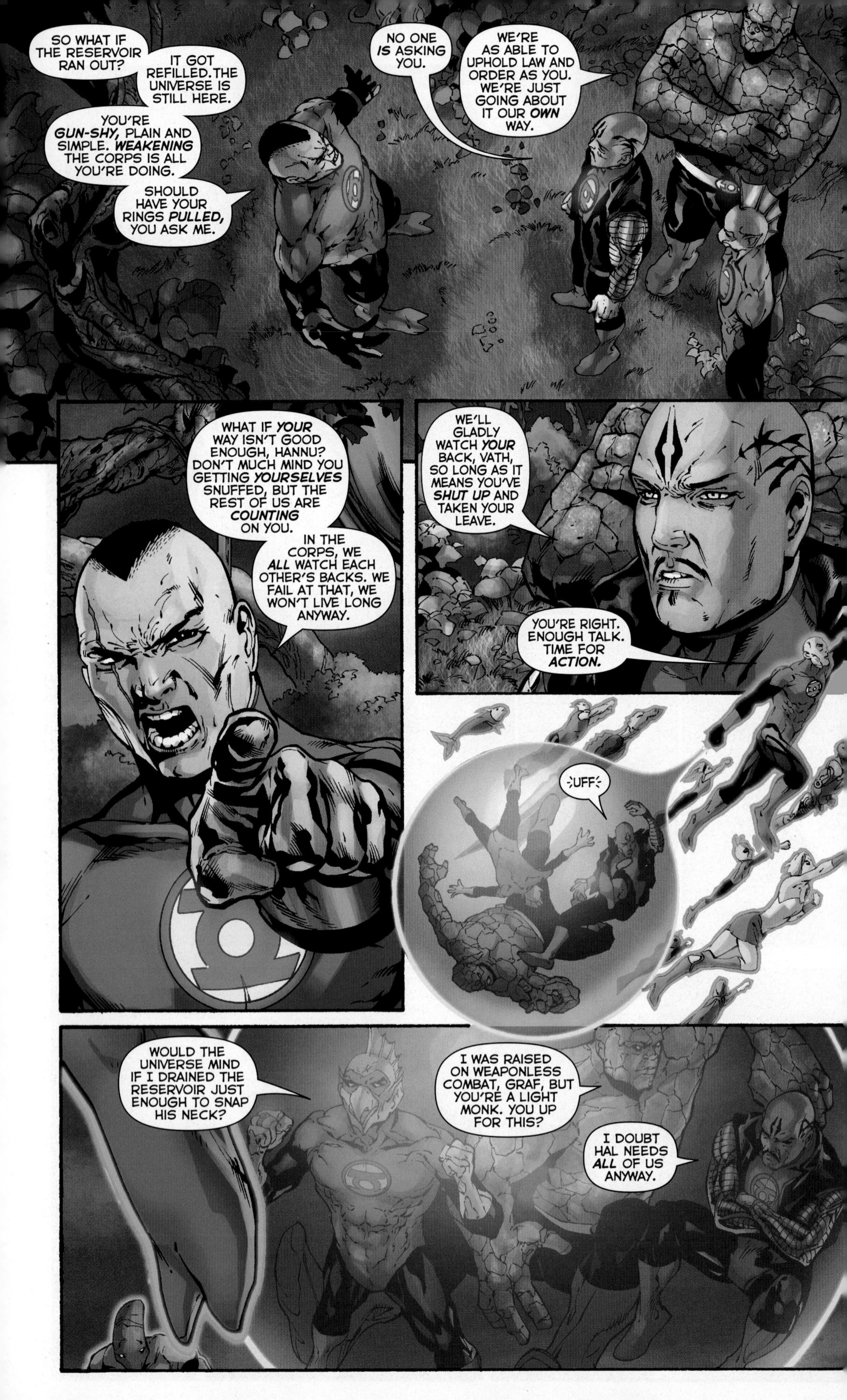
SO WHAT IF THE RESERVOIR RAN OUT?
IT GOT REFILLED. THE UNIVERSE IS STILL HERE.
YOU'RE GUN-SHY, PLAIN AND SIMPLE. WEAKENING THE CORPS IS ALL YOU'RE DOING.
SHOULD HAVE YOUR RINGS PULLED, YOU ASK ME.
NO ONE IS ASKING YOU.
WE'RE AS ABLE TO UPHOLD LAW AND ORDER AS YOU. WE'RE JUST GOING ABOUT IT OUR OWN WAY.
WHAT IF YOUR WAY ISN'T GOOD ENOUGH, HANNU? DON'T MUCH MIND YOU GETTING YOURSELVES SNUFFED, BUT THE REST OF US ARE COUNTING ON YOU.
IN THE CORPS, WE ALL WATCH EACH OTHER'S BACKS. WE FAIL AT THAT, WE WON'T LIVE LONG ANYWAY.
WE'LL GLADLY WATCH YOUR BACK, VATH, SO LONG AS IT MEANS YOU'VE SHUT UP AND TAKEN YOUR LEAVE.
YOU'RE RIGHT. ENOUGH TALK. TIME FOR ACTION.
UFF
WOULD THE UNIVERSE MIND IF I DRAINED THE RESERVOIR JUST ENOUGH TO SNAP HIS NECK?
I WAS RAISED ON WEAPONLESS COMBAT, GRAF, BUT YOU'RE A LIGHT MONK. YOU UP FOR THIS?
I DOUBT HAL NEEDS ALL OF US ANYWAY.

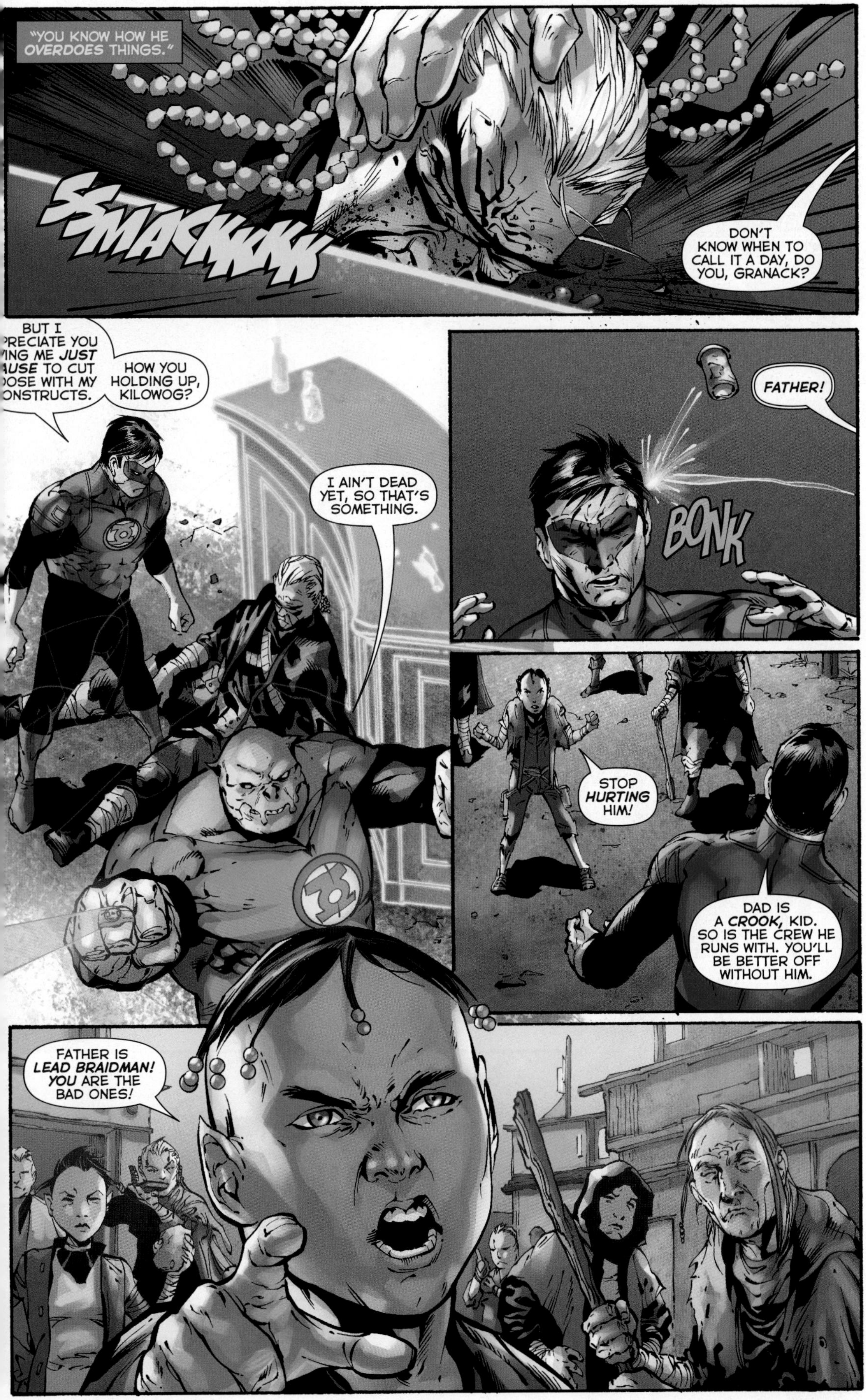
"YOU KNOW HOW HE OVERDOES THINGS."
SSMACKKKK
DON'T KNOW WHEN TO CALL IT A DAY, DO YOU, GRANACK?
BUT I PRECIATE YOU VING ME JUST AUSE TO CUT OOSE WITH MY ONSTRUCTS.
HOW YOU HOLDING UP, KILOWOG?
I AIN'T DEAD YET, SO THAT'S SOMETHING.
FATHER!
BONK
STOP HURTING HIM!
DAD IS A CROOK, KID. SO IS THE CREW HE RUNS WITH. YOU'LL BE BETTER OFF WITHOUT HIM.
FATHER IS LEAD BRAIDMAN! YOU ARE THE BAD ONES!

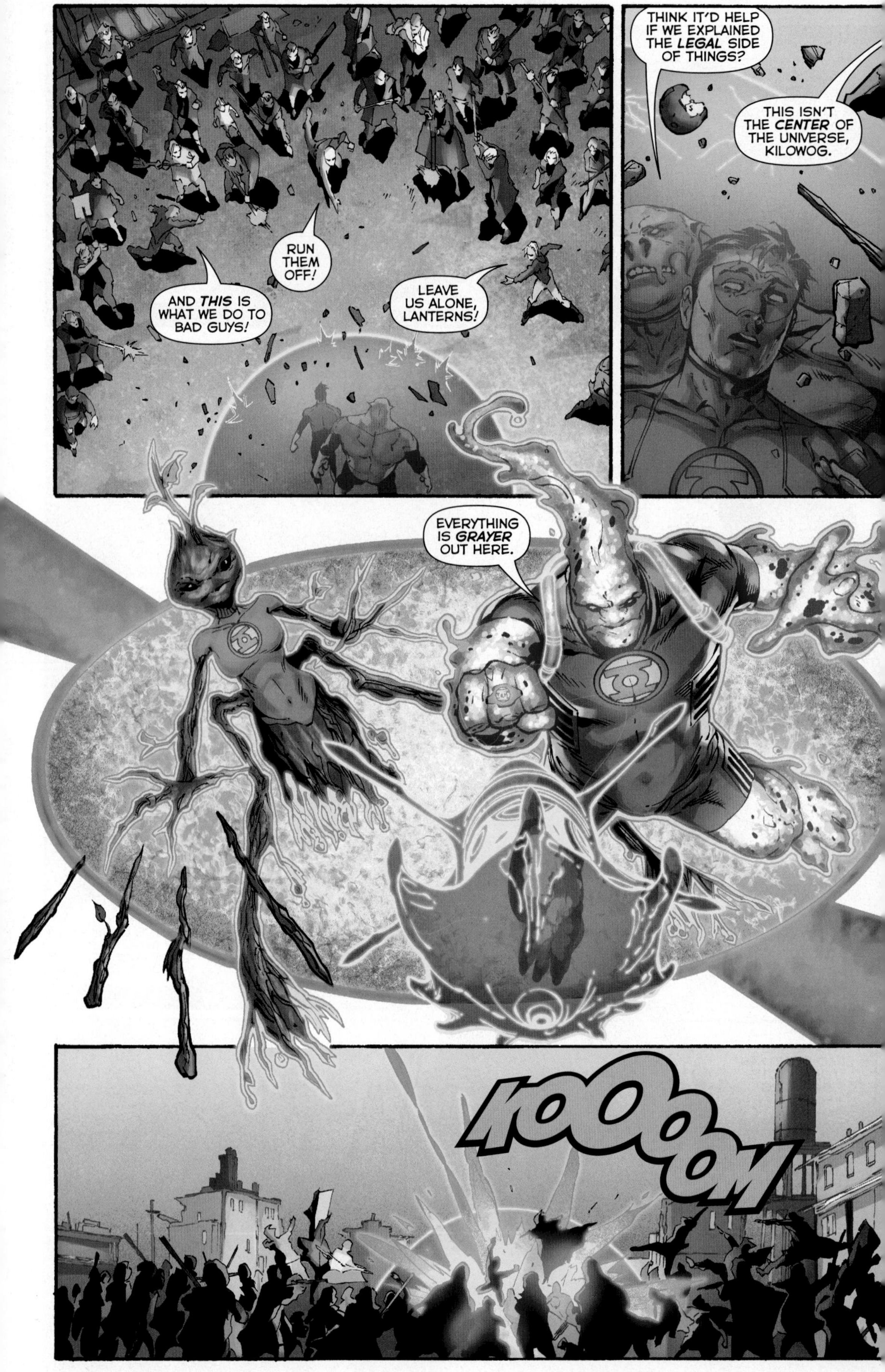
AND THIS IS WHAT WE DO TO BAD GUYS!
RUN THEM OFF!
LEAVE US ALONE, LANTERNS!
THINK IT'D HELP IF WE EXPLAINED THE LEGAL SIDE OF THINGS?
THIS ISN'T THE CENTER OF THE UNIVERSE, KILOWOG.
EVERYTHING IS GRAYER OUT HERE.
KOOOOOM

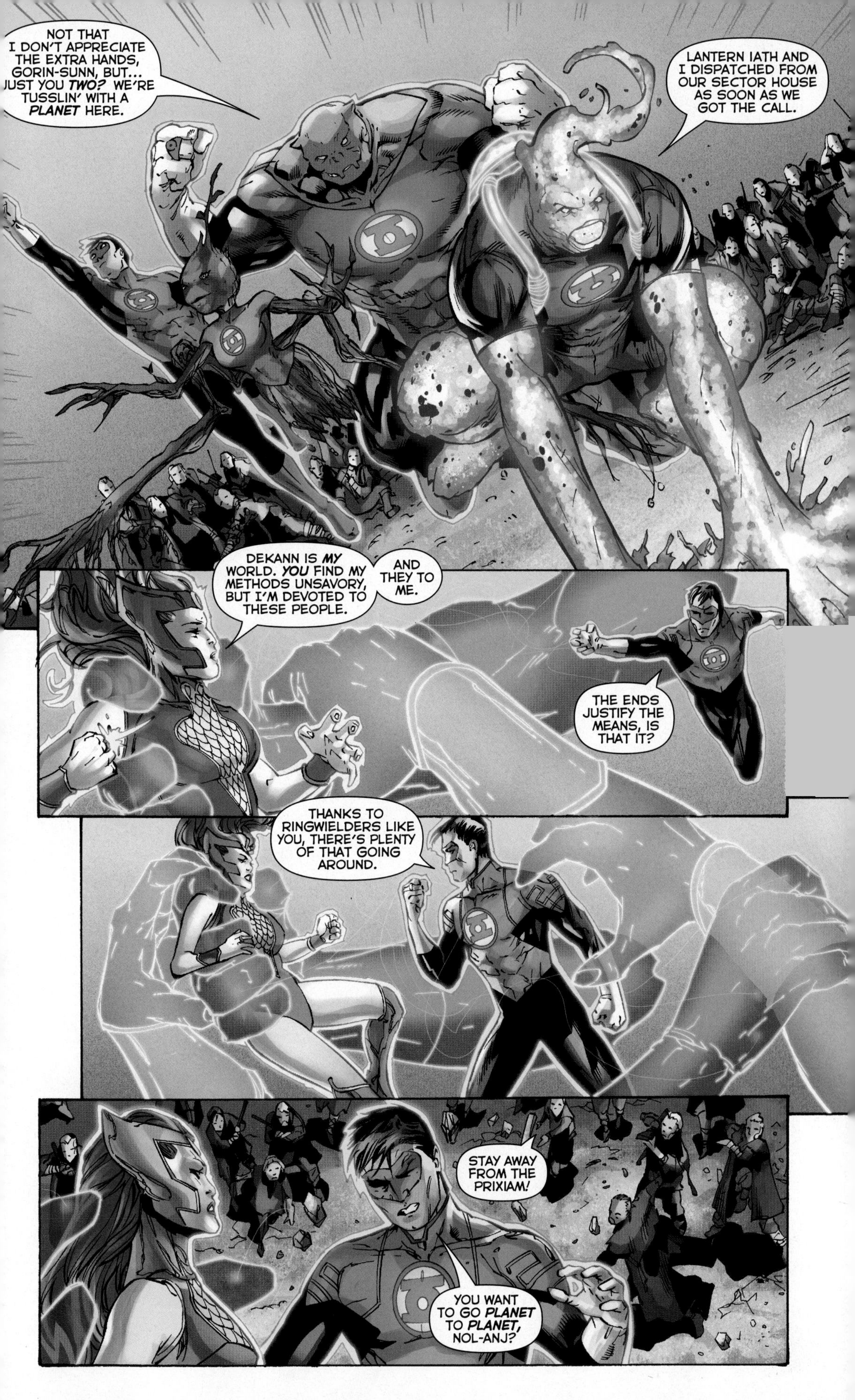
NOT THAT I DON'T APPRECIATE THE EXTRA HANDS, GORIN-SUNN, BUT... JUST YOU *TWO?* WE'RE TUSSLIN' WITH A *PLANET* HERE.
LANTERN IATH AND I DISPATCHED FROM OUR SECTOR HOUSE AS SOON AS WE GOT THE CALL.
DEKANN IS *MY* WORLD. *YOU* FIND MY METHODS UNSAVORY, BUT I'M DEVOTED TO THESE PEOPLE.
AND THEY TO ME.
THE ENDS JUSTIFY THE MEANS, IS THAT IT?
THANKS TO RINGWIELDERS LIKE YOU, THERE'S PLENTY OF THAT GOING AROUND.
STAY AWAY FROM THE PRIXIAM!
YOU WANT TO GO *PLANET* TO *PLANET,* NOL-ANJ?

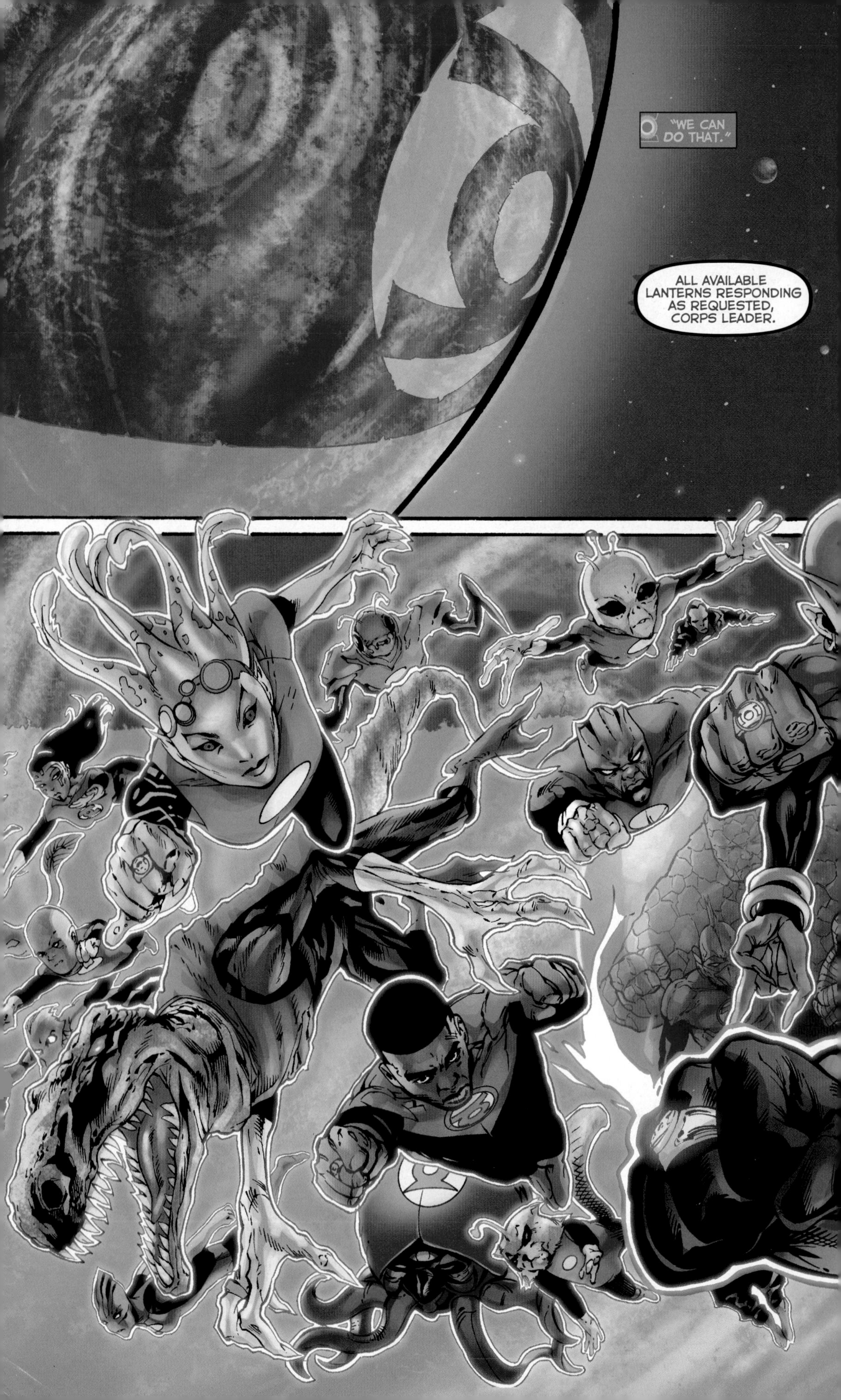

"WE CAN DO THAT."
ALL AVAILABLE LANTERNS RESPONDING AS REQUESTED, CORPS LEADER.

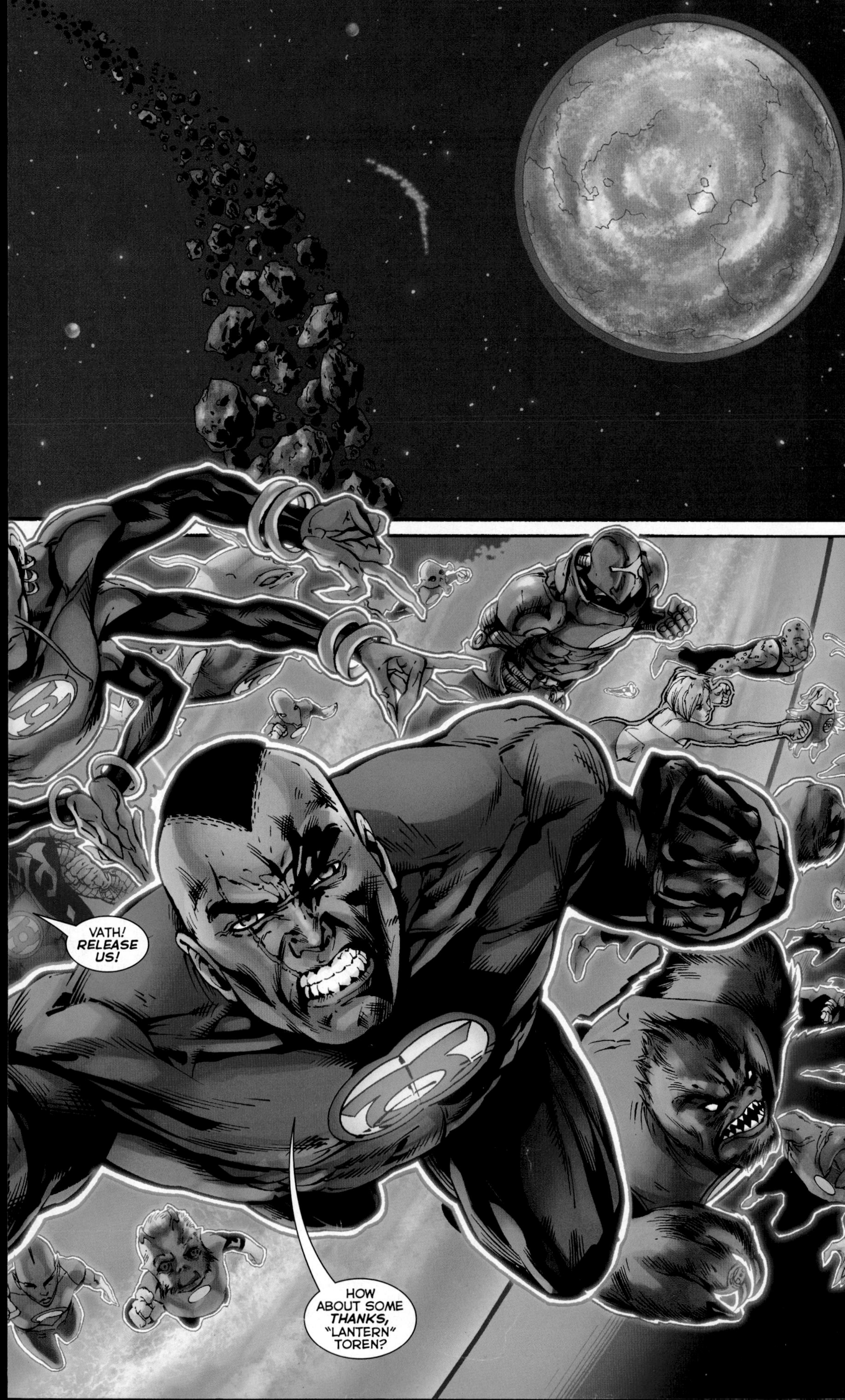
VATH! RELEASE US!
HOW ABOUT SOME THANKS, "LANTERN" TOREN?

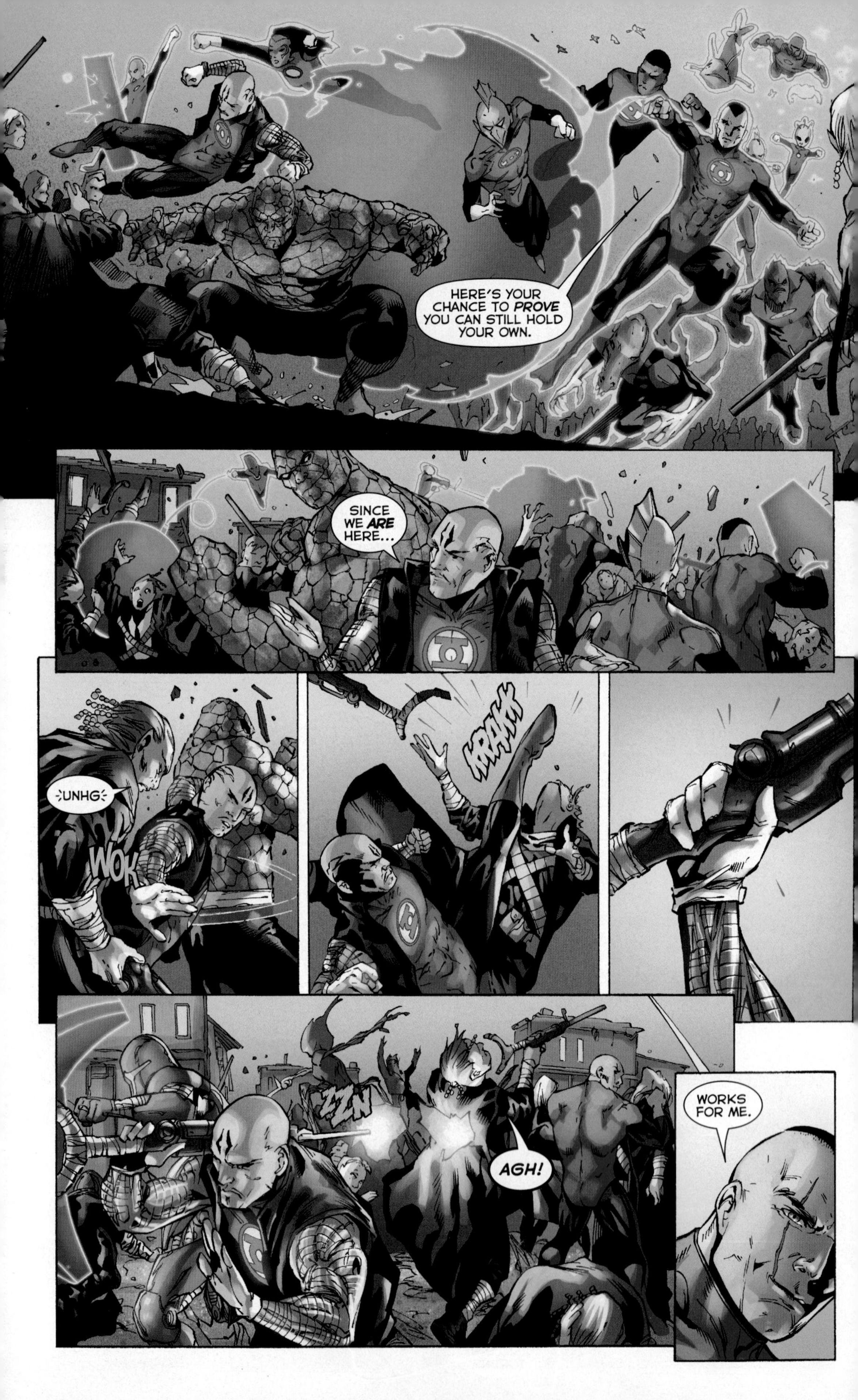
HERE'S YOUR CHANCE TO PROVE YOU CAN STILL HOLD YOUR OWN.
SINCE WE ARE HERE...
UNHG
WOK
KRAKK
ZZZN
AGH!
WORKS FOR ME.

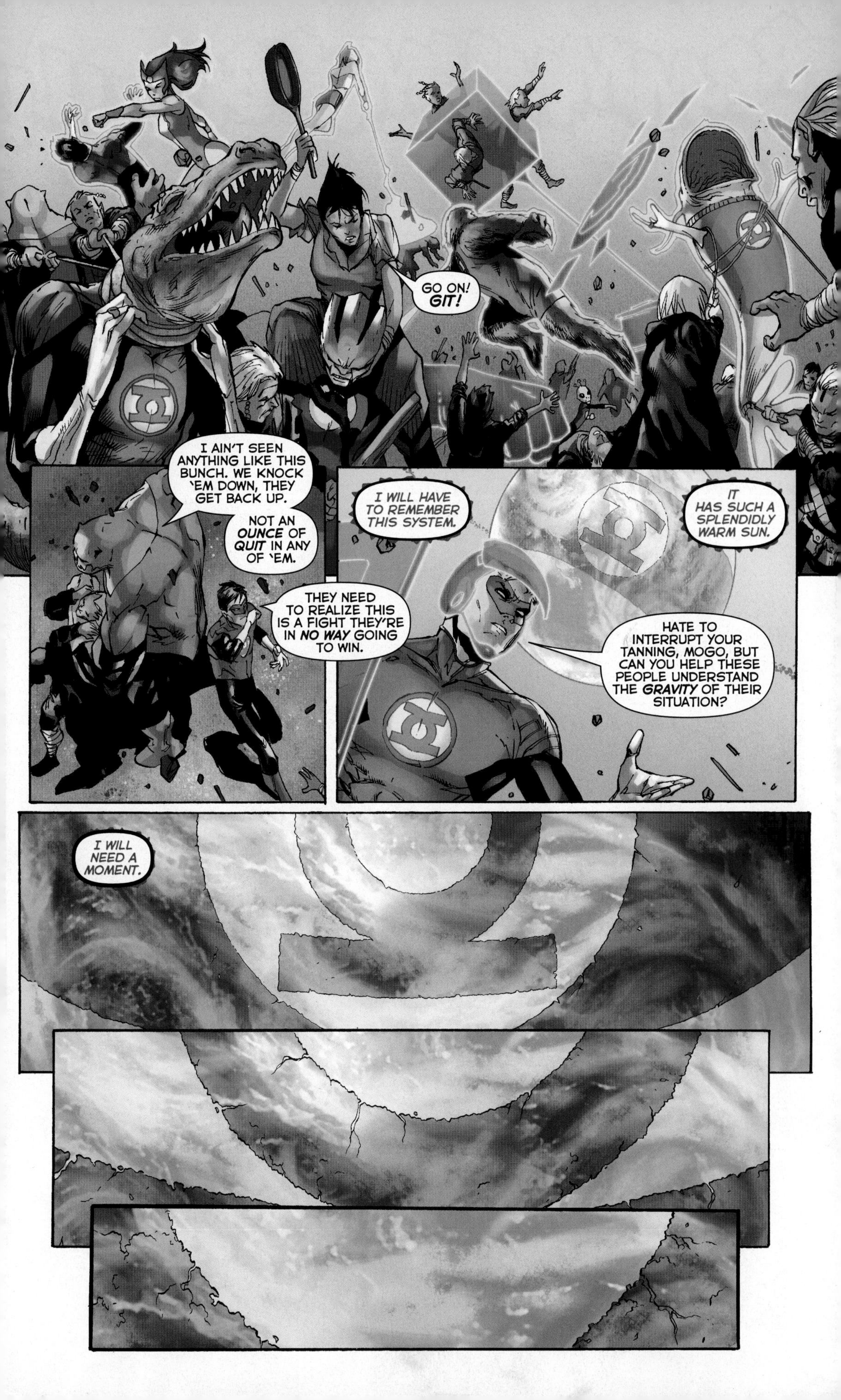
GO ON! GIT!
I AIN'T SEEN ANYTHING LIKE THIS BUNCH. WE KNOCK 'EM DOWN, THEY GET BACK UP.
NOT AN OUNCE OF QUIT IN ANY OF 'EM.
THEY NEED TO REALIZE THIS IS A FIGHT THEY'RE IN NO WAY GOING TO WIN.
I WILL HAVE TO REMEMBER THIS SYSTEM.
IT HAS SUCH A SPLENDIDLY WARM SUN.
HATE TO INTERRUPT YOUR TANNING, MOGO, BUT CAN YOU HELP THESE PEOPLE UNDERSTAND THE GRAVITY OF THEIR SITUATION?
I WILL NEED A MOMENT.

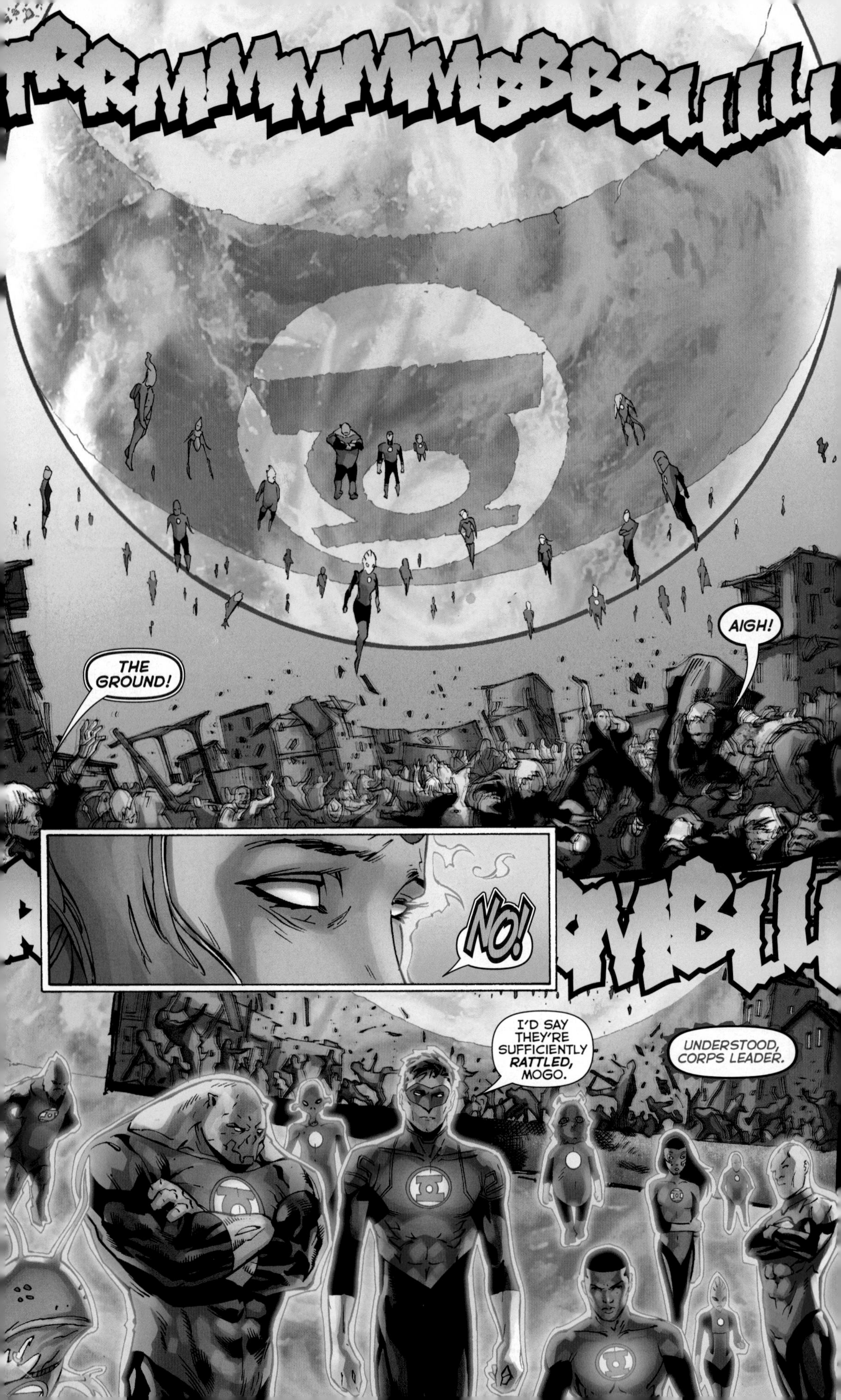
TRRMMMMMMBBBLLLL
THE GROUND!
AIGH!
NO!
I'D SAY THEY'RE SUFFICIENTLY RATTLED, MOGO.
UNDERSTOOD, CORPS LEADER.

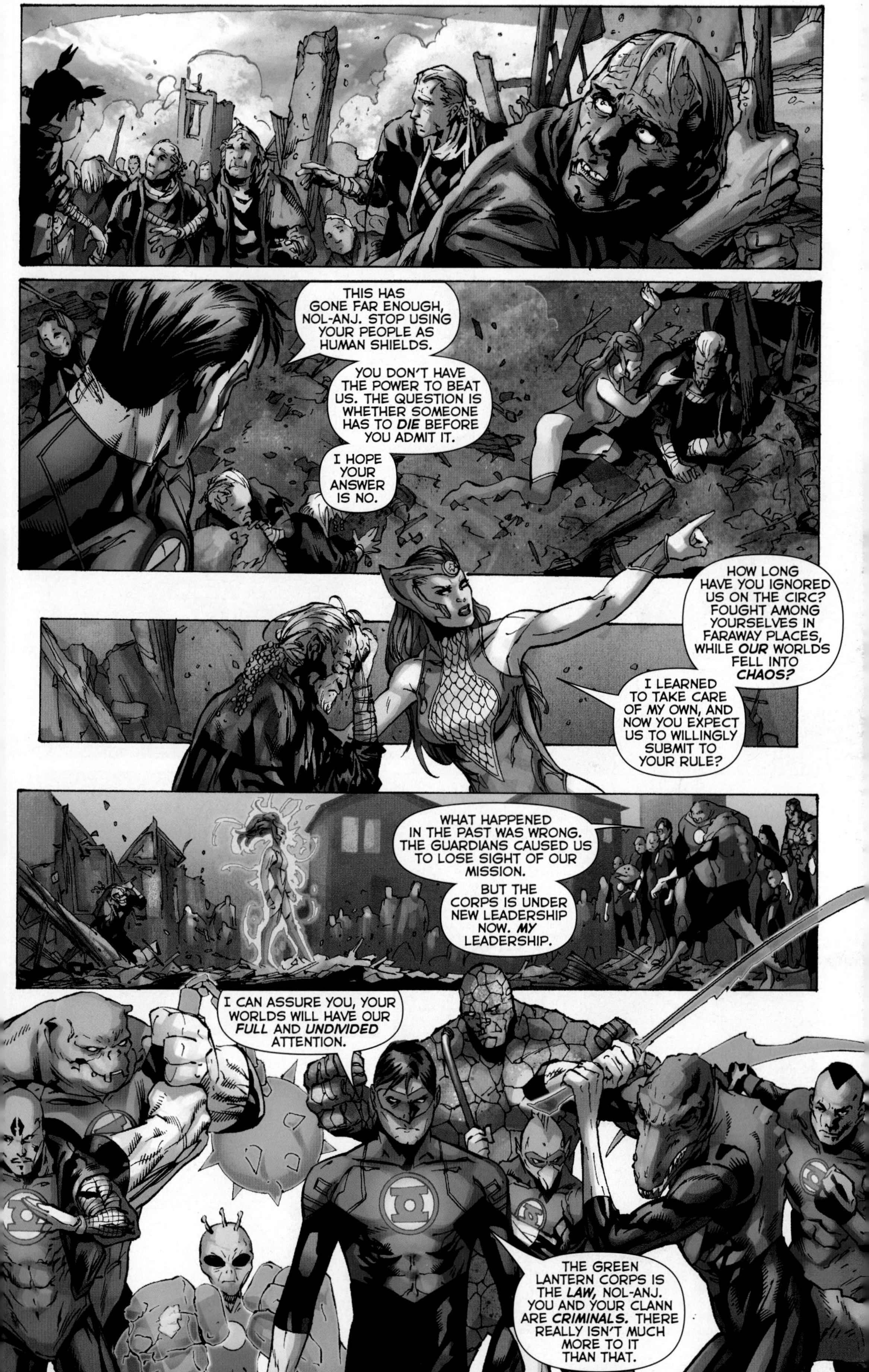

THIS HAS GONE FAR ENOUGH, NOL-ANJ. STOP USING YOUR PEOPLE AS HUMAN SHIELDS.
YOU DON'T HAVE THE POWER TO BEAT US. THE QUESTION IS WHETHER SOMEONE HAS TO DIE BEFORE YOU ADMIT IT.
I HOPE YOUR ANSWER IS NO.
HOW LONG HAVE YOU IGNORED US ON THE CIRC? FOUGHT AMONG YOURSELVES IN FARAWAY PLACES, WHILE OUR WORLDS FELL INTO CHAOS?
I LEARNED TO TAKE CARE OF MY OWN, AND NOW YOU EXPECT US TO WILLINGLY SUBMIT TO YOUR RULE?
WHAT HAPPENED IN THE PAST WAS WRONG. THE GUARDIANS CAUSED US TO LOSE SIGHT OF OUR MISSION.
BUT THE CORPS IS UNDER NEW LEADERSHIP NOW. MY LEADERSHIP.
I CAN ASSURE YOU, YOUR WORLDS WILL HAVE OUR FULL AND UNDIVIDED ATTENTION.
THE GREEN LANTERN CORPS IS THE LAW, NOL-ANJ. YOU AND YOUR CLANN ARE CRIMINALS. THERE REALLY ISN'T MUCH MORE TO IT THAN THAT.

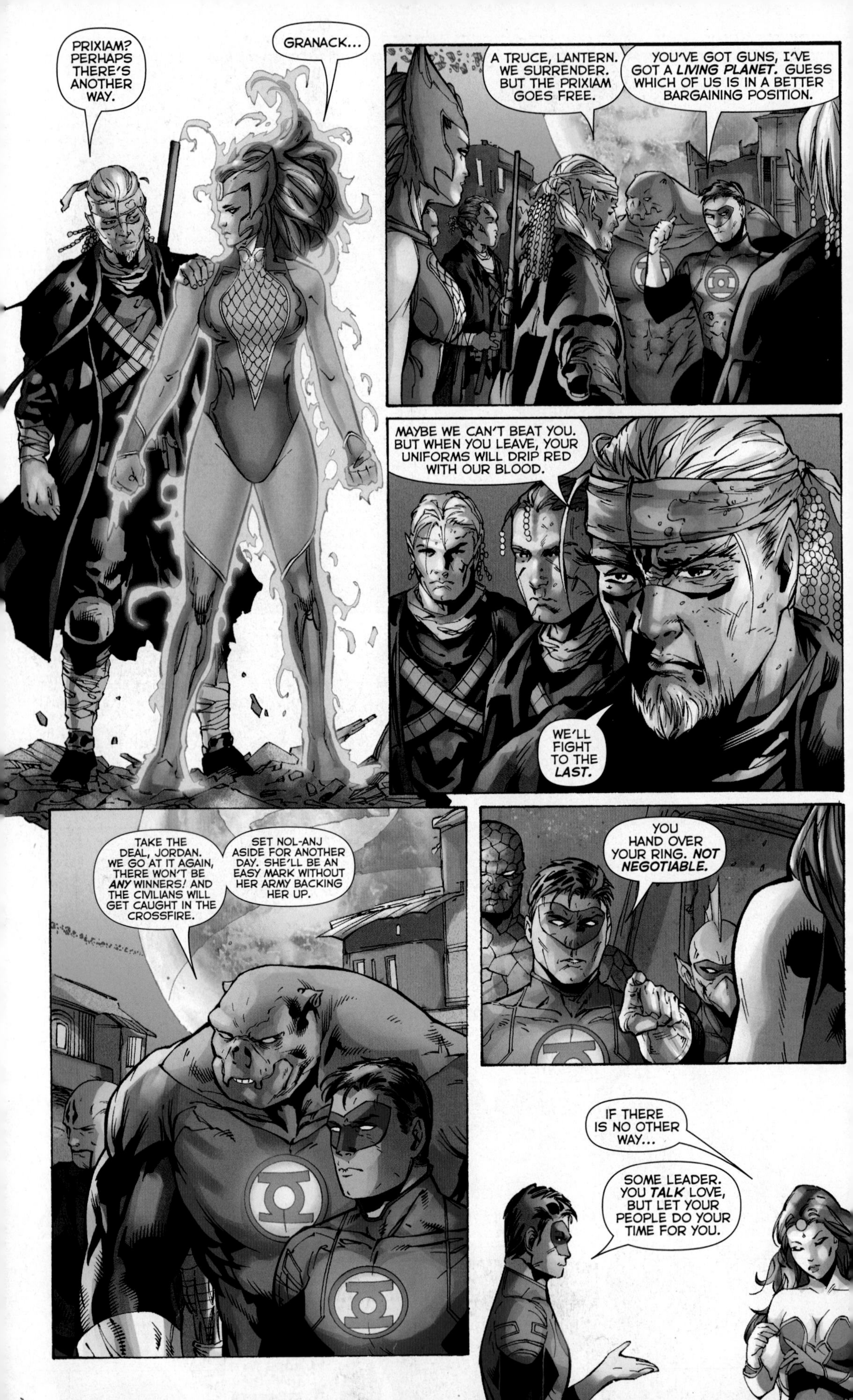
PRIXIAM? PERHAPS THERE'S ANOTHER WAY.
GRANACK...
A TRUCE, LANTERN. WE SURRENDER. BUT THE PRIXIAM GOES FREE.
YOU'VE GOT GUNS, I'VE GOT A *LIVING PLANET.* GUESS WHICH OF US IS IN A BETTER BARGAINING POSITION.
MAYBE WE CAN'T BEAT YOU. BUT WHEN YOU LEAVE, YOUR UNIFORMS WILL DRIP RED WITH OUR BLOOD.
WE'LL FIGHT TO THE *LAST.*
TAKE THE DEAL, JORDAN. WE GO AT IT AGAIN, THERE WON'T BE *ANY* WINNERS! AND THE CIVILIANS WILL GET CAUGHT IN THE CROSSFIRE.
SET NOL-ANJ ASIDE FOR ANOTHER DAY. SHE'LL BE AN EASY MARK WITHOUT HER ARMY BACKING HER UP.
YOU HAND OVER YOUR RING. *NOT NEGOTIABLE.*
IF THERE IS NO OTHER WAY...
SOME LEADER. YOU *TALK* LOVE, BUT LET YOUR PEOPLE DO YOUR TIME FOR YOU.

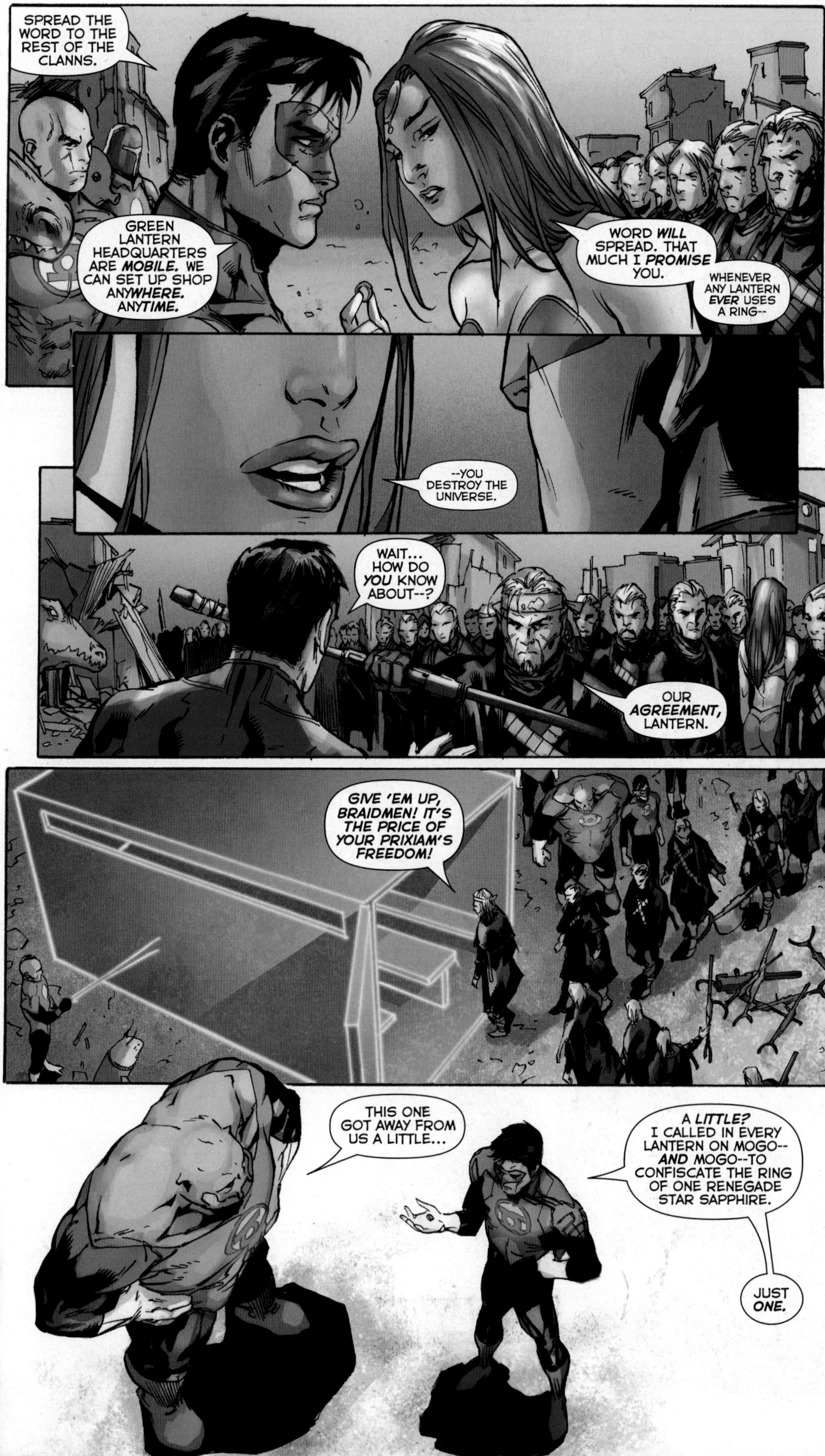
SPREAD THE WORD TO THE REST OF THE CLANNS.
GREEN LANTERN HEADQUARTERS ARE MOBILE. WE CAN SET UP SHOP ANYWHERE. ANYTIME.
WORD WILL SPREAD. THAT MUCH I PROMISE YOU.
WHENEVER ANY LANTERN EVER USES A RING--
--YOU DESTROY THE UNIVERSE.
WAIT... HOW DO YOU KNOW ABOUT--?
OUR AGREEMENT, LANTERN.
GIVE 'EM UP, BRAIDMEN! IT'S THE PRICE OF YOUR PRIXIAM'S FREEDOM!
THIS ONE GOT AWAY FROM US A LITTLE...
A LITTLE? I CALLED IN EVERY LANTERN ON MOGO-- AND MOGO--TO CONFISCATE THE RING OF ONE RENEGADE STAR SAPPHIRE.
JUST ONE.

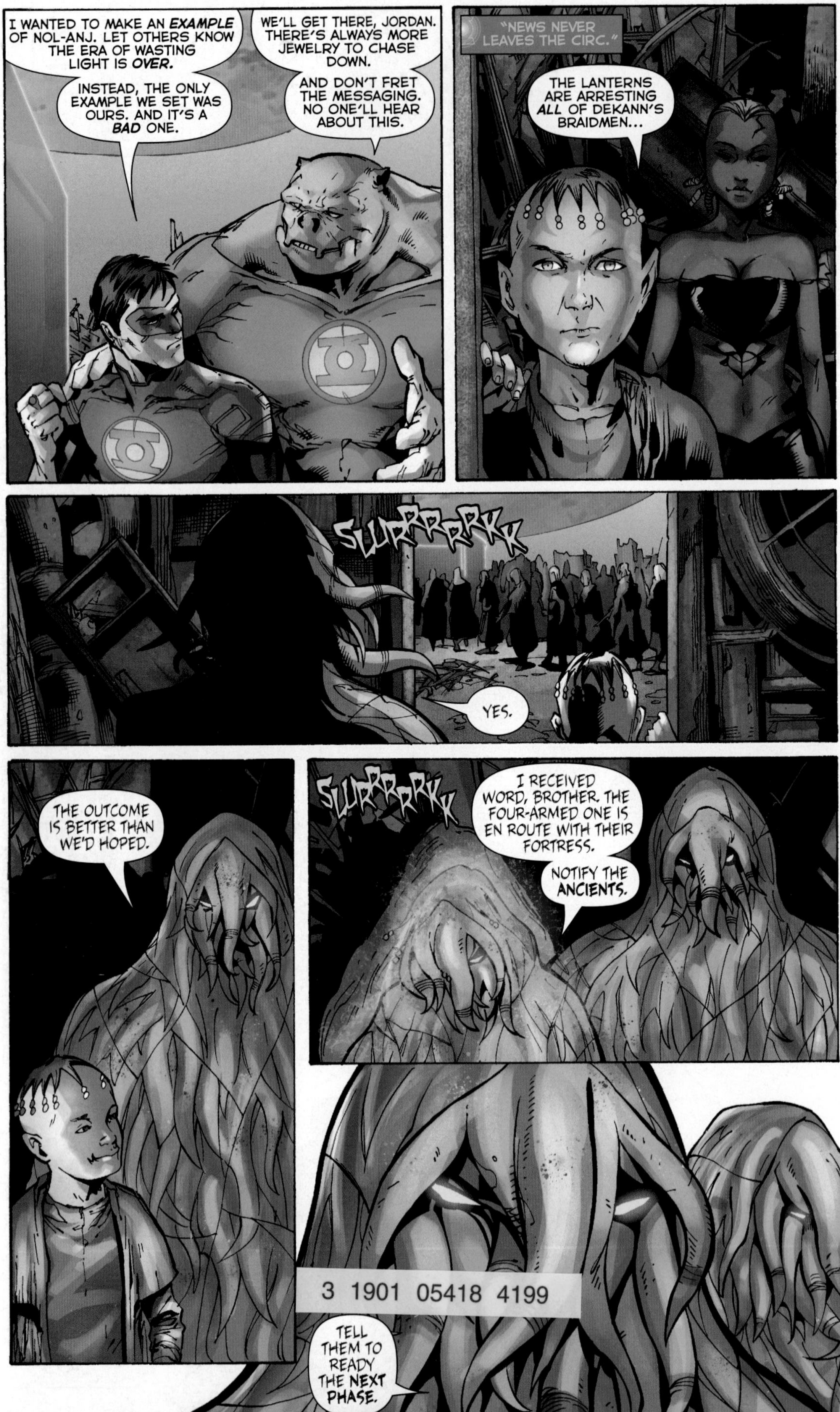
I WANTED TO MAKE AN EXAMPLE OF NOL-ANJ. LET OTHERS KNOW THE ERA OF WASTING LIGHT IS OVER.
INSTEAD, THE ONLY EXAMPLE WE SET WAS OURS. AND IT'S A BAD ONE.
WE'LL GET THERE, JORDAN. THERE'S ALWAYS MORE JEWELRY TO CHASE DOWN.
AND DON'T FRET THE MESSAGING. NO ONE'LL HEAR ABOUT THIS.
"NEWS NEVER LEAVES THE CIRC."
THE LANTERNS ARE ARRESTING ALL OF DEKANN'S BRAIDMEN...
SLURRRRRKK
YES.
THE OUTCOME IS BETTER THAN WE'D HOPED.
SLURRRRRKK
I RECEIVED WORD, BROTHER. THE FOUR-ARMED ONE IS EN ROUTE WITH THEIR FORTRESS.
NOTIFY THE ANCIENTS.
TELL THEM TO READY THE NEXT PHASE.